Climb Abo[ard]

The California State Rai[lroad Museum]

The Largest and Finest Interpretive Railroad Museum in the Nation

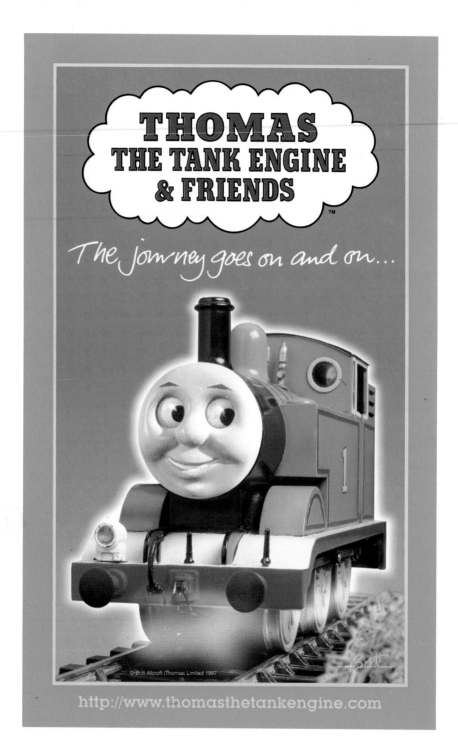

THOMAS
THE TANK ENGINE
& FRIENDS
™

The journey goes on and on...

© Britt Allcroft (Thomas) Limited 1997

http://www.thomasthetankengine.com

32nd ANNUAL

Steam Passenger Service

DIRECTORY

A Guide to Tourist Railroads and Railroad Museums

KALMBACH BOOKS

Assistant Editor: Julie LaFountain
Cover Design: Kristi Ludwig   ISSN: 0081–542X

To the Museums and Tourist Railroads

Listings: We would like to consider for inclusion every tourist railroad, trolley operation, railroad museum, live-steam railroad, and toy train exhibit in the United States and Canada that is open to the public and has regular hours and about which reliable information is available. If you know of an operation that is not included in the book, please send information to the address above.

1998 *Directory*: To be published in February 1998. A packet that includes all pertinent information needed for inclusion in the 1998 *Directory* will be mailed to all organizations listed in this book. New listings are welcomed. For information, please write to:

> Assistant Editor—Steam Passenger Service Directory
> Books Division
> Kalmbach Publishing Co.
> P.O. Box 1612
> Waukesha, WI 53187–1612

Advertising: Advertising space for the 1998 *Directory* must be reserved by November 14, 1997. Please contact Mike Yuhas at 1-800-558-1544, extension 625.

Publisher's Cataloging in Publication
(Prepared by Quality Books, Inc.)

Steam passenger service directory
    32nd annual steam passenger service directory: a guide to tourist railroads and railroad museums / [assistant editor, Julie LaFountain].
    p. cm.
    ISBN: 0–89024–309–3
    Includes indexes.

    1. Railroad museums--United State--Directories. 2. Railroad museums--Canada--Directories. I. LaFountain, Julie.

TF6.U5S84 1997   625.1'0075
                                  QBI96-40798

Contents

U.S. Railroads and Museums 1
Canadian Railroads and Museums .366
Index 400

Symbols

D   Display

M   Museum

R   Ride

♿   Handicapped accessible

P   Parking

Bus/RV parking

Gift, book, or museum shop

Refreshments

Restaurant

Dinner train/dining car

Guided tours

Picnic area

Excursions

 Arts & crafts

 National Register of Historic Places

 Brochure available; send SASE

M Memberships available

arm Association of Railway Museums, member

TRA👆N Tourist Railway Association, Inc., member

 Amtrak service to nearby city

VIA VIA service to nearby city

 Credit cards accepted

 VISA

To the Reader

Tourist railroads and railroad museums don't have a long history—most are creations of the past five decades. Until about 1950, if you wanted to ride a train, you went down to the station. There were plenty of old locomotives and passenger cars to ride in or just to look at.

Then diesels replaced steam locomotives. Passenger trains were discontinued. Lines were abandoned. As it became more and more difficult to see and ride trains, more and more people said, "They were interesting" and "They were fun to ride."

And that, quite simply, is what railroad museums and tourist railroads are about. They preserve some of the most fascinating machinery ever devised; they re-create an enjoyable aspect of the past; and they give us insight into the history and development of North America.

Guest Coupons: The reduced-rate coupons provided by many operations in this edition of the *Steam Passenger Service Directory* will be honored by the museums. Be sure to present them when purchasing tickets.

Brochures: Many operations listed in the *Directory* offer brochures and/or timetables. Please see the symbol sections in the listings for those operations that provide brochures. ▶ ◀

Every effort has been made to ensure the accuracy of the contents. However, we depend on the information supplied by each operation. We cannot assume responsibility for errors, omissions, or fare and schedule changes. In some cases, updated information was unavailable, so 1996 information has been used. Be sure to write or phone ahead to confirm hours and prices.

Advertising Contents

APPAREL
BC Junction A-15
Daylight Sales A-7
J-Bar Rail Boutique A-8

BED & BREAKFAST
Ron & Rita Hatch's Bed & Breakfast A-24

CONSULTANTS
Centennial Rail Ltd. A-24
Stone Consulting & Design, Inc. A-30

PUBLICATIONS
Kalmbach Publishing Co. A-6, A-9, A-12, A-18, A-23
Live Steam Magazine A-22

RAILROAD ASSOCIATIONS
Association of Railway Museums, Inc. .A-27
Tourist Railway Association, Inc. A-20

RAILROAD EQUIPMENT REPAIR & SALES
Anderson Steel Company A-19
Backshop Enterprises A-21
Benson Mountain Co. A-11
D.F. Barnhardt & Associates A-22

RAILROAD INSURANCE
Hamman-Miller-Beachamp-Deeble, Inc. A-14

RAILROADIANA
The Depot Attic A-10
Innovative Rail Works A-3
Milepost 1 . . . . .Inside back cover
Smith-Thompson A-31
Walter E. Lee Inc. A-17

TOURIST RAILROADS

California State Railroad Museum . . . . .Inside front cover, i
California Western Railroad (The Skunk Train) A-26
Colorado Railroad Museum A-16
National Railroad Museum A-1

TRAVEL

Kalmbach Publishing Co. A-29
Rail Travel Center A-30
Trains Unlimited Tours A-25

VIDEO

Clear Block Productions Inc. A-13
Herron Rail Services A-2
Historic Railroad Shops A-19
Kalmbach Publishing Co. A-4
Penn Valley Pictures A-5
Video Ed A-26

WHOLESALERS

Britt Allcroft Inc. ii
E&M Specialty A-28
Railfan Specialties A-28

To recall the <u>real</u> glory days of railroading, stop in at the gift shop and select one of our videos. Our programs were all filmed when the great trains roamed the country by dedicated photographers who preserved the images of railroading from the 1930s to the 1960s. All transferred from film to video by studios such as Disney/MGM and narrated with sound and appropriate music to create the highest acclaimed railroad videos available. Available at better tourist railroads.

If the store you visit doesn't have our tapes, write for a free catalog.

Over 30 titles/More coming.
Most railroads covered.

2016 N. Village Ave.
Tampa, FL 33612
(813)932-3887

Quality, the difference is on the screen.

RAILROAD HISTORY COMES ALIVE

Wisconsin Central: Railroad Success Story
By Otto Dobnick and Steve Glischinski

Discover how Wisconsin Central was transformed into the most successful regional railroad in the country. Learn about the history of Wisconsin Central's predecessors and the events leading to the new Wisconsin Central. 11 x 8⁷⁄₁₆; 160 pgs.; 106 color photos; 3 maps; hardcover with dust jacket. Available May 1997.
#01069 . . . . $49.95

The Iron Horse: An Illustrated History of Steam Locomotives
By Henry B. Comstock

Enjoy the complete story of steam power on American railroads. Follow the majesty of steam locomotives and the history of their development. Includes locomotives from the 1820s through the 1950s. 8½ x 11; 224 pgs.; 25 color photos; 187 illustrations; hardcover.
#10-7090 . . . . Price: $49.95

The Nickel Plate Story
By John A. Rehor

Explore the remarkable story of an independent railroad that fought for its life throughout its competitive history. Traces the history of the famed New York, Chicago & St. Louis Railroad (the "Nickel Plate"). 8½ x 11; 484 pgs.; 527 photos; 15 illus.; hardcover with dust jacket.
#01059 . . . . Price: $74.95

Authentic T-Shirts • Children's T-Shirts • Collectible Railroad Art

Note: This is the Daylight T-Shirt design, Available in Children's Medium through XXXL

(510) 680-1791 • Fax (510) 825-8466

VIGNETTES

(vin - yetz´) *n.*

1. A short descriptive scene, as from a movie.
2. Clear Block Productions' popular video tape series on vintage railroading, including the following roads:

Also from Clear Block -
"Into the 90's", series, on today's railroads:

The Grand Trunk -
(Volumes I, II & III)

Dusk to Dawn - Railroading after dark. Includes a handy after dark "shooting tips" pamphlet.

CSX's Indiana Mainlines-
(Volumes I & II)

SOO Line -
(Volumes I & II)

COMING SOON!
Kansas City Southern

NEW!
Vignettes of the JERSEY CENTRAL

Baltimore and Ohio
(Volumes I & II)

Reading
(Volumes I & II)

Chesapeake and Ohio

Missouri Pacific

Erie Lackawanna
(Volumes I & II)

Detroit, Toledo & Ironton

COMING SOON!
Lehigh Valley
Western Maryland

Available at your dealer or direct. Call or write for your *free* catalog listing these and over 500 titles from other producers including Pentrex, Sunday River, Mark I Video, Rail Innovations, WB Video, Green Frog and Greg Scholl.

PH 1-800-645-5813 • FAX (614)389-6091

CLEAR BLOCK PRODUCTIONS, INC. P.O. Box 527, Marion, OH 43301-0527

A-14

Discover the Fascination of Railroading at the

Colorado Railroad Museum

You can ring the bell on some of Colorado's oldest steam locomotives or climb into a red caboose. See over sixty cars and engines displayed in an authentic setting at the foot of the Rocky Mountains. The museum building, a replica of an 1880 style masonry depot, houses more than 50,000 rare old photographs, papers and artifacts. There's fun for the entire family!

Steam Train Runs
April 12-13
June 21-22
August 2-3
October 4-5
December 6-7

Open Every Day
9 a.m. - 5 p.m.
(to 6p.m. in June,
July, August)

Colorado Railroad Museum
Book Store and Gift Shop <u>The</u> Railroad Book Source

CALL US FIRST! 800-365-6263

Best Selection of Railroad Books
We stock over 1000 titles from throughout the country, hundreds of videos, calendars and gifts available *FAST PERSONAL SERVICE!*

Biggest & Best RR Book Catalog $2.00
(refundable with first purchase)

Members Receive Discounts!
Call for information about becoming a member, and charge to your Visa, Mastercard, or Discover today!

*Purchase from us
and help to preserve railroad heritage!*

Colorado Railroad Museum
P.O. Box 10, Golden, CO 80402-0010
17155 W. 44th Ave / 303-279-4591
800-365-6263 / fax 24 hours 303-279-4229
Email corrmus@aol.com

HISTORIC RAILROAD SHOPS

Georgia's State Railroad Museum -- The oldest and most complete Antebellum railroad manufacturing and repair facility still in existence in the U.S. Collection highlights southern industrial technology. Included are the massive Roundhouse, Operating Turntable, and the125-foot Smokestack. Also, an HO scale layout of Savannah, shaft and belt driven machinery exhibit, and the oldest portable steam engine in the U.S.
Open daily from 10:am - 4:pm. Blacksmithing every Thursday.

For information on tours and private parties:

601 West Harris Street	**Phone:** **(912) 651-6823**
Savannah, GA 31401	**Fax:** **(912) 651-3691**

TRAIN

You are invited to join TRAIN
THE TOURIST RAILWAY ASSOCIATION, INC.

TRAIN is the one trade association that is serving the growing needs of tourist rail lines, railroad museums, excursion operators, private car owners and suppliers - the multi-faceted groups that make up creative railroading.

With over 350 member organizations, and growing every month, our Roster is too long to print in the Steam Directory. Our members included in the STEAM PASSENGER SERVICE DIRECTORY may be identified by the **TRAIN** logo on their listing page.

TRAIN members receive our bi-monthly newsletter— *TRAINLINE,* filled with articles relating to the tourist railway industry.

TRAIN is an action association dealing decisively in the areas of
- Legislation
- Insurance
- Mechanical-steam
- Mechanical-electric
- Advertising
- Safety
- Operations
- Mechanical-diesel
- Mechanical-passenger cars
- Promotion

For further information on this important alliance of professionals write:

Tourist Railway Association, INc.
P.O. Box 28077
Denver, CO 80228-0010
1(800) 67-TRAIN
(303) 988-7764
FAX (303) 989-2192

A-28

TRAINS'
Steam Locomotive Tour
of Eastern Germany

Join TRAINS' Editor Kevin P. Keefe and railroad historian George H. Drury this October as they explore the wonders of Germany by train. For 12 action-packed days, you'll see some of the most beautiful and interesting sights in all of Europe!

Harz Narrow Gauge Railways' afternoon train from Brocken arrives in Wernigerode.

Board a new train every day for another exciting adventure:
- Enjoy the Selke Valley and Cross-Harz Railways, both part of the Harz Narrow Gauge Railways network
- Ride an InterCity Express, the fastest thing on German rails
- Experience the Rübelandbahn, an electrically operated DB line noted for its steep grades
- Ride behind one of the few remaining 0-4-4-0T Mallets built for the Saxon narrow gauge lines
- Explore the sights on rural streetcars and suburban trains throughout the region

Take in the history of German railroading at these exciting stops:
- The German Transportation Museum in Nuremberg
- Europe's largest train station at Leipzig
- A German Steam Locomotive Museum at Neuenmarkt-Wirsberg
- Tour a city's streetcar system in Nordhausen
- Visit a model railroad equipment factory at Kurort Oybin

Take the whole family and enjoy these fun-filled activities:
- The Doll and Toy Museum in Nuremberg
- A castle tour in Wernigerode
- Bach's church in Arnstadt
- A city tour including two narrow gauge lines just outside of Dresden
- Plus many opportunities to explore picturesque villages and medieval cities

For a brochure and additional information on this exciting trip through eastern Germany, call A1 Tours & Travel at
1-800-677-9412

0868-9611KCPad

NORTH ALABAMA
RAILROAD MUSEUM, INC.
Diesel, scheduled
Standard gauge

NORTH ALABAMA RAILROAD MUSEUM, INC.

Ride/Operation: Our train operates over 3½-miles (an additional ½ mile under construction) of the former NC&StL Railway Hunstville Branch. The round trip lasts 1¼-hours. The train travels through woodland, pastures, urban and industrial areas.

Displays/Exhibits: Display/exhibits include the restored Chase depot which was the smallest union station in the country serving the NC&StL Railway and the Southern Railway, a walk-through passenger train, 1926 boxcab locomotive, ice bunker refrigerator, A/V car, RPO Car, coach, dining car and 10-6 Pullman sleeper, historic photos of area's railroads, graphic displays, items of railroad materials and equipment.

Schedule: Museum open for tours 9:30 a.m.-2:00 pm each Wednesday and Saturday, year around except holidays and bad weather. Train excursions on 2nd and 4th weekend, April-October.

Fare/Admission: $4 adults, $2 children under 12. Train Ride $10 adults, $5 children under 12, also incudes museum tour.

Locomotives: 1926 Boxcab switcher (60 ton), 1949 Alco S-2.

Rolling Stock/Equipment: 6 passenger cars, 1 ea. RPO, Pullman 10-6 sleeper, 2 former troop sleepers, 1 ice bunker refrig. car, 4 cabooses, 1 tank car, 1 flat car, 2 box cars and 3 baggage cars, 3 Fairmont motor cars, 2 push cars a Chevelle rail car.

Special Events: Mothers' Day special, Goblin special and the annual Santa Train.

Location: Take I-565, go to east end, continue 2 miles east on U.S. Highway 72 for 1.8 miles to traffic light, take left (north) on Moores Mill Rd. for 1.9 miles, take left (west) on Chase Road for .5 miles, museum on left.

P 🚌 ✳ 📷 🏕 🚂
▶ ◀ M TRAIN

Contact: Hugh J. Dudley
Director Museum Operations

Mailing Address:
P.O. Box 4163
Huntsville, AL 35815
Telephone Museum: (205) 851-6276
Home: (205) 851-6276
Fax: (205) 895-0222
E-mail: duaned@hiwaay.net
Internet: http://hiwaay.net/sunrise/narm/main.htm

HUNTSVILLE DEPOT

Displays/Exhibits: The station built at Huntsville, Alabama, in 1860 by the Memphis & Charleston Railroad is now a museum, with emphasis on the relationship of the railroad to the commerce, industry, and development of the surrounding area. The museum exhibits include a 20-minute multimedia presentation and a ticket office brought to life through robotics. The museum operates a replica of a 1920s trolley on a 30-minute tour of downtown and the ante-bellum area.

Schedule: March-December, Tuesday-Saturday, 10 a.m.-4 p.m. Closed during January and February.

Fare/Admission: Adults $4.50, children 4-12 $3.50, age 65 and over $3.50. Checks accepted. Group discounts available. Trolley: adults $2, children $1.

Special Events: Civil War Jubilee (fourth weekend in April), Roundhouse Roundup and Harvest Festival (fourth weekend in October), Christmas celebration (second weekend in December).

Notes: Nearby attraction-Alabama Space and Rocket Center, Constitution Hall Village,

Location: Huntsville is only a few miles south of the Tennessee border, on I-565 and U. S. Routes 72, 231, and 431. Food and lodging can be found within a mile of the museum.

Mailing Address:
320 Church Street
Huntsville, AL 35801

Telephone: (205) 539-1860
(800) 239-8955

ALASKA RAILROAD

Ride/Operation: The Alaska Railroad, established in 1914 with railroad equipment used in the construction of the Panama Canal, provides passenger service between Anchorage and Seward and between Anchorage, Denali National Park and Fairbanks. Scenic rides on 469 miles of mainline track through state and national parks offer passengers an opportunity to view wildlife such as bear, moose, beavers, and birds. Spectacular mountain terrain and optional tours are also available at stops along the way.

Displays/Exhibits: Potter Section House State Historic Park, ten miles south of Anchorage, features rail cars depicting the history of the Alaska Railroad. Small gift shops on the Express Trains.

Schedule: Anchorage-Denali National Park-Fairbanks: Daily express, May 16-September 17. Anchorage-Seward: Daily, May 17-September 1. Anchorage-Fairbanks: Weekends, September 17-May. Winter Tours: Weekends, September 19-May.

Fare: Call or write for information.

Locomotives: Four rail diesel cars; 48 locomotives of various types.

Passenger Cars: Three Vista-Dome cars; seven coaches; six new coaches constructed in 1990; five diners/food-service cars.

Rolling Stock/Equipment: 1,222 pieces of all types, including owned and leased freight cars.

Special Events: Special rates and promotional packages available in late May, June, late August, and September; available in Anchorage Depot only.

   (some routes)

(summer only)   (Express Train)

TRAIN

Contact: Janet Swanson
Customer Service Supervisor

Mailing Address:
P.O. Box 107500
Anchorage, AK 99510
Telephone: (907) 265-2494
(800) 544-0552

Alaska, Skagway
D-R

WHITE PASS & YUKON ROUTE
Steam, diesel, scheduled
36" gauge

GEORGE A. FORERO, JR.

Ride/Operation: Built in 1898 to supply the Klondike Gold Rush, the White Pass & Yukon Route is one of the most spectacular mountain railroads in the world. Declared an International Historical Civil Engineering Landmark by the American and Canadian Society of Engineers, the WP&YR offers round-trip excursions from Skagway to White Pass Summit and through rail/bus connections to Whitehorse, Yukon. Steam engine No. 73 pulls trains 1½ miles to the edge of town, where it is cut off to let diesels tackle the 4-percent grade to the summit. The WP&YR carried more than 160,000 passengers during the 1996 season, breaking all previous ridership records.

Displays/Exhibits: A four-panel mural in the WP&YR depot depicts the complete history of the North and of the railroad. Next door is the visitors' center for the Klondike Gold Rush National Historical Park, which contains comprehensive displays about the 1898 Gold Rush, the railroad, and the area.

Train: Parlor cars from many narrow-gauge railroads, including the Sumpter Valley, the Pacific Coast, the Northwestern Pacific, the Utah & Northern, and the Los Angeles & Redondo, most dating from the 1880s and 1890s; nine steel cars, one built by Pacific Car & Foundry in 1935. (The newer cars retain "old" styling.)

Schedule: Daily, May 15-September 15. Excursion trains: Lv. Skagway 8:30 a.m. & 1:00 p.m. for a 40.8-mile, 3-hour round trip. Through service, northbound: Lv. Skagway 12:40 p.m. (train); arr. Fraser, B.C., 2:00 p.m. (change to bus); arr. Whitehorse, Yukon, 6:30 p.m. Through service, southbound: Lv. Whitehorse, Yukon, 8:15 a.m. (bus); arr. Fraser, B.C., 10:20 a.m. (change to train); arr. Skagway, Alaska, 12:10 p.m.

Fare: Summit excursion: Adults $75.00, children $37.50. Through service: Adults $95.00, children $47.50. Reservations recommended.

Locomotives: No. 73, 1947 Baldwin 2-8-2—last White Pass steam engine; 11 General Electric 90 Class boxcab diesel locomotives; 4 Alco MLW 101 Class road diesels.

Rolling Stock/Equipment: WP&YR freight operations were suspended in 1982, but equipment remains on the property. Oahu railway flats, Colorado & Southern boxcars, strings of ore flats, container flats, cabooses. Restored No. 1 1898 steam driven rotary snowplow is displayed at Depot.

Location: Railroad Depot, 2nd & Spring streets.

Radio Frequency: 160.325

Contact: Tina Cyr
Director of Marketing
Mailing Address:
P. O. Box 435
Skagway, AK 99840
Telephone: (800) 343-7373 &
(907) 983-2217
Fax: (907) 983-2734
E-mail: ngauge73@aol.com
Internet: http://www.whitepassrailroad.com

4

Transportation museum
Standard gauge

MUSEUM OF ALASKA TRANSPORTATION & INDUSTRY

Ride/Operation: The Alaska Live Steamers operate the 7½-inch-gauge Alaska Central Railroad on the site. Rides are offered on an irregular schedule of weekends and holidays.

Displays/Exhibits: The machines and vehicles that built Alaska are displayed outdoors and in a large, new exhibition hall on this park-like 10-acre site. More than 30 pieces of railroad equipment on view are joined by more than 200 other transportation and industrial artifacts. Aircraft, boats, tractors, heavy machinery, engines, and vehicles are included. Indoor exhibits include a history of local gold mining, restored vehicles, Alaska bush pilot Hall of Fame, early communications equipment, and more.

Schedule: May 1-Sept. 30, daily 9:00 a.m.-6:00 p.m.; Oct. 1-April 30, Tues.-Sat. 9 a.m.-5:00 p.m. Alaska Live Steamers operate unscheduled weekends and holidays May to Sept.

Admission: Adults $5.00, family rate $12.00, students & seniors $2.50. Reduced rates for tour groups.

Locomotives: (5): Alaska R.R. #1000, first diesel in Alaska; #1500, star of the film, *The Runaway Train*; 1944 General Electric center cab; and two Baldwin S-12's.

Rolling Stock: Four WWII Troop Cars house an exhibit on Alaska RR history. Bureau of Mines Safety Car, Lake Minchumina Pullman Car, 1917 box cars, 1930 caboose, Jordan Spreader, steam wrecker, speeders, and more.

Special Events: Open house with demonstrations, July 4th weekend. Antique Power Show mid-August.

Location: Off mile 47 Parks Highway, next to Wasilla Airport.

Contact: Harrison Yost
Curator

Mailing Address:
P.O. Box 870646
Wasilla, AK 99687
Telephone: (907) 376-1211
Internet: http://www.alaska.net/~rmorris/mati1.htm

SAN PEDRO & SOUTHWESTERN RAILROAD
Diesel, scheduled
Standard gauge

SAN PEDRO & SOUTHWESTERN RAILROAD

Ride/Operation: San Pedro & Southwestern's Gray Hawk Excursion train departs Benson for a four hour, 50-mile round trip throughout pristine San Pedro Riparian National Conservation Area. Here, lush cottonwoods and mesquite thrive among various species of birds, mammals, and reptiles. Travel through an area speckled with the remains of once powerful silver mills. Pass the ruins of Contention City and the historic ghost town of Fairbank. Expert narration of western and railroad history and folklore throughout trip. Stop at Fairbank on return to Benson for western entertainment and optional barbecue.

Train: Former Southern Pacific *Daylight* cars, Illinois Central heavyweight coach, Lackawanna coach, bar car, open observation cars.

Schedule: Trains operate year-round on Thursdays, Friday, Saturdays and Sundays. Times vary with season. Please call for departure times.

Fare: Adults, $24; Seniors (60 and over), $21; Students (K-12) $15. Children under school age travel free when accompanied by a fare-paying passenger.

Locomotives: 1961 EMD GP-20s No. 2039 and 2044.

Special Events: Moonlight runs on selected full moon evenings in warm weather. Holiday specials and other theme trains operate periodically throughout the year. Please call for information.

Notes: Please write or call for free brochure.

Location: The SPSW depot is located at 796 E. Country Club Drive. From I-10 Business loop take State Route 80 one mile south to Country Club Drive, then one block east to depot.

Contact: General Manager

Mailing Address:
P.O. Box 1420
Benson, AZ 85602
Telephone: (520) 586-2266

THE ARIZONA RAILWAY MUSEUM
Railway museum
Standard gauge

STEVE WHISEL

Displays/Exhibits: The museum building, reminiscent of an early Southwestern railway depot, houses railroad memorabilia and artifacts from railways of the Southwest and elsewhere. The museum is expanding its trackage to exhibit additional equipment.

Schedule: Weekends, 12:00-4:00 p.m. (except holidays). Please call for summer hours.

Admission: Free; donations welcomed.

Rolling Stock/Equipment: 1906 Baldwin 2-8-0 No. 2562, idler car No. 7131, steam derrick No. 7130 and caboose No. 413, all former Southern Pacific; 1943 Plymouth gas-mechanical switch engine; GRYX No. 799, three-compartment tank car; Southern Pacific tank car No. 60157, single dome; former Santa Fe pulpwood car No. 320219, caboose No. 999741, boxcars No. 600197 and No. 202493, and coach No. 2870; former Seaboard 10-6 sleeper "West Palm Beach"; SFRD No. 16811, ice bunker refrigerator car; former Rio Grande caboose No. 01469; 1950 Baldwin DRS 6-6-1500, former Magma Arizona Railroad No. 10; 1949 observation car, former Pennsylvania Railroad "Frank Thompson"; 1933 UTLX tank car.

Notes: The museum is a nonprofit volunteer organization.

Location: In Chandler at Erie and Delaware Streets, adjacent to the Southern Pacific tracks one-half mile east of state route 87. From I-10, take Chandler Boulevard east to Chandler. About 20 miles southeast of downtown Phoenix.

Contact: President

Mailing Address:
P.O. Box 842
Chandler, AZ 85224
Telephone: (602) 821-1108

VERDE CANYON RAILROAD
Diesel, scheduled
Standard gauge

TOM JOHNSON-RED ROCK STOCK

Ride/Operation: The Verde Canyon Railroad offers a panoramic rail experience into Arizona's other grand canyon, accessible only by rail. The flora, fauna and rugged high desert rock faces are distinctive to this geological area. The train rolls past looming crimson cliffs, near ancient ruins and passes through a 680 foot man made tunnel. Coach and first class seating both access open air viewing cars. Souvenir car and deli on board. Year-round departures. Reservations required.

Schedule: Open year-round. Trains depart 11:00 a.m. Wednesday - Sunday. Mondays added in spring and fall. Two departures on Saturday (depart 9:00 a.m. and 2:30 p.m.) March, April, May, October, November. Starlight trains one Saturday per month, May through October. Reservations required.

Fare/Admission: First class: adult $52.95, adult coach $34.95, senior (65+) coach $30.95, children (12 and under) coach $19.95

Locomotives: FP7 locomotives, 1510 and 1512.

Rolling Stock/Equipment: 5 Pullman Standard, 1 Budd stainless steel; 5 flatcars converted to open-air viewing cars; 1 bunkcar converted to souvenir and deli car.

Special Events: Starlight trains during the summer; "Throw Mama on the Train" in May; Firecracker Barbecue on July 4th; Early Bird New Year's Eve Party on December 31.

Location: Two hours north from Phoenix on I-17, take Hwy 260 to Clarkdale or 89A from I-10 at Flagstaff through Sedona to Clarkdale; 20 miles west of Sedona on 89A.

Flagstaf, 40 miles away

Contact: Janet Clark
Excursion Manager

Mailing Address:
300 North Broadway
Clarkdale, Arizona 86324
Telephone: (800) 293-6245
(520) 639-1653

ARIZONA TRAIN DEPOT

Displays/Exhibits: 8 x 24-foot, 20 x 50-foot overhead.

Schedule: Monday-Friday 10:00 a.m.- 5:00 p.m., Wednesday 1:00-8:00 p.m., Saturday 10:00 a.m.- 3:00 p.m.

Fare: Free

Locomotives/Trolleys: LGB Mogul, Circus display with Wilson brothers limited edition set, Gandy Dancer, LGB Coca-Cola Set, Aristocraft Pacific Rio Grande & Santa Fe, LGB Colorado & Southern Mogul.

Special Events: Monthly meetings. Garden railroad tours. Call for dates and details.

Notes: Come and relax in the hobo's corner and talk trains or watch a collection of train videos.

Location: 755 East McKellips Road, Suite #5, Mesa, Arizona 85203.

   ✳   **M**

Contact: Lee DeGroff
Owner

Mailing Address:
755 East McKellips
Mesa, AZ 85203
Telephone: (602) 833-9486
Fax: (602) 834-4644

GPD

Ride/Operation: Four model train layouts. Main layout is O-gauge 19' x 35' featuring hands-on operation by the visiting public. Other layout are HO, G, and prewar standard gauge.

Displays/Exhibits: Several show cases display unique and sometimes rare examples of our hobby and railroadiana. Exhibits change with the season.

Schedule: Wednesday 5:00-9:00 p.m., Friday 10:00 a.m.-7:00 p.m., Saturday 10:00 a.m.-6:00 p.m., Sunday 12:00-5:00 pm.

Fare/Admission: Free.

Special Events: Semi Annual Swap Meet, January & June. Monthly meeting, 7:00 p.m., first Friday of the month.

Location: Foothills Mall. Ina Rd & La Cholla Blvd., Tucson Arizona. Ina Road. exit I-10 approx 3 miles east on Ina Road.

Tucson, 12 miles away

Contact: Warren Reynolds

Mailing Address:
7401 N. La Cholla Blvd. #181
Tucson, AZ 85741

OLD PUEBLO TROLLEY

Electric, scheduled
Standard gauge

R.G. GUTHRIE

Ride/Operation: 1.1 mile (one-way) ride on historic trolley through historic business district and historic neighborhood.

Displays/Exhibits: Three trolleys under restoration: 1912 Los Angeles Huntington Standard; 1935 Brussels, Belgium; 1951 Toronto, Canada.

Schedule: Friday: 6:00-10:00 p.m. Saturday: noon-midnight. Sunday: noon-6:00 p.m.

Fare: Adults $1.00 (one-way), children $.50 (one-way). $2.50 unlimited all-day pass. Sunday $.25, sponsored by local merchants.

Locomotives/Trolleys: All trolleys. 1912 Los Angeles (long term restoration), 1935 Belgium, 1951 Toronto PCC, 1953 Kyoto, Japan, rebuilt.

Rolling Stock/Equipment: 1912 electric mining locomotive plus other miscellaneous work cars.

Special Events: Annual Fourth Avenue Street Fair, all holidays.

Notes: All-volunteer operations, restoration, overhead, and track construction.

Location: Car barn located at 4th Avenue and 8th Street. Operates on 4th Avenue from 8th Street north to University Boulevard and east 0.6 mile to main gate of the University of Arizona.

Contact: Gene Cagwood or Dick Guthrie

Mailing Address:
P.O. Box 1373
Tucson, AZ 85702
Recording: (520) 792-1802
Voice: (520) 792-0225
Fax: (520) 791-3189/Attn: Dick Guthrie
Internet: http://www.azstarnet.com/~bnoon/opthome.html

WILLIAM RAMSEY

Ride/Operation: The Grand Canyon Railway operates a turn-of-the-century steam train Memorial Day weekend through September and vintage 1950s diesel locomotives the remainder of the year. Passengers ride in authentically restored 1923 Harriman coaches across 65 miles of pine forests, grassy plains, and small canyons, arriving at the 1910 Grand Canyon depot, just steps from the canyon rim. Western characters, strolling musicians, and interpretive programs combine to make this an unforgettable journey.

Displays/Exhibits: The Williams Depot, listed on the National Register of Historic Places, was once a bustling Harvey House and depot. Today it offers visitors a free museum, a year-round engine display, gift shop, and the Depot Cafe. Wild West performances take place daily, prior to train departure. Adjacent to the historic depot is the new Fray Marcos Hotel which combines turn-of-the-century elegance with modern day amenities. The new hotel is home to Spenser's, where casual dinner is available and drinks are served from a beautiful 19th century bar which celebrates a colorful history.

Schedule: Daily, (except December 24-25). Depart Williams 9:30 a.m., arrive Grand Canyon 11:45 a.m.; depart Grand Canyon 3:15 p.m., arrive Williams 5:30 p.m.

Fare: Adults $49.50 plus applicable National Park Service entrance fee, children $19.50. Club Class (pastries and coffee served in the morning; fully stocked bar): $12.00 additional. Chief Class (first-class service; complimentary continental breakfast; afternoon hors d'oeuvres; cocktails available): $50.00 additional. Rates do not include tax.

Locomotives: Steam: Nos. 18 and 20, 1910 Alco SC-4 2-8-0s; No. 29, 1906 Alco SC-3 2-8-0; No. 4960, 1923 Baldwin O1A 2-8-2 Diesel: No. 2134 GP7 Electro-Motive Division of General Motors Corporation, Nos. 6773 and 6793, 1959 MLW (6793 is the last in the series).

Passenger Cars: Coach Class: 1923-vintage Harriman-type passenger car. Club Class: converted 1923 Harriman passenger car with mahogany bar.

Chief Class: 1954 CN converted open platform parlor car, 30-passenger.

New Service: 1954 Budd Heritage short dome coach, 66-passengers.

Location: Williams is on I-40, 35 miles west of Flagstaff.

Mailing Address:
123 North San Francisco, Suite 210
Flagstaff, AZ 86001
Telephone:
1-800-THE-TRAIN (843-8724)
Other Inquiries: (520) 773-1976

MIKE ORVIK

Displays/Exhibits: Vintage railroad equipment.

Ride/Operation: Two- or three-hour 22 mile round trip. Railroad follows Colorado River on Arizona side across from Old Mexico.

Schedule: Weekends, October 1 through June.

Fare/Admission: Adults $10, seniors $9, children to age 12 $5, under age 4 are free.

Locomotives: 1941 Whitcomb Diesel, 1952 Davenport Center Coach, 1922 Pullman Chair Coach, 1952 ACF Club Car.

Special Events: Available for special charter groups.

Telephone: (520) 783-3456

EUREKA SPRINGS & NORTH ARKANSAS RAILWAY
Steam, scheduled
Standard gauge

GEORGE A. FORERO, JR.

Ride/Operation: A 4-mile, 45-minute round trip through a wooded valley next to a winding creek in the heart of the Ozarks. During the "turn-around" trip, the steam engine is turned on a turntable at one end of the line and on a wye at the other end. Visitors may also ride the train, then take the city-operated trolley through downtown Eureka Springs.

Displays/Exhibits: The Eureka Springs depot, built in 1913 of locally cut limestone; operating turntable from the Frisco Lines; 1896 smoker coach, former Central of Georgia; two steam tractors.

Train: Steel coaches, former Rock Island; wooden caboose, former Cotton Belt.

Schedule: Monday-Saturday, April-November 2, on the hour, 10:00 a.m.-4:00 p.m. Dining car: Monday-Saturday; lunch, 12:00 & 2:00 p.m.; dinner, 5:00 & 8:00 p.m.

Fare: Adults $8.00, children (4-11) $4.00, children under 4 ride free. Call or write for dining-car fares.

Locomotives: No. 1, 1906 Baldwin 2-6-0, former W.T. Carter; No. 201, 1906 Alco 2-6-0, former Moscow, Camden & San Augustine; No. 226, 1927 Baldwin 2-8-2, former Dierks For. & Coal.

Passenger Cars: Six commuter cars, former Rock Island.

Rolling Stock/Equipment: No. 4742, 1942 EMD SW1.

Location: In northwest Arkansas, a short distance from the Missouri border. Take highway 23 north to the city limits.

Radio Frequency: 151.655

Contact: Robert L. Dortch, III
Depot Manager

Mailing Address:
P.O. Box 310
299 North Main Street
Eureka Springs, AR 72632
Telephone: (501) 253-9623

WHITE RIVER RAILWAY
Diesel, scheduled
Standard gauge

WHITE RIVER RAILWAY

Ride/Operation: On your four hour round-trip excursion you'll enjoy the Cotter tunnel, the historic Cotter railroad bridge crossing, and the beautiful White River of the Ozarks.

Schedule: Year round. Call for schedule.

Fare/Admission: Adults $23.00, seniors 55+, $21.00, children under age 12 $15.00, under age 3 are free.

Location: Flippin, Arkansas ticket office is located on Highway 62, one block from Jct. Highways 62 and 178. Calico Rock, Arkansas ticket office is located at Kountry Kreation on Highway 5.

P

Contact: Robert Prendeville

Mailing Address:
P.O. Box 1093
Flippin, AR 72634
Telephone: (800) 305-6527
(501) 453-3000

FORT SMITH TROLLEY MUSEUM
Electric, scheduled
Railway museum

BRADLEY MARTIN

Ride/Operation: Passengers take a 1-mile, 20-minute round trip on a restored Fort Smith Birney Safety Car from "Hanging" Judge Parker's Court Room and Gallows at the Fort Smith National Historic Site, then past the trolley museum and the Fort Smith National Cemetery. The National Historic Site is adjacent to the Old Fort Museum, which features the colorful history of Fort Smith's frontier days.

Displays/Exhibits: Original Fort Smith and Hot Springs streetcars, three internal-combustion locomotives, three cabooses, former Missouri-Kansas-Texas diner, power car. Memorabilia and photos are also displayed.

Schedule: Daily, May-October; Monday-Saturday, 10:00 a.m.-5:00 p.m.; Sunday, 1:00-5:00 p.m. Weekends, November-April; Saturday, 10:00 a.m.-5:00 p.m.; Sunday, 1:00-5:00 p.m. Group tours available at other times by special arrangement.

Fare: Adults $1.00, children $.50.

Trolleys: No. 225 (operational and on Historic Register), No. 221, No. 205, and No. 10, all former Fort Smith Light and Traction; No. 50, former Hot Springs Street Railway; No. 1545, former Kansas City Public Service.

Locomotives: General Electric 44-ton, former United States Air Force No. 1247; No. 6, 8-ton Plymouth, former Augusta Railroad; No. 7, 35-ton Vulcan.

Rolling Stock: Diner bunk car, former MKT; converted troop sleeper power car and caboose; cabooses, former Burlington Northern and Union Pacific; 5 motor cars, former Frisco.

Special Events: Annual Open House, April 30.

Location: 100 South 4th Street, 3 blocks south of Garrison Avenue in Fort Smith's historic downtown.

   ♿ **P**

M ar n

Contact: Bradley Martin
General Manager

Mailing Address:
2121 Wolfe Lane
Fort Smith, AR 72901
Telephone: (501) 783-0205
(501) 783-1237
E-mail: bmartin@fs.cei.net
Internet: http://www.fs.cei.net/trolley/

READER RAILROAD

Steam, scheduled

Standard gauge

W. D. CAILEFF, JR.

Ride/Operation: Reader Railroad, the oldest all-steam, standard-gauge common carrier to operate in the United States, offers a 7-mile, 1-hour round trip. Open platform wooden coaches are drawn by veteran logging engines, operations reminiscent of the railroad's earliest days.

Train: Open-platform wooden coaches; open-air car; caboose.

Schedule: Write or call for information.

Fare: Adults $6.00, children (4-11) $3.60, children under 4 ride free with parent. Group rates available. Fares may be slightly higher for special events.

Locomotives: No. 7, 1907 Baldwin 2-6-2, former Victoria, Fisher & Western.

Location: Off state route 24 between Camden and Prescott on highway 368.

Contact: R. A . Grigsby

General Manager

Mailing Address:

P.O. Box 507

Hot Springs, AR 71902

Telephone: (501) 624-6881

ARKANSAS & MISSOURI RAILROAD
Diesel, scheduled
Standard gauge

ARKANSAS & MISSOURI RAILROAD

Ride/Operation: Visitors can choose either a 134-mile journey from Springdale or a 70-mile journey from Van Buren, both crossing over trestles and passing through Winslow Tunnel on their way to the top of the Ozark Mountains. The 134-mile round trip includes complimentary breakfast and snacks; the 70-mile trip includes snacks.

Schedule: April-November; Wednesday & Saturday. Second half of October: Tuesday, Wednesday, Friday-Sunday. *Springdale* ride from 8:00 a.m.-4:00 p.m. *Van Buren* ride from 10:30 a.m.-1:30 p.m.

Reservations are taken Mondays through Fridays, 8:00 a.m. to 4:00 p.m. Please call or write for complete schedule.

Fare: April-September and November: $29.00 (Springdale), $19.00 (Van Buren). October: Second, third, fourth weeks add $5.00; Saturday add $10.00.

Locomotives: Alco RS-1 (1943 and 1951)

Rolling Stock/Equipment: No. 102, 1899 combination coach/baggage, former Boston & Maine; No. 104, 1917 Pullman coach; Nos. 105 & 106, 1920s Harlan & Hollingsworth.

Special Events: Please call or write for information.

Location: 306 East Emma Street.

Contact: Dana Turney
Passenger Operations Manager

Mailing Address:
306 East Emma Street
Springdale, AR 72764
Telephone: (800) 687-8600

DESCANSO, ALPINE & PACIFIC RAILWAY

Scheduled
24" gauge

WEBB PHOTOGRAPHY

Ride/Operation: Passengers ride an industrial 2-foot-gauge railway to yesteryear among 100-year-old Engelman oaks in San Diego County's foothills. The train leaves Shade Depot and makes a ½-mile round trip, climbing the 6½-percent grade to High Pass/Lookout and crossing a spectacular 100-foot-long wooden trestle, giving passengers magnificent views of the surrounding area.

Displays/Exhibits: At Shade Depot and Freight Shed is a display of railroad artifacts, including those of the DA&P. Mail service with mailer's postmark permit canceling is available.

Train: Gasoline-powered engine, open-type industrial/passenger cars.

Schedule: June-August: Sundays, 1:00-3:00 p.m., every half hour. September-May: Intermittent Sunday operation. Rides and tours may be scheduled at other times with advance notice; please call to arrange.

Fare/Admission: No charge.

Locomotives: No. 2, 1935 2½-ton Brookville, SN 2003, powered by original McCormick-Deering 22½-horsepower P-12 gasoline engine, former Carthage (Missouri) Crushed Limestone Company.

Location: Thirty miles east of San Diego. Take Tavern Road exit off I-8, travel south on Tavern 1.9 miles, turn right on South Grade Road and travel .6 mile, turn left onto Alpine Heights Road; the DA&P is the fifth driveway on the right.

P ☕ 📷 ✳ ▶ ◀

 San Diego

Contact: Roy Athey
Superintendent of Operations

Mailing Address:
1266 Alpine Heights Road
Alpine, CA 91901
Telephone: (619) 445-4781

19

GOLDEN GATE LIVE STEAMERS, INC.

Steam, scheduled
2½", 3¼", 4¾", 7½" gauges

GOLDEN GATE LIVE STEAMERS

Ride/Operation: Established in 1936, this club promotes interest in live steam and has a stationary boiler to operate stationary steam engines. The club's Tilden Park site has steaming bays for thirty to forty engines as well as raised track in 2½-inch, 3¼-inch, and 4¾-inch gauges and ground-level track in 4¾-inch and 7½-inch gauges. Valid boiler certificates from other clubs are accepted; IBLS wheel standards are enforced.

Schedule: Sundays, year round, 11:00 a.m.-3:00 p.m., weather permitting.

Fare: Donations welcomed.

Locomotives: More than 275 locomotives are running or under construction. Weights of the locomotives range from 14 pounds to almost a ton. The club has a 1½-inch Atlantic and a 1½-inch Pacific. Privately owned engines range from small 4-4-0s to a big 4-8-4. Steam boats, stationary engines, and steam traction are also modeled.

Special Events: Spring Meet, May 10-11. Fall Meet, October 11-12.

Note: Monthly meetings, second Friday of each month, 8:00 p.m., at St. Christopher's Church at Hacienda and Via Toledo in San Lorenzo.

Location: Corner of Grizzly Peak Boulevard and Lomas Cantadas in Tilden Park, Oakland.

Contact: Jim Dameron
Secretary

Mailing Address:
130 Pereira Avenue
Tracy, CA 95376
Telephone: (209) 835-0263

REDWOOD VALLEY RAILWAY CORP.

Steam, scheduled
15" gauge

REDWOOD VALLEY RAILWAY

Ride/Operation: A 1¼-mile, 12-minute ride through redwoods, laurels, and the scenic wilds of Tilden Park, passing through a tunnel, over a trestle, up and down grades, and around many curves. The operation re-creates an old-time narrow-gauge atmosphere with authentically designed locomotives, wooden cars, realistic trackwork, and scale buildings.

Train: Most trains are twelve cars long plus a caboose.

Schedule: Weekends and holidays, 11:00 a.m.-6:00 p.m., weather permitting (no trains after dark). Weekdays, Easter and summer vacations, 12:00-5:00 p.m. Closed Thanksgiving Day, Christmas Day.

Fare: Single-ride ticket $1.50, five-ride ticket $6.00, under age two ride free.

Locomotives: 0-4-0 No. 2, "Juniper," internal-combustion switcher; 2-4-2 No. 4, "Laurel"; 4-4-0 No. 5, "Fern"; 4-6-0 No. 11, "Sequoia."

Passenger Cars: Freight-type cars with wood bodies, truss rods, and archbar trucks. Capacity eight adults each.

Rolling Stock/Equipment: One Denver & Rio Grande Western-style eight-wheel caboose; 9 four-wheel work "Jimmies"; weed-spray car; tie-inserter car; ballast-regulator car; push car.

Note: The current project is a 2-6-2 locomotive.

Location: Tilden Regional Park.

P

Contact: Ellen E. Thomsen
President

Mailing Address:
2950 Magnolia Street
Berkeley, CA 94705
Telephone: (510) 548-6100

LAWS RAILROAD MUSEUM
& HISTORICAL SITE

Railway museum
36" gauge

LAWS RAILROAD MUSEUM & HISTORICAL SITE

Displays/Exhibits: In 1960, the Southern Pacific Railroad abandoned "The Slim Princess," its famed narrow-gauge line from Keeler to Laws. At the time of the abandonment, the railroad deeded 1909 Baldwin 4-6-0 No. 9, the Laws station building, rolling stock, and other property to the city of Bishop and Inyo County. The 1883 depot, the reception center, and the station agent's residence are open to the public. Outside is the hand-operated gallows-type turntable, used until the last day of operation. The train, headed by No. 9, includes several freight cars and a caboose. Other narrow-gauge rolling stock on display includes a rare cupola caboose, passenger and freight equipment, and a Brill self-propelled car. Also at the site are the Wells Fargo building, library and arts building, assay house, Chalfont General Store, bottle house, country store, doctor's office, carriage house, Conway house, Laws post office, farm machinery, pioneer display building, firehouse, print shop, and stove house.

Schedule: Daily, 10:00 a.m.-4:00 p.m., weather permitting.
Admission: Donations welcomed.

Location: From Bishop, follow U.S. Highway 6 north 4.5 miles to the junction of Silver Canyon Road, then turn right.

Contact: Alice J. Boothe
Administrator

Mailing Address:
P.O. Box 363
Bishop, CA 93515
Telephone: (619) 873-5950

KNOTT'S BERRY FARM
Steam, scheduled
Narrow gauge

KNOTT'S BERRY FARM

Ride/Operation: Gasoline-driven railway car originally used by the Rio Grande Southern and other lines as a more cost-effective passenger alternative to the high operating cost of the steam train. Built in 1931. Original body/engine: Pierce-Arrow "33" 6 cyl. Rebuilt engine: GMC Truck. Operates in place of steam passenger train weekdays in January and February only.

Train: The Ghost Town & Calico Railway is held up by bandits more than 10,000 times a year, giving it the highest crime rate of any railroad in the world.

Schedule: Open daily except Christmas.
Fare/Admission: Adults $29.95, seniors (60 +) and children ages 3-11 $19.95.

 Fullerton, 8 miles away

Contact: Robert Ochsner

Mailing Address:
8039 Beach Blvd.
Buena Park, CA 90620
Telephone: (714) 220-5130
Fax: (714) 220-5124

SAN DIEGO RAILROAD MUSEUM

Ride/Operation: A 16-mile, 1½ hour round trip from Campo to Miller Creek through the scenic hills of San Diego back country, over the San Diego & Arizona (former San Diego & Arizona Eastern, former Southern Pacific). Day trips to Tecate, Mexico are also offered. The museum also maintains a restored depot at La Mesa. Administrative offices and research library are located in the historic Santa Fe Depot.

Displays/Exhibits: Large collection at Campo includes: No. 11, 1929 Alco 2-8-2T, former Coos Bay Lumber Co.; No. 46, 1937 Baldwin 2-6-6-2, former California Western Railroad; No. 104, 1904 Baldwin 2-8-0, former Southern Pacific Railroad; many historic passenger cars and freight and work equipment from area railroads. Walking tours of the Campo collection are featured every weekend.

Schedule: Open weekends and certain holidays; train leave Campo Depot at 12:01 and 2:30 p.m.

Fare/Admission: Adults $10.00, seniors $8.00, children 6-12 $3.00, under six ride free.

Locomotives: No.3, 1923 Lima 3-truck Shay, former Hutchinson Lumber; No. 1366, 1947 Fairbanks-Morse H20-44, former Union Pacific; No. 1809, EMD MRS-3, former U.S. Army (SD&A); No. 2353, 1912 Baldwin 4-6-0, former SP & SD & AE; No. 7485, 45-ton General Electric, former U.S. Army (SD&A); No. 2093, 1949 Alco RS-2, former Kennecott Cooper.

Special Events: Mexico day trips: one or two Saturdays per month, by reservation only-$35 adults, $20 children.

Location: 70 miles from downtown San Diego. Take the Buckman Springs exit off I-8 east and travel south 10 miles to state highway 94, then one mile west to Campo.

Contact: Win Mott
Executive Director

Mailing Address:
1050 Kettner Boulevard
San Diego, CA 92101
Telephone: Tape: (619) 687-7762
Campo Depot: (619) 478-9937
Admin. Office & Sales: (619) 595-3030
Fax: (619) 595-3034

NORTHERN COUNTIES LOGGING MUSEUM
Steam, scheduled
Standard gauge

EILEEN FAHEY

Ride/Operation: Fort Humboldt State Historic Park, in southwestern Eureka, hosts a small logging exhibit emphasizing historic steam artifacts, primarily from local redwood lumber companies. Some equipment has been restored by the Northern Counties Logging Interpretive Association and is steamed on occasion. Visitors can enjoy a short ride behind a steam locomotive, usually two round trips to the end of the 400 feet of track.

Displays/Exhibits: One and one-half acres of display area contain six steam donkeys, from a small 3-ton vertical spool to a 110-ton Washington Iron Works "Slackliner," and two small (9- and 12-ton) steam locomotives of unique design. A walkway around the grounds includes display panels that take visitors from logging's earliest days to today's modern mechanized methods.

Schedule: Park: daily, 9:00 a.m.-5:00 p.m., availability of staff permitting. Steam-ups: April 26-27, May 17, June 21, July 19, August 16, and September 20, 10:00 a.m.-4:00 p.m.

Fare: A donation of $1.00 (adults) and $.50 (children) is requested to help with equipment maintenance.

Locomotives: No. 1, 1892 Marshutz & Cantrell 12-ton 0-4-0, former Bear Harbor Lumber Company; 9-ton 0-4-0, former Elk River Mill & Lumber Co. No. 1, "Falk." The NCLIA has several other locomotives at a separate location, including No. 2, 1898 Baldwin 2-4-2T, former Bear Harbor Lumber Co.; No. 15, 1916 Baldwin 2-8-2, and No. 33, 3-truck Shay, both former Hammond Lumber Co.; No. 29, 1910 Baldwin 2-6-2, former Pacific Lumber Co.; No. 7, 2-truck Shay, former Arcata & Mad River (being restored to operating condition); No. 54, 28-ton Heisler converted to diesel, former Mutual Plywood Corp.

Rolling Stock/Equipment: At a separate location are several steam, diesel, and gasoline donkeys of various sizes, a steam sawmill (under restoration), and a Clyde track-laying machine, one of only two known to exist.

Special Events: Annual Dolbeer Steam Donkey Days, held in conjunction with Eureka's Rhododendron Festival. Other steam-ups may be scheduled for special events such as Rotary International District Conventions, Humboldt County School Day, etc.; please call for information.

Location: 3431 Fort Avenue.

Eureka (bus service)

Contact: Bill Fahey

Mailing Address:
NCLIA
3431 Fort Avenue
Eureka, CA 95503
Telephone: (707) 445-6567

ROARING CAMP & BIG TREES
NARROW GAUGE RAILROAD

Steam, scheduled
36" gauge

ROARING CAMP & BIG TREES NARROW GAUGE RAILROAD

Ride/Operation: Trains leave from the 1880 South Pacific Coast depot at Felton and make a 6-mile, 1 ¼-hour round trip from Roaring Camp to Bear Mountain in the Santa Cruz Mountains. The route, which has a maximum gradient of 8½ percent, passes directly through the Welch Big Trees Grove of California Redwoods, the first grove purchased for preservation of the redwoods, in 1867. A spectacular mountainside switchback is located at Spring Canyon.

Displays/Exhibits: Steam sawmill, 1880 general store, covered bridge, red caboose saloon, chuck-wagon barbecue, linotype/print exhibit, photo booth. Henry Cowell State Park is adjacent.

Train: Open excursion-type cars; side-door caboose; observation car.

Schedule: January-March & October-December, weekends & holidays, 12:00, 1:30 & 3:00 p.m.; April-June 6, weekdays, 11 a.m.; weekends & holidays, 12 noon, 1:30 p.m., & 3 p.m.; June 7-September 2, weekdays, 11:00 a.m., 12:15 p.m., 1:30 p.m. & 3 p.m.; weekends and holidays, 11:00 a.m., 12:15 p.m., 1:30 p.m., 2:45 p.m. & 4 p.m. September 2-September 30, weekdays, 11:00 a.m.; weekends & holidays 11:00 a.m., 12:15 p.m., 1:30 p.m., 2:45 p.m., and 4 p.m.; October-November, weekdays 11:00 a.m. (No trains Christmas day)

Fare: Adults $13.50, children (3-12) $9.75.

Locomotives: No. 1, 1912 Lima 2-truck Shay, former Coal Processing Corp. No. 2593; No. 2, 1899 2-truck Heisler, former West Side Lumber Co. No. 3; No. 5, 1928 2-truck Climax, former Elk River Coal & Lumber No. 3; No. 6, 1912 Lima 2-truck Shay, former W.M. Ritter No. 1; No. 7, 1911 Lima 3-truck Shay, former West Side & Cherry Valley Ry. No. 7; No. 40, 1958 Plymouth diesel switcher, former Kaiser Steel Co. No. 2.

Special Events: Civil War Reenactment. 1830s Mountain Man Rendezvous. Fourth of July Frog Jump. Moonlight Steam Train Parties.

Location: Six miles north of Santa Cruz on Graham Hill Road.

Contact: Georgiana P. Clark
Chief Executive Officer

Mailing Address:
P.O. Box G-1
Felton, CA 95018
Telephone: (408) 335-4484
Fax: (408) 335-3509
E-mail: RCamp448@aol.com

**SANTA CRUZ, BIG TREES &
PACIFIC RAILWAY**
*Diesel, scheduled
Standard gauge*

GEORGE A. FORERO, JR

Ride/Operation: Built in 1875 as the Santa Cruz & Felton Railroad and considered one of the most scenic railroads in the West, this line offers a 14-mile, 2½–hour round trip along the spectacular San Lorenzo River Canyon to the beach at Santa Cruz. The train travels across two wooden trestles, crosses the San Lorenzo River on a long steel bridge, traverses a tunnel, passes the fabled Big Trees stand of California redwoods, and rolls down quiet Santa Cruz streets lined with Victorian homes. The SCBT&P is a working 10-mile common carrier railroad that provides freight and passenger service. Plans are under way to operate a steam locomotive on the line.

Train: Three 1900-era wooden passenger coaches; two 1920s-era steel coaches; four open-air cars; restored 1895 caboose, former Lake Superior & Ishpeming.

Schedule: Daily in summer; weekends and holidays in spring and fall; 10:30 a.m. & 2:30 p.m. from Felton, 12:30 p.m. from Santa Cruz. Additional trains may operate depending on the season.

Fare: Adults $15.00, children (3-12) $11.00.

Locomotives: Nos. 2600 & 2641, CF7 1500-horsepower diesels, former Santa Fe; No. 20, 50-ton centercab Whitcomb. Steam locomotive to be announced.

Location: 6 miles inland from Santa Cruz, California, on Graham Hill Road.

Contact: Georgiana P. Clark
Chief Executive Officer

Mailing Address:
P.O. Box G-1
Felton, CA 95018
Telephone: (408) 335-4484
Fax: (408) 335-3509

FILLMORE & WESTERN RAILWAY
Diesel, scheduled
Standard gauge

FILLMORE & WESTERN RAILWAY

Ride/Operation: This railway offers rides through the citrus groves on a former Southern Pacific branch line. Fillmore and Santa Paula still have their original 1887 depot buildings as centerpieces in downtown districts featuring museums and shopping. The trains you will ride have appeared in over 150 Hollywood motion pictures, television series, and commercials.

Train: Heavyweight and/or streamlined passenger cars pulled by model F7 diesels and/or an Alco RS-32. Steam locomotive No. 51 is fired up for occasional special events.

Schedule: Two-hour-long daytime trips between Fillmore and Santa Paula on weekends, year round. Special three-hour "Theater on Rails" Murder Mystery or Vaudeville trips featuring dinner in the diner on Saturday evenings and some Fridays, Spring and Fall. Bar-B-Que dinner trips during the Summer. Call or write for a current timetable.

Fare: Excursion fares vary depending upon length and type of trip. Group rates and charters are available year round.

Locomotives: No. 1, 1891 Porter 0-4-0, former Rogue River Valley; No. 51, 1906 Baldwin 2-8-0, former Great Western Railway; Nos. 100 & 101, 1949 EMD F7As, former Chicago & North Western; No. 4009, 1961 Alco RS-32, former Southern Pacific.

Rolling Stock: Heavyweight passenger cars built in the 1920's and lightweight cars built in the 1940's and 1950's.

Special Events: Fillmore Orange Festival, May 3-4, July 4th day and evening trips, Pumpkin Patch Special, three weekends in October, Santa Claus Specials three weekends in December; and the New Year's Eve Party Train on December 31. Other events to be announced.

Location: Approximately forty-five miles northwest of Los Angeles in rural Ventura County. Fillmore is located on S.R. 126, between I-5 and U.S. 101. Most trains depart from Central Park in Fillmore's Old Town District, but Santa Paula departures are also available on some trains.

Oxnard

Contact: Marketing Manager

Mailing Address:
351 Santa Clara Avenue
Fillmore, CA 93015
Telephone: (805) 524-2546
Fax: (805) 524-1838

YOSEMITE MOUNTAIN-
SUGAR PINE RAILROAD
Steam, scheduled
36" gauge

JOSEPH T. BISPO

Ride/Operation: From 1899 to 1931 the Madera Sugar Pine Lumber Company logged more than thirty thousand acres of timber, using wood-burning Shay locomotives to haul logs to the sawmill at Sugar Pine. The YM-SP operates a narrated, 4-mile, 45-minute round trip over the restored line of the Madera Sugar Pine Lumber Company. Track runs through the scenic Sierra Nevada at an elevation of 5,000 feet, winds down a 4-percent grade into Lewis Creek Canyon, passes Horseshoe Curve, crosses Cold Spring Crossing, and stops at Lewis Creep Loop.

Displays/Exhibits: A museum housed in an 1856 log cabin displays railroad artifacts, antique Yosemite photos, and many relics of sawmill life. Steam donkey engine and assorted rolling stock on display.

Schedule: Railcars: Daily, April-October. Steam train: Daily, May 12-September; Weekends, early May and October.

Fare: Railcars: Adults $6.75, children (3-12) $3.75. Steam train: Adults $10, children (3-12) $5.

Locomotives: No. 10, 1928 Lima 3-truck Shay (largest narrow-gauge Shay built) & No. 15, 1913 Lima 3-truck Shay, both former Westside Lumber Co.; No. 5, 1934 Vulcan 10-ton gas-mechanical; three former WL Model A powered railcars.

Passenger Cars: Logging cars; covered and open converted flatcars, former Westside Lumber Co.

Rolling Stock/Equipment: Wedge snowplow, oil tank car, refrigerator cars, parts car, Model A speeder, side dump car, crane/handcar.

Special Events: Moonlight Special with steak barbecue and music every Saturday night in summer; reservations advised.

Notes: Operating in the Sierra National Forest.

Location: Four miles south of Yosemite National Park on Highway 41.

Contact: Max Stauffer
President
Mailing Address:
56001 Yosemite Highway 41
Fish Camp, CA 93623
Telephone: (209) 683-7273

California, Folsom
(Folsom City Zoo)
R

TOM PANIAGUA

FOLSOM VALLEY RAILWAY
DIV. OF GOLDEN SPIKE ENTERPRISES
Steam, scheduled
12" Narrow gauge

Ride/Operation: A ¾mile trip (10 minute ride) through a 50-acre city park features vintage wooden freight cars drawn by a 1/3 scale coal-burning locomotive representative of late nineteenth-century steam motive power.

Displays/Exhibits: Old-time freight wagons and horse-drawn farm implements on display near the railroad. Also, adjacent to the railroad is the Folsom City Zoo and Park.

Schedule: February-November, Tuesdays-Fridays from 11:00 a.m.-2:00 p.m.; Saturdays, Sundays, and Holidays from 11:00 a.m.-5:00 p.m.; December-January Saturdays, Sundays and School Holidays. (Weather Permitting)

Fare: $1.00 per person

Rolling Stock: 1950 Ottawa old-time wooden, truss rod style freight cars, cattle car, hopper car, 5 open gondola cars, bobber caboose.

Locomotives: 4-4-0 Coal Fired Ottawa (The Cricket)

Special Events: The week of 4th of July celebration, the train will operate all day until 10:00 p.m.

Notes: Planning to expand railway to 2-3 miles and enlarging gift center.

Location: Folsom is approximately 25 miles east of Sacramento off of U.S. 50. Folsom Valley Railway is next to the Folsom Zoo, which is located at 50 Natoma Street.

Contact: Terry and Geri Gold
Owners

Mailing Address:
121 Dunstable Way
Folsom, CA 95630
Telephone & Fax: (916) 983-1873
(Call before sending fax)

THE SKUNK TRAIN
CALIFORNIA WESTERN RAILROAD
Diesel, steam, scheduled
Standard gauge

GARY RICHARDS

Ride/Operation: 40 mile scenic ride through the redwoods.

Schedule: Open year round, call for details.

Fare/Admission: Full day adults $26, children 5-11 $12; half day adults $21, children 5-11 $10.

Locomotives: Steam locomotive, historic motor rail cars.

Location: Highway 1 in Fort Bragg, CA, or Highway 101 in Willits.

Contact: Lynn A. Hakin
Chief Operating Officer

Mailing Address:
P.O. Box 907
Fort Bragg, CA 95437
Telephone: (707) 964-6271
Fax: (707) 964-6754

NILES CANYON RAILWAY
Steam, diesel, scheduled
Standard gauge

GEORGE A. FORERO, JR.

Ride/Operation: A 12-mile, 1-hour round trip through scenic Niles Canyon over a portion of the original transcontinental railroad, built in the 1860s.

Displays/Exhibits: Three operating trains plus steam engines, diesel engines, and cars are on display at the terminal area.

Train: Several consists: a four- or five-car train of a 2 coach plus open excursion cars, pulled by a vintage 80-ton diesel (to be replaced or supplemented by a steam engine); a 1926 diesel railbus.

Schedule: First and third Sundays of every month, 10:00 a.m.-4:00 p.m. Charters available.

Fare: Suggested donations are adults $6.00, children (3-12) $3.00.

Locomotives: Nos. 1 & 5, 3-truck Heislers, and Nos. 7 & 12, 3-truck Shays, all former Pickering Lumber; 2-6-2T No. 2, former Quincy Railroad; 0-4-0TNo. 3, former Steptoe Valley; 2-6-2TNo. 4, former Clover Valley; 2-6-2No. 30, former Sierra Railroad; 2-6-2T No. 233, former Central Pacific; 0-6-0No. 1269 and 4-6-2No. 2467, both former Southern Pacific.

Passenger Cars: 1911 Harriman coach, former Southern Pacific; 1910 open excursion cars (former flatcars); homemade coach; others.

Special Events: Spring Wildflower excursion. Fall Color excursion. Christmas Train of Lights, December.

Location: Sunol, southern Alameda County, between Pleasanton and Fremont.

Contact: Alan Ramsay
Director of Public Relations

Mailing Address:
P.O. Box 2247, Niles Station
Fremont, CA 94536-0247
Telephone: (510) 862-9063

SOCIETY FOR THE PRESERVATION OF CARTER RAILROAD RESOURCES

Horse, scheduled
36" gauge

BRUCE MAC GREGOR

Ride/Operation: This group is dedicated to acquiring and restoring railroad cars constructed by Carter Brothers of Newark, California, in the late 1800s. The society currently has seven Carter cars and three other cars. The cars are restored using appropriate hand tools, following the techniques used in the original construction.

The 1 ½-mile ride is powered by one of the Society's two draft horses, making this the only regularly scheduled horse-drawn railroad in the United States; the line is a re-creation of the nearby Centerville Branch of the South Pacific Coast Railroad, which was horse-drawn for more than 25 years. The trip takes passengers through the Ardenwood Historic Farm, a 200-acre working farm.

Displays/Exhibits: The open-air restoration shop is open to the public and contains two boxcars, two flatcars, a combine, and a handcar. The Ardenwood Historic Farm, which consists of a historic farmhouse, a blacksmith shop, farmyard, and operating Best steam tractor, demonstrates life on a farm at the turn of the century.

Schedule: Train: April-October; Thursday & Fridays, 10:30 a.m.-3:00 p.m.; weekends, 10:30 a.m.-4:00 p.m.

Admission: Adults $6.00, senior citizens $4.00, children (4-17) $3.50. Train fare is included with park admission. Admission for special events is $1.00 extra.

Locomotives/Trolleys: "Robbie", 1989 Percheron; "Tucker", 1990 Belgian, both 0-2-2-0T hayburners. No. 2, 1940 Whitcomb 14 ton, former ASARCO.

Rolling Stock/Equipment: No. 47, 1881 caboose and No. 1725, 1888 15-ton flat car, both former South Pacific Coast; No. 1010, 1882 combine, former San Joaquin & Sierra Nevada; No. 253, 1874 8-ton boxcar, former Monterey & Salinas Valley; Nos. 10 & 472, 1880 10-ton boxcars, and No. 444, 1880 10-ton combination boxcar, all former Oregonian; No. 439, 15-ton flatcar, former Diamond & Caldor; No. 8, 1885 single-truck horsecar, former Oakland Railroad.

Special Events: Railroad Heritage Fair and Exposition, April 5 (tentative-please call). Harvest Festival, early October.

Location: 34600 Ardenwood Boulevard, 15 miles south of Oakland at the intersection of I-880 and highway 84.

Fremont (Centerville)

Contact: Rich Hill

Mailing Address: SPCRR
P.O. Box 783
Newark, CA 94560
Telephone: (408) 370-3555

SOUTH COAST RAILROAD MUSEUM
Railway museum
Standard gauge

DAVID HIETER

Ride/Operation: The Goleta Depot, built in 1901 by the Southern Pacific Railroad, was relocated in 1981 to Lake Los Carneros County Park and restored; it now houses a museum. A 7½-inch-gauge train operates over one-third of a mile of track, and handcar rides are given.

Displays/Exhibits: A central exhibit is the 300-square-foot HO-scale model railroad. Visitors can also see the refurnished depot office, operating signal and communications equipment in the building and on the grounds, and various small exhibits and displays of railroad artifacts, rare photographs, and memorabilia.

Schedule: Museum: Wednesday-Sunday, 1:00-4:00 p.m. Miniature train: Wednesdays & Fridays 2:00-3:30 p.m.; Saturdays & Sundays, 1:00-4:00 p.m. Handcar rides: Third Saturday of every month, 1:00-4:00 p.m.

Fare/Admission: Museum: donation ($1 suggested for adults). Miniature train: $1.00. Handcar rides: No charge.

Rolling Stock/Equipment: 1960s Southern Pacific bay-window caboose No. 4023.

Special Events: Depot Day, September 28, 11:00 a.m. to 4:00 p.m., features rides on handcar, inspection car, and miniature steam trains; barbecue; special one-day exhibits; and silent auction.

Location: 300 North Los Carneros Road (7 miles west of Santa Barbara on U.S. 101).

Contact: Gary B. Coombs
Director

Mailing Address:
300 North Los Carneros Road
Goleta, CA 93117
Telephone: (805) 964-3540

TED BENSON

Ride/Operation: Operated by the California State Railroad Museum, Railtown 1897 Historic Sierra Railway Shops is enjoying its Centennial Year as a continuously operated steam locomotive maintenance complex established in 1897, now a California State Historic Park. Railtown 1897 and the Sierra Railway is also one of Hollywood's most popular feature film and television locations. Over 200 movies, television programs and commercials have been filmed at Railtown, including *The Unforgiven, Back to the Future III, High Noon, The Virginian, Petticoat Junction,* and *Wild, Wild West.*

Displays/Exhibits: Continuously worked steam locomotive roundhouse and shops of the Sierra RR.

Train Schedule: Weekends, April-September; Saturdays, October-November. Trains depart on the hour between 11:00 a.m. and 3:00 p.m. for a 6-mile, 40 minute round trip excursion. Call for "special trains."

Roundhouse and Maintenance Shops Tours: Weekends, year round. 45 minute guided tours of the entire working roundhouse and maintenance shop complex. Self-guided tours available daily.

Fares: Train: adults $6.00, children (6-12) $3.00, 5 and under free. Tours: adults $2.00, children (6-12) $1.00, 5 and under free.

Passenger Cars: No. 5 combine and No. 6 coach "shorty" cars built in San Francisco, 1903 by Holman; original Sierra Railroad parlor car and four suburban coaches, all former Southern Pacific; 1869 "Wason" coach, former Central Pacific; two former CP mountain observation cars; 1910 Harriman-type coach; circa 1919 baggage car; Pullman "Dover Patrol."

Location: 5th Avenue at Reservoir Road. Five blocks from Hwy 49/108.

Riverbank (bus connection)

Business Operations: Joe Nemmer
Media Calls: Nanci Kramer

Mailing Address: P.O. Box 1250
Jamestown, CA 95327
Business Telephone: (209) 984-3953
Media Telephone: (916) 445-1705

LOMITA RAILROAD MUSEUM
Railway museum
Standard gauge

LOMITA RAILROAD MUSEUM

Displays/Exhibits: This museum is a replica of the Boston & Maine station at Greenwood, Massachusetts. No expense was spared to create a suitable treasury for the railroad artifacts on display, which include many live-steam models as well as a huge collection of railroadiana. The station agent's office is complete in every respect. Outside, a 1902 Southern Pacific Mogul and a 1910 Union Pacific caboose wait at the station platforms. A 1913 wooden boxcar and a 1923 oil tank car are also on display at the museum's Annex Park, a charming recreation park decorated with benches, a water fountain, lights, and brickwork of the Victorian era.

Schedule: Wednesday-Sunday, 10:00 a.m.-5:00 p.m. Closed Thanksgiving and Christmas.

Admission: Adults $1.00, children $.50.

Locomotives: No. 1765, 1902 Baldwin 2-6-0, former Southern Pacific, with a large whaleback tender.

Rolling Stock/Equipment: 1910 Union Pacific class CA-1 caboose No. 25730; 1910 wooden boxcar; 1923 oil tank car, former Union Oil Company (Alaska).

Location: 250th & Woodward avenues; just south of Los Angeles.

Contact: Alice Abbott
Manager

Mailing Address:
250th & Woodward Avenue
Lomita, CA 90717
Telephone: (310) 326-6255

DALE L. BROWN, JR.

Ride/Operation: Founded in 1952 as a last resting place for steam locomotives and other railroad and obsolete transportation equipment, the Travel Town Museum now boasts a fine collection of rare, valuable pieces that is being used to educate the public about railroad history as well as to entertain. Visitors may take a 10-minute, propane-powered ride with covered cars on 16-inch-gauge track around the perimeter of the museum. Docent Tours of the passenger cars are offered the third Sunday of each month.

Displays/Exhibits: Fourteen steam locomotives; one electric; eight passenger cars; five cabooses; eight freight cars; five other major pieces; two operating diesel switchers.

Schedule: Daily except Christmas, 10:00 a.m.-4:00 p.m. Summers: Daily, 10:00 a.m.-5:00 p.m.

Fare/Admission: Museum: No charge. Scale Train Ride: Adults $1.75, children $1.25. Group rates available.

Locomotives/Trolleys: No. 1, 1864 Norris-Lancaster 4-4-0, former Stockton Terminal & Eastern; No. 664, 1899 Baldwin 2-8-0, former Santa Fe; No. 3025, 1904 Alco 4-4-2, former Southern Pacific; No. 1544, 1902 steeple-cab electric, former Pacific Electric; newly acquired 1955 Baldwin RS-12, former McCloud River No. 33, later California Western No. 56; others.

Rolling Stock/Equipment: "The Little Nugget," club-dorm No. 701 from the Union Pacific Streamliner *City of Los Angeles*, and sleeping cars "Rose Bowl" (1937) and "Hunters Points" (1940), both originally on *City of San Francisco;* others.

Notes: Persons interested in Travel Town improvements may join the American Southwestern Railway Association (213) 668-0104. Those interested in operations the Southern California Scenic Railway Association, (213) 667-1423.

Location: Northwest corner of Griffith Park. Take Zoo Drive west or exit from the 134 freeway at Forest Lawn Drive and follow signs to Griffith Park.

Los Angeles, Glendale

Contact: Operations Manager

Mailing Address:
3900 W. Chevy Chase Drive
Los Angeles, CA 90039
Telephone: (213) 662-5874

TRAVEL TOWN MUSEUM
CRYSTAL SPRINGS & CAHUENGA VALLEY RAILROAD
Diesel, scheduled

ED SIKORA

Ride/Operation: The Crystal Springs & Cahuenga Valley Railroad is the excursion railroad of the Travel Town Museum. When complete, it will provide a rail connection between the Travel Town Museum and the Los Angeles Zoo-Autry Museum of Western Heritages, a distance of about 2 miles. At this time, the operating track extends only to the Museum boundary, but each year will see additional track extensions.

Train: SP and AT&SF cabooses.

Schedule: First Sunday of every month, 10:00 a.m.-5:00 p.m. (Second Sunday if Easter or Christmas fall on first Sunday.)

Fare: Free. Donations accepted.

Locomotives: No. 1, 1942 Electromotive Corp. 40-ton industrial switcher; No. 56, 1955 Baldwin-Lima-Hamilton RS-12.

Notes: Persons interested in equipment restoration, railway operations and track construction may join the Southern California Scenic Railway Association, (213) 667-1423.

Location: Northwest corner of Griffith Park. Exit the eastbound or westbound 134 Freeway at Forest Lawn Drive, and follow the signs to Griffith Park and Museums.

Los Angeles, Glendale

Contact: Operations Manager

Mailing Address:
3900 W. Chevy Chase Drive
Los Angeles, CA 90039
Telephone: (213) 662-5847

BILLY JONES WILDCAT RAILROAD
Steam, scheduled
18" gauge

BILLY JONES WILDCAT RAILROAD

Ride/Operation: A 1-mile, 8-minute loop through a park, featuring a 40-foot wooden trestle, a 2-percent grade, and a hand-operated turntable. The railroad crosses Los Gatos Creek on an 86-foot-long bridge. The railroad is a 1/3-scale operation.

Displays/Exhibits: A 1910 Savage carousel is also operated.

Schedule: Train: March 15-beginning of school summer vacation and September 6-October 31, weekends, 10:30 a.m.-4:30 p.m.; beginning of school summer vacation-September 5, daily, 10:30 a.m.-4:30 p.m.; November 1-March 14, weekends, 11:00 a.m.-3:00 p.m. Carousel: March 15-beginning of school summer vacation and September 6-October 31, Tuesday-Sunday, 10:30 a.m.-4:30 p.m.; beginning of school summer vacation-September 5, daily, 10:30 a.m.-4:30 p.m.; November 1-January 1, Tuesday-Sunday, 11:00 a.m.-3:00 p.m.; January 2-March 14, weekends, 11:00 a.m.-3:00 p.m. Weather permitting.

Fare: Train and carousel: $1.00; handicapped persons and children under 2 ride free.

Locomotives: No. 2, 1905 Johnson Machine Works 2-6-2, former Venice miniature railroad; No. 2502 Diesel Hydraulic.

Passenger Cars: 1915 MacDermott San Francisco Overfair Railway; wheelchair-accessible car available.

Location: Oak Meadow Park, one block west of state highway 17; entrance is on Blossom Hill Road.

Contact: Jerry Kennedy
General Manager

Mailing Address:
P.O. Box 234
Los Gatos, CA 95031
Telephone: (408) 395-RIDE

MC CLOUD RAILWAY COMPANY
Steam, scheduled and irregular
Standard gauge

MC CLOUD RAILWAY COMPANY

Ride/Operation: Open air excursion rides, mostly to Signal Butte (approximately 5 miles toward Mt. Shasta). Special steam runs also.

Schedule: June & September, Saturday, 4:00 p.m. July & August, Saturday-Sunday, 4:00 p.m. Special excursions on Memorial Day weekend, Labor Day weekend, and others.

Fare: Adults $9.00, children under 12 $6.00. Call for steam fares.

Locomotives: No. 25 steam engine (only steam engine retained by MCRR); Nos. 36, 37, 38, 39 diesel; No. 30 former MCRR.

Passenger Cars: Open air flatcar with theater seats and fenced perimeter. Diner cars (see Shasta Sunset Dinner Train).

Special Events: 1997 Centennial celebration for railroad and town of McCloud.

Notes: See Shasta Sunset Dinner Train, page 41. Forty-five miles from Yreka Western (Blue Goose) Excursion.

Location: I-5 to Mt. Shasta, CA (60 miles north of Redding, CA and 90 miles south of Medford, OR), then 10 miles east on Highway 89 South. In McCloud trains load on Main Street across from the post office, bank, and McCloud Hotel.

Dunsmuir

Contact: Jeff Forbis
President

Mailing Address:
P.O. Box 1500
McCloud, CA 96057
Telephone: (916) 964-2141
Fax: (916) 964-2250
E-mail: train@macshasta.com
Internet: http://www.mtshasta.com/mcrail/mcrail.html

MC CLOUD RAILWAY COMPANY

Ride/Operation: Four-course gourmet meal served in elegantly restored 80-year old dining cars. Three-hour ride with meal.

Schedule: April, November, December: Saturday; May, June, September, October: Friday & Saturday; July, August: Friday-Sunday. Times: Friday & Saturday 6:00 p.m. except October-December, 5:00 p.m.; Sunday, 1:00 p.m.

Fare: Dinner with 3 hour ride: Adults $70.00, children under 12 $35.00. Lunch with 2 hour ride: $49.00, children under 12 $29.00. Tax, tip, and standard beverages included. Beer and wine extra.

Locomotives: No. 25 steam engine; Nos. 36, 37, 38, 39 diesel; No. 30 former MCRR.

Passenger Cars: 1916 IC coaches furnished in mahoghany and antique brass.

Special Events: 1997 is centennial for town of McCloud and railroad. Steam Engine no. 25 will run again (no action since 1986). Debut of No. 25 on Memorial Day weekend.

Notes: See McCloud Railway, page 40. Forty-five miles from Yreka Western (Blue Goose) Excursion.

Location: I-5 to Mt. Shasta, CA (60 miles north of Redding, CA and 90 miles south of Medford, OR), then 10 miles east on Highway 89 South. In McCloud trains load on Main Street across from the post office, bank, and McCloud Hotel.

P 🚌 ✳ ♁ ⚓ 🏛

▶ ◀ 🚂 Dunsmuir

Contact: Verline Forbis
President

Mailing Address:
P.O. Box 1500
McCloud, CA 96057
Telephone: (916) 964-2141
Fax: (916) 964-2250
E-mail: train@macshasta.com
Internet: http://www.mtshasta.com/mcrail/mcrail.html

NAPA VALLEY WINE TRAIN
Diesel, scheduled
Standard gauge

NAPA VALLEY WINE TRAIN

Ride/Operation: Gourmet dining excursions aboard lavishly restored 1915 Pullman cars for lunch, brunch or dinner year-round while gently gliding past picturesque vineyards.

Schedule: Year round, brunch, lunch and dinner, call for details.

Fare/Admission: Range from $22-$33, children 12 and under half-price Monday-Thursday only.

Locomotives: (4) 1951 Alco Diesel engines.

Rolling Stock/Equipment: (8) 1915-1917 Pullman dining coaches.

Special Events: Themed holiday cuisine, weekly vintners, luncheons, monthly Murder Mystery dinner theatre, regional cuisine cooking classes.

Location: 54 miles north of San Francisco. Connection with Amtrak or by car. Weekday tour bus packages with Grayline of San Francisco.

connection for Amtrak bus

Contact: Erica Ercolano

Mailing Address:
1275 McKinstry St.
Napa, CA 94559
Telephone: (707) 253-2160
(707) 253-9264
E-mail: wtsales@napanet.net
Internet: http://napavalley.com/winetrain.html

IRVINE PARK RAILROAD
Propane
Scheduled
24" gauge

JOHN FORD

Ride/Operation: Irvine Park Railroad is located on 500 acres in Irvine Regional Park, the oldest county park in the state of California. The train departs from an old fashioned depot, where railroad folk songs fill the air. The locomotive will make a scenic one-mile journey around the park during which riders can view two lakes complete with waterfalls and fountains, a grove of oak trees, and the Orange County Zoo. The ride is narrated by the engineer and lasts approximately 12 minutes.

Schedule: Winter: daily except Thanksgiving and Christmas, 10:00 a.m.-4:00 p.m. Summer: daily, 10:00 a.m.-4:30 p.m.

Fare/Admission: $2, children under age one are free. School and group rates are available. Call for prices.

Locomotives: A 1/3 scale replica of the 1863 C.P. Huntington.

Rolling Stock/Equipment: Four coaches.

Location: From State Highway 55 take the Chapman Avenue exit and drive east to Jamboree Road. Turn left into the park entrance.

Contact: John Ford or Steve Horn

Mailing Address:
1 Irvine Park Road
Orange, CA 92669
Telephone: (714) 661-5892
Fax: (714) 997-3035

California, Orland
R

ORLAND, NEWVILLE & PACIFIC RAILROAD
Steam, scheduled
15" gauge

BILL HOLLIDAY

Ride: The ON&P is an all-volunteer railroad operating in the Glenn County Fairgrounds. A 1-mile ride takes visitors past the original Orland Southern Pacific depot, the picnic site, and the demonstration orchard, then through a tunnel and along Heritage Trail. The train is normally pulled by a magnificent 5/12th-scale live-steam model of the North Pacific Coast's 1875 Baldwin narrow-gauge locomotive "Sonoma." The picnic grounds at Deadowl Station are open whenever the train is running.

Displays/Exhibits: Former Orland Southern Pacific depot, 1918 Southern Pacific 2-8-0 No. 2852, caboose, schoolhouse, blacksmith shop, print shop, 1920s gas station, miscellaneous steam machinery, old farm equipment. Livestock is also exhibited at fair time, during May and October.

Train: Two fifteen-inch-gauge (5 inches = 1 foot) locomotives, four open cars, caboose.

Schedule: Every Weekend March 29-30 thru May 10-11; June 16; July 4; Every Weekend-August 30-31, Sept. 1 thru Oct. 11-12. Hours 12:00 noon til 5:00 p.m. each day. Private parties by appointment.

Fare/Admission: $1.00, children under 2 ride free. Admission charged for Glenn County Fair and Harvest Festival.

Locomotive: Replica of 1876 Baldwin narrow-gauge 4-4-0 "Sonoma"; gas-powered work-train engine; 1938 15-inch gauge amusement park 4-4-0 steam locomotive.

Passenger Cars: Wood-sided gondolas, covered excursion car; one car is equipped to carry wheelchairs.

Rolling Stock: Caboose.

Special Events: Easter Egg Hunt, March 29; Glenn County Fair, May 14-18; Harvest Festival, October 18-19; Halloween Ghost Train, Oct. 31. (Fair & Festival Hours-Call for specific information.)

Location: Glenn County Fairgrounds, Woodruff Avenue and East Yolo Street, two blocks south of highway 32. Orland is 100 miles north of Sacramento on I-5 and 20 minutes west of Chico on 32.

 M

📷 (Heritage Trail, by appointment)

Contact: Frank Allen
Manager

Mailing Address:
221 East Yolo
P.O. Box 667
Orland, CA 95963
Telephone: (916) 865-9747
(916) 865-1168

44

ORANGE EMPIRE RAILWAY MUSEUM
Electric, diesel, steam, scheduled
Standard gauge, 42" gauge

ORANGE EMPIRE RAILWAY MUSEUM

Ride/Operation: Interurbans and trains operate on a 2-mile former railroad right-of-way; streetcars operate on a half-mile route around the museum.

Displays/Exhibits: More than 150 pieces of equipment, including streetcars; interurbans; work cars; electric, steam, and diesel locomotives; and passenger and freight cars. Grizzly Flats enginehouse with three-foot-gauge equipment is on display, including the steam engine "Emma Nevada" from the Ward Kimball collection.

Train: Santa Fe and Union Pacific coaches; U.S. Navy flatcar; UP vintage flatcar; Santa Fe, Southern Pacific, and Union Pacific cabooses.

Schedule: Equipment: Weekends and some school holidays, 11:00 a.m.-5:00 p.m. Museum grounds: Daily, 9:00 a.m.-5:00 p.m. Closed Thanksgiving and Christmas.

Fare/Admission: Equipment rides, all-day pass: Adults $6.00, children (6-11) $4.00, children under 6 ride free when accompanied by an adult. Admission: No charge except for special events. Prices vary for special events. Call or write for specific information.

Locomotives/Trolleys: No. 2, 1922 Baldwin 2-6-2, former Ventura County Railroad; No. 653, 1928 General Electric, former Sacramento Northern; No. 1624, 1925 Pacific Electric Shops; Nos. 498, 418 & 717, all former PE Shops; No. 8580, 1944 General Electric, former U.S. Air Force; No. 3165, former Los Angeles Transit Lines; Nos. 665, 1160, 1201 & 3100, all former Los Angeles Railway; No. 19, former Kyoto (Japan) Street Railway; No. 167, former Key System; RPO car, former Santa Fe; first-generation diesels.

Special Events: Rail Festival, April. Fall Festival, October. Spring and Fall Swap Meets. Santa Train, December. Write for dates.

Location: One mile south of Perris at 2201 South "A" Street, about 18 miles southeast of Riverside on Interstate 215. Perris has Greyhound bus service from Los Angeles and San Diego.

Contact: Olivette Shannon
Gift Shop Manager

Mailing Address:
P.O. Box 548
2201 South A Street
Perris, CA 92572
Telephone: (909) 943-3020

RAILWAY & LOCOMOTIVE
HISTORICAL SOCIETY
SOUTHERN CALIFORNIA CHAPTER
Railway display, Standard gauge

Displays/Exhibits: Motor cars; berth section of business car displaying various day and night arrangements; horse car with stabling section. Former Atchison, Topeka & Santa Fe Arcadia Station has many displays.

Schedule: Second Sunday of every month, 10:00 a.m.-3:30 p.m. Daily during Los Angeles County Fair, September 5-September 28. Other times by request. Call for schedule updates.

Admission: No charge other than general admission to L.A. County Fair during September.

Locomotives: "Big Boy" 4-8-8-4 No. 4014, largest steam engine built, "Centennial" No. 6915, largest diesel engine built, and 4-12-2 No. 9000, all former Union Pacific; 4-10-2 No. 5021, former Southern Pacific; 4-6-4 No. 3450, former Santa Fe; 1887 0-6-0 No. 2, former Outer Harbor Term; No. 3, 3-truck Climax, former Fruit Growers Supply; narrow-gauge 2-8-0 No. 3, former U.S. Potash.

Passenger Cars: Pullman business car, former Nickel Plate.

Rolling Stock/Equipment: Six-bunk drover's caboose No. 1314 & 1990 horse express car (used as library), both former Santa Fe; GATX ice refrigerator car.

Special Events: Open daily during L.A. County Fair.

Note: Meetings are held in the basement Carillon Room of the Glendale (CA) Federal Savings, 401 North Brand Boulevard, first Tuesday of every month, September 1-June 30, 7:30 p.m.

Location: Enter through gate 12 at White Avenue on the east side of the Los Angeles County Fairgrounds in Pomona.

Contact: Ted Liddle

Mailing Address:
R&LHS
L.A. County Fairplex
P.O. Box 2250
Pomona, CA 91769
Telephone: (818) 917-8454

GEORGE A. FORERO, JR.

Ride/Operation: A 1-mile ride around a balloon turning track through pine forest.

Displays/Exhibits: More than 70 freight cars representing nearly every car type of the Western Pacific Railroad; several passenger cars; other rolling stock; railroad artifacts in the diesel shop building.

Train: Diesel locomotive; cabooses.

Schedule: Daily, year-round, 10:00 a.m.-5:00 p.m. Train operates weekends, May 25-September 8, every half-hour, 11:00 a.m.-4:00 p.m.

Fare/Admission: Train ride: Adults $2.00, family rate $5.00 (valid all day). Museum: Free admission; donations welcomed.

Locomotives: One electric locomotive and 35 diesels of all types: 14 Electro-Motive Division engines, including a former Western Pacific SW1, an NW2, a GP7, an F7, a former Union Pacific GP30, a DDA40X, a GP9, and a former Southern Pacific SD9; 9 Alcos, including a former Western Pacific S-1, a former Southern Pacific RS-32, a former VIA FPA-4 & FBB-4, and a former Kennecott Copper RS-3; 5 Baldwins, including a former Oregon & North Western AS616 and a former U.S. Steel S-12; 5 General Electrics, including a former Western Pacific U30B and a former Milwaukee Road U25B; a Fairbanks Morse, former U.S. Army H-12-44; a 1929 IR 600-horsepower engine; and a Plymouth, former U.S. Army ML8.

Location: Fifty miles northwest of Reno, Nevada, on the main line of the former Western Pacific Railroad, near the Feather River Canyon in the Sierra Nevada. The museum is in the former Western Pacific diesel service facility west of the Portola depot. From state route 70, travel one mile south on county road A-15 (Gulling) across the river and through town. Follow signs to the museum.

Radio Frequency: 161.01

Contact: Norman W. Holmes
Executive Director

Mailing Address:
P.O. Box 608
Portola, CA 96122
Telephone: (916) 832-4131

POWAY -MIDLAND RAILROAD

Ride/Operation: The Poway-Midland Railroad began operation on July 4, 1993, on a half-mile narrow-gauge loop around Old Poway Park. The Park has been developed by the City of Poway to look like a turn-of-the-century small American town.

Displays/Exhibits: Poway Historical Society museum, operating replica nineteenth-century train barn, water tower, windmills, band gazebo, and a 1937 Southern Pacific caboose. Planned displays include a train depot and a boxcar housing a railroad equipment museum.

Trains: 1907 Baldwin 0-4-0 steam locomotive with either 1880s mine gondolas or a relica passenger coach, 1894 Los Angeles Yellow Car Trolley, or a 1950 Fairmont Speeder with 1880s mine gondolas.

Schedule: Saturdays, 10:00 a.m.-4:00 p.m. Sundays, 11:00 a.m.-2:00 p.m. Holidays, 9:00 a.m.-5:00 p.m. Closed second Sunday of each month. Steam locomotive is scheduled to run the second and fourth weekend of each month. All equipment subject to availability. Call during hours of operation to confirm.

Fare/Admission: Locomotive: Adults $2.00, children $.50. Trolley: Adults $1.50, children $.50. Speeder and gondolas: Adults $1.00, children $.50.

Locomotives/Trolleys: 1907 Baldwin 0-4-0, former Cowell Portland Cement Company Railroad No. 3; 1894 narrow-gauge Los Angeles "Yellow Car" trolley

Rolling Stock: Four 1880s Mining Gondolas converted for passenger use and one 1950 Fairmont Speeder.

Passenger Cars: Replica 1900 passenger car.

Special Events: Farmers' Market, Saturdays. Street Fairs, Memorial Day weekend. Fourth of July. Poway Days, third week of September. Christmas in the Park, second Saturday in December.

Location: Midland Road between Temple and Aubry. Poway is 20 miles north of San Diego.

San Diego

Contact: PMRR Volunteers

Mailing Address:
P.O. Box 1244
Poway, CA 92074-1244
Telephone: (619) 486-4063

BAY AREA ELECTRIC RAILROAD ASSN.
WESTERN RAILWAY MUSEUM
Electric, scheduled; diesel, irregular
Standard gauge

BAY AREA ELECTRIC

Ride/Operation: Streetcars and interurbans carry passengers on a 6-mile round trip circling the museum grounds and extending south on the former Sacramento Northern Railway. The museum's line is being re-electrified 6.5 miles south towards Montezuma; diesel-powered excursion trains operate on another 6-mile portion of the line north of the museum.

Displays/Exhibits: More than 50 pieces of historic rolling stock on display, including former SN wooden combine No. 1005 and steel coach 1020; Oregon Electric parlor-observation car "Champoeg"; and Peninsular Railway 1903 wooden interurban No. 52. Also "Transportation History of Solano County" and in the Streetcar Theater, "Bay Area Transportation Retrospective."

Schedule: Streetcars and interurbans: Weekends, September-May; Wednesday-Sunday, July 4-Labor Day; 11:00 a.m.-5:00 p.m., at 10- to 20-minute headways. Diesels: spring and winter; coach and first-class available.

Fare: Museum (including streetcar/interurban rides): Adults $6.00, seniors $5.00, children (3-11) $3.00, families $18.00 maximum. Excursion trains: Please call or write for information.

Locomotives/Electric Cars: Express Motor #7, former Central California Traction Co., former San Francisco-Oakland Terminal freight motor No. 1001, Sacramento Northern freight motors Nos. 652 and 654, interurbans 1005 and 1020 and Birney No. 62. Wooden interurbans from the Peninsular Railway and the Petaluma & Santa Rosa; "Bay Bridge" articulated units Nos. 182 and 187 and Key System streetcars 271, 362 and 987. Former "Crandic" interurban 111. S.F. Muni streetcars 178, 1003, 1012 and 1153. Blackpool England open "boat" car No. 602 and Melbourne W-2 tram No. 648.

Rolling Stock/Equipment: Observation No. 751, former Salt Lake & Utah; Bamberger coach No. 400; "Harriman" coaches, former Southern Pacific; heavyweight Pullman lounge and sleeper-diner; large freight-car collection.

Location: About 30 miles northeast of San Francisco on state route 12, between Suisun and Rio Vista in Solano County, twelve miles from I-80.

Suisun-Fairfield

Radio Frequency: 161.355

Contact: Bart C. Nadeau
Secretary

Mailing Address:
5848 State Highway 12
Suisun City, CA 94585
Telephone:
Weekends: (707) 374-2978
Fax: (707) 374-6742

CALIFORNIA STATE RAILROAD MUSEUM

Displays/Exhibits: One of the finest railroad museums in the country, CSRM features more than 30 meticulously restored locomotives and cars from the beginning of railroading in the West to the present day. The museum complex, located on an 11-acre site in Old Sacramento, includes the reconstructed 1870s Central Pacific Railroad freight and passenger stations, the Big Four Building, housing the museum's extensive library and archive, and the 100,000-square-foot Museum of Railroad History.

Schedule: Daily, 10:00 a.m.-5:00 p.m. Closed Thanksgiving, Christmas & New Year's Day.

Fare/Admission: Adults $6.00, children (6-12) $3.00, children under 6 admitted free.

Locomotives: Diminutive "C.P. Huntington," 1863 Cooke 4-2-4T, former Southern Pacific No. 1; "Gov. Stanford," 1862 Norris 4-4-0, former Central Pacific No. 1; "Genoa," "Empire," and "J.W. Bowker," all former Virginia & Truckee; giant 1944 Baldwin cab-forward 4-8-8-2, former Southern Pacific No. 4294; E9A passenger diesel; "Warbonnet" F7's Nos. 347C & 347B, former Santa Fe; others.

Rolling Stock/Equipment: Atchison, Topeka & Santa Fe premiere "Super Chief"; diner "Cochiti"; the 1929 heavyweight sleeping car "St. Hyacinthe," which gives the illusion of speeding through the night, with simulated sound, light, and motion; a completely equipped Great Northern Railway Post Office car; "The Gold Coast," Lucius Beebe and Charles Clegg's famous private car; many others.

Special Events: California Railroad Festival, a 3-day event held every Father's Day weekend. The museum also runs steam-powered excursions. See next page.

Note: The museum is the home of the California Railroad Festival, the U.S. National Handcar races and the annual National Railway Preservation Symposium. Museum membership, volunteer programs available.

Sacramento

Radio Frequencies: 160.335, 160.440

Media Contact: Nanci Kramer Director of Public Relations and Marketing

Mailing Address:

111 "I" Street
Sacramento, CA 95814
Telephone: (916) 552-5252 ext. 7245

CALIFORNIA STATE RAILROAD MUSEUM
SACRAMENTO SOUTHERN RAILROAD

Steam, diesel, scheduled
Standard gauge

CALIFORNIA STATE RAILROAD MUSEUM

Ride/Operation: The Sacramento Southern is the excursion railroad of the California State Railroad Museum. The line was built as a subsidiary of the Southern Pacific at the turn of the century; museum trains have been in regular service since 1984. A 6-mile, 40-minute round trip takes passengers along the historic Sacramento River. Extension of the line is planned to the towns of Freeport and Hood, 17 miles down the river.

Train: Open and closed excursion-type cars.

Schedule: Weekends, April 1-September, departures on the hour, 10:00 a.m.-5:00 p.m. First weekend of the month, October-December, departures on the hour, 12:00-3:00 p.m. Also Thanksgiving weekend and selected weekends.

Fare: Adults $5.00, children (6-12) $2.00, children under 6 ride free.

Locomotives: No. 4466, 1920 Lima 0-6-0, former Union Pacific; diesel locomotives from the collection of the California State Railroad Museum.

Location: Northern terminus is the reconstructed Central Pacific Railroad Freight Depot at Front and "K" Streets in Old Sacramento.

  Sacramento

Radio Frequencies: 160.335, 160.440

Media Contact: Nanci Kramer
Director of Public Relations and Marketing

Mailing Address:

111 "I" Street
Sacramento, CA 95814
Telephone: (916) 552-5252 ext. 7245
Fax: (916) 327-5655
Beeline: (916) 552-5252 ext. 7245

SAN DIEGO MODEL RAILROAD MUSEUM
Model railroad

T. J. WEGMANN

Operation: The world's largest indoor model railroad museum includes four large model railroad exhibits, toy trains, educational displays, and a railroad-themed gift shop.

Displays/Exhibits: Cabrillo Southwestern O-scale layout, San Diego & Arizona Eastern and Southern Pacific/Santa Fe Tehachapi Pass HO-scale layouts, and Pacific Desert Lines N-scale layout; the HO exhibits are of railroads that run through southern California. On the SD&AE, trains leave San Diego heading east and descend into the desert over the huge wooden trestle in spectacular Carriso Gorge. A narrow-gauge railroad connects with the standard-gauge trains on the final leg of the journey. The SP/SF layout models southern California's busiest rail artery—nearly all north-south rail traffic passes through this notch in the Tehachapi mountains northeast of Los Angeles. Leaving the yards in Bakersfield, trains roll through California's Central Valley to the Caliente Creek, where a steep, winding climb begins. The PDL, an alternative route east from San Diego, includes scale models of many downtown buildings circa 1950 and a view of Carriso Gorge modeled in 1/160 size. Also featured are G-gauge exhibits and interactive Lionel model trains in a new "Toy Train Gallery."

Schedule: Tuesday-Friday, 11:00 a.m.-4:00 p.m.; Saturday-Sunday, 11:00 a.m.-5:00 p.m.

Admission: Adults $3.00; discounts for senior citizens, military personnel, and students; children under 15 admitted free.

Location: Off I-5 or California route 163. Take Park Boulevard to Space Theater Way; museum is located in the Casa de Balboa Building at 1649 El Prado in Balboa Park.

San Diego

Contact: John Rotsart
Mailing Address:
1649 El Prado
San Diego, CA 92101
Telephone: (619) 696-0199
Gift Shop: (800) 446-8738

Internet: http://www.globalinfo.com/noncomm/SDMRM/sdmrm.html

SAN FRANCISCO MUNICIPAL RAILWAY
F-MARKET carline
Electric, regular
Standard gauge

Ride/Operation: The F MARKET is a regular Municipal Railway line, operating between the Transbay Terminal at 1st & Mission Streets and Castro & Market Streets via Market Street. Most service is with rehabilitated ex-Philadelphia PCC cars painted to represent US cities where PCCs served. Occasionally, a car from the historic fleet takes the place of a PCC.

Schedule: Every day from about 6:30 a.m. to 12:30 a.m.

Fare/Admission: Regular Municipal Railway fares: adults $1.00; seniors (65 and over), youths (5-17), and disabled with ID, $.35. For full Muni fare information, write to the address below.

Historic collection of electric streetcars from San Francisco and seven foreign countries: single-truck "California" configuration No. 578, built in 1895; Muni's first car, double-truck No. 1; Muni double-truck No. 130; Muni PCCs No. 1006 (double-ended) and No. 1040 (the last American PCC); former St. Louis PCC No. 1704; Johnstown, PA No. 351; Hamburg, Germany, V6 No. 3557; Oryol, Russia, single-truck No. 106; Milan, Italy, Peter Witt No. 1834; Blackpool, England, boat tram No. 228; Hiroshima, Japan, former Kobe double-truck No. 578; Osaka, Japan, Hankai Railway double-truck No. 151; Porto, Portugal, single-truck No. 187; and Melbourne, Australia, W2 No. 496; Muni line car No. 0304 and flatcar No. C1,which are work cars. Not all are operational. (On some holidays, several historic cars may also operate as chartered additions to the regular F-line service. Call (415) 552-3055 for information.)

Rolling Stock/Equipment: PCC cars: 14 from Philadelphia, 3 from San Francisco (double-end); occasional operation of one or more historic cars.

Note: Volunteers work on some cars at Market and Duboce. Support group for historic vehicle maintenance can be contacted at the Market Street Railway, (415) 552-3055.

 San Francisco, Oakland/Emeryville

Contact: Nicolas Finck
or Alan Siegel

Mailing Address:
949 Presidio Avenue, Room 238
San Francisco, CA 94115
Telephone: (415) 923-6162

KELLEY PARK TROLLEY
Electric, scheduled
Standard gauge

FAWNA FERGUSON

Ride/Operation: Since 1984 California Trolley and Railroad Corporation volunteers have restored six trolley cars for operation in the downtown San Jose Transit Mall, on the tracks of the new light rail system. Kelley Park trolleys operate on ¼ mile of track through the grounds of the San Jose Historical Museum.

Displays/Exhibits: Visitors can watch volunteers restore cars and artifacts for the San Jose Historical Museum.

Schedule: Weekends, 12:00-4:00 p.m., except Thanksgiving, Christmas & New Year's Day.

Fare: Included with admission to the San Jose Historical Museum: Adults $4.00, senior citizens $3.00, children $2.00, children under 6 ride free.

Trolleys: Operational trolley No. 168, former Porto, Portugal No. 154; No. 129, former Sacramento No. 35. Horse car runs on special occasions.

Special Events: Civil War Days, May 24-26. Chinese Festival, call for date. Victorian Christmas, December 13-14.

Note: The California Trolley and Railroad Corporation is currently developing a railroad museum at the Santa Clara County Fairgrounds. Southern Pacific Railroad's six stall San Jose Roundhouse and 85 foot turntable will be relocated to the fairground site. Additionally, the corporation is restoring Southern Pacific steam locomotive No. 2479, 123 Baldwin 4-6-2, to operating condition.

Location: The museum is located in Kelley Park, a short distance from the intersection of highways 280, 680, and 101.

    P   ✳   ◑   🍴   ▶   ◀

ar n   San Jose

Contact: Fred Bennett
Project Manager
Mailing Address:
1600 Senter Road
San Jose, CA 95112
Telephone:
Museum: (408) 287-2290
Trolley Barn: (408) 293-2276

TRAIN TOWN

Ride/Operation: Train Town is a 10-acre railroad park filled with thousands of trees, animals, lakes, bridges, tunnels, waterfalls, and historic replica structures. Fifteen-inch-gauge live-steam locomotives and diesel replicas pull long passenger trains through the park.

Displays/Exhibits: Railroad shops and a complete miniature town, built to the same ¼ scale as the railroad. Full-sized rail equipment includes Santa Fe caboose No. 999648; Union Pacific caboose No. 25155; and Southern Pacific's first steel caboose, No. 11.

Train: Sixteen scale-reproduction passenger and freight cars.

Schedule: Daily, June 1-September 30; Friday-Sunday, year-round; 10:30 a.m.-5:00 p.m. Closed Christmas and Thanksgiving.

Fare: Adults $3.50, senior citizens & children (16 months-16 years) $2.50.

Locomotives/Trolleys: Replica of No. 5212, 1937 Alco J-1a 4-6-4, former New York Central; No. 1, 1960 Winton Engineering 2-6-0; SW 1200, 1992 custom locomotive; No. 401, 1975 gas-electric motor car.

Location: Sonoma is in wine country, less than an hour north of San Francisco. Train Town is on Broadway, one mile south of the Sonoma Town Square.

Contact: Robert Frank
Superintendent

Mailing Address:
P.O. Box 656
Sonoma, CA 95476
Telephone: (707) 938-3912

SONORA SHORT LINE RAILWAY
12" gauge
Steam, scheduled

JAMES HOBACK

Ride/Operation: Scenic 10-minute steam powered train ride through a working apple ranch in the foothills of California's Sierra Nevada Mountains. Train is ⅓ full size, 12" gauge.

Display/Exhibits: Apple ranch has farm animals on display.

Schedule: 11 a.m. to 5 p.m. weekends and holidays, mid-February through Thanksgiving.

Fare: $1.50 single ticket, $6.25 for a 5-ride ticket. Children under 12 months of age-free.

Locomotives/Trolleys: 1/3 scale: 4-4-0 steam locomotive, oil fired, 1910 era Baldwin narrow gauge styling; Plymouth, 1927, diesel powered. (Locomotives are 12" gauge.)

Rolling Stock/Equipment: 5 Hurlbut built excursion cars

Special Events: September through October, apple harvest season.

Notes: Apple ranch has pastry shop and gift shop. Special group train rides with reservations.

Location: Sonka's Apple Ranch, 19200 Cherokee Road, Tuolumne, CA, 5 miles east of Sonora, CA

 Riverbank

Contact: James L. Hoback
Owner

Mailing Address:
19720 Tuolumne Road, North
Tuolumne, CA 95379
Telephone: (209) 928-4689

YOLO SHORTLINE
RAILROAD COMPANY
Steam, diesel, scheduled
Standard gauge

RICHARD JONES

Ride/Operation: This common-carrier freight railroad offers a 28-mile, 2½-hour round trip between Woodland and West Sacramento over the former Sacramento Northern's Woodland Branch. The trip begins in Woodland, crosses the Yolo bypass on an 8,000-foot trestle, and offers views of scenic Yolo County farmlands and wetlands and the Sacramento River.

Displays/Exhibits: Near the parking and passenger-loading area are the Hayes Truck Museum (admission separate) and the Southern Pacific Depot (under restoration).

Schedule: Passenger trains operate May-October; Saturdays, Sundays and holidays, Trains depart 10:00 a.m. & 2:00 p.m.

Fare: Adults $13.00, senior citizens $11.00, children (4-14) $8.00, children under 4 ride free. $2 off ticket if diesel is used instead of steam locomotive. Charter and special excursions have separate fares.

Locomotives: No. 1233, 0-6-0 S-10 Switcher, and Nos. 131, 132 & 133 GP9 diesels, EMD, all ex-Southern Pacific. No. 50, 50-ton General Electric (1939), exSpreckels Sugar. No. 101, Alco S-1, ex-Western Pacific. Other "guest" locomotives occasionally used.

Passenger Cars: No. 701, Budd coach, former Seaboard; No. 702, Pullman coach, former Santa Fe; No. 501, maintenance-of-way flatcar converted to open-air car, and No. 502, gondola converted to open-air car, both former Southern Pacific; No. 801 baggage car/commissary car, former Northwestern Pacific; No. PPCX 800591, PV "Burrard," former CN.

Special Events: Special Clarksburg trips leave West Sacramento and go to Clarksburg on selected days.

Other special passenger runs and charter trips are scheduled from time to time. Please call or write for information.

Note: Beer, wine, snacks and souvenirs are available on board.

Location: East Main Street and Thomas Street. The site is about 1 mile west of the East Main Street exit of I-5, about 20 miles northwest of Sacramento.

Contact: David Magaw
President

Mailing Address:
P.O. Box 724
West Sacramento, CA 95891
Telephone: (916) 372-9777
Fax: (916) 372-3545

YREKA WESTERN RAILROAD
Steam, scheduled
Standard gauge

YREKA WESTERN RAILROAD

Ride/Operation: Constructed in 1888 as the Yreka Railroad Company, this line began operations on January 8, 1889, providing rail service between the city of Yreka and the newly constructed California & Oregon Railroad 7.4 miles to the east at the cattle town of Montague, California. Today's YWR offers a 15-mile, 3-hour round trip between Yreka and Montague, including a one-hour stopover at Montague. The train travels through local lumber mills and across the scenic Shasta Valley, where passengers see panoramic views of 14,162-foot Mount Shasta.

Displays/Exhibits: One-thousand-square-foot model railroad; historic displays.

Train: Open-air car; two 1948 former Milwaukee Hiawatha cars; two former Southern Pacific Harriman cars.

Schedule: May 24-June 15 & September 13-October 26, weekends; June 18-September 8, Wednesday-Sunday; all departures 10:00 a.m.

Fare: Adults $9.00; Children (3-12) $4.50.

Locomotives: No. 19, 1915 Baldwin 2-8-2, and No. 18, 1914 Baldwin 2-8-2, both former McCloud River Railroad; Nos. 20 & 21, EMD SW8s.

Special Events: Dinner Trains - please call or write for information. Great Wild Goose Chase - August 24; runners race the train to Montague and return by train.

Location: On the east side of the central exit off I-5 in Yreka.

Contact: Larry G. Bacon
General Manager

Mailing Address:
P.O. Box 660
Yreka, CA 96097
Telephone: (916) 842-4146

PIKE'S PEAK HISTORICAL STREET RAILWAY FOUNDATION, INC.

Electric, PCC Streetcar scheduled
Standard gauge

PIKES PEAK HISTORICAL STREET RAILWAY FOUNDATION, INC.

Ride/Operation: Several trips over 500' test track. Operation and history of car explained during ride.

Display/Exhibits: Interpretive center displaying street railway history with a strong emphasis on Colorado Springs street railway history. Also lecture on history and return of streetcars to Colorado Springs.

Schedule: Saturday, 10:00 a.m.-4:00 p.m., year round except Thanksgiving, Christmas and New Year's week. Other times please write or call. Groups tours please call ahead for special showing.

Fare/Admission: Adults $2.00, children (12 and under) $1.00.

Locomotives/Trolleys: 9 Southeastern Pennsylvania Transportation Authority PCC's (Philadelphia) 1947; 1 Los Angeles Railways PCC 1943; 1 Colorado Springs Double Truck, 1901 Laclede Car Co.; 1 Ft. Collins Municipal Railway, Single Truck, 1919 Birney, American Car Co.

Notes: Visit a working car house (former Rock Island Engine House) built in 1888. See cars under restoration. Guided tour of cars on hand and shop area.

Location: 2333 Steel Dr. Use Fillmore St. exit from I-25, east on Fillmore 4 blocks to Cascade. South on Cascade 2 blocks to Polk St. West on Polk. When forced to turn South, you will automatically be on Steel Dr. We're located at the very end of Steel Dr.

Contact: H. H. Noble
Vice President of Operations

Mailing address:
P.O. Box 544
Colorado Springs, CO 80901
Telephone: (719) 475-9508
Fax Number: (719) 635-3179

CRIPPLE CREEK
NARROW GAUGE RAILROAD

Steam, scheduled
24" gauge

CRIPPLE CREEK NARROW GAUGE RAILROAD

Ride/Operation: A 4-mile, 45-minute round trip over a portion of the old Midland Terminal Railroad. The train runs south out of Cripple Creek, past the old MT wye, over a reconstructed trestle, and past many historic mines to the deserted mining town of Anaconda.

Displays/Exhibits: A museum is located in the former Midland Terminal depot.

Train: Open excursion-type cars.

Schedule: Daily, May 22- October 11, every 45 minutes, 9:30 a.m.-5:30 p.m.

Fare: Adults $7, senior citizens $6.50, children (3-12) $3.50, children under 3 ride free.

Locomotives: No. 1, 1902 Orenstein & Koppel 0-4-4-0, No. 2, 1936 Henschel 0-4-0; No. 3, 1927 Porter 0-4-0T; No. 13, 1946 Bagnall 0-4-4-0T

Location: Trains leave from the former Midland Terminal Railroad Bull Hill depot.

Contact: James Birmingham
General Manager

Mailing Address:
Box 459
Cripple Creek, CO 80813
Telephone: (719) 689-2640

FORNEY HISTORIC TRANSPORTATION MUSEUM
Railway museum
Standard gauge

FORNEY HISTORIC TRANSPORTATION MUSEUM

Displays/Exhibits: This museum features three steam locomotives: former Union Pacific "Big Boy" No. 4005, built by Alco in 1941; former Chicago & North Western 4-6-0 No. 444; and an 0-4-0T locomotive from Germany. The collection also includes four executive and business cars, two dating from the 1890s; a dining car; a rotary snowplow; and three cabooses. The museum has a fine collection of horse-drawn vehicles and a large display of antique automobiles.

Schedule: Monday-Saturday, except Easter, Thanksgiving, Christmas, and New Year's Day, 10:00 a.m.-5:00 p.m.; Sunday, 11:00 a.m.-5:00 p.m.

Admission: Adults $4.00, children (12-18) $2.00 and (5-11) $1.00. Group rates available.

Location: Near I-25 and Speer Boulevard in Denver. From I-25 take exit 211 (23rd Avenue) and travel 5 blocks east on Water Street to 1416 Platte Street.

P   🚌   ✳   ▶   ◀

 Denver

Contact: Rob Etherington
Business Manager

Mailing Address:
1416 Platte Street
Denver, CO 80202
Telephone: (303) 433-3643

PLATTE VALLEY TROLLEY
Electric, scheduled
Standard gauge

PLATTE VALLEY TROLLEY

Ride/Operation: A 25-minute, 2.5-mile round trip along the west bank of the South Platte River between 15th and Decatur streets. One-hour route 84 excursions are made to Lakewood at specified times.

Schedule: April, May & September-November: weekdays, 11:00-3:00 p.m.; weekends, 11:00-4:00 p.m.; every half hour. June-August: daily, 11:00 a.m.-4:00 p.m., every half hour. Route 84 excursion: April-October; weekdays, 12:00 p.m.; weekends, 2:00 p.m.

Fare: Adults $2.00, senior citizens & children $1.00. Route 84 excursion: Adults $4.00, senior citizens $3.00, children $2.00. Group and charter rates available.

Trolleys: No. 1977, built in 1986 by the Gomaco Trolley Company of Ida Grove, Iowa, is an authentic reproduction of open-air cars once produced by the J.G. Brill Company; a built-in diesel-electric generator provides power. Denver & Intermountain interurban No. 25, built in 1911 by the Woeber Carriage Company of Denver, is being restored by its owner, the Rocky Mountain Railroad Club, and is anticipated to be operational by fall 1995.

Notes: The Platte Valley Trolley is a project of the Denver Rail Heritage Society, a nonprofit, educational, volunteer organization.

Location: West of downtown Denver with stops at 15th Street & Speer Boulevard (Confluence Park near the Forney Transportation Museum), 7th Street, and the Children's Museum. Just east off exit 211 of I-25.

Denver

Contact: Mike Heirty
General Manager

Mailing Address:
2200 7th Street
Denver, CO 80211-5215
Telephone: (303) 458-6255

THE SKI TRAIN

Ride/Operation: The Ski Train, a Colorado tradition since 1940, offers a 120-mile round trip from Denver's Union Station over the main line of the Rio Grande, passing through the famous Moffat Tunnel and stopping at West Portal, the location of Winter Park Resort.

Train: First-class, coach-class, and cafe-lounge cars.

Schedule: Weekends, mid December to early April. Lv. Denver Union Station 7:15 a.m., arr. Winter Park 9:15 a.m.; lv. Winter Park 4:15 p.m., arr. Denver 6:15 p.m.

Fare: Coach: $35.00; first class: $55.00.

Locomotives: Varies.

Note: Nonskiers are also welcome and may take a guided tour of the ski slopes or spend the day shopping or relaxing. Snowmobiling and cross-country skiing are also available.

Location: Train departs from Denver Union Station.

 Denver

Contact: Jim Bain

Mailing Address:
555 17th Street, Suite 2400
Denver, CO 80202
Telephone: (303) 296-4754

DURANGO & SILVERTON
NARROW-GAUGE RAILROAD

Steam, scheduled
36" gauge

AMOS CORDOVA

Ride/Operation: The Durango & Silverton was established in 1881 to transport miners to and from Silverton and to haul precious metals to smelters. Today, a coal-fired, steam-powered, narrow-gauge train travels through the wilderness of the two-million-acre San Juan National Forest, following the Animas River through breathtaking Rocky Mountain scenery, where the only noises are those of the working locomotives, the river, and their echoes. The 90-mile round trip, which originates at Durango, takes approximately nine hours, including a 2 1/4-hour lay-over at Silverton for lunch and sightseeing. A half-day winter trip to Cascade Canyon is also offered.

Displays/Exhibits: Daily tours are offered of the roundhouse, car shop, and yards, May-October.

Train: Coaches; open-side observation car; coach for handicapped; parlor car; concession cars; rail camp (camping car); 1886 caboose in daily service; two private coaches.

Schedule: Daily, April 26-October 8, lv. Durango 8:30 a.m.; May 13-October 25, 9:15 a.m. train added; June 2-August 14 & August 30-September 28, 10:10 a.m. train added; June 17-August 14, 7:30 a.m. train added but will run Monday-Friday only. Consult timetable for exact schedule on day of your visit. Winter Train: November 28-April 25, except Christmas Day, 10:00 a.m.

Fare/Admission: Silverton: Adults $42.70, children (5-11) $21.45; parlor car $73.40; caboose $67.85. Cascade Canyon: Adults $36.15, children (5-11) $18.00. Yard Tours: Adults $5.00, children (5-11) $2.50.

Locomotives: Nos. 473, 476 & 478, 1923 Alco class K-28 2-8-2s; Nos. 480, 481 & 482, 1925 Baldwin class K-36 2-8-2s; Nos. 493, 498 & 499, 1930 Burnham Shops class K-37 2-8-2s; all former Denver & Rio Grande Western.

Location: In the southwestern part of the state on U.S. 160 & 550.

Contact: Amos Cordova
Vice President

Mailing Address:
479 Main Avenue
Durango, CO 81301
Telephone: (303) 247-2733

FORT COLLINS MUNICIPAL RAILWAY
Electric, scheduled
Standard gauge

AL KILMINSTER

Ride/Operation: A 3-mile ride on a restored portion of the historic Fort Collins trolley system on a painstakingly restored 1919 trolley. The tracks are in a grass median down the center of Mountain Avenue, then down the center of Roosevelt Avenue to City Park. Passengers board at the City Park terminus.

Schedule: Weekends & holidays, May 1-September 30, 12:00-5:00 p.m., weather permitting.

Fare: Adults $1.00, children (under 12) $.50. Group charters and special rates available.

Trolleys: No. 21, 1919 American single-truck Birney Safety Car, purchased new by the city of Fort Collins and in daily service until 1951.

Note: The Fort Collins Municipal Railway Society is a nonprofit group of volunteers. The streetcar and railway are the property of the city of Fort Collins.

Location: In the northern part of the state. Take exit 269-B off I-25 and proceed west on state route 14 to Mountain Avenue, then west on that street.

Contact: Robert Hutchison
President

Mailing Address:
P.O. Box 635
Fort Collins, CO 80522
Telephone: (970) 224-5372
Internet: http://www.fortnet.org/CITY/Trolley/

Colorado, Georgetown
D-R

GEORGETOWN LOOP RAILROAD
Steam, scheduled
36" gauge

GEORGE A. FORERO, JR.

Ride/Operation: A 6.5-mile, 70-minute round trip over the right-of-way of the former Colorado & Southern. The train travels through highly scenic, mountainous terrain and over the reconstructed Devil's Gate Viaduct, a spectacular 96-foot-high curved trestle. Located in the Old Georgetown Station are the railroad's headquarters, the Depot Express Cafe with an operating LGB model, and Baggage Cart Gifts. The Georgetown Loop Railroad is a project of the Colorado Historical Society.

Displays/Exhibits: Displayed at the Old Georgetown Station (the original Colorado & Southern depot) are 2-8-0 No. 44, a rail and tie car, former Rio Grande Southern caboose No. 0400, and a 1"-to-100'-scale diorama of the Clear Creek valley from Georgetown to Silver Plume, depicting the historic and present-day railroad. The Colorado Historical Society's 80-minute mine tour and exhibit can be reached by train.

Train: Open excursion-type cars.

Schedule: Daily, May 24-October 5; lv. Silver Plume 9:20 & 10:40 a.m., 12:00, 1:20, 2:40 & 4:00 p.m.; lv. Devil's Gate 10:00 & 11:20 a.m, 12:40, 2:00 & 3:20 p.m. Limited schedule weekdays in September. No mine tours after Labor Day.

Fare/Admission: Train: Adults $11.95, children $7.50, children under 3 ride free. Charters available year-round. Group rates available. Mine tour: Adults $4.00, children $2.00.

Locomotives: No. 40, 1920 Baldwin 2-8-0 & No. 44, 1921 Baldwin 2-8-0, both former International Railways of Central America; No. 8, 1922 Lima 3-truck Shay, No. 12, 1926 Lima 3-truck Shay & No. 14, 1916 Lima 3-truck Shay, all former West Side Lumber Co.; Nos. 130 & 140, 54-ton General Electric diesels, former U.S. Gypsum Company.

Notes: Trails and Rails Downhill Mountain Bike Tours trace the historic Argentine Central Railway. Reservations can be made with the Georgetown Loop Railroad.

Location: West of Denver. Take exit 226 off Interstate 70 for Silver Plume, exit 228 for Georgetown.

 Denver

Radio Frequency: 161.115

Contact: Lindsey G. Ashby
President & General Manager

Mailing Address:
P.O. Box 217
Georgetown, CO 80444
Info & Reservations: (303) 670-1686
(303) 569-2403
Outside Colorado: (800) 691-4386
Fax: (303) 569-2894
Internet: http://www.gtownloop.com

COLORADO RAILROAD MUSEUM

Ride/Operation: This 38-year-old museum, oldest and largest in the Rocky Mountain area, houses an extensive collection of Colorado railroad memorabilia as well as the layout of the Denver HO Model Railroad Club. On outdoor trackage are more than 50 cars and locomotives, both narrow- and standard-gauge, including the oldest locomotives and cars in the state. No. 346, an 1881 Baldwin 2-8-0, and a Rio Grande "Galloping Goose" operate on selected weekends.

Schedule: Museum: daily; June-August, 9:00 a.m.-6:00 p.m.; September-May, 9:00 a.m.-5:00 p.m. Train: 1997-call, fax, or write for schedule. HO Model Railroad: First Thursday of every month, 7:30-9:30 p.m.

Admission: Adults $3.50, senior citizens (over 60) $3.00, children (under 16) $1.75, family rate (parents and children under 16) $7.50.

Locomotives: Include 4-6-0 No. 20 (Schenectady, 1899), former Rio Grande Southern; 2-8-0 No. 583 (Baldwin, 1890), former Denver & Rio Grande—the only surviving D&RG standard-gauge steam locomotive; and 4-8-4 No. 5629 (West Burlington, 1940), former Chicago, Burlington & Quincy.

Passenger Cars: Former Rio Grande Southern Galloping Geese Nos. 2, 6 & 7; former Colorado Midland observation car No. 111, used on wildflower trains; and former Santa Fe observation car "Navajo" (Budd, 1937), from the original streamlined *Super Chief;* others.

Location: Twelve miles west of downtown Denver. Take I-70 westbound exit 265 or eastbound exit 266 to 17155 West 44th Avenue.

P 🚌 ✳ ☕ ▶ ◀ 🎪

M ar n TRAIN Denver

Contact: Charles Albi
Executive Director

Mailing Address:
P.O. Box 10
Golden, CO 80402
Telephone: (303) 279-4591
(800) 365-6263
Fax: (303) 279-4229
Internet: http://www.nyx.net/~dpitts/crrm.html

NATIONAL HISTORIC ARGO GOLD MILL
Model, scheduled
Half scale

BOB BOWLAND

Ride/Operation: Visitors ride in half-scale models of 1800s mining cars behind a gas-powered model of the 0-4-0 "H.K. Porter" to the Double Eagle gold mine, then to world-famous Argo Tunnel and the Argo gold mill.

Displays/Exhibits: Mining museum, gold and gemstone panning.

Train: Models of locomotive, ore cars, passenger car, cattle car, caboose.

Schedule: Year-round, 10:00 a.m.-7:00 p.m.

Admission: Year-round pass: Adults $10.00, children (7-12) $8.00 & (1-6) $5.00. Pass includes train ride and tour of mine, mill, and museum.

Special Events: Monthly themes include: Horseback riding, Wild West days, gunfights (June); Gold Rush days, mining events (July); Pow-wow (August).

Location: 2350 Riverside Drive.

Contact: Darrell Chauncey
Program Director

Mailing Address:
P.O. Box 1503
Idaho Springs, CO 80452
Telephone: (303) 567-2421

LEADVILLE, COLORADO & SOUTHERN RAILROAD
Diesel, scheduled
Standard gauge

LEADVILLE, COLORADO & SOUTHERN RAILROAD

Ride/Operation: The 22½-mile, 2½-hour train trip follows the headwaters of the Arkansas River to an elevation of 11,120 feet, over an old narrow-gauge roadbed converted to standard gauge in the 1940s. Train leaves from the restored 1894 railroad depot (formerly Colorado & Southern, built originally for the Denver, South Park & Pacific) in Leadville, highest incorporated city in the United States.

Displays/Exhibits: No. 641, 1906 Brooks 2-8-0, former Colorado & Southern.

Train: GP9 with open and enclosed excursion cars; boxcar with concessions.

Schedule: Daily, May 24-June 15, 1:00 p.m.; June 16-September 1, 10:00 a.m. & 2:00 p.m.; September 2-September 28: 1:00 p.m.

Fare: Adults $22.50, children (4-12) $12.50, children 3 and under free. Group rates available.

Locomotives: No. 1714, 1955 EMD GP9, former Burlington Northern.

Passenger Cars: Six excursion cars, boxcar, caboose.

Location: Depot at 326 East 7th Street.

    ⅃   **P**   ✱   🏛   TRAIN

Contact: Stephanie Olsen
President

Mailing Address:
P.O. Box 916
Leadville, CO 80461
Telephone: (719) 486-3936

MANITOU & PIKE'S PEAK RAILWAY
Diesel, scheduled
Standard gauge (cog)

MANITOU & PIKE'S PEAK RAILWAY

Ride/Operation: The M&PP, the highest cog railway in the world, was established in 1889 and has been operating continuously since 1891; it celebrated its centennial of passenger operations in June 1991. A 3¼-hour round trip takes passengers to the summit of Pike's Peak (elevation 14,110 feet) from Manitou Springs (elevation 6,575 feet) and includes a 40-minute stop at the summit.

Train: Twin-unit diesel hydraulic railcars and single unit diesel electric railcars.

Schedule: Daily; May-mid June, September & October, 9:20 a.m. & 1:20 p.m.; mid June-August, every 80 minutes, 8:00 a.m.-5:20 p.m.

Fare: Adults: $21.00, children (5-11) $9.50; July 1st to Aug. 15th - Adults: $22.00, children (5-11) $10.00. Group rates available.

Special Events: Occasional steam-up of former M&PP steam locomotive No. 4, built by Baldwin in 1896.

Location: Six miles west of Colorado Springs at 515 Ruxton Avenue.

Radio Frequency: 161.55 and 160.23

Contact: D. M. Doane, General Manager or W. Spencer Wren, Traffic Manager

Mailing Address:
P.O. Box 351
Manitou Springs, CO 80829
Telephone: (719) 685-5401

TINY TOWN RAILROAD

Ride/Operation: Tiny Town Railroad, a 1/4-scale live-steam railroad, takes passengers from its full-sized station on a 1-mile loop ride around Tiny Town. The railroad carried more than 75,000 riders in its 1995 season.

Displays/Exhibits: At 75 years old, Tiny Town is the oldest miniature town in the United States. It features more than 100 hand-crafted, 1/6-sized structures laid out in the configuration of a real town.

Train: Two live-steam and two gas-powered 1/4-scale locomotives.

Schedule: Daily, Memorial Day through Labor Day; Weekends, May, September & October; 10:00 a.m.- 5:00 p.m. Train runs continuously.

Fare/Admission: Train rides: $1.00. Admission: Adults $2.50, children (3-12) $1.50, children under 3 admitted free.

Locomotives: 1970 standard-gauge 4-6-2 "Occasional Rose," propane-fired; 1970 narrow-gauge 2-6-0 "Cinderbell," coal-fired; 1954 F-unit "Molly," gas-powered; 1952 A- & B-unit "Betsy," gas-powered.

Passenger Cars: Open amusement-park-style cars; caboose.

Notes: Tiny Town is operated by the nonprofit Tiny Town Foundation.

Location: Twenty-five minutes southwest of downtown Denver.

 Denver

Contact: Jack Bradley
Park Manager

Mailing Address:
6249 South Turkey Creek Road
Morrison, CO 80465
Telephone: (303) 697-6829

BILL GUIDER

Ride/Operation: Excursions over Metro-North commuter routes, or the seldom traveled Beacon branch (former New Haven Maybrook line), connecting with Hudson River cruises or other attractions.

Displays/Exhibits: Locomotive, RDC's, FCD railbus, coaches, caboose, freight and maintenance of way cars in ex-New Haven yard. Exhibits in Danbury Union Station.

Schedule: Station- April-Thanksgiving, Tuesdays-Sundays, 10 a.m.-4 p.m.; Thanksgiving-New Year extended holiday hours; January-March, Thursdays-Sundays, 10 a.m.-4 p.m. Yard- Same as station, conditions permitting. Closed holidays.

Admission: Adults $2; children 5-15 $1; 4 and under free.

Locomotives/Trolleys: Alco RS-1 400, Ex-Green Mountain 400, ex-Illinois Central Gulf 1053, ex-Gulf, Mobile and Ohio 1053, nee-Illinois Terminal 753, ex-New Haven RDC-1s 32 and 47. Ex-New Haven FCD railbus 15.

Rolling Stock/Equipment: Five ex-Reading coaches, two ex-New York Central Burro cranes, ex-New Haven NE-5 caboose, ex-New Haven gondola and ex–Pennsylvania boxcar.

Special Events: Easter Bunny Trains, March 22. Spring Train Show/Railfan Excursions, April 26, 27. Fall Train Show/Foliage Excursions, October 18, 19. Halloween Ghost Trains, October 24, 25, 26. Holiday Model Railroad Display, November 28-December 31. Holiday Express to New York, December 6, 7. Santa Claus Trains, December 13, 14.

Notes: 1) Danbury Union Station was the site of several scenes in Alfred Hitchcock's 1951 film, "Strangers on a Train." 2) Send name and address to be included on excursion mailing list. 3) Metro-North service to Danbury. 1/4 mile walk to museum. Connect with Amtrak at Stamford, CT

Location: 120 White Street, Danbury, CT - I-84 exit 5, right on Main St., left on White St.

Mailing Address:
P.O. Box 90
Danbury, CT 06813-0090
Telephone: (203) 778-8337
Fax: (203) 778-1836
Internet: http://www.danbury.org/org/drm

72

SHORE LINE TROLLEY MUSEUM
Electric, scheduled
Standard gauge

T. SHADE

Ride/Operation: The Shore Line Trolley Museum operates the sole remaining segment of the historic 97-year-old Branford Electric Railway. The 3-mile ride passes woods, salt marshes, and meadows along the scenic Connecticut shore. Trolley operator escorts passengers and provides interpretation for a cross section of the extensive collection.

Displays/Exhibits: Parlor car No. 500, Atlanta No. 948, work cars, and the world's first electric locomotive. The restoration shop, which is on the guided tour, houses cars undergoing restoration or maintenance. Automated sound show, "Birth of the Trolley Era"; hands-on exhibits; a slide/video theater.

Schedule: Daily, May 29-September 4; weekends and holidays, September & October; weekends, May. Sundays, April & November; 11:00 a.m.-5:00 p.m. Trolleys run every 30 minutes.

Fare: Unlimited rides and guided tour: Adults $5.00, senior citizens $4.00, children (2-11) $2.00, children under 2 ride free. Rates and program may vary on special-event weekends. Group charter rates available (203-467-7635).

Trolleys: Connecticut Co. open car No. 1414; Connecticut Co. suburban No. 193; Montreal double-truck No. 2001; Johnstown lightweights No. 356 & 357; Brooklyn (NY) convertible No. 4573; Third Avenue Railway No. 629. Other cars may be operated.

Special Events: Write for flyer.

Location: Take exit 51 east or 52 west off the Connecticut Turnpike (I-95) and follow signs to the museum.

P ✳ ☕ 📷 ⛱ ⛪ ▶ ◀

M New Haven

Contact: George T. Boucher
Director

Mailing Address:
17 River Street
East Haven, CT 06512-2519
Telephone: (203) 467-6927

CONNECTICUT TROLLEY MUSEUM
Electric, scheduled
Standard gauge

SCOTT R. BECKER

Ride/Operation: A 3-mile, 25-minute round trip through scenic woodlands over a rebuilt portion of the former Rockville branch of the Hartford & Springfield Street Railway, originally built in 1906. The ride often includes meets with other trolleys, and the line features a historic working semaphore signal system. Trolleys leave from the "Isle of Safety" trolley-stop shelter built in 1913 for downtown Hartford, Connecticut, and from the CTM North Road terminal.

Displays/Exhibits: More than 60 pieces of rolling stock, including streetcars, interurbans, rapid-transit cars, electric freight equipment, work cars, steam and diesel locomotives, wooden passenger cars from the 1890s, and freight cars. A 1910 Climax geared steam locomotive (former Middle Fork Railroad) is on display. The new exhibit building includes the "Great Trolley Exhibit Hall," with display cars from the storage barn, as well as a picture history of the trolley.

Schedule: Daily, May 25-September 2 weekdays, 10 a.m.-5 p.m.; thereafter Weekends 10 a.m.-5 p.m. (months of January and February by reservation and charter only). Closed Thanksgiving, Christmas Eve and Christmas Day.

Fare: Adults $6.00, senior citizens $5.00, children (5-12) $3.00, children under 5 ride free. Group rates available.

Trolleys: Nos. 65, 355, 840 & 1326, former Connecticut Co.; Nos. 4, 2056 & 2600, former Montreal Tramways; No. 1850, former Rio de Janeiro; Nos. 4436 & 4284, former Chicago Transit Authority; No. 451, former Illinois Terminal.

Passenger Cars: Two 1899 Jackson & Sharp coaches; 1890 wooden open-vestibule combine, former New Haven; 1894 coach, former Philadelphia & Reading.

Rolling Stock/Equipment: Wooden boxcars built before 1880; steel and wooden cabooses.

Special Events: Halloween Program, "Rails to the Dark Side," Fri.-Sun. last two weekends in October, Winterfest, 1 1/2 mile tunnel of lights, nightly operation November 29-December 31.

Location: Halfway between Hartford, Connecticut,

and Springfield, Massachusetts. Take exit 45 off I-91 and travel 3/4 mile east on route 140.

Windsor Locks

Contact: Business Office

Mailing Address:
P.O. Box 360
East Windsor, CT 06088-0360
Telephone: Gift Shop: (860) 623-7417
Office: (860) 627-6540

Connecticut, Essex
R

VALLEY RAILROAD COMPANY
Steam, scheduled
Standard gauge

HOWARD PINCUS

Ride/Operation: A 2½-hour excursion along the scenic banks of the Connecticut River on restored 1920s-vintage cars. All trains except the last of the day connect with a riverboat cruise at Deep River.

Train: Open gondola car; restored coaches; extra-fare Pullman parlor car "The Great Republic."

Schedule: May 3-June 13: Wednesday-Friday, 2:00 & 3:30 p.m.; weekends & May 30, 12:00, 1:30, 3:00 & 4:30 p.m. June 14-September 1: weekdays, 10:30 a.m., 12:00, 1:30, 3:00 & 4:30 p.m.; weekends, July 4 & September 1, 6:00 p.m. train added. September 3-October 26: Wednesday-Sunday & October 13, 10:30 a.m., 12:00, 1:30, 3:00 & 4:30 p.m. November 28-December 23: Friday, 5:30 & 7:00 p.m.; weekends & November 28, 11:00 a.m., 12:30, 2:00, 3:30, 5:30, & 7:00 p.m. December 15-18 & 22-23: 5:30 & 7:00 p.m.

Fare: Train and boat: adults $14.00, children (3-11) $7.00, children under 3 ride free. Train only: adults $10.00, children (3-11) $5.00, children under 3 ride free. Parlor car: extra fare. Discounts for senior citizens. Group rates for groups of 25 or more.

Locomotives: No. 97, 1926 Alco 2-8-2, former Birmingham & Southeastern; No. 40, 1920 Alco 2-8-2, former Aberdeen & Rockfish; 44-ton diesel No. 0800; 80-ton diesel No. 0900.

Special Events: President's Weekend, February 15-17. St. Patrick's Day, March 15-16. Easter Eggspress, March 22-23, 28-29. Antique Machinery and Transportation Day, May 4. Hot Steamed Music Festival, June 27-29. Ghost Train, October 24-25. North Pole Express, November 29-December 22. Tuba Concert, December 14. Call for schedules.

Location: From shoreline, take exit 69 off I-95, then travel north on state route 9 to exit 3. From Hartford, take exit 22 off I-91, then travel south on state route 9 to exit 3. Valley Railroad is a half-mile west of route 9 on state route 154.

 Old Saybrook

Contact: Staci M. Roy
General Manager

Mailing Address:
P.O. Box 452
Essex, CT 06426
Telephone: (860) 767-0103

75

CONNECTICUT ANTIQUE MACHINERY ASSOCIATION, INC.
Railway exhibit
36" gauge

Ride/Operation: A short stretch of three-foot-gauge track is in operation during this group's popular Fall Festival, with a locomotive shunting ore cars from their turn-of-the-century operating rock crusher to the end of the line (currently being extended; plans call for a loop around the museum grounds).

Displays/Exhibits: A wide range of exhibits showing the development of the country's agricultural and industrial technology from the mid 1800s to the present, including a collection of large stationary steam engines in the Industrial Hall; a display of large gas-engines; a tractor and farm-implement display in the large tractor barn; and the reconstrucrted Cream Hill Agricultural School buildings, which housed an early agricultural school that was the forerunner of the University of Connecticut, and a large engine-pumping exhibit. Future plans include a sawmill.

Train: 1921 8-ton Plymouth diesel; three Koppel tip cars.

Schedule: Museum: Saturdays and Sundays, Memorial Day-Labor Day and by appointment. Train: Spring Gas Up, call for information; Fall Festival, September 27-28.

Admission: Adults $3.00, children (5-12) $1.50, children under 5 admitted free.

Locomotives: No. 4, 1908 Porter 2-8-0, former Argent Lumber Co.; No. 16, 1921 Plymouth D1, former Hutton Brick Co.; No. 18, 1917 Vulcan limited-clearance 0-4-0T, former American Steel & Wire Co.

Rolling Stock: No. 111, caboose, former Tionesta Valley Railway; miscellaneous ore cars.

Special Events: During Spring Gas-Up and Fall Festival, grounds are filled with restored, operating antique machinery, including gas engines, steam engines, cars, trucks, tractors, hot-air engines, steam launches, and more.

Location: One mile north of the village on route 7; adjacent to the Housatonic Railroad.

Contact: Bob Hungerford
President

Mailing Address:
P.O. Box 1467
New Milford, CT 06776
Telephone: (203) 927-0050

RAILROAD MUSEUM OF NEW ENGLAND
Railway museum
Standard gauge

HOWARD PINCUS

Ride/Operation: Ten miles along the scenic Naugatuck River through the Mattituck State Forest to Thomaston culminating across the face of the Thomaston Dam.

Displays/Exhibits: New location! Historic equipment, display of a B&M Milk Car with restored interior, and a MEC Baggage RPO with exhibits.

Schedule: Weekends, May-October.

Fares: Adults $7.50, children 12 and under $5.00. Senior citizen discount.

Locomotives/Trolleys: Diesel locomotives include RS-3 No. 529, Alco FA-1 No. 0401, and General Electric U25B No. 2525, all former New Haven; EMC SW1 No. 1109, former Boston & Maine; and E-33 No. 4601, former Conrail and New Haven electric freight locomotive. Steam locomotives include No. 1246, 1946 Montreal 4-6-2, former Canadian Pacific Railway, and 2-6-2 No. 103, former Sumter & Choctaw, which heads a display train of vintage freight cars.

Rolling Stock/Equipment: Numerous cars from northeastern railroads, including passenger, head-end, and freight cars and cabooses.

Special Events: Railfan Days, special excursions to Torrington, Plow Xtras, Caboose Hops.

Location: I-84 or I-95 to Rt. 8 North. Exit 36, Huntingdon Ave. Right at light. Left on Chase Rd to Jay-Mar.

Contact: Howard Pincus
President

Mailing Address:
P.O. Box 4658
Waterbury, CT 06704
Telephone: (203) 395-0615

SMITHSONIAN INSTITUTION

Displays/Exhibits: The Smithsonian's Railroad Hall symbolizes the achievements of railroads and rail transit in the United States from the 1820s to about 1965. On display are original pieces of the "Stourbridge Lion" and the "Dewitt Clinton," a complete Winton 201-A engine from the Pioneer Zephyr, a series of ½-inch-scale models showing locomotive development from the earliest steam engine to present-day diesels, and many other exhibits.

Schedule: Daily 10:00 a.m.-5:30 p.m. except Christmas Day.

Fare/Admission: Free.

Locomotives: No. 1401, 1926 Alco 4-6-2, former Southern Railway; "John Bull," 1831 Stephenson 4-2-0, former Camden & Amboy Railroad. "Pioneer," 1851 Wilmarth 2-2-2, former Cumberland Valley Railroad; "Olomana," 1883 Baldwin 2-4-2T, former plantation locomotive; "Jupiter," 1876 Baldwin narrow gauge 4-4-0 (in Arts & Industries Building).

Notes: Information leaflet No. 455, available on request, describes the railroad exhibits. (Extensive research inquiries cannot be answered.)

Location: National Museum of American History, 14th Street and Constitution Avenue.

 Washington D.C.

Contact: William L. Withuhn
Supervising Curator
Division of Transportation

Mailing Address:
National Museum of American History
Washington, DC 20560

AVONDALE RAILROAD CENTER, DELAWARE PROJECT
Railway museum
Standard gauge

LINDA A. WOODCOCK

Displays/Exhibits: This display, a component of the Avondale Railroad Center of Avondale, Pennsylvania, features a Pennsylvania Railroad class B-6sa 0-6-0, the only surviving locomotive of its class, which is being cosmetically restored; a Union Pacific caboose; a PRR baggage car; and two Reading Railroad passenger cars. The equipment is located on the siding of the Minker Construction Company's Stone Mill Business Center, and Minker's offices are housed in a newly built replica of a turn-of-the-century railroad station. The facility is on the main line of the Wilmington & Western Railroad.

Schedule: Year-round.

Admission: Free.

Special Events: Art shows, seasonal celebrations. Please write for information.

Location: Route 41, in the center of town.

Mailing Address:
P.O. Box 809
Avondale, PA 19311

QUEEN ANNE'S RAILROAD
Steam, diesel, scheduled
Standard gauge

QARR

Displays/Exhibits: The Queen Anne Railroad's excursion train takes passengers on a 1¼-hour ride in open-window coaches through southern Delaware countryside on the former Pennsylvania Railroad Lewes-Georgetown line. The *Royal Zephyr* travels a 2½-hour course, during which passengers enjoy a full dinner with linen and silver service and live musical entertainment. A murder mystery dinner theater is featured on selected trains. A cash bar is available on all dinner trains.

Train: Excursion: open-window heavyweight coaches. Royal Zephyr: climate-controlled dining cars.

Schedule: Office: May-December. Royal Zephyr: May-December, weekends. Excursion: June-September. Write or call for current schedule.

Fare/Admission: Write or call for current prices.

Locomotives: No. 3 1943 Vulcan locomotive works 0-6-0T U.S. Navy; No. 19 1959 Alco T-6 PRR.

Passenger Cars: 1947 Pullman Standard coaches, former New Haven; MP-54 coach, former PRR; coach, former New York Central; heavy combine, former Norfolk & Western; baggage car, former Amtrak/U.S. Army.

Note: The railroad reserves the right to make equipment and schedule changes without notice. Full refunds are given if train is cancelled.

Location: From Route 1 follow Cape May-Lewes ferry signs to Kings Highway station site.

Contact: Mark Jordan, General Manager
or Keith Cranor, Assistant Manager

Mailing Address:
730 Kings Highway
Lewes, DE 19958
Telephone: (302) 644-1720

WILMINGTON & WESTERN RAILROAD
Steam, scheduled
Standard gauge

EDWARD J. FEATHERS

Ride/Operation: A 10-mile, 1¼-hour round trip over a portion of the former Baltimore & Ohio Landenberg Branch, from Greenbank Station to the Mt. Cuba Picnic Grove. Also offered are occasional trips past Mt. Cuba along the Red Clay Creek Valley to either Yorklyn or Hockessin.

Displays/Exhibits: Original W&W Yorklyn station serves as the Greenbank Gift Shop.

Train: Steel open-platform combine and coaches, former Delaware, Lackawanna & Western; closed-platform coaches, former Pennsylvania Railroad and DL&W; wood-sided cabooses, former B&O.

Schedule: Saturday and/or Sunday, April-October. Trip includes one hour round trip to Mount Cuba Picnic Grove or two hour round trip to Yorklyn and Hockessin. The diesel engine normally runs on Saturdays and the steam engine runs on Sundays. Please call or write for latest timetable.

Fare: Please call for fares. Caboose rentals, group rates, and private charters are available.

Locomotives: No. 98, 1909 Alco 4-4-0, former Mississippi Central; No. 37, 1924 Alco 2-8-2T, former Sugar Pine Lumber Co.; No. 8408, 1942 EMD SW1, former B&O; No. 114, EMD SW1, former Lehigh Valley; No. 4662, 1929 Pullman Standard doodlebug, former PRR.

Special Events: Easter Bunny Specials, Wild West Robberies, Autumn Leaf Specials, Santa Claus Specials, Tuesday School Trains and Epicurean Express Dinner Trains. Call for information.

Location: Trains leave from Greenbank Station, on route 41 just north of route 2, four miles southwest of Wilmington. Take exit 5 off I-95, follow route 141 north to route 2 west, then follow route 41 north.

Wilmington

Radio Frequency: 160.755

Contact: David L. Ludlow
Executive Director

Mailing Address:
P.O. Box 5787
Wilmington, DE 19808
Telephone: (302) 998-1930
Fax: (302) 998-7408

FLORIDA CENTRAL
ADVENTURE DINNER TRAIN
Scheduled
Standard gauge

FLORIDA CENTRAL ADVENTURE DINNER TRAIN

Ride/Operation: A 2½-hour, 54-mile round trip dinner train serving a four-course meal. The train travels through the heart of Central Florida on former SAL and ACL trackage.

Schedule: Wednesday, October 2-November 20, 3:30 p.m.; Thursday-Saturday, 6:30 p.m.; Sunday, 1:00 p.m.

Fare/Admission: From $44.95 to $49.95 plus tax and gratuity, seasonal specials and group rates available.

Locomotives: Nos. 47 & 53 diesels CF7s.

Rolling Stock/Equipment: Air-conditioned dining cars. Nos. 300 & 301 former PRR dining cars; No. 303 Pullman former ATSF; No. 302 Pullman former ACL.

Special Events: Special holiday trains Thanksgiving through New Year's.

Note: Nearby attractions include Walt Disney World, Universal Studios, Sea World, Kennedy Space Center.

Location: Located on Orange Avenue. Off SR 434 west, 1/4 mile south of junction SRs 434 and 436.

♿ call for information

P   ♟   TRAIN   Orlando

Radio Frequency: 161.475 and 160.545

Contact: General Manager

Mailing Address:
P.O. Box 967
Plymouth, FL 32768-0967
Telephone: (407) 889-7005
Fax: (407) 880-8500

JEANNE HICKAM

Ride/Operation: The museum sponsors a 12-to-15-minute, 1⅛-mile ride at the Train Village in Lakes Park.

Displays/Exhibits: Historical exhibits feature railroads that operated in South Florida, artifacts, and steam locomotive operation.

Train: Three 7½ inch gauge FP7A diesels with four cars each. One 7½ inch gauge replica of 0-6-0 ACL143 with four cars.

Schedule: Weekdays, 10:00 a.m.-2:00 p.m. Closed Mondays mid April-mid October; Saturdays & holidays, 10 a.m.-4:00 p.m.; Sundays, 12:00-4:00 p.m. Closed Christmas Day. Charters & groups by special arrangement.

At press time Museum was seeking a new location. Call or write for information.

Fare/Admission: Train: $2.50 Daytime; $3.00 Special night rides, children 3 and under ride free accompanied by an adult; Lakes Park parking $0.75/hour.

Locomotives: Nos. 1994, 1995, 1996, FP7A diesels; No. 143 7-1/2 inch gauge; No. 143, 1905 Baldwin 0-6-0, former Atlantic Coast Line displayed at Lakes Park, awaiting cosmetic restoration.

Special Events: Valentine Special (night ride), Feb. 14-17; Easter Bunny Express, March 28-30; American Liberty Express, July 4-27; Halloween Express (night ride), Oct. 18-31, Holiday Express (night ride), Nov. 29-Jan. 11, 1998. Night rides feature lighted miniature villages and holiday displays (Christmas over 125,000 lights).

Note: Lakes Park and any future Museum location are wheelchair-accessible. Train: limited handicapped access.

Location: Train Villiage & Museum Office: Lakes Park, 7330 Gladiolus Dr. Between Rt. 41 & Summerlin Dr.

 Tampa

Contact: Kent Schneider, President
Jeanne Hickam, Treasurer

Mailing Address:
P.O. Box 7372
Fort Myers, FL 33911-7372
Telephone: (941) 267-1905
Fax: (941) 267-0225

SEMINOLE GULF RAILWAY
Diesel, scheduled
Standard gauge

SEMINOLE GULF RAILWAY

Ride/Operation: Excursion trains between Bonita Springs, Ft. Myers colonial station and down-town Ft. Myers station. Across street from Ft. Myers Imaginarium, Hands-on museum and Aquarium. Dinner trains with Murder Mystery show runs 6:30 pm friday and saturday night. Sunday has 5:30 pm twilight dinner to the Caloosahatchee river and back. We also have a Jazz train with featured musicians from local jazz society every thursday night for $10 and food is available from menu.

Schedule: We are open year around. Feature Christmas rail/boat rides in December are very popular. Murder Mystery year round and special events. Dinner trains for Valentine's Day, Mother's Day, Father's day and Thanksgiving.

Fare/Admission: Adult $11 excursion, children $6 + tax. Dinner train from $29.75 + tax to $44.75 on Saturday.

Locomotives: 8 GP9s, 3 RDCs

Rolling Stock/Equipment: Dinning cars Sanibel, Gasparilla, and Captiva; kitchen car Marco

Special Events: Offers great hotel stay rates for our Get-a-Way program for persons in the 1-3 hour driving distance who desire to ride the train and stay overnight.

Location: Exit 22 from I -75.

Contact: Carl J. Appelberg

Mailing Address:
4410 Centerpointe Drive
Ft. Myers, FL 33916

Telephone: (941) 275-6060
1-800-SEM-GULF
Fax: (941) 275-0581
E-mail: JAppelberg@AOL.Com

HIGH SPRINGS STATION MUSEUM

Displays/Exhibits: Real artifacts of the American railroad heritage. From whistles to cabooses, hand car to velocipede, dishes, silver, tools, uniforms, signals, telegraph, motorcars and more.

Schedule: Wednesday-Saturday, 10:00 a.m.-5:00 p.m. Sunday, 12:00-5:00 p.m.

Fare/Admission: Adults $3.00; children 12 and under $2.00. Family discounts available.

Locomotives: 5-ton Plymouth narrow gauge engine.

Rolling Stock/Equipment: Wooden caboose, motorcars.

Location: I-75 exit 79. Five miles west to center of High Springs. Turn right before the railroad tracks.

Contact: Ric Tritsch
President

Mailing Address:
P.O. Box 2008
High Springs, FL 32655-2008
Telephone: (904) 454-5377

GOLD COAST RAILROAD MUSEUM
Diesel, scheduled
Standard and narrow gauge

GOLD COAST RAILROAD EXHIBIT

Ride/Operation: The Gold Coast Railroad Museum, a non-profit, volunteer organization, has been in existence for over 35 years. Located on approximately 60 acres, which formerly housed the N.A.S. Richmond base in World War II, the museum has over 30 pieces of rolling stock on display, hundreds of railroad memorabilia, and a 20-minute train ride into a scenic pineland on both standard and narrow gauge trains. Self guided tours of railroad cars and engines dating from the 1920s to 1950s are available. Railroad artifacts are displayed in one of the baggage cars, while exhibits of N.A.S. Richmond and the early lumbering industry in South Florida, as well as several layouts of model railroads including one which visitors can operate are displayed in the buildings.

Schedule: Monday-Friday: 11:00 a.m.-3:00 p.m. Train rides by reservation only. Weekends: 11:00 a.m.-4:00 p.m. Train rides on the hour beginning at noon.

Fare/Admission: Adults $5.00, children 12 and under $2.00.

Locomtoves: Nos. 113 and 153 Florida East Coast steam engines.

Rolling Stock/Equipment: Ferdinand Magellan, also known as U.S. Presidential Car No. 1, and the only Pullman car ever custom built for the President of the U.S. The Silver Crescent built in 1948 for the California Zephyr.

Special Events: Mystery on the Sunshine Express is a monthly program of participatory murder mysteries held on board a Tri-Rail train combined with dinner at a hotel destination. Railroad Days, Western Days. Call for dates.

Notes: Group/school tours, birthday parties, photo shoot location also available.

Location: Florida Turnpike or U.S. 1 to S.W. 152nd Street. Head west on S.W. 152nd Street to the Metrozoo entrance. Take Metrozoo entrance drive and follow signs to Gold Coast Railroad Museum.

Miami Airport, Hialeah

Contact: Connie Greer

Mailing Address:
12450 S.W. 152nd Street
Miami, FL 33177
Telephone: (305) 253-0063
Fax: (305) 233-4641

L&N DEPOT

Displays/Exhibits: Louisville & Nashville Depot was restored in 1992. It houses a telegraph office, exhibits, and a gift/hobby shop. Four former L&N passenger cars are being renovated, as are a restored L&N steel caboose and a former L&N bridge tender's house which contains an HO model diorama, as a Gallery of Railroad History.

Schedule: Friday & Saturday, 10:00 a.m.-4:30 p.m., other times by appointment.

Fare/Admission: Adults $2.00, children $1.00.

Rolling Stock/Equipment: No. 2722 L&N diner; Nos. 1652 & 1653 L&N dorm car; No. 2715 L&N diner; No. 1148 L&N bay-window caboose; No. 1102 SL-SF caboose; No. 18050 L&N PS-1 boxcar.

Special Events: Depot Days Arts & Crafts Festival, November 8-9.

Location: Exit 8 from I-10 north on 191 to Milton. South of Highway 90 on Canal Street to Henry Street.

Pensacola

Contact: L.S. Panzik

Mailing Address:
L&N Depot
206 Henry Street
Milton, FL 32570
Telephone: (904) 623-3645
(904) 623-0793

THE HENRY MORRISON FLAGLER MUSEUM

Ride/Operation: Whitehall, a 55-room Gilded Age estate, was the winter home of Henry M. Flagler, developer of the Florida East Coast Railway that linked the entire east coast of Florida.

Displays/Exhibits: Visitors to the Flagler Museum experience life during America's Gilded Age through the eyes of one of its most important citizens, Henry Flagler. Flagler, with partners John D. Rockefeller and Samuel Andrews, founded Standard Oil. Displays and exhibits focus on the contributions Flagler made to the state of Florida by building the Florida East Coast Railway and developing tourism and agriculture as the state's major industries.

Schedule: Tuesdays-Saturdays, 10 a.m.-5 p.m., Sundays noon-5p.m. Museum is closed Thanksgiving, Christmas Day and New Year's Day.

Fare/Admission: Adults $7.00, children 6-12 $3.00

Passenger Cars: Henry Flagler's private railcar, built in 1886.

Location: I-95 to exit 52A(Okeechobee Blvd. E.). Cross bridge onto island of Palm Beach. Turn left at first light on Cocoanut Row. Left turn on Whitehall Way.

West Palm Beach

Contact: Jessica Johnston

Mailing Address:
PO Box 969
Palm Beach, FL 33480
Telephone: (561) 655-2833
Fax: (561) 655-2826
Email: flagler@emi.net
Internet: http://www.emi.net/palm_beach/flagler_museum

88

FLORIDA GULF COAST RAILROAD MUSEUM, INC.

Diesel, scheduled
Standard gauge

FLORIDA GULF COAST RAILROAD MUSEUM. INC.

Ride: A 12-mile, 1½-hour ride through rural Florida on pre-1950s and 1950s passenger equipment—a museum where you ride the exhibits.

Schedule: January through April: Saturday 11:00 a.m., 1:00, and 3:00 p.m.; Sunday 1:00 & 3:00 p.m. May through December: Saturday 11:00 a.m. & 1:00 p.m.; Sunday 1:00 & 3:00 p.m.

Fare/Admission: Adults $8.00, children ages 3-11 $5.00.

Locomotives: Alco RS-3 diesel. EMD GP7 diesel.

Rolling Stock/Equipment: Open window coach, caboose, air-conditioned lounge car.

Location: From I-75, take exit 45 (Moccasin Wallow Road) to U.S. 301, turn south ¼ mile to the Parrish Post Office. Turn east to the train.

P   🚌   ✳   ☕   🛤   **M**

ar n   TRAIN   Tampa, 40 miles away

Contact: Mike Warren

Mailing Address:
P.O. Box 355
Parrish, FL 34219
Telephone: (941) 722-4272

CENTRAL FLORIDA RAILROAD MUSEUM
CENTRAL FLORIDA CHAPTER, NRHS
Model railroad musem and display

CENTRAL FLORIDA RAILROAD MUSEUM

Displays/Exhibits: The museum is housed in the former Tavares & Gulf R.R. Depot which was constructed in 1913. Displays include a pictorial history of the Tavares & Gulf R.R., a subsidiary of the Seaboard Air Line R.R., as well as many historic photographs of early central Florida railroading. An extensive collection of railroad memorabilia and equipment is also displayed which includes a 1938 Fairmont motor car, a 1900 velocipede hand Car and a caboose. The depot/museum is on an active branch line operated by the Florida Central R.R., a short line operated by the Pinsly R.R. Co.

Schedule: Sundays 2:00-5:00 p.m. except some holiday weekends. Other times by appointment. Call (407) 656-8749.

Fare/Admission: Free, donations appreciated.

Rolling Stock/Equipment: Clinchfield Caboose No. 1073.

Location: Take exit 267 off Florida. Turnpike, then west 2 miles on state road 50 to Winter Garden. Turn right on Vineland Rd. (RT 535) and proceed north (535 will become Main St.) to railroad crossing. Cross tracks and turn left on Joiner St. and proceed one block to museum entrance on Boyd Street.

P Orlando, 12 miles away

Contact:
R.K. Murdock
Curator

Mailing Address:
1227 Marscastle Avenue
Orlando, FL 32812
Telephone: (407) 656-8749

MICHAEL DZIADIK

Ride/Operation: At the museum, locomotives No. 2 and No. 5 pull cabooses around a half-mile loop, and the North Georgia Live Steamers operate a 1 1/2-inch-scale live-steam train over 4,000 feet of track.

Displays/Exhibits: Twelve-acre museum site at Duluth features steam and diesel locomotives and passenger and freight cars. The museum library, housed in former Southern RPO No. 153, is open by appointment.

Train: Cabooses Nos. X-92, former Central of Georgia; No. 1064, former Clinchfield Railroad; No. 2866, former Georgia Railroad; No. 7871, former Southern Railway.

Schedule: April-November, Saturdays 9:00 a.m.-5 p.m. and Sundays of third full weekend each month 12:00-5:00 p.m. Train rides included with admission. North Georgia Live Steamers operate third weekend of each month. December-March, exhibits only.

Fare: Adults $5, Children (2-12) $3, Seniors $3. December-March exhibit is free admission; donations welcomed.

Locomotives: No. 97, 1943 Porter 0-6-0T, former Georgia Power; No. 9, 1924 Heisler, former Campbell Limestone Co.; No. 8202, 1950 EMD SW7 diesel, former Southern Railway; Nos. 2 & 5, 1948 & 1941, 44-ton General Electric center-cab diesels, former Hartwell Railroad.

Location: At 3966 Buford Highway, Duluth, about 10 miles north of Atlanta and 1/4 mile south of Pleasant Hill Road.

 Atlanta

Mailing Address:
Southeastern Railway Museum
or Atlanta Chapter, N.R.H.S.
P.O. Box 1267
Duluth, GA 30136-1267
Telephone: (770) 476-2013

KENNESAW CIVIL WAR MUSEUM
Railway museum
Standard gauge

KENNESAW CIVIL WAR MUSEUM

Operation: The Andrews Raid and the Great Locomotive Chase, one of the unusual episodes of the Civil War, has been much publicized over the years. The "General," now one of the most famous locomotives in American history, is enshrined in a museum within 100 yards of the spot where it was stolen on April 12, 1862. The old engine, still operable, last ran in 1962. The Kennesaw Civil War Museum was officially opened on April 12, 1972, 110 years after the historic seizure of the "General."

Displays/Exhibits: Locomotive "General" and tender; train and Civil War memorabilia; video show about the Great Locomotive Chase.

Schedule: March 1-November 30: Monday-Saturday, 9:30 a.m.-5:30 p.m.; Sunday, 12:00-5:30 p.m. December 1-February 28: Monday-Saturday, 10:00 a.m.-4:00 p.m.; Sunday, 12:00-5:30 p.m.

Admission: Adults $3.00, senior citizens & AAA service $2.50, children $1.50, children (under 7) admitted free.

Locomotives: The "General," No. 3, 1855 Rogers, Ketchum & Grosvenor 4-4-0, former Western & Atlantic Railroad.

Location: Off highways 41 & 75 about 25 miles north of Atlanta. Take exit 118 off I-75 north, turn left, and travel 2 1/2 miles.

Contact: Dawn K. Collins
Dir. Museum & Preservation Services

Mailing Address:
2829 Cherokee Street
Kennesaw, GA 30144
Telephone: (770) 427-2117
(800) 742-6897
Fax: (770) 429-4559

HISTORIC RAILROAD SHOPS

Displays/Exhibits: Savannah's *Historic Railroad Shops* are an antebellum railroad manufacturing and repair facility. Construction of the site was begun in 1845 and thirteen of the original structures are still standing. Included in these structures are the massive a roundhouse and operating turntable, and the 125 ft. smokestack.

The Railroad Shops make up the oldest and most complete railroad repair and manufacturing facility still standing in the United States, and are a National Historic Landmark. The site, owned by the City of Savannah, was used for the filming of the motion picture "Glory" in 1988. On August 1, 1989, operation of the *Railroad Shops* was taken over by the Coastal Heritage Society.

Since 1989, approximately one million dollars has been spent on capital improvements at the site in an effort to protect and expand its resources.

The goal of the site is to present a resource that protects its structures and its history, including artifacts, and written history. The site is a multiple use facility and, therefore, dedicates its mission to serving as wide a range of public and private use as possible. Permanent exhibits in five of the structures on the site. The *Shops* are open for self-guided tours.

Schedule: Self-guided tours daily, 10:00 a.m.-4:00 p.m. Group tours and special daytime functions are available at the *Shops* as well as "After Hours" functions and dinner programs. Groups are welcomed to enjoy a variety of menus and historic programs. Please call for more information or reservations.

Contact: Robert Edgerly

Mailing Address:
601 West Harris Street
Savannah, GA 31402
Telephone: (912) 651-6823
Fax: (921) 651-3691

HAWAIIAN RAILWAY SOCIETY

Ride/Operation: This site offers a 90-minute, 6 1/2-mile ride from the historic plantation town of Ewa to the water's edge, where passengers can witness the surf crashing against the rocks. The train travels along the fence and main gate of Barbers Point Naval Air Station and through cane fields, the old town sites of Gilberts and Sisal, and the Ko Olina Resort and golf course. Passengers also get a view of pre-World War II Fort Barrette not normally available to the public. Narration on the ride provides the history of the area and railroading in Hawaii.

Displays/Exhibits: Nos. 6 and 12, former Oahu Railway & Land Co.; No. 6, former Waialua Agricultural Co.; No. 1, former Ewa Plantation Co.; No. 65-00174, former U.S. Navy; Hawaii's 40 & 8 "Merci" boxcar.

Train: No. 65-00302, former U.S. Navy; Whitcomb 0-4-4-0; converted U.S. Army flatcars, three covered and two open.

Schedule: Sundays (except major holidays), 12:30 & 2:30 p.m. Group charters available.

Fare: Adults $8.00, senior citizens (62+) and children (2-12) $5.00.

Location: Take exit 5A off freeway H-1; travel south on Fort Weaver Road to the fourth stoplight (Renton Road); turn right onto Renton Road and travel all the way to the end; the site is on the left.

Contact: Jan Lorimer
Administrator

Mailing Address:
P.O. Box 1208, Ewa Station
Ewa Beach, HI 96706
Telephone: (808) 681-5461
Fax: (808) 681-4860

LAHAINA, KAANAPALI & PACIFIC RAILROAD

Steam, scheduled
36" gauge

LAHAINA, KAANAPALI & PACIFIC RAILROAD

Ride/Operation: The LK&P offers an old-fashioned passenger-train ride behind steam locomotives. Passengers are entertained by a singing conductor as the train passes through fields of sugar cane and the Kaanapali Golf Courses. The 12-mile, 1-hour round trip takes passengers between the historic old town of Lahaina and the resort of Kaanapali Beach. During busy periods, trains pass each other at Hahakea siding, the midpoint of the ride. The train crosses a 400-foot-long trestle, and the trip features spectacular views of the West Maui Mountains and the neighboring islands of Molokai and Lanai. Locomotives are turned on a turntable at Lahaina station at the end of each trip.

Train: Open-window coaches are patterned after 1880 Kalakaua-style coaches that ran on the Hawaiian Railroad. Nos. 101, 102, and 103 were built in 1969, No. 104 in 1983, Nos. 105 and 106 in 1991, Nos. 107 and 108 in 1995, and No. 109 in 1996.

Schedule: Daily Twenty-four one-way trips per day between 8:55 a.m. and 5:30 p.m.

Fare: Round trip: adults $13.50, children $7.00. One way: adults $9.50, children $5.00.

Locomotives: No. 1, "Anaka," 1943 Porter 2-4-0 & No. 3, "Myrtle," 1943 Porter 2-4-0, both former Carbon Limestone Co.; No. 45, "Oahu," 1959 Plymouth diesel, former Oahu Railway; No. 5, "Waikakalaua," 1908 Baldwin, former Oahu Sugar Company; No. 85, "Iniki," 1910 Alco Cooke Works, former Oahu Railway.

Special Events: Train Package Tours-Land/Sea Adventure, Adult $39.50, Child $19.75; Hawaii Experience, Adult $17.50, Child $9.25; Lahaina Town Tour, Adult $17.50, Child $7.00. Group rates available. Chartered trains run evenings (5-8 pm) for groups (up to 300). Catered parties and receptions at Kaanapali Station. Call for further information.

Notes: The Lahaina, Kaanapali & Pacific Railroad is operated by Railroads of Hawaii, Inc., a subsidiary of Kyle Railways, Inc.

Location: Kaanapali Beach Resort, Maui.

   ♿   **P**   🚌   ✳   ☕

▶ ◀ **Radio Frequency:** 154.540

Contact: Marty Garelick
General Manager
Mailing Address:
P.O. Box 816
Lahaina, HI 96767-0816
Telephone: (808) 667-6851

SILVERWOOD CENTRAL RAILWAY

Steam, scheduled
36" gauge

SILVERWOOD CENTRAL RAILWAY

Ride/Operation: A 3.2-mile, 20-minute ride around the perimeter of Silverwood Theme Park, crossing a trestle and passing through wooded areas.

Displays/Exhibits: Silverwood Theme Park, an upscale Victorian mining town, includes several gift shops, a full-service restaurant, an old-time theater, professional entertainment, a daily air show, and the Country Carnival, which includes the corkscrew rollercoaster, the whitewater raft ride "Thunder Canyon," and an indoor ice show. The park is also beginning construction of its new "Woodie Rollercoaster."

Train: Typical train consists of an engine, two roofed cars, and one open car.

Schedule: Daily, Memorial Day through Labor Day. Weekends, May and September.

Fare: Included in park admission. Call for rates.

Locomotives: No. 7, 1915 Porter 2-6-0, former Eureka & Palisade Railroad; No. 12, 1928 Baldwin 2-6-2, former Kahului Railroad.

Passenger Cars: Enclosed car; two roof cars; three open cars.

Rolling Stock/Equipment: Flatcar; three boxcars, former Southern Pacific; coal car, former East Broad Top.

Location: In northern Idaho, 15 miles north of Coeur d'Alene on highway 95.

Contact: Jane A. Thompson
Administrative Assistant

Mailing Address:
North 26225 Highway 95
Athol, ID 83801
Telephone: (208) 683-3400
Fax: (208) 683-2268

Idaho, Wallace
M-D

NORTHERN PACIFIC DEPOT
RAILROAD MUSEUM
Railroad display, museum

Displays/Exhibits: Contain many photographs and other related artifacts (ex: telegraph machine, maps, pen, patches, matches etc.) We have an old time office set up downstairs that looks like the real thing from the past. We also have the original blue prints for the Depot on display.

Schedule: Summer and fall hours: 9:00 a.m.-7:00 p.m., seven days a week. Spring and winter hours vary.

Fare/Admission: Spring and summer; $2 adults, $1.50 seniors, $1 children 6-16, free for children under 6, families $6.

Special Events: Annual Depot days, held in May, celebrate the moving and restoration of the Depot in 1986.

Contact: Linda Brunette

Mailing Address: P.O. Box 469
Wallace, ID 83873
Telephone: (208) 762-0111

HISTORIC PULLMAN FOUNDATION

Displays/Exhibits: This organization offers guided tours of the historic Pullman district. The tour begins with an introductory video and a view of the interior of the HPF Visitor Center and the Greenstone Church; it then continues with the visitor's choice of a walk or a bus trip through the area, taking in the Pullman Suite at the Hotel Florence (once reserved for George M. Pullman), a Victorian furniture display room, and a "wood display" room containing actual pieces from Pullman's home on Prairie Avenue. Tour/luncheon packages are available, with lunch at the Hotel Florence restaurant; also, Sunday tours from May through October are scheduled to coincide with brunch hours at the Hotel Florence.

Schedule: Hotel Florence Restaurant and Museum open year-round, Monday-Friday, 11 a.m.-2 p.m.; Saturday, 10 a.m.-2 p.m.; Sunday, 10 a.m.-3 p.m. Visitor Center Exhibit and Video open year round, Saturday, 11 a.m.-2 p.m.; Sunday, 12-3 p.m. Guided Walking Tour offered 1st Sunday of the month, May-October at 12:30 p.m. and 1:30 p.m. Group Tours may be arranged; call 312-785-8181 or write for further information.

Admission: Hotel Florence Museum-Donations accepted; Visitor Center-Adults $3.00 donation, students $1.00, children free. Guided Walking Tour-Adults $4.00, seniors $3.00, students $2.50. Rates subject to change.

Location: 11111 South Forrestville Avenue.

♿ (limited)   **P**   🚌   ❊   ◗

Chicago

Contact: Deborah Bellamy
Executive Director

Mailing Address:
11111 South Forrestville Avenue
Chicago, IL 60628-4649
Telephone: (773) 785-8181
Fax: (773) 785-8182

ALEX TREML

Displays/Exhibits: The Museum of Science and Industry's model railroad exhibit was originally installed in 1941. The layout is approximately 3,000 square feet. Features include an "O" gauge track that is 1/48 the actual size, totaling 1,200 feet, in addition to 10,000 feet of switchboard wire, 350 relays, 5,500 trees, 150 telegraph poles, as well as a host of freight cars.

Schedule: Labor Day - Memorial Day: 9:30 a.m.-4:00 p.m. Monday-Friday; 9:30-5:30 Saturday and Sunday

Fare/Admission: General admission: adults $6, seniors $5, children (5-12) $5.50, children under 5 are free. Members free. General admission free on Thursdays. Combination tickets (General admission and Omnimax): Adults $10, seniors $8, children (5-12) $5.50, children under 5 are free; must share seat.

Locomotives: Engine 999 was the first vehicle to go over 100 mph. The pioneer Zephyr was the first streamlined diesel - electric train Zephyr exhibit opens in December 1997.

Location: From the north, proceed south on Lake Shore Drive past 57th Street and turn right at a new traffic signal at Science Drive. From south, follow Cornell Drive north to 57th Street and enter Museum grounds by making a right turn at Everett Drive.

Contact: Francesca Sgambati
Public Relations Coordinator

Mailing Address:
57th Street and Lake Shore Drive
Chicago, IL 60637
Telephone: (312) 684-1414 Ext. 2477 or
Direct line (312) 947-3734
Fax: (312)-684-2907
Internet: http://www.msichicago.org.

SILVER CREEK & STEPHENSON RAILROAD

Steam, scheduled
Standard gauge

GEORGE A. FORERO, JR

Ride/Operation: The train departs from the replica Silver Creek Depot, then travels on a 4-mile round trip through Illinois farmland and stands of virgin timber known as "Indian Gardens." From there, the train journeys across the Yellow Creek on a 30-foot-high cement and stone pier bridge.

Displays/Exhibits: The "turn-of-the-century" Silver Creek Depot is a tribute to an important part of our country's transportation history. Displayed inside are lanterns, locks and keys, whistles, sounders, tickets, advertising, couplers, and much more, representing railroads from across the country. Visitors taking in the exhibits can hear the clicking of the telegraph as the telegrapher taps out messages.

Train: 1912 36-ton Heisler; 1941 bay-window caboose, former Chicago, Milwaukee, St. Paul & Pacific; 1889 wooden caboose with cupola, former Hannibal & St. Joseph, reported to be the oldest caboose running in the state; 1948 caboose, former Illinois Central Gulf; covered flatcar.

Schedule: May 25-26; June 14-15; July 4; July 25-27; Sept. 26-27; Oct. 11-12; Oct. 25-26; 11:00 a.m.-5:00 p.m.

Fare: Adults $4.00, children (under 10) $1.50.

Locomotives: 1912 36-ton Heisler; 14-ton Brookville switch engine; 12-ton Plymouth switch engine.

Rolling Stock/Equipment: Work cars.

Notes: The Silver Creek & Stephenson Railroad and the Silver Creek Depot are projects of the Stephenson County Antique Engine Club. Information about the railroad can also be obtained from the Stephenson County Convention & Visitor Bureau, 2047 AYP Road, Freeport, IL 61032.

Location: Half-mile south of the Stephenson County Fairgrounds, at Walnut & Lamm Roads.

Contact: Peggy S. Althoff
Secretary

Mailing Address:
SCAEC
P.O. Box 255
Freeport, IL 61032
Telephone: (800) 369-2955
(815) 232-2306
Operating Days: (815) 235-2198

GALESBURG RAILROAD MUSEUM

Displays/Exhibits As you visit the Galesburg Railroad Museum, you will experience railroading of the early 1900's. The Museum has restored an engine and three cars built in the 20's and 30's and maintains an extensive collection of railroad memorabilia.

Schedule: Open Tuesday-Sunday 12:00 p.m.-5:00 p.m. Memorial Day-Labor Day and other times when requested for group tours.

Fare/Admission: Not for profit corporation requests $1.00 donation for adults and $.50 for children.

Locomotives: CB&Q 3006, Hudson Class 4-6-4. Built in 1930 by the Baldwin Locomotive Works, one of 12 built for the CB&Q.

Rolling Stock/Equipment: None of the rolling stock is operational; for exhibit only. CB&Q 2645, the Meath, a pullman parlor car built in 1921. CB&Q 1945, a combination railway post office and baggage express car built in 1924 by American Car & Foundry.

CB&Q 13501, one of the first steel waycars built by CB&Q in 1930.

Special Events: Railroad days - fourth full weekend in June, annual Railroad and city wide celebration drawing some 50,000 persons.

Location: In downtown Galesburg, get off I-74 exit 48 at Main St. go west to Seminar St. and left or south one block to museum.

P M

Contact: John Stablein
President

Mailing Address:
P.O. Box 947,
Galesburg, IL 61402-0947
Telephone: (309) 342-9400
or (309) 289-2661

MONTICELLO RAILWAY MUSEUM
Diesel, scheduled
Standard gauge

PAUL YOOS

Ride/Operation: This museum, incorporated in 1966, offers a 50-minute round trip over former Illinois Central and Illinois Terminal trackage. Passengers board at the Illinois Central Depot at the museum or at the 1899 Wabash Depot in downtown Monticello.

Displays/Exhibits: 1907 Baldwin 2-8-0, former Southern Railway No. 401; Shedd Aquarium's "Nautilus" (fish car); Nickel Plate RPO; Santa Fe Pullman "Pleasant Valley"; 1931 Alco 0-4-0 tank engine No. 1; 1944 Industrial Brownhoist; freight equipment; cabooses.

Train: No. 1189, former Wabash F7A, or No. 301, former Long Island RS-3; commuter coach, former Rock Island No. 2541, and/or baggage/coach combine, former IC No. 892, and/or vista gon, former Nickel Plate Road No. 1907; caboose No. 500836, former Norfolk & Western.

Schedule: Weekends & holidays, May 4-Oct. 31; 1:00, 2:00, 3:00 & 4:00 p.m. at museum site; 1:30, 2:30 & 3:30 p.m. in town. Charters/private cars/birthday caboose on request. Throttle times available.

Admission: Adults $5.00, senior citizens & children (4-12) $3.00, children under 3 accompanied by an adult ride free.

Locomotives: No. 1, 1930 Alco 0-4-0, former Montezuma Gravel Co.; No. 191, 1916 Alco 0-6-0, former Republic Steel Corp.; No. 301, 1955 Alco RS-3, former Long Island Railroad; No. 401, 1907 Baldwin 2-8-0, former Southern Railway; No. 44, 1940 Davenport 44-ton diesel; No. 1189, 1953 GMD F7A, former Wabash No. 725; No. 6789, 1959 Alco FPA-4, former Canadian National/VIA; CTA "Skokie Swift," one of four articulated car sets.

Passenger Cars: Pullman No. 2910 & dormitory car No. 1906, both former IC; passenger coach No. 1238 & parlor car "City of Decatur," both former Wabash; others.

Rolling Stock/Equipment: Wooden vinegar tank car No. 1655, former Standard Brands; wedge snowplow No. 40065, former Canadian Pacific; 4-wheel caboose, former Baltimore & Ohio; others undergoing restoration.

Special Events: Throttle Time, April 26-27 & November 8-9. Throw Momma ON the Train, May 10-11. Father's Day Bluegrass & More, June 14-15. Caboose Trains, August 16-17. Railroad Days, September 20-21. Depot Day, October 4. Ghost Trains & Haunted Boxcar, October 24-26 & 31. Please call for more information.

Notes: Monticello Railway Museum is a nonprofit volunteer organization.

Location: 20 miles southwest of Champaign; 20 miles northeast of Decatur. Take Exit 166 off I-72.

Champaign

Radio Frequency: 160.635

Contact: Barbara A. Mann

Mailing Address:
P.O. Box 401
Monticello, IL 61856-0401
Telephone: (217) 762-9011
800-952-3396

102

RAYVILLE RAILROAD MUSEUM
(PIATT COUNTY MUSEUM)
Model railroad
HO gauge

Displays/Exhibits: Rayville is a 10 x 36-foot miniature town hand-crafted by and named after the museum's curator, Ray McIntyre. The town of Rayville, which opened in 1966, is an HO-scale community that features a ball park, a drive-in movie, a race track, a circus, a lake and much more. In addition, the museum has a collection of railroad memorabilia. Campaign buttons, miniature trains, railroad books and photographs line the walls along with cast iron banks, car models, music boxes, old toys and postcards.

Rayville is one of three museums that make up the Piatt County Museum.

Schedule: 8:00 a.m.-11:00 a.m. and 12:00-4:00 p.m., seven days a week.

Fare/Admission: Adults $2, Children $0.50.

Location: 20 miles southeast of Champaign, 20 miles northeast of Decatur, on Interstate 72.

P M Champaign

Contact: Lila Miller

Mailing Address:
315 W. Main St.
Monticello, IL 61856
Telephone: (217) 762-4731

RICHARD M. SCHROEDER

Displays/Exhibits: Displays show the history of former C&EI railroad and other area railroads. The Baggage Room contains a HO model railroad. The Depot Museum preserves the railroad history of east Central Illinois and western Indiana in a former Chicago and Eastern Illinois Railroad Depot.

Schedule: Memorial Day through Labor Day, weekends, 12:00-4:00 p.m, and by appointment.
Fare/Admission: No charge.

Location: In Rossville, Illinois, one block north on Illinois Route No. 1 to Benton Street, east 3 blocks to CSX transportation tracks.

Contact: Richard M. Schroeder

Mailing Address: P.O. Box 1013
Danville, IL 61834-1013
Telephone: (217) 442-1374
E-mail: Rickschro@AOL.com
Internet: http://www.prairienet.org/djc-nrhs/

FOX RIVER TROLLEY MUSEUM
Electric, scheduled
Standard gauge

FRED LONNES

Ride/Operation: The Aurora, Elgin & Fox River country trolley line has been operating since 1896, first as a passenger interurban, later with electric freight, then as a diesel freight line. Chicago-area interurban and rapid-transit cars currently demonstrate the trolley era by operating from Castlemuir (South Elgin) to Coleman and Coleman Grove (Kane County Blackhawk Park). The nostalgic, 3-mile, 25-minute round trip takes passengers along the scenic Fox River.

Displays/Exhibits: 1926 Chicago, South Shore & South Bend coach No. 14; 1908 Chicago Transit Authority electric locomotive No. L-202; 1957 Illinois Central-built caboose No. 9648; 1895 Chicago Street Railway Post Office car No. 6 (used on special occasions).

Schedule: Sundays, May 12-November 3, plus May 27, July 4 & September 2, 11:00 a.m.-5:00 p.m. Saturdays, June 29-August 31, 11:00-5:00 p.m.

Fare: All-day pass: $6.00. Single ride: Adults $2.50, seniors (65+) $2.00, children (3-11) $1.50. Children must be accompanied by an adult. Charter and group rates available.

Locomotives/Trolleys: No. 20, 1902 Niles interurban, former Chicago, Aurora & Elgin—oldest operating interurban in America; No. 4451, 1924 Cincinnati, former Chicago Transit Authority; No. 5001, 1947 Pullman all-electric rapid-transit, former Chicago Rapid Transit; No. 715, 1926 Cincinnati, former Chicago North Shore & Milwaukee; Nos. 6101 & 6012, 1950 rapid transit cars, former St. Louis, former CTA.

Rolling Stock/Equipment: Diesel locomotive and additional interurban, rapid transit, and streetcar rolling stock on site or undergoing restoration.

Special Events: Mother's Day—free rides for Mom with paid child's fare. Spring Caboose Day. Father's Day—free rides for Dad with paid child's fare. Red, White & Blue Dollar Day, July 4, all rides $1.00. Trolley Folk Music Fest. Fall Caboose Sundays. Haunted Trolley. Call for dates and information.

Notes: The museum is operated by the volunteer, non-profit Fox River Trolley Association, Inc.

Location: 375 LaFox Street (Illinois route 31), 6 miles south of I-90, 3 miles south of U.S. 20. South Elgin is about 35 miles northwest of Chicago.

Contact: Ticket Agent

Mailing Address:
P.O. Box 315
South Elgin, IL 60177-0315
Telephone: (847) 697-4676

ILLINOIS RAILWAY MUSEUM
Steam, electric, diesel, scheduled
Standard gauge

THE ILLINOIS RAILWAY MUSEUM

Ride/Operation: A 5-mile, 25-minute round trip over the reconstructed right-of-way of the former Elgin & Belvedere, featuring steam and/or diesel trains and electric interurbans on weekends and streetcars on weekdays.

Displays/Exhibits: This extensive museum displays more than 300 pieces of rail equipment of all types. The museum also has a depot built in 1851, a signal tower, and an "el" station that have been moved to the site and restored.

Schedule: Daily, May 27-September 1. Weekends only, May, September & October.

Admission: Weekends when steam or diesel trains are operated: Adults $8.00, children (5-11) $6.00. Weekdays: Adults $6.00, children (5-11) $3.50. Maximum family admission: $30.00.

Locomotives/Trolleys: Midwestern interurbans and streetcars; Chicago elevated cars; North Shore, South Shore, Chicago, Aurora & Elgin, and Illinois Terminal interurbans. No. 1630, 1918 Baldwin 2-10-0, former Frisco Lines; No. 101, 1926 Baldwin 2-6-2, former Tuskegee Railroad; No. 5, 1929 Lima 3-truck Shay, former St. Regis Paper Co.; No. 8380, 1929 Baldwin 0-8-0, former Grand Trunk Western; No. 265, 1944 Alco 4-8-4, former Milwaukee Road; No. 16, 1915 Baldwin 4-4-0, former Detroit, Toledo & Ironton; No. 2050, 1922 Alco 2-8-8-2, former Norfolk & Western; No. 3719, 1900 Brooks 2-6-0, former Illinois Central; No. 2707, 1943 Alco 2-8-4, former Chesapeake & Ohio; No. 3001, 1926 Ingersoll Rand boxcab, former Delaware, Lackawanna & Western; No. 760, 1944 Fairbanks-Morse H-10-44 diesel, former Milwaukee Road; No. 9001, 1937 Electro-Motive Corporation SC-600, former Missouri Pacific; 1892 Rogers 4-6-0, 1923 Baldwin 2-8-2, 1930 Baldwin 4-6-4, and No. 9911-A, 1940 Electro-Motive Division E-5, all former Chicago, Burlington & Quincy.

Passenger Cars: Commuter cars from the Rock Island, the Chicago & North Western, and the Lackawanna; a train of heavyweight equipment; private cars; and 1936 Budd articulated stainless-steel Burlington *Nebraska Zephyr*.

Rolling Stock/Equipment: Large collection, including refrigerator cars, cabooses, two milk cars, and steam and electric work equipment.

Special Events: Scout Day, May 17. Railroad Day, May 26. Chicago Day, June 22. Trolley Pageant, July 4. Diesel Weekend, July 19-20. Vintage Transport Extravaganza, August 3. Railfan Weekend, August 30-31 & September 1. Members' Weekend, September 20-21.

Location: 7000 Olson Road, 1 mile east of town.

Contact: Nick Kallas
General Manager

Mailing Address
P.O. Box 427
Union, IL 60180
Recorded message: (815) 923-4000
Business office: (815) 923-4391
Fax: (815) 923-2006

VALLEY VIEW MODEL RAILROAD
Model railroad

VALLEY VIEW MODEL RAILROAD

Displays/Exhibits: This display is modeled after the Chicago & North Western's Northwest line, with accurate track layouts of some of the towns modeled. Three to four trains operate simultaneously over the railroad, which has eight scale miles of track, 16 ever-changing trains, 250 buildings, 64 turnouts, 250 vehicles, 450 people, 84 operating signal lights, 250 pieces of rolling stock, and operating grade crossings with flashers and gates. Extra equipment is on static display in the gift shop.

Schedule: Wednesdays and weekends, Memorial Day through Labor Day, 1-6 p.m.

Admission: Adults $4.00, children (5-12) $2.00, children under 5 admitted free.

Location: Valley View Farm, 17108 Highbridge Road - 3/4 mile straight north of the Illinois Railroad Museum on Olson and Highbridge Rd. in Union, Illinois--beautiful McHenry County.

Contact: Ted Voss

Mailing Address:
17108 Highbridge Road
Union, IL 60180
Telephone: (815) 923-4135

WHITEWATER VALLEY RAILROAD

Ride/Operation: This line offers a 32-mile, 5 1/2-hour round trip to Metamora, Indiana, a restored canal town that features one hundred shops and a working grist mill. A 2-hour stopover at Metamora gives passengers a chance to tour the town.

Displays/Exhibits: A small museum is located in the gift shop.

Train: No. 25, 1951 Lima; 1930s open-window coaches.

Schedule: Weekends and holidays, 12:01 p.m.

Fare: Adults $11.00, children (2-12) $5.00.

Locomotives: No. 6, 1907 Baldwin 0-6-0, former East Broad Top; No. 8, 1946 General Electric, former Muncie & Western; No. 11, 1924 Vulcan 0-4-0T; No. 100, 1919 Baldwin 2-6-2; No. 25, 1951 Lima SW7.5; No. 210, 1946 General Electric 70-ton; No. 709, 1950 Lima SW10; No. 2561, 1931 Plymouth 32-ton gas engine; No. 9339, 1948 Alco S1; No. 9376, 1950 Lima SW12, former Baltimore & Ohio.

Special Events: Christmas Trains, Weekends, 11/29-12/1, 12/6-12/8, 12/13-12/15 & 12/21-12/22.

Location: 300 South Eastern Avenue.

Radio Frequency: 160.650

Contact: Maurice E. Hensley
President

Mailing Address:
P.O. Box 406
Connersville, IN 47331
Telephone: (317) 825-2054

CORYDON SCENIC RAILROAD
Diesel, scheduled
Standard gauge

CORYDON SCENIC RAILROAD

Ride/Operation: A 1-½-hour, 16-mile ride over part of the 114-year-old Louisville, New Albany & Corydon Railroad from Corydon (the state's first capital) to Corydon Junction. Air conditioned trains with guides aboard to answer passengers' questions as the train travels along Big Indiana Creek into the southern Indiana woods and hills, crossing two major bridges and passing many sink holes.

Train: RDC coaches.

Schedule: May, Saturday-Sunday 1:00 & 3:00 p.m.; June, September, October & November 1-16, Friday 1:00 p.m., Saturday-Sunday 1:00 & 3:00 p.m.; July & August, Wednesday-Friday, 1:00 p.m., Saturday-Sunday 1:00 & 3:00 p.m.

Fare: Adults $9.00, senior citizens $8.00, children $5.00, age 3 and under free. Discount for groups of 20 or more.

Locomotives: Two 44-ton General Electric center-cab diesels; 2 Alco 1000-horsepower RS-1s.

Passenger Cars: 1952 & 1953 RDCs, Nos. 9801 & 9802; 1920 & 1930 Erie Lackawanna coaches.

Special Events: Civil War Weekend, September 27-28.

Notes: Schedule and equipment subject to change. Visa and Master Charge accepted.

Location: Walnut and Water streets. One mile south of I-64, in downtown Corydon.

Contact: Richard P. Pearson
Public Relations

Mailing Address:
P.O. Box 10
Corydon, IN 47112
Telephone: (812) 738-8000

Indiana, Elkhart
M

NATIONAL NEW YORK CENTRAL
RAILROAD MUSEUM
Railway museum

NATIONAL NEW YORK CENTRAL RAILROAD MUSEUM

Displays/Exhibits: Housed in ca. 1915 coaches and former NYC freighthouses, Museum traces local railroad history from 1833 to present as well as the NYC roles on local and national level. Many interactive exhibits also.

Schedule: Tuesday-Friday, 10:00 a.m.-2:00 p.m.; Saturday-Sunday, 10:00 a.m.-3:00 p.m. Closed Mondays and major holidays.

Fare/Admission: Adults $2, senior citizens (55+) $1, students (6-14) $1, and under 5 free. Special group rates available.

Locomotives/Trolleys: Mohawk No. 3001, former NYC L3a; No. 4882, former PRR GG1, No. 4085, former NYC E8.

Rolling Stock/Equipment: Steam wrecker, former NYC, c. 1926; wooden caboose, former NYC, c. 1915; bay window caboose, former NYC, c. 1960.

Special Events: 20 Years of Conrail Exhibit, through June 1.

Notes: New interactive exhibits are open. Call or write for specific information.

Location: 721 S. Main Street, Elkhart.

     P   🚌   ✳   📷   ▶   ◀

M   TRAIN   Lakeshore and Capitol Limited's stop at Elkhart

Contact: David M. Bird
Executive Director

Mailing Address:
P.O. Box 1043
Elkhart, IN 46515
Telephone: (219) 294-3001

110

FORT WAYNE RAILROAD HISTORICAL SOCIETY
Steam, irregular
Standard gauge

Ride/Operation: The FWRHS is America's most successful all-volunteer mainline steam operator. Since 1979 the Society has operated over 300 mainline excursions carrying 250,000 passengers over 50,000 miles on over a dozen different railroads from Wisconsin to New Jersey and Alabama. No. 2716 began a new service career in 1996 after being stored since 1982. No. 2716 is on long term lease from the Kentucky Railway Museum, Inc.

Train: Varies with trips and sponsors.

Schedule: Varies. For trip announcements, please send a self-addressed stamped envelope. Tentatively planned is a return visit to the Iron Horse Festival, Logansport, IN, on July 19-20. Informal tours may be taken on most Saturdays between 10:00 a.m.-4:00 p.m.

Fare: Varies with trip.

Locomotives: No. 765, 1944 Lima 2-8-4, former Nickel Plate; maintained and operated by the society.

No. 2716, 1944 Alco 2-8-4, former Chesapeake & Ohio, newly restored to operation. No. 1, 1906 Alco, Rhode Island, former Lake Erie and Fort Wayne. This is one of only two former Wabash steam locomotives in existence now undergoing cosmetic restoration. Various rolling stock on hand.

Special Events: The Society's Annual Open House is held the first weekend after Labor Day.

Location: The Society's home shop is located east of New Haven, Indiana. Take State Route 14 east three miles to Ryan Road, north one mile on Edgerton Road, east two miles to the Jefferson Park Shop.

Contact: Wayne York

Mailing Address:
P.O. Box 11017
Fort Wayne, IN 46855
Telephone: (219) 493-0765

FRENCH LICK, WEST BADEN & SOUTHERN RAILWAY
Diesel, electric, scheduled
Standard gauge

FRENCH LICK, WEST BADEN & SOUTHERN RAILWAY

Ride/Operation: A 20-mile, 1 3/4-hour round trip between the resort town of French Lick and Cuzco, site of Patoka Lake. The train traverses wooded Indiana limestone country and passes through one of the state's longest railroad tunnels. The trolley makes a 2-mile round trip from French Lick to West Baden.

Displays/Exhibits: The French Lick, West Baden & Southern Railway is operated by the Indiana Railway Museum, which owns 57 pieces of railway equipment.

Train: Erie and Rock Island coaches.

Schedule: Train: Weekends, April thru October, plus May 26, July 4 & September 1, 10:00 a.m., 1:00 & 4:00 p.m.; November, 1:00 p.m.; Tuesdays, June 3-October 28, 1:00 p.m.

Trolley: Call for schedule. Times are Eastern Standard Time.

Fare: Train: Adults $8.00, children (3-11) $4.00, children under 3 ride free. Trolley: $1.00, children under 3 ride free.

Locomotives/Trolleys: No. 3, 1947 General Electric 80-ton diesel; No. 208, 1912 Baldwin 2-6-0, former Angelina & Neches River Railroad; No. 97, 1925 Baldwin 2-6-0, former Mobile & Gulf Railroad; No. 1, Alco S-4 diesel, former Algers, Winslow & Western Railway; No. 313, 1930 former Porto, Portugal.

Special Events: Wild West Hold-ups are scheduled on major holiday weeks during the operating season. Call for specific dates and information.

Location: Trains depart from the old Monon Railroad passenger station in French Lick, located on state route 56 in southwestern Indiana, about an hour's drive from Louisville.

Radio Frequency: 160.635

Contact: G. Alan Barnett
General Manager

Mailing Address:
P.O. Box 150
French Lick, IN 47432
Telephone: (812) 936-2405
(800) 74-TRAIN

KENNETH HOUGH

Ride/Operation: A 2¼-mile, 15-minute trip over unique dual-gauge (24-inch and 36-inch) trackage through the scenic 155-acre grounds in LaPorte County; a 1½-inch-scale train that travels over a figure-eight layout and passes over and under a trestle bridge; a 14-inch-gauge train that runs over a 5,000-foot loop of track. All trains are live steam.

Displays/Exhibits: A large collection of steam-powered equipment, including a 92-ton railroad steam crane, a 350-horsepower Allis-Chalmers Corliss steam engine, steam traction engines, water pumps, sawmill, electric light plant, and antique gas engines and tractors.

Train: Open excursion-type cars.

Schedule: Weekends, May 24-September 7; Sundays, September 14-October 26; 12:00-5:00 p.m.

Fare: Train: $3.00 or $2.00, depending on choice of gauge. Steam Show: $3.00 (visitors over 12 years old).

Locomotives: No. 2, 1911 Porter 36-inch 2-6-0, former United Fruit, Guatemala; No. 1, 1935 Henschel (Germany) 24-inch 0-4-0T; No. 7, 1929 Lima 36-inch 3-truck Shay, former New Mexico Lumber Co.; No. 19-B, 1889 Sharp & Stewart (Glasgow, Scotland) 24-inch 0-4-0T, former Darjeeling & Himalayan Railway; 1940 Czechoslovakia CSK 0-4-0; Henschel (Germany) 0-4-0T. Two German-built locomotives are being restored for 24-inch-gauge use.

Special Events: Annual Steam Show, four-day Labor Day weekend show.

Location: Take exit 49 off the Indiana Toll Road, travel north on state route 39 approximately 6½ miles to county road 1000N, turn right and travel 2½ miles to the grounds. Alternate route: Take exit 1 (New Buffalo, Michigan) off I-94, travel south 2 miles to county road 1000N, turn left and travel 2½ miles to grounds.

Contact: John P. Edris
General Manager

Mailing Address:
2946 Mt. Claire Way,
Long Beach, IN 46360
Telephone: (219) 872-7405

THE CHILDREN'S MUSEUM
OF INDIANAPOLIS
Railway museum
Toy trains

Displays/Exhibits: In 1868 the "Reuben Wells" (named after its designer) was the most powerful engine in the world. Its job was to push freight and passenger cars to the top of Indiana's Madison Hill, which had a grade of 5.9 percent. The 35-foot-long, 55-ton steam engine reduced to fifteen minutes what would have taken a team of horses half a day to complete. The "Reuben Wells" was retired in 1905. The Children's Museum acquired the Reuben Wells in 1968, and in 1975 workers built the new museum around it. The museum also contains an 1890s train station complete with blacksmith shop and offers a view of the Ohio River and the One Spot Repair shed, where a tool car awaits.

The Toy Train Treasures exhibit at the Children's Museum is the nation's largest public display of pre-World War II toy trains. Visitors can see more than 5,000 cars, engines, and accessories in a collection of more than 1,500 train sets. Toy Train Treasures traces the rise and fall of the toy train industry, with special emphasis on trains made by Lionel, Ives, and American Flyer.

Schedule: Open Daily: 10:00 a.m.-5:00 p.m.; closed Mondays September-February; 1st Thursday of each month: 10:00 a.m.-8:00 p.m.

Admission: Adults $6.00, senior citizens $5.00, children (2-17) $3.00, children under 2 admitted free.

Location: 3000 North Meridian Street.

Contact: Tonya Woodard
Media Coordinator

Mailing Address:
P.O. Box 3000
Indianapolis, IN 46206
Telephone: (317) 924-5431

CARTHAGE, KNIGHTSTOWN & SHIRLEY RAILROAD
Diesel, scheduled
Standard gauge

CARTHAGE, KNIGHTSTOWN & SHIRLEY RAILROAD

Ride/Operation: A 10-mile, 1 1/4-hour round trip over the former Cleveland, Cincinnati, Chicago & St. Louis Michigan Division through scenic country, crossing the Big Blue River into Carthage, Indiana. Trains leave from the former New York Central freight house in Knightstown.

Train: Open-window coaches; open-platform transfer and cupola cabooses.

Schedule: May-October; weekends & holidays, 11:00 a.m., 1:00 & 3:00 p.m.; Fridays, 11:00 a.m.

Admission: Adults $6.00, children (3-11) $4.00, children under 3 ride free. Group rates available.

Locomotives: No. 215, 45-ton General Electric, former Air Force No. 1215.

Location: Thirty-three miles east of Indianapolis on U.S. 40; 3 miles south of I-70 on state route 109.

Contact: Marion J. Allison
President

Mailing Address:
112 West Carey Street
Knightstown, IN 46148
Telephone: (317) 345-5561

LINDEN RAILROAD MUSEUM
Railway museum

LINDEN RAILROAD MUSEUM

Displays/Exhibits: Operated by the Linden-Madison Township Historical Society, this museum is housed in the former Linden depot built by the Chicago, Indianapolis & Louisville Railway and the Toledo, St. Louis & Western Railroad in 1908. Restored to its 1950s appearance, the depot houses a collection of railroadiana from the Nickel Plate and Monon railroads. The Monon agent's room houses the E. E. Kauffman Monon collection, including a ¾-inch-scale model of the Louisville, New Albany & Chicago "Admiral" locomotive and cars and a ¾-inch-scale live-steam model of Monon Pacific No. 440 and the observation car "Babe." A HO railroad club operates a 1950s depiction of Linden in the Monon baggage room. Numerous Nickel Plate artifacts are displayed in the Nickel Plate agent's room including R. W. Schaller's early Indiana Railroad photos. An O gauge model layout is featured in the Nickel Plate baggage room. Outside, railway equipment and buildings are on display. The depot sits adjacent to the present-day Indianapolis-Chicago CSX main line (former Monon).

Schedule: April-October, Friday-Sunday, 1:00-5:00 p.m. June 11-September 2, Wednesday-Sunday, 1:00-5:00 p.m. Group tours by appointment.

Admission: Adults $2.00, teens (13-17) $1.00, children (6-12) $.50.

Rolling Stock/Equipment: Caboose No. 497, former Nickel Plate; Fairmont A-3 motor car.

Special Event: The Lincoln Funeral Train model exhibit, June 11-September 2.

Location: Linden is located south of Lafayette on U.S. 231 and is 7.9 miles north of the Crawfordsville exit of I-74. The depot is across from Jane Stoddard Park, at 514 North Main Street.

Contact: Bob Straw
President

Mailing Address:
P.O. Box 154
Linden, IN 47955
Telephone: (317) 339-RAIL (7425)
(800) 866-3973

INDIANA TRANSPORTATION MUSEUM
Steam, electric, diesel, scheduled
Standard gauge

JIM VAWTER

Ride/Operation: This 37½-mile tourist railroad offers passengers a trip through Indianapolis and rural Hamilton and Tipton counties; excursions vary in length. Visitors can also enjoy a 20-minute electric trolley ride through Forest Park aboard vintage trolleys and interurbans.

Displays/Exhibits: Many railroad cars are on display, including Henry M. Flagler's business car No. 90 from the Florida East Coast Railway (on special occasions), cabooses, boxcars, and passenger equipment.

Train: Mainline excursions with restored Budd coaches, former Burlington combine, former Louisville & Nashville heavyweight dining car, Pullman heavyweight coaches and Chesapeake & Ohio/Nickel Plate cabooses.

Schedule: Friday: Train to dinner at various restaurants along the line. Saturday & Sunday: excursion trips to various locations along the line.

Fare/Admission: Train: Adults $8-12 depending on destination; Children $5-7; Seniors & members $1 discount. Dinner Train: $45-55 depending on restaurant. Museum only: Adults $3.00; Children (3-12) $2.00.

Locomotives/Trolleys: U.S. Navy Baldwin VO-1000, Monon SW1 DS-50; no. 587, 1918 Baldwin 2-8-2, former Nickel Plate Road; FP7 no. 96C and F7 no. 83A, and other electric locomotives.

Passenger Cars: Budd coaches, former Santa Fe; 1937 Pullman heavyweight coaches.

Special Events: Many excursions and special events, call or write for specific information.

Location: On State Route 19 at Forest Park, 20 miles north of Indianapolis.

Indianapolis

Contact: Richard Howell
Interim Director

Mailing Address:
P.O. Box 83
Noblesville, IN 46061-0083
Telephone: (317) 773-6000

HOOSIER VALLEY RAILROAD MUSEUM
Railway display
Standard gauge

BRUCE EMMONS

Displays/Exhibits: Established in North Judson since 1988. The organization has been in the process of building the physical plant for a working railroad museum. The collection today consists of 30 pieces of railroad rolling stock. This includes the former 2-8-4 Chesapeake & Ohio steam locomotive No. 2789, which is under roof and being restored.

Schedule: Saturday: 8:00 a.m.-5:00 p.m. Call or write for information.

Admission: No charge.

Locomotives/Trolleys: No. 6, 0-4-2-T Porter; 44-ton Whitcomb diesel; 2-8-4 No. 2789, former Chesapeake & Ohio; No. 11, 95-ton General Electric, former Acme Steel.

Passenger Cars: Parlor car, former Gulf, Mobile & Ohio; baggage car, former Nickel Plate; coach, former New York Central; two coaches, former South Shore.

Rolling Stock/Equipment: World War II troop sleeper; transfer caboose, former Elgin, Joliet & Eastern; caboose, former Bessemer & Lake Erie; caboose, former Illinois Central; two steel boxcars, former NKP and Wabash; boxcar, former Pennsylvania Railroad; 1937 wood boxcar, former NKP; bunk car, former Norfolk & Western; 20-ton Orton rail crane; 40-foot wood boxcar, former Wabash; caboose, former Erie C345; caboose, former NKP 471.

Special Events: Membership Day & Annual Dinner Party, date to be announced.

Location: 507 Mulberry Street.

P M ✳ ▶ ◀

Contact: Bruce Emmons
Treasurer

Mailing Address:
P.O. Box 75
North Judson, IN 46366
Telephone: (219) 223-3834

TIM BAINTER

Ride/Operation: This railroad opened in 1989 on the grounds of the famous "Come and Dine" restaurant and gift shop. The train takes passengers on a 25-minute, 1 ½-mile ride, traveling across two bridges, through a 100-foot curved tunnel, crossing City Street, and making a 10-minute stop at a miniature farm.

Displays/Exhibits: On display are 30 to 40 antique farm tractors (fully restored), along with other antiques and collectibles. The gift shop is located within a one-third-scale depot.

Schedule: April 1-October 31, Monday-Saturday, 11:00 a.m.-dark; train leaves the station every 30 minutes.

Fare/Admission: $3.00; children under 4 ride free. Winter Wonderland Train, $4 per person, children under 5 ride free.

Locomotives: One-third-scale, 15"-gauge 4-4-0 built in 1957 by Elmer and Norman Sandley; GP38 diesel-hydraulic.

Passenger Cars: Three 1/3-scale, 8-passenger coaches, built in Old Wakarusa Shop.

Rolling Stock/Equipment: Two 1/3-scale stock cars, caboose, gondola, and hopper, all built in Old Wakarusa Shop.

Special Events: Pumpkin Trains, mid-September to October. Train makes a stop at a pumpkin patch. Winter Wonderland Train, December, train rides from 6:00 to 9:00 p.m. through 100,000 Christmas lights.

Location: On the grounds of "Come and Dine" restaurant on highway 19.

Nappanee

Contact: Tim Bainter
General Manager

Mailing Address:
P.O. Box 591
Wakarusa, IN 46573
Telephone: (219) 862-2714
(219) 862-2136

BOONE & SCENIC VALLEY RAILROAD
IOWA RAILROAD HISTORICAL SOCIETY

Steam, electric, scheduled
Standard gauge

IOWA RAILROAD HISTORICAL SOCIETY

Displays/Exhibits: Iowa Railway Museum, small items and rolling stock.

Ride/Operation: A 14 mile, 1½-hour trip through the Des Moines River Valley crossing a 156 foot-high trestle and the "Y" camp river bridge.

Train: Chinese steam locomotive.

Schedule: Memorial Day weekend-October 31. Daily: 1:30 p.m. Weekends: 11:00 a.m., 1:30 and 4:00 p.m.

Fare/Admission: Weekdays: Adults $8.00, children 5-12 $4, under 5 are free. Weekends: Adults $10.00.

Locomotives: No. JS8419 Chinese steam locomotive, Datong, China. Nos. 1003 & 1103 diesels, former C&NW. Trolleys: No. 50, former Charles City & Western. No. 106, former Chicago South Shore & South Bend.

Rolling Stock/Equipment: Lackawanna commuter cars and RI passenger cars.

Special Events: Pufferbilly Days, second weekend in September, a four day railroad heritage event.

Notes:

Location: I-35 to Ames, Iowa. U.S. 30 west to Boone, Iowa. North on Story Street (through business district) to 11th Street, turn west and go six blocks.

Oceola, Iowa 50 miles away

Contact:
Fenner Stevenson
General Manager

Mailing Address:
11th & Division Streets
Box 603
Boone, IA 50036
Telephone:
(515) 432-4249 or (800) 626-0319
Fax: (515) 432-4253

MASON CITY & CLEAR LAKE ELECTRIC
RAILWAY HISTORICAL SOCIETY

Electric, scheduled
Standard gauge

MASON CITY & CLEAR LAKE RAILWAY

Displays/Exhibits: We are adjacent to the nation's oldest continuously operating, electrical freight railroad (private property). Opportunities to view and photograph the railroad in operation occur almost daily.

Ride/Operation: One mile of electric travel from our carbarn and collection of historic trolley equipment/cars. Historic Baldwin-Westinghouse steeple cab power (five and support equipment.

Schedule: Memorial Day through Labor Day; charter trips any day April-October.

Fare/Admission: $3.50 adult, $2.00 children under 12.

Locomotives: 1927 Chicago North Shore and Milwaukee Interurban #727, 1948 PCC Trolley car, wooden trolley car (circa 1890s electric sweeper car 1900, Fairmont motor car.

Special Events: Group tours April - October any day of the week. Call (507) 373-5867 or CUB of Mason City or Clear Lake

Location: East end of Main Street, Clear Lake, Iowa. ½ mile east of I-35.

Contact:
Robert Entorf
President

Mailing Address:
P.O. Box 956
Mason City, IA 50401-0956

TRAINLAND U.S.A.

Displays/Exhibits: In 1964 Red Atwood became interested in Lionel trains. He built two small lay-outs and began to think of building a large one—which he completed in 1981. The O gauge layout measures 44x96 feet and has 22 trains, operating simultaneously.

Schedule: Memorial Day to Labor Day, daily. Weekends in September, 9:00 a.m.-7:00 p.m. Also open the Friday, Saturday and Sunday after Thanksgiving, noon -6:00 p.m. Group tours available with advance notice April-October.

Fare/Admission: Adults $3.50, seniors 55+ $3.00, children 4-12 $1.50, under age 4 are free. Checks accepted. Group discounts available.

Notes: Adventure Land Park, Maytag Museum are nearby attractions.

Location: State Highway 117, two miles north of Exit 155 of I-80.

nearby

Contact: Red Atwood
Owner/President

Mailing Address:
3135 Highway 117 N
Colfax, IA 50054
Telephone: (515) 674-3813

RAILSWEST RAILROAD MUSEUM
Railway museum
Model railroad

RAILSWEST RAILROAD MUSEUM

Displays/Exhibits: The RailsWest Railroad Museum and HO model railroad are housed in an 1899 former Rock Island depot. The museum contains displays of historic photos, dining-car memorabilia, uniforms, and many other interesting items used during the steam era. The 22-foot by 33-foot model railroad depicts scenery of the Council Bluffs/Omaha area, featuring train lines that served the heartland: Union Pacific; Missouri Pacific; Chicago & North Western; Wabash; Norfolk & Western; Chicago and Great Western; Rock Island; Milwaukee Road; and Chicago, Burlington & Quincy.

Schedule: May & December: Saturday-Sunday, 1-5 p.m. Memorial Day-Labor Day: Monday-Tuesday & Thursday-Saturday, 10:00 a.m.-4:00 p.m.; Sunday, 1:00-5:00 p.m.

Admission: Adults $3.00, senior citizens (60+) $2.50, children (6-12) $1.25, children under 6 admitted free.

Rolling Stock/Equipment: Burlington route handcar (velocipede); No. 903690, 1963 Budd RPO car, former Union Pacific No. 5908; No. 24548, 1967 caboose, Rock Island No. 17130; No. 462536, 1969 UP boxcar.

Special Events: Depot Days, September 27-28; Christmas at the Depot, November 29-December 28, Saturday & Sunday, 1:00-5:00 p.m.

Location: 1512 So. Main Street. Take exit 3 off I-80.

P 🚌 ✳ ▶ ◀ 📷 ⛩

M Omaha, Nebraska

Contact: Marcia Hastings

Mailing Address:
72 Bellevue Avenue
Council Bluffs, IA 51503
Telephone: Depot (712) 323-5182
Marcia Hastings: (712) 322-0612

FORT MADISON, FARMINGTON & WESTERN RAILROAD
Diesel, scheduled

FORT MADISON, FARMINGTON & WESTERN RAILROAD

Ride/Operation: The FMF&W is an old-time country railroad with tracks relaid on an abandoned Chicago, Burlington & Quincy branch chartered under its present name in 1869. A 2-mile ride takes passengers through the woods, up a 1.3-percent grade, and over a newly built trestle.

Displays/Exhibits: Exhibits include an extensive collection of memorabilia, a hand-pump car that visitors can operate, work equipment, and rolling stock. An authentic, re-created depot and enginehouse are open for viewing, and visitors can also see a display of rare velocipedes and very early section cars in the section house. A 1920s-era filling station showcases the Model T depot hack and other antique cars and is part of the growing, re-created, early-1900s town on the grounds. A 30-ton steam crane is demonstrated on select days as is a steam sawmill.

Train: 1926 Edwards Railway Motor Car Company "doodlebug" or open-air cars and caboose.

Schedule: Weekends and holidays, May 24-October 26, 12:00-5:00; trains depart hourly on the half hour.

Fare/Admission: Adults $4.00, students (5-18) $3.00, children (under 5) admitted free with paying adult. Price includes ride and museum admission.

Locomotives: 1913 Baldwin 0-4-0 tender locomotive; 1927 Vulcan 8-ton gas-mechanical; 1941 Davenport diesel-mechanical.

Rolling Stock/Equipment: 1914 wood caboose, former Chicago, Burlington & Quincy; 1890s wood truss-rod boxcar; automobile boxcar; U.S. Army flatcar; various speeders; work equipment.

Special Events: Antique Machinery Show, September 27-28; Santa Train, December 7,14 & 23.

Notes: A 115-acre park and lake are just across the road from the railroad. Camping, with all hookups, is available at the park.

Location: Southeast Iowa. Five and one-half miles east of Donnellson or 3 miles west of U.S. Rt. 61/Iowa Rt. 2 junction off Iowa Highway 2. Follow signs.

Ft. Madison, Mt. Pleasant

Contact: Dave Miner
President

Mailing Address:
2208 220th Street
Donnellson, IA 52625
Telephone: (319) 837-6689
Fax: (319) 837-6080

SANTA FE DEPOT MUSEUM
& HISTORIC CENTER
Railroad museum

DAVE SALER

Displays/Exhibits: The former Santa Fe depot in Fort Madison, a building in the mission revival style, is the nucleus of Fort Madison's historic district. It is a museum of railroad history, fire-fighting equipment, and fountain pens, reflecting Fort Madison's industrial history. Recently added to the museum is a section on the great floods of 1993. Outside is a Santa Fe caboose which is open to view.

Schedule: Daily: May through September; Weekends: October. 12:00-4:00 p.m.

Fare/Admission: Adults $2.00; children under age 12 are 50 cents. Group rates available.

Location: The historic district is at the foot of Ninth Street. Fort Madison is in the southeast corner of Iowa on U.S. Route 61 and State Route 2.

Mailing Address:
North Lee County Historical Society
P.O. Box 285
Fort Madison, IA 52627
Telephone: (319) 372-7661
Fax: (319) 372-1825

MIDWEST CENTRAL RAILROAD
Steam, irregular
36" gauge

PAUL A. KNOWLES

Ride/Operation: A 1-mile steam train ride with two station stops, through the grounds of the Midwest Old Settlers & Threshers Reunion. The reunion, held August 31 to September 4, features a large display of steam-powered farm equipment, antique cars, and an old Midwest farm village. This year is the 35th anniversary of the MCRR, a nonprofit educational organization.

Displays/Exhibits: The world's largest steam show, featuring more than 100 operating steam traction engines, dozens of models, antique tractors, cars, trucks, and all kinds of powerhouse and farm equipment.

Train: Three vintage locomotives; six wooden coaches; two cabooses.

Schedule: May 26- July 4, 10:00 a.m.-5:00 p.m. August 28-September 1, 8:30 a.m.-9:30 p.m.; during the reunion, rides operate on 10-minute schedules.

Fare: Adults $2.00, children $1.00. Admission to grounds: $7.00 one day; $10.00 for all five days.

Locomotives: No. 6, 1891 Baldwin 2-6-0, former Surry, Sussex & Southampton Railway, Dendron, Virginia; No. 9, 1923 Lima 3-truck Shay, former West Side Lumber Company; No. 16, 1951 Henschel 0-4-0ST, Kassel, West Germany.

Location: Southeast Iowa.

Mt. Pleasant

Mailing Address:
Box 102
Mt. Pleasant, IA 52641
Telephone: (319) 385-2912

STU PALMER

Displays/Exhibits: In addition to electric rail equipment, there are over 100 steam tractor engines, over 100 gas tractors, many agricultural history exhibits.

Ride/Operation: 1-1/2 miles of electric trolley mainline, with carbarn and 9 electric trolleys. Main event each year last 10 days ending Labor Day. Service compound and other displays at the Old Thresher's Reunion.

Schedule: Memorial Day-Labor Day, Sunday, 12:00-4:00 p.m. August 23-September 1, daily, 8:00 a.m.-8:30 p.m.

Fare/Admission: Adults $1, children under 6 are free. $7.00 admission to Old Thresher's Reunion.

Locomotives: Nos. 3093 & 3226 PCC cars from Boston MBTA; No. 4476 PCC car from Toronto; Nos. 1718 & 1779 Narragansett open cars from Rio de Janeiro, Brazil.

Special Events: Midwest Old Thresher's Reunion, August 27-September 1.

Location: Intersection of US highways 34 and 218 in southeast Iowa.

Contact:
Lennis Moore or Tom Boland

Mailing Address:
Old Thresher's Reunion
Mt. Pleasant, IA 52641
Telephone: (319) 385-8937
Fax: (319) 385-0563

Iowa, Waverly
D-R

IOWA STAR CLIPPER DINNER TRAIN
Diesel, scheduled
Standard gauge

IIOWA STAR CLIPPER DINNER TRAIN

Ride/Operation: The *Iowa Star Clipper* Dinner Train has the distinction of being the first dinner train in the United States. The *Star Clipper* began operation in May 1985 and has been running year-round ever since. The train, which departs from the historic depot in Waverly, a quaint Midwestern town of 8,000, runs leisurely through the Iowa countryside along rolling hills, plains, and valleys. Each 3-hour dinner excursion includes elegant 5-course cuisine served by candlelight on fine china and linen. A variety of entertainment is featured throughout the year, such as musical reviews, murder mysteries, and piano playing.

Displays/Exhibits: Depot designated Waverly Visitor and Information Center. Brochure displays for Iowa attractions; decorative railroad paraphernalia.

Schedule: Year-round, 11:30 a.m. & 7:00 p.m.

Fare: $42.50 per person, plus state tax. Group rates available; call for information.

Locomotives: Nos. 407 & 416, F7 diesel-electrics.

Passenger Cars: Two 1950s Pullman passenger cars converted to 1950s-style dining cars; 1950s Pullman passenger car converted to full-service kitchen.

Special Events: Murder mysteries. Musical reviews. Events for children. Please call or write for more information.

Location: One mile east of Highway 218 and Highway 3 intersection, on Bremer Avenue (Main Street) and 4th Street.

♿ (with prior arrangements) P

✳ 🚶 Chicago

Contact: Elloha Quigley
Sales Director

Mailing Address:
311 East Bremer Avenue
Waverly, IA 50677
Telephone: (800) 525-4773
(319) 352-5467

ABILENE & SMOKY VALLEY RAILROAD
Diesel, scheduled
Standard gauge

DALE OLIVER

Ride/Operation: A 10-mile, 1-1/2 hour round trip over former Chicago, Rock Island & Pacific track. Passengers can ride the train from Abilene, the premier "Cow Town," where longhorns first boarded Kansas Pacific cattle cars. The A&SV is located next to the Eisenhower Presidential Library, Museum, and Home and is adjacent to the Dickinson County Heritage Center, which includes the Museum of Independent Telephony, the operating 1900 C. W. Parker steam carousel, the Greyhound Hall of Fame, plus shops, art galleries, mansions, restaurants, bed & breakfasts, and more..

Train: No. 4, Alco S-1, former Hutchinson & Northern; No. 2002, 1903 wooden coach/diner, former Missouri-Kansas-Texas; No. 381, 1942 Whitcomb 45-ton side-rod, former Ideal Cement; No. 6004, arch-windowed combine, former Rock Island; No. 466, caboose, former Union Pacific.

Schedule: Weekends, May and October; daily, June-August. Dinner train, weekends. Charter trips available. Please call or write for more information.

Fare/Admission: Adults $7.50, children $5.50.

Locomotives: No. 3415, 1921 Baldwin 4-6-2, former Atchison, Topeka & Santa Fe; No. 93, 1940 G.E. 44-tonner, former Arkansas Valley Railroad.

Rolling Stock/Equipment: No. 3883 caboose, former Union Pacific; No. 1000 unique Kansas Grain Inspection Car; No. 89427 covered hopper shop converted by Rock Island.

Special Events: Chisholm Trail and Dickinson County Heritage Day, October 5.

Location: I-70 to Abilene exit, South on K-15 to 417 South Buckeye Street.

  P 🚌 ☕ 🍴 ▶ ◀ M

TRAIN

Contact: F. W. Schmidt
Vice President

Mailing Address:
P.O. Box 744
Abilene, KS 67410
Telephone: (913) 263-1077

Kansas, Baldwin City
D-R

MIDLAND RAILWAY
Diesel, scheduled
Standard gauge

E. N. GRIFFIN

Ride/Operation: This line was constructed in 1867 as the Leavenworth, Lawrence & Galveston, the first railroad south of the Kansas River. The Midland Railway, which began service in 1987 as Kansas's first excursion railway, is an intrastate common-carrier railroad. The 7-mile round trip to "Nowhere" passes through scenic eastern Kansas rolling farmland and woods and crosses a 250-foot wooden trestle.

Displays/Exhibits: Railroad equipment, photos, and memorabilia, including photographs of two U.S. presidents arriving in Baldwin.

Schedule: Weekends, May 17-October 26, 11:30 a.m., 1:30 & 3:00 p.m. (subject to change).

Fare: Adults $5.50, children (4-12) $2.50, children under 4 ride free. All-day fare, $8.00 (4 and older). Discounts for groups of 25 or more.

Locomotives: No. 524, 1946 EMD NW2, former Chicago, Burlington & Quincy; No. 142, 1950/59 Alco/EMD RS-3, former Missouri-Kansas-Texas; No. 652, 1952 EMD E8, former Chicago, Rock Island & Pacific; No. 460, 1942 44-ton General Electric, former Atchison, Topeka & Santa Fe; No. 8255, Alco RS-3, former New York Central; No. 28, 1944, 45-ton General Electric, former U.S. Army.

Passenger Cars: Heavyweight coach No. 3106 & commuter coach No. 2507, former CRI&P; combine No. 441, former Chicago, St. Paul, Minneapolis & Omaha; steel caboose No. 32, former Northern Pacific; transfer caboose No. 55, former MKT.

Rolling Stock/Equipment: GE 20-ton boxcab diesel-electric; 2-8-2T No. 10, former Coos Bay; RPO No. 30, former Kansas City Railway; wood caboose, former CRI&P; others.

Special Events: Hobo Days, August 16-17. Maple Leaf Festival, October 18-19. Halloween Train, October 24, 25, 26. Railfans Weekend, TBA.

Note: A major rehabilitation project is scheduled for 1997, extending the ride from to Norwood via "Nowhere." Train schedules and fares are subject to change. SASE after May 15 for current information.

Location: About 30 miles southwest of Kansas City on U.S. 56 at the 1906 former AT&SF depot, 1515 High Street, 7 blocks west of downtown.

Radio Frequency: 161.055

Contact: Allen D. Maty
Manager of Passenger Traffic

Mailing Address:
P.O. Box 412
Baldwin City, KS 66006
Telephone:
Depot: (913) 594-6982
Kansas City area: (913) 371-3410

THE GREAT PLAINS TRANSPORTATION
MUSEUM, INC.

Railway museum

L. L. CLERICO

Operation: The museum was established in 1985 with the help of the local National Railway Historical Society chapter to preserve and display transportation history as it relates to Kansas. The museum is one of the sponsors of the annual Air Capital Train Show.

Displays/Exhibits: Recently repainted, former ATSF 3768 is the highlight of our outdoor display. The indoor display is housed in a former railroad hotel that is currently being remodeled.

Schedule: Saturdays, year-round, 9:00 a.m.-3:00 p.m., except Christmas and New Year's Day; Sundays, April-October, 1:00-4:00 p.m.

Admission: Adults $2.50, senior citizens $2.00, children (5-12) $1.50. Group rates available.

Locomotives: 4-8-4 No. 3768, former Atchison, Topeka & Santa Fe; electric No. 603, former Kansas Gas & Electric; NW2 diesel-electric No. 421, former Burlington Northern; Whitcomb 30-ton No. 3819, former Mobil Oil.

Passenger Cars: Heavyweight baggage car, former AT&SF.

Rolling Stock/Equipment: Combine No. 2312, former AT&SF; wood caboose No. 876, former Frisco; bay-window caboose No. 17120, former Rock Island; steel caboose No. 13495, former Missouri Pacific; steel caboose No. 13519, former Chicago, Burlington & Quincy; carbody No. 12, former AVI; S-2 Fairmont motor car; M-9 Fairmont motor car.

Bus: 1954 Flexible Twin Coach Model FT-33P, 40 seats, operated occasionally, former Wichita Transportation Corp.

Location: 700 E. Douglas, Upper Level, Union Station Complex.

Contact: Ted Grosvenor
Director

Mailing Address:
P.O. Box 2017-C
Wichita, KS 67201-5017
Telephone: (316) 263-0944

RAILWAY EXPOSITION COMPANY

Ride/Operation: The Railway Exposition Company, a nonprofit organization founded in 1975, is dedicated to the preservation, restoration, and operation of historic rail equipment. Railway Expo sponsors and/or provides equipment for special charter and excursion trips operated in the Ohio-Kentucky-Indiana region.

Displays/Exhibits: Six locomotives and seventy cars from various railroads and time periods. Interiors included on the guided tour are a Seaboard Air Line locomotive training car; the cab of an SW1 locomotive and a Railway Post Office from the Pennsylvania Railroad; a 1938 streamlined Pullman; a 1923 heavyweight Pullman; a WWII Pullman troop sleeper; a 1906 open-platform office car; the streamlined Rock Island "El Comedor" dining car; and displays of artifacts and memorabilia. A half-hour tour takes visitors around and through ten cars and two locomotives.

Schedule: Weekends, May 1-October 31, 1:00-4:30 p.m. Tour lasts about 30 minutes. Closed holidays.

Admission: Adults $4.00, children $2.00.

Locomotives: Baldwin VO-1000 diesel, former Patapsco & Back River Railroad; an E8A passenger diesel and an SW1 diesel switcher, both former Pennsylvania Railroad; a 15-ton Brookville industrial locomotive; Alco S-4 diesel, former Grand Trunk Western railroad; a Plymouth industrial locomotive.

Location: South of Cincinnati. Take I-75 south to exit 189 and travel east on route 1072 to Kentucky route 17. Travel 2 miles north (left) on route 17; turn right onto Latonia Avenue; at the first stop sign, turn left onto West Southern Avenue and travel to the end of the street.

Contact: Tim Hyde
Vice President, Museum Operations

Mailing Address:
P.O. Box 15065
Covington, KY 41015-0065
Telephone: (606) 491-RAIL

HARDIN SOUTHERN RAILROAD

Ride/Operation: This line is a working common-carrier railroad offering seasonal *Nostalgia Train* passenger service for a 2-hour, 18-mile journey to the past. Built in 1890, the railroad was once a portion of the Nashville, Chattanooga & St. Louis Railway's Paducah main line through the Jackson Purchase in western Kentucky. The railroad is a designated Kentucky State Landmark. Today's trip features the rural farms and lush forests of the Clarks River Valley.

Train: Historic first-generation diesel; open-window and air-conditioned coaches.

Schedule: Weekends, May 25-October 31, midday & late afternoon.

Fare: Adults $9.75, children (3-12) $6.00. Tour, group, and charter rates available.

Locomotives: No. 863, 1940 Electro-Motive Corporation SW1, former Milwaukee Road; one of the oldest examples of this model still in common-carrier service.

Passenger Cars: Former main-line transcontinental equipment.

Special Events: Easter. Mother's Day. Halloween. Christmas.

Location: In western Kentucky, southeast of Paducah via I-24 and state route 641; six miles from the Tennessee Valley Authority's Land Between the Lakes national recreation area. Hardin at the junction of state routes 641 and 80. The depot is in the center of town.

Fulton, Kentucky

Contact: Karl R. Koenig
Vice-President & General Manager

Mailing Address:
P.O. Box 20
Hardin, KY 42048
Telephone: (502) 437-4555

ELMER KAPPELL

Ride/Operation: Steam alternates weekends with diesel on a 20-mile, 1 1/2-hour round trip through scenic Rolling Fork River Valley, from nostalgic New Haven to Boston, Kentucky, over former Louisville & Nashville trackage initially constructed in 1857. Official Railway Museum of the Commonwealth of Kentucky, near Lincoln's birthplace and boyhood home in historic Nelson County.

Displays/Exhibits: Our new brick depot is a replica of the original New Haven depot, complete with a Station Masters Office from the 1930s. More than 5,000 square feet of artifacts and memorabilia depicting Kentucky railroad history. Special programs for students. More than 60 pieces of equipment displayed, stored, or under restoration.

Schedule: Museum: Daily, with special holiday hours (call for schedule). Train: Weekends, April, May & September-November; Tuesday-Sunday, June-August. Groups and tours by appointment. Call for complete schedule.

Fare/Admission: Please call or write for information.

Locomotives: No. 152, 1905 Rogers 4-6-2 No. 152, EMD E3 No. 770 (first diesel for the *Pan-American*), and 1925 Alco 0-8-0 No. 2152, all former L&N; No. 32, 1948 EMD BL2, former Monon; CF7 No. 2546, former Santa Fe; 1952 Fairbanks-Morse, former USA No. 1846; No. 11, 1923 Vulcan 0-4-0T, former Louisville Cement; No. 2716, 1943 Alco 2-8-4, former C&O (stored off-site).

Passenger Cars: Former L&N and other open and closed window cars; diner "Kentucky Colonel," former Southern Pacific; Pullman solarium-lounge "Mt. Broderick"; 1910 Jackson & Sharp, "Itsuitsme," former Bangor & Aroostook No. 100.

Special Events: Kentucky Homecoming Festival, May 31-June 7. Murder Mystery Weekend, fall. Rolling Fork Iron Horse Festival, September 14. Kentucky Bourbon Festival, September 20-22. Halloween Trains. Christmas Trains. Civil War Train Robberies, to be announced. Please call or write for specific information.

Location: Less than one hour south of Louisville on U.S. 31E; 30 minutes from I-65. Take exit 112 off I-65 to Bardstown, then U.S. 31E south.

Radio Frequency: 160.545

Contact: Karl Lusk, Jr.

Mailing Address:
P.O. Box 240
New Haven, KY 40051-0240
Telephone: (502) 549-5470
(800) 272-0152

KENTUCKY CENTRAL RAILWAY
Steam, scheduled
Standard gauge

RUTH ANN COMBS

Ride/Operation: The Kentucky Central Railway is operated by the Kentucky Central Chapter of the National Railway Historical Society. Trips typically originate in Paris and run to Carlisle, Ewing, or Maysville. The 50-mile "Bluegrass Route," now operated by the Transkentucky Transportation Railroad, was part of the original Kentucky Central Railway, which later became part of the Louisville & Nashville Railroad. It passes through some of Kentucky's most beautiful horse farms and through two tunnels.

Schedule: Train: To be announced; please call for information. Museum: Most Sunday afternoons and by appointment.

Fare: Please call for information.

Locomotives: 1925 Baldwin 2-6-2, former Reader No. 11; No. 9, VO, 1000 Baldwin diesel, former LaSalle & Bureau County Railroad, former TransKentucky Transportation Railroad; 1951 SW8, former U.S. Army.

Passenger Cars: Three coaches, former Erie Lackawanna; KCR No. 1, former Southern Railway concession/observation car.

Rolling Stock/Equipment: Bay-window caboose No. 225, former Southern Railway; caboose No. 904055, former Baltimore & Ohio.

Special Events: To be announced.

Location: U.S. 460 East (North Middletown Road).

Cincinnati, OH and Maysville, KY

Contact: Shirley Ross
Public Relations

Mailing Address:
1749 Bahama Road
Lexington, KY 40509
Telephone: (606) 293-0807

BIG SOUTH FORK SCENIC RAILWAY

Ride/Operation: Passengers enjoy a narrated trip reminiscent of rail travel in the early 1900s as the Big South Fork Scenic takes them through the gorge area near Roaring Paunch Creek. The 3-hour trip features a 1½-hour stop at the restored mining community of Blue Heron, where oral interpretations are offered.

Displays/Exhibits: Interpretive exhibits at the Blue Heron Mining Community tell the stories of miners and their families living and working in the mining camp.

Schedule: April, May & September; Wednesday-Sunday, 10:00 a.m.; weekends, 10:00 a.m. & 2:00 p.m. June-August & October; Monday-Friday, 10:00 a.m.; weekends, 10:00 a.m. & 2:00 p.m. November 1, 10:00 a.m; November 2 (last day of season), 10:00 a.m. & 2:00 p.m.

Fare: Adults $10.00, senior citizens $9.50, children (4-12) $5.00, children under 3 ride free.

Locomotives: 1942 Alco.

Passenger Cars: Covered flatcars.

Contact: Della Jones

Mailing Address:
P.O. Box 368
Stearns, KY 42647
Telephone: (800) 462-5664

136

BLUEGRASS RAILROAD MUSEUM

Ride/Operation: This museum, founded in 1976, offers a 1 1/2-hour, 11 1/2-mile round trip through Kentucky's famed horse country, including a stop to view the Kentucky River Palisades and the 104-year-old Louisville Southern Railroad "Young's High Bridge," 281 feet high and 1,659 feet long.

Displays/Exhibits: Limestone sills from the Lexington & Ohio Railroad, built 1831-35; air-conditioned display car with railroad artifacts; diner "Duncan Tavern," baggage express car and caboose, all former Louisville & Nashville; baggage car, former Southern Railway.

Train: 1931 Pullman Standard commuter coaches, former New Jersey Central.

Schedule: Weekends, early May-late October; Saturdays, 10:30 a.m., 1:30 & 3:30 p.m.; Sundays, 1:30 & 3:30 p.m.

Fare: Adults $7.00, senior citizens (62+) $6.00, children (2-12) $4.00; children under 2 not occupying a seat ride free. Additional fare possible for some special events.

Locomotives: Nos. 2043 & 2086, 1953 Alco MRS-1s, and No. 1849, Fairbanks-Morse H12-44, all former U.S. Army.

Special Events: Halloween Ghost Train. Santa Express. Train robberies. Hobo Days. Clown Days. Please send SASE for complete listing.

Location: Woodford County Park, U.S. 62 (Tyrone Pike).

Radio Frequency: 160.275

Contact: Don Scalf

Mailing Address:
P.O. Box 27
Versailles, KY 40383
Telephone: (606) 873-2476

NOSTALGIA STATION
TOY AND TRAIN MUSEUM
Railroad display, museum, model railroad display

NOSTALGIA STATION TOY AND TRAIN MUSEUM

Displays/Exhibits: Nostalgia Station feature antique toys and trains from 1900 to the present, housed in a vintage Louisville & Nashville railroad depot. One hundred linear feet of train and toy displays are on exhibit, featuring Lionel, American Flyer, Ives, Marx and other makes. In the toy gallery vintage toys and dolls are on display, including tin, cast iron, wood, plastic and glass playthings from 1900 to the present. See a 1/4 scale live steam locomotive, built in 1904 by the State College of Kentucky-College of Electrical and Mechanical Engineers. Also featured in the exhibits are railroadiana and memorabilia of local interest.

Schedule: Wednesday through Saturday, 10:00 a.m.-5:00 p.m. Sunday, 1:00-5:00 p.m.

Admission: Adults $3.00, seniors $2.50, children $1.50, under age 5 free with adult. AAA member discount available.

Location: Versailles is located 10 miles south of I-64 (Midway exit) or 16 miles west of I-75 (exit 110 Newton Pike, Lexington). From US 60 bypass (Versailles) take Douglas Avenue west ¼ mile. Museum is on right at Depot Street intersection.

Contact: Winfrey or Wanda Adkins
Owners

Mailing Address:
279 Depot Street
Versailles, KY 40383
Telephone: (606) 873-2497

DEQUINCY RAILROAD MUEUM

Ride/Operation: Nestled among tall pines at the beginning of Louisiana's foothills in north Calcasieu County, the city of DeQuincy was at the intersection of two major railroads in 1895. Its turn-of-the-century beginnings have been preserved, including two major historical landmarks—the All Saints Episcopal Church and the Kansas City Southern Railroad Depot. Both structures are on the National Register of Historic Places, and the depot now houses the railroad museum.

Displays/Exhibits: 1913 steam locomotive; vintage caboose; passenger coach; a host of railroad artifacts.

Schedule: Monday-Friday, 9:00 a.m.-4:00 p.m.; weekends, 1:00-4:00 p.m.

Admission: No charge; donations welcomed.

Special Events: State-approved Railroad Days Festival, second weekend in April.

Location: At the intersection of state routes 12 and 27; 20 miles north of Lake Charles, Louisiana, 47 miles east of Beaumont, Texas, and 130 miles west of Baton Rouge, Louisiana.

Lake Charles

Contact: Mrs. Fred B. Fluitt, Jr.
Treasurer

Mailing Address:
P.O. Box 997
DeQuincy, LA 70633
Telephone: (318) 786-2823
(318) 786-7113

Maine, Alna
(Sheepscot Station)
M-R

BRUCE N. WILSON

WISCASSET, WATERVILLE &
FARMINGTON RAILWAY MUSEUM
Gas mechanical
24" gauge

Ride/Operation: Ride on a restored flatcar hauled by Brookville gas-mechanical 1 1/2 ton engine. Former SR & RL Model T inspection car operates on special occasions; write for schedule.

Displays/Exhibits: Portland Co. steam locomotive built in 1891 and last used by the WW & F Railway, boxcar 309, original section house, replica Sheepscot Station, Weeks Mills freight shed.

Schedule: Saturdays 9:00 a.m.-5:00 p.m.; Sundays (Memorial Day to Labor Day) 12 noon -5:00 p.m.

Fare/Admission: Donations accepted.

Special Events: Annual picnic in August, other events as scheduled in Museum newsletter. Write for further information.

Notes: All volunteer effort to lay rail on original right of way and build rail yard into replica three stall Wiscasset Car Shop. Visitors are welcomed to participate with our volunteers and to walk the grade.

Location: 4.7 miles north of Wiscasset on the Crossroad. Take Rt. 218 north off Rt. 1 opposite the Wiscasset Post Office, follow Rt. 218, left on the Crossroad.

Contact: Bruce N. Wilson
Secretary

Mailing Address:
P.O. Box 12
Hanover, MA 02339-0012
Telephone: (207) 774-4971

GEORGE A. FORERO, JR

Ride/Operation: A 1.5-mile, 15-minute trip through woods and a covered bridge and past many railroad structures. The railroad is reminiscent of the many 2-foot-gauge lines that formerly ran in Maine.

Displays/Exhibits: The 8-acre village complex includes two restored railroad stations, an 1847 town hall, an exceptional display of more than 55 antique vehicles, a schoolhouse, and 26 other buildings.

Train: Closed coach; open coach; caboose.

Schedule: Daily, June 10-October 13, 9:30 a.m.-5:00 p.m., every half hour. Also May 25-27.

Fare: Adults $6.00, children (2-12) $3.00, children under 2 ride free. Yearly Membership: $30 family, $20 individual. Group rates available.

Locomotives: No.12313, 1913 Henschel 0-4-0T, former city of Hamburg; No. 22486, 1934 Henschel 0-4-0T; No. 24022, 1938 Henschel 0-4-0T; No. 24023, 1938 Henschel 0-4-0T; No. 14283, Baldwin 0-4-0ST; No. 14522, Baldwin 0-4-0ST; Plymouth 0-4-0; Ford Model T inspection car.

Rolling Stock/Equipment: Two-foot-gauge equipment includes 1908 Sandy River & Rangeley Lakes combination car No. 11 (former Franklin & Megantic No. 1); SR&RL boxcar No. 147; Wiscasset & Quebec boxcar No. 312; Wiscasset, Waterville & Farmington handcar; dump cars; and flatcars. Standard-gauge equipment includes cabooses Nos. 563 & 653, both former Maine Central; a circa 1920 Fairmont railcar; a "40 & 8" car, built in 1885; and a velocipede.

Special Events: Scottish Festival, Father's Day Special. Antique Engine Meet. Annual Fund Raising Auction, Annual Antique Auto Days, Firefighters' Benefit Circus, Children's Day, Firefighters' Day, Maine Narrow-Gauge Railroad Day, Fall Foliage Festival and Ghost Train.

Location: On state route 27, eight miles from U.S. route 1.

Contact: Robert Ryan
Director

Mailing Address:
P.O. Box 123
Boothbay, ME 04537
Telephone: (207) 633-4727

141

FORT FAIRFIELD RAILROAD MUSEUM
Motor car, railroad display, museum, irregular
Standard gauge

BRUCE NETT

Ride/Operation: 8 mile round trip (25 min.) motor car rides on former Bangor & Aroostook tracks.

Displays/Exhibits: Former CP station a CP caboose with numerous artifacts. Mockup of CP diesel locomotive cab. 1/2 mile away at former BAR station we have a former CP sleeping car built in 1921 and converted to an outfit car in 1965. We restored it to a dining car open only for special occasions. Also a CP diesel, a boxcar and a BAR reefer.

Schedule: Usually on weekend but on request anytime.

Fare/Admission: Free. Motor car rides are $3.00

Locomotives: CP RS-23 diesel (shell).

Rolling Stock/Equipment: CN caboose, BAR reefer, CAR/CP boxcar (the only one ever run).

Special Events: Maine Potato Blossom Festival 3rd weekend in July.

Location: Along Main Street in town.

Contact: Bruce Nett

Mailing Address:
Box 269
Fort Fairfield, ME 04742
Telephone: (207) 473-4045

CHARLES WOOLNOUGH

Ride/Operation: A 3 3/4-mile round trip takes passengers over the former Atlantic Shore Line interurban right-of-way, where they can experience the trolley era through the "National Collection" spanning a century of mass-transit vehicles. Visitors can also learn to operate a trolley in the museum's "Be a Motorman" program; please call or write for details.

Displays/Exhibits: Visitors can tour the huge exhibit barn, filled with restored trolleys from Boston to Budapest, New York to Nagasaki, and Sydney to San Francisco. A fascinating part of the visit is the world-famous Town House Restoration Shop, where "junk" is turned into gems. Also, visitors can see the trolley station that traveled by sea—the Victorian copper-clad Northampton Station from Boston's elevated railway—and many other artifacts of our history.

Schedule: Times indicated are: opening time/time of last ride. Museum store open one hour past last departure. May 1-24: weekdays, 12:00/1:30 p.m.; weekends, 11:00 a.m./3:30 p.m. May 25-27 (Memorial Day Weekend): daily 11:00 a.m./4:30 p.m. May 28-June 30: weekdays, 11:00 a.m./3:30 p.m.; weekends, 11:00 a.m./4:30 p.m. July 1-September 2: daily, 10:00 a.m./5:30 p.m.July 24-August 28 (Wed. only)-Ice Cream Night at 7:30 p.m. September 3-October 14: weekdays, 10:00 a.m./3:30 p.m.; weekends, 10:00 a.m./4:30 p.m. October 15-November 15 (weather permitting): weekdays, by chance or appointment; weekends, 11:00 a.m./3:30 p.m. Other times by appointment.

Admission: Adults $7.00, senior citizens $5.00, children (6-16) $4.00, family pass $25.00. Group rates: Adult $4.50, children (6-16) $3.00. Special admission prices, special events, call for specific information.

Locomotives/Trolleys: More than 200 pieces from the United States, Canada, Australia, Japan, Germany, Hungary, Italy, England, and New Zealand: horse cars, city cars, buses, interurbans, rapid-transit cars, work equipment, trackless trolleys, locomotives, and freight cars.

Special Events: June, Maine Museum Day. July, USA Trolley Parade, Trolley Birthday Party, Moxie Day,

Maine Antique Power Days. August, Vidbels Olde Tyme Circus. September, Fall Foliage Tours. October, Members Day (Columbus Day weekend), Ghost Trolley. December, Christmas Prelude. Promotional days TBA. Call for dates and details.

Location: 195 Log Cabin Road; 1.5 miles off U.S. Route 1, 3 miles north of Kennebunkport, and 20 miles south of Portland.; Short distance from exits 3 and 4 of the Maine Turnpike.

Contact: Donald Curry, Director

Mailing Address: P.O. Box A
Kennebunkport, ME 04046-1690
Recorded Info: (207) 967-2800
Reservations: (207) 967-2712
Internet: http://www.biddeford.com/trolley

143

SANDY RIVER RAIL ROAD MUSEUM DIVISION
PHILLIPS HISTORICAL SOCIETY
Railway museum, gas replica of steam
24" gauge

Ride/Operation: A 6/10 mile ride on original road bed. Passengers ride in a 111 year old Laconia coach that is a sister to the coach being restored in our shops.

Displays/Exhibits: 30 sq. foot museum full of original Sandy River memorabilia.

Schedule: 1st and 3rd Sundays, June-September & 3rd week of August.

Fare/Admission: Train Ride $3.00. Museum and other displays are donation only.

Locomotives: 1 Brookville, 1 Plymouth, 1 gas powered replica of SR & RL No. 4, 1 rail bus.

Rolling Stock/Equipment: 5 box cars, 2 coaches, 2 cabooses, 1 tool car and 1 flanger.

Special Events: Old Home Days, three weeks in August. Fall Foliage, last weekend in August, first weekend in September.

Notes: We can always use volunteers for painting.

Location: 18 miles north of Farmington on Rt. 4.

Contact: Kenneth Teele
Director

Mailing Address:
P.O. Box B
Phillips, ME 04966
Telephone: (207) 639-3352
Fax: (207) 639-2553

MAINE NARROW GAUGE RAILROAD
COMPANY AND MUSEUM
Steam, diesel, scheduled
24" gauge

J.E. LANCASTER

Ride/Operation: A two-foot-gauge train takes passengers on a 2-mile round trip along Casco Bay.

Displays/Exhibits: Sandy River & Rangley Lakes Railroad parlor car No. 9, 100 year old Bridgton & Harrison, Sandy River & Rangley Lakes and Wiscasset & Quebec coaches; other rolling stock; antique freight-hauling trucks; railroad artifacts and photos.

Train: Steam- or diesel-powered passenger trains.

Schedule: Weekends February 15-May 16, October 14-December 12. Daily May 17-October 13, December 13-January 1. Also during Maine and New Hampshire school vacation weeks.

Fare/Admission: Train: Adults $4.00, children $3.00. Museum: free. Fares subject to change.

Locomotives: No. 3, 1913 Vulcan 0-4-4T; No. 4, 1918 Vulcan 0-4-4T, former Monson; No. 8, 1924 Baldwin 2-4-4T, former B&SR; No. 1, 1949 General Electric B-B diesel.

Passenger Cars: Circa 1890 coaches Nos. 4, 19 & 20 and Combine No. 14, former SR&RL; coaches Nos. 15, 16 & 18, former B&SR; replica coaches, excursion cars, former Edaville.

Rolling Stock/Equipment: Railbus No. 4, Model T track car and cabooses Nos. 551, 553 & 557, former SR&RL; tank cars Nos. 21 & 22, flanger No. 40; snow plow No. 2, box cars, former B&SR.

Special Events: Railfair; All Aboard Auction Day; Send SASE for list of dates and events.

Location: 58 Fore Street (off Franklin Arterial-US Rt. 1A).

Contact: J. Emmons Lancaster
Superintendent

Mailing Address:
58 Fore Street
Portland, ME 04101
Telephone: (207) 828-0814

BELFAST AND MOOSEHEAD LAKE RAILROAD
Steam
Standard gauge

BELFAST & MOOSEHEAD LAKE RAILROAD

Ride/Operation: 1-1/2 hour narrated ride with train robbery, dining car, beer and wine offered.

Displays/Exhibits: Armstrong turntable, original station.

Train: The only Swedish steam train in the U.S.

Schedule: Mid-May through late October. Call for dates and times.

Fare/Admission: Adult $14.00, children (16 and under) $7.00, under 3 free.

Locomotives: 1913 Swedish S.L., 4-6-0.

Rolling Stock/Equipment: Sleeper car, dining car, first class, second class and open air cars.

Special Events: Mother's Day. Father's Day. Lobster Trains.

Notes: Belafast and Moosehead Lake Railroad offers diesel diesel-powered train rides in Belfast, Maine.

Location: 1 Depot Square, Unity.

Contact: Elizabeth Roy
Director of Marketing

Mailing Address:
P.O. Box 555
Unity, ME 04988
Telephone: (800) 392-5500
Fax: (207) 948-5903

THE B&O RAILROAD MUSEUM
Railway museum
Steam scheduled, irregular
Standard gauge

THE B&O RAILROAD MUSEUM

Ride/Operation: Excursion trains depart Mt. Clare Station each Saturday and Sunday for a 3-mile round trip over the first mainline in America.

Displays/Exhibits: The B&O Railroad Museum's collection of locomotives, cars, artifacts, and archives originated as an exhibit at the 1893 Columbian Exposition in Chicago. With additional pieces, the collection was opened to the public in 1953 at Mt. Clare, the site from which the nation's first mainline railroad began building west in 1828. The museum underwent a substantial renovation in the 1970s and now operates as a tax-exempt educational foundation. A variety of equipment and interpretive exhibits, model railroads, toy-train exhibits, railroad artifacts are displayed, including 48 locomotives, 146 cars and 20 miscellaneous vehicles.
Buildings include the 1851 Mt. Clare Station, the 1884 Annex Building, the 1884 covered passenger-car roundhouse, and a large 1870 car shop currently used for equipment storage.

Schedule: Daily, 10:00 a.m.-5:00 p.m. Open everyday except Thanksgiving and Christmas.

Fare/Admission: Museum: adults $6.00, senior citizens $5.00, students (5-12) $3.00, children 4 and under free. Train: additional $2.00 (children under 4 ride free). Group rates available; call 752-2463.

Locomotives: Two replicas of early nineteenth-century locomotives; 9 original nineteenth-century locomotives; 12 twentieth-century steam locomotives; 14 diesel-electric locomotives; 3 electric locomotives; 2 electric m-u cars; RDC; locomotive crane; diesel tractor switcher; Vanderbilt tender.

Passenger Cars: The oldest passenger car in North America; 5 nineteenth-century cars; 15 additional passenger cars representing all significant twentieth-century types.

Rolling Stock/Equipment: Cabooses; wide variety of historic freight cars; work equipment; giant Pennsylvania Railroad 200-ton steam wreck crane; special cars such as a molten steel car and dynamometer car.

Special Events: All Aboard Days, April. New Exhibit: "When the Whistle Broke into a Scream: Trainwrecks 2nd-The Evolution of Railroad Safety 1830-1910," July-December. Wine Tasting, November. Holiday Happenings, December.

Location: Pratt and Poppleton Streets, 10 blocks west of the Inner Harbor.

Baltimore

Contact: Dorothy Fuchs
Marketing Director

Mailing Address:
901 West Pratt Street
Baltimore, MD 21223-2699
Telephone: (410) 752-2490
Fax: (410) 752-2499

BALTIMORE STREETCAR MUSEUM
Electric, scheduled
5' 4 1/2" gauge

ANDREW S. BLUMBERG

Ride/Operation: A streetcar leaves the visitors' center every fifteen minutes for a 1 1/4-mile round trip alongside Falls Road.

Displays/Exhibits: In a modern carhouse are 13 cars (11 electric and 2 horse-drawn) tracing street-rail transit in the city of Baltimore from 1859 to 1963; tours are available. The visitors' center contains displays and a video presentation.

Schedule: Weekends, June 1-October 31; Sundays, November 1-May 31; 12:00-5:00 p.m. Groups at these and other times by prior arrangement.

Admission: Adults $4.00, senior citizens (65+) and children (4-11) $2.00, maximum family charge $12.00.

Trolleys: No. 554, 1896 single-truck summer car, No. 1050, 1898 single-truck closed car & No. 264, 1900 convertible car, all Brownell Car Co.; No. 1164, 1902 double-truck summer car, No. 3828, 1902 double-truck closed car & No. 6119, 1930 Peter Witt car, all J.G. Brill Co.; No. 7407, 1944 Pullman-Standard PCC car.

Special Events: Mother's Day. Father's Day. Grandparents' Day. Museum Birthday Celebration, usually first Sunday in July. Antique Auto Meets, three times a year. Dixieland Concert, July or August. Christmas, Visits from Santa. Please call or write for a complete listing.

Location: Former Maryland & Pennsylvania Railroad terminal at 1901 Falls Road, three blocks from Amtrak station (Penn Station).

   P *   ☂ ▶ ◀

M ar n   Baltimore

Contact: Andrew S. Blumberg
Director of Public Affairs

Mailing Address:
P.O. Box 4881
Baltimore, MD 21211
Telephone: (410) 547-0264

CHESAPEAKE BEACH RAILWAY MUSEUM
Railway museum
Standard gauge

CHESAPEAKE BEACH RAILWAY MUSEUM

Displays/Exhibits: This museum preserves and interprets the history of the Chesapeake Beach Railway. The CBR, which was built by a group of Colorado financiers and railroad builders that included Otto Mears and David Moffat, brought people from Washington, D.C., to the resorts of Chesapeake Beach and North Beach from 1900 until 1935. Housed in an 1898 CBR station, the museum contains photographs and artifacts from the days of the railroad and the resort, including photos of the steamships that brought visitors by water and the early amusements on the boardwalk.

Schedule: Daily, May 1-September 30, 1:00-4:00 p.m. Weekends, April & October, 1:00-4:00 p.m. By appointment at all other times.

Admission: No charge.

Passenger Cars: The Chesapeake Beach Railway car "Dolores," the last known surviving piece of CBR rolling stock, is under restoration by museum staff and volunteers.

Special Events: Hike on abandoned CBR right-of-way, first Saturday in April (raindate, second Saturday). Antique Car Show & Founders Day third Sunday of May. Concerts, second Thursday evening of June, July & August; please call or write for details. Children's Railroad History Program, Thursdays, 10:00 a.m., mid-June to mid-August. Holiday Open House, first Sunday of December.

Location: Chesapeake Beach (Calvert County).

Contact: Harriet M. Stout
Curator
or Bernard Loveless

Mailing Address:
P.O. Box 783
Chesapeake Beach, MD 20732
Telephone: (301) 257-3892

WESTERN MARYLAND
SCENIC RAILROAD
Steam, diesel, scheduled
Standard gauge

TIM WILSON

Ride/Operation: A 32-mile, 3-hour round trip over tracks of the former Western Maryland Railway and Cumberland & Pennsylvania Railroad. The excursion includes a 1 1/2-hour layover at Frostburg, the site of The Old Depot restaurant, the Depot Center Shops, Thrasher Carriage Museum, and an active turntable. The route passes through the Cumberland Narrows, traverses the famous Helmstetter's Horseshoe Curve and the 914-foot length of Brush Mountain Tunnel-- all while climbing nearly 1,300 feet in elevation. Trains depart from downtown Cumberland's Western Maryland Station Center, which houses the Transportation and Industrial Museum, the Allegany Arts Council Gallery, the Western Maryland gift shop, the Allegany County Tourism Information Center, the Western Maryland Chapter of the National Railway Historical Society, and a National Park Service Chesapeake & Ohio Canal Visitors Center. The western terminus of the C&O Canal is adjacent to the station.

Schedule: May-September, steam locomotive, Tuesday-Sunday, 11:30 a.m.; October, Tuesday-Sunday, 11:00 a.m. & 4:00 p.m.; After October 27, 11:00 a.m. only; November 1-December 15, weekends only, 11:30 a.m.

Fare: April-September: Adults $14.75, senior citizens (60+) $13.25, children (2-12) $9.50. October-December: Adults $16.75, senior citizens (60+) $16.25, children $10.50. Children under 2 not occupying a seat ride free. Call for reservations, group rates, and charter information.

Special Events: Mother's Day (Mom rides free), May 11. Murder Mysteries, monthly. Dinner Trains, monthly. Heritage Days Train Raid. Father's Day (Dad rides free), June 15. July 4 (everyone rides at child's price). Children's Ghost Train. Santa's Express.

Location: Take exit 43-C off I-68 (downtown Cumberland); follow signs to Tourist Information.

Cumberland

Contact: Ed Kemmet, General Manager or Margy Pein, Dir. Marketing & Sales

Mailing Address:
13 Canal Street
Cumberland, MD 21502
Telephone: 1-800-TRAIN-50
Local: (301) 759-4400
Fax: (301) 759-1329
Internet: http://www.wmsr.com

THE ELLICOTT CITY B&O RAILROAD
STATION MUSEUM
Railway museum

THE ELLICOTT CITY B&O RAILROAD STATION MUSEUM

Displays/Exhibits: Built in 1831, this stone station is the oldest surviving railroad station in America and is a registered National Historic Landmark. Visitors may tour the restored building and see many railroad displays. An HO-gauge model-railroad layout of the 13 miles from Baltimore to Ellicott City is housed in the restored 1885 freight house.

Schedule: Changes seasonally. Please call or write for current information.

Admission: Adults $3.00, senior citizens $2.00, children (5-12) $1.00, children under 5 admitted free. Group rates available.

Special Events: Please call or write for schedule.

Location: At Maryland Avenue and Main Street in Ellicott City. Take exit 13 via Catonsville off the Baltimore Beltway (I-695) and travel west 4 1/2 miles.

Contact: Ed Williams
Director

Mailing Address:
2711 Maryland Avenue
Ellicott City, MD 21043
Telephone: (410) 461-1944

ELLIS DAVISON

Ride/Operation: One hour rides aboard vintage heavyweight Pullmans. Ride "Defender," a 1912 Pullman parlor/diner/lounge car or "Catoctin," an original 1923 Pullman office car with observation platform. Special two hour railfan trips are run throughout the year as well as special events.

Schedule: June through December: Weekends at designated times for regular runs. Saturday: dinner train and other railfan specials. Call for times.

Fare/Admission: Adults $10.00, children under 10 $5.00 (children limited to Catoctin only). Locomotive cab ride with engineer $15.00. Summer Rail Fan Extravaganza, $20.00.

Locomotives: Nos. 85 & 95 center cab 80-ton diesel electric Whitcombs, former U.S. Navy.

Special Events: Fall Foliage Trains, October weekends. Annual Santa Express, December 6. Candy Cane Trains, December 7, 13, 14, 20 & 21. Summer Rail Fan Extravaganza, May-September, last Saturday of month. Photo run-by opportunities. Photo contest winner receives two free dinner train tickets.

Location: Located on the Delmarva Peninsula. Excursion trains depart from Ridgely, 3-1/2 miles northeast of the junction of Maryland Routes 404 and 480.

P   🚌   🍴 nearby   👤   📷

🪑   🚂   🎅 Santa Express only   ▶ ◀

Contact: William G. Bartosh

Mailing Address:
P.O. Box 586
Ridgely, MD 21660
Telephone: (410) 482-2330
Fax: (410) 482-7075

WESTERN MARYLAND AND RAILWAY HISTORICAL SOCIETY, INC.

Displays/Exhibits: The Western Maryland Railway Historical Society was founded in 1967 to preserve the heritage of the WM, now part of CSX. It has established a museum in the former general office building of the railway at Union Bridge, next to the Maryland Midland station. On exhibit are Western Maryland artifacts and an N scale model railroad. The museum includes a library and an archives collection which are available for research by appointment.

Schedule: May-October, Sundays 1:00-4:00 p.m.
Fare/Admission: Free, donations welcomed.

Location: On Main Street (State Route 75) at railroad tracks.

P ✳ 🏛 ▶ ◀ M

Contact: Henry E. Hess
Recording Secretary

Mailing Address:
8600 Midi Avenue
Baltimore, MD 21234-4011
Telephone: (410) 668-4349

WALKERSVILLE SOUTHERN RAILROAD
Diesel & gasoline, scheduled
Standard gauge

PAUL J. BERGDOLT

Operation: Walkersville Station is a "turn of the century" small-town railroad station built by the Pennsylvania Railroad in the late 1800s. Next to the station is a small freight house built in the same period.

Train: A former Western Maryland troop sleeper has been converted into an enclosed riding coach and a former B&O flatcar has been converted into an open air excursion car. In addition, a mixed train is sometimes run with a boxcar and a caboose.

Schedule: May through September: Saturday. October: Saturday & Sunday. One hour excursions depart every 1½ hours.

Fare/Admission: Adults $6.50, children under 12 $3.50.

Special Events: Saturday evening Mystery Trains, Father's and Mother's Day Specials, and Santa Claus Trains. Call for times.

Location: Located 50 miles west of Baltimore and 50 miles northwest of Washington D. C., northeast of Frederick on MD Route 194.

Contact:
Vaughn Rockney

Mailing Address:
P.O. Box 651
Walkersville, MD 21793-0651
Telephone: (301) 898-0899
E-mail: ROCKNEY@GEIS.GEIS.COM

BOB FLACK

Ride/Operation: A 1¾-mile, 20-minute round trip in Northwest Branch Park on cars selected from the museums collection of 15 streetcars. Passengers board the trolleys at the Visitors Center Station.

Displays/Exhibits: *Washington Trolleys: Rediscovered,* a 10-minute slide show; an operating gauge O-streetcar layout; *Radio Theatre,* recalling Glen Echo Amusement Park; displays interpreting streetcar and interurban systems of the national capital region; architecture reminiscent of the turn of the century.

Schedule: Weekends, January 2-December 1, plus Memorial Day, July 4 & Labor Day, 12:00-5:00 p.m. Wednesdays, July 1-August 31, 11:00 a.m.-3:00 p.m. Also December 7-8, 14-15, 21-22, 28-29, 5:00-9:00 p.m. Selected school days; please call or write.

Fare: Adults $2.50 (5-ride $6.25), children (2-17) $2.00 (5-ride $5.00), children under 2 and those presenting valid membership cards from the Association of Railway Museums, the National Railway Historical Society, or the Railroad Enthusiasts ride free.

Trolleys: No. 678, New York City; No. 352, Johnstown; No. 120, Graz, Austria; No. 955, Dusseldorf, Germany; No. 5954, Berlin, Germany; No. 6062 with trailer No. 7802, Vienna, Austria; Nos. 766, 1053, 1101 & 1540, Washington, D.C.

Rolling Stock/Equipment: Sweepers Nos. 07 & 51 and work cars Nos. 0509 & 0522, former Washington, D.C.

Special Events: Cabin Fever Day, February 22. Snow Sweeper Day, March 22. Trolley Car Spectacular, April 20. Antique Auto Gathering, July 13. Fall Open House, October 19. Holly Trolleyfest, December.

Notes: Bus service on route 26 from Twinbrook Station is available Saturdays and Sundays from 12:00 to 5:00 p.m.

Location: On Bonifant Road between Layhill Road (Maryland route 182) and New Hampshire Avenue (Maryland route 650), north of Wheaton.

P 🚌 ✳ ⛱ ▶ ◀ M

ar ll Washington

Contact: Kenneth Rucker
Curator

Mailing Address:
P.O. Box 4007
Silver Spring, MD 20914
Telephone: (301) 384-6088

WALKER TRANSPORTATION COLLECTION
BEVERLY HISTORICAL SOCIETY
& MUSEUM

WALKER TRANSPORTATION COLLECTION-O. C. LEONARD

Railway museum

Displays/Exhibits: The Walker Transportation Collection has been preserving items of New England railroading since 1969. Thousands of photographs and color slides, as well as a complete library, motion pictures, videotapes, and recordings, are available to researchers; copies of photos can be obtained at a reasonable charge. The collection also contains material on street railways, coastal and lake shipping, aviation, industrial and firefighting equipment, and the great hotels and resorts where travelers of yesteryear spent their vacations. Rotating displays of transportation artifacts and models are featured, as are periodic exhibits of various transportation modes relating to New England.

Schedule: Wednesdays, 7:00-10:00 p.m. Other times by appointment.
Admission: Adults $2.00, children (under 16) $1.00.

Location: 117 Cabot Street.

&. (partially)   **P** 🏛 ▶ ◀ **M**

Contact: Richard W. Symmes
Curator

Mailing Address:
117 Cabot Street
Beverly, MA 01915
Telephone: (508) 922-1186

OLD COLONY & FALL RIVER RAILROAD MUSEUM

Railway museum
Standard gauge

DAVID SOUZA

Displays/Exhibits: The museum, located in railroad cars that include a renovated former Pennsylvania Railroad coach, features artifacts of the Old Colony, New Haven, and Penn Central railroads, Conrail, and other New England lines. Also on display is New Haven rail diesel car No. 42, "Firestone"; New Haven boxcar No. 33401, which houses a video theater and displays; and caboose No. 21052.

Schedule: Weekends, April 19-June 29 & September 6-December 2, Saturdays 10:00 a.m.-4:00 p.m., Sundays 12:00-4:00 p.m. Daily, June 30-September 1; Sunday-Friday, 12:00-5:00 p.m.; Saturday, 10:00 a.m.-5:00 p.m.

Admission: Adults $1.50, children (5-12) $.75, children under 5 admitted free.

Special Events: Annual Railroad Show, third weekend in January. Fall River Celebrates America, mid-August waterfront celebration with craft fair, exhibits, Tall Ships, fireworks, and more.

Notes: Battleship Cove, which houses the *U.S.S. Massachusetts* and other warships, is directly across the street from the railroad museum. Also within walking distance is Heritage State Park (with picnic area and boat rides), the Marine Museum at Fall River with a large *Titanic* display, the Fall River carousel, and the Tall Ship *H.M.S. Bounty*.

Location: The museum is located in a railroad yard at the corner of Central and Water streets, across from the entrance to Battleship Cove.

  (ramp to car but small door clearance)

  (walking distance)

Contact: Jay K. Chatterton
Curator

Mailing Address:
P.O. Box 3455
Fall River, MA 02722
Telephone: (508) 674-9340

CAPE COD RAILROAD

Ride/Operation: A two-hour scenic train ride through the heart of Cape Cod. Enjoy entertaining commentary while viewing sites such as the Cape Cod Canal, Great Salt Marsh, and cranberry bogs.

Schedule: June-October, daily except Mondays. 10:00 a.m., 12:30 & 3:00 p.m. from Hyannis. 11:10 a.m. & 1:40 p.m. from Sandwich. Call for spring and winter hours.

Fare/Admission: Adults $11.50, seniors, $10.50, children 3-12 $7.50.

Locomotives: Nos. 1100 & 1114 1946 F10s. No. 1789 1955 GP9.

Rolling Stock/Equipment: Dome car, two Budd cars, Nobska, several others.

Special Events: Evening Gourmet Dinner Train, February-December, days and hours vary.

Location: Mid Cape Highway (Route 6), exit no. 7 (Willow Street), turn south on Willow, right on Main Street for one block.

Contact: Brenda Johnson

Mailing Address:
252 Main Street
Hyannis, MA 02601
Telephone: (508) 771-3788
(508) 771-0760

BILL SEXTON

Ride/Operation: Fifteen-minute short shuttle train ride within Lenox station yard, with narrative of Berkshire railroading and Lenox station history. Locomotive cab tours for youngsters. The museum is in the restored Lenox station.

Displays/Exhibits: Restored former New York, New Haven & Hartford NE-5 caboose; Fairmont speeder and track-gang train; displays about Berkshire railroading history; railroad videos; two model railroads.

Train: Fifty-ton General Electric; one former Erie-Lackawanna coach.

Schedule: Memorial Day-October 26; every half hour,10:00 a.m.-4:00 p.m.

Fare/Admission: Train ride: adults $1.50, children $1.00. Museum admission: no charge.

Locomotives: No. 67, 1957 50-ton General Electric, former United Illuminating; No. 8619, 1953 EMD SW8, former New York Central; No. 954, Alco S-1, former Maine Central.

Special Events: Santa Runs, the three weekends before Christmas.

Location: At the foot of Housatonic Street, east off U.S. route 20; five miles north of exit 2 (Lee) of Massachusetts Turnpike.

Pittsfield

Mailing Address:
P.O. Box 2195
Lenox, MA 01240
Telephone: (413) 637-2210

LOWELL NATIONAL HISTORICAL PARK
Electric, scheduled
Standard gauge

LOWELL NATIONAL HISTORICAL PARK

Ride/Operation: Lowell National Historical Park, established in 1978 as part of the National Park Service, U.S. Department of the Interior, encompasses a canal system, restored mill buildings, and nineteenth-century commercial buildings. Two circa 1901 open-air trolleys, Nos. 1601 and 1602, and one circa 1919 closed car, No. 4131, provide transportation through this historic mill town.

Displays/Exhibits: A display in former Boston & Maine combine/tool car No. M3031, staffed by the Boston & Maine Railroad Historical Society. Former B&M 0-6-0 No. 410, a restored 1911 Manchester Locomotive Works G-11, is displayed next to the tool car.

Schedule: Changes seasonally. The trolley operates daily, March through November; the combine exhibit has infrequent hours.

Fare/Admission: No charge for these items, although a fee is charged for other tours and museums affiliated with the National Park Service.

Locomotives/Trolleys: Two circa 1901 open-air trolleys; one circa 1919 closed trolley; 1911 0-6-0, former Boston & Maine.

Rolling Stock/Equipment: Combine/tool car, built in 1907 by Pullman as a 72-passenger open-platform coach, remodeled in 1946.

Special Events: The combine is usually staffed by the B&M Railroad Historical Society during the Lowell Folk Festival (last full weekend in July). Trolleys are used for special events.

 Boston

Mailing Address:
67 Kirk Street
Lowell, MA 01852
Telephone: (508) 970-5000

Michigan, Blissfield R

ADRIAN & BLISSFIELD RAILROAD
Diesel, scheduled
Standard gauge

ADRIAN & BLISSFIELD RAIL ROAD

Ride/Operation: This working, common-carrier freight and passenger railroad offers 14-mile, 1 1/2-hour round trips from Blissfield to Lenawee Junction over a former New York Central line—the first railroad built west of the Allegheny Mountains and the oldest in the former Northwest Territory. The train travels through the village of Blissfield, crosses the River Raisin, and runs through Lenawee County farmland to Lenawee Junction. The "Old Road Dinner Train" is a 2- to 3-hour round trip featuring traditional, impeccable dining-car service including an elegant four-course dinner. Murder mystery dinner train service is also available.

Train: Open-window coaches and dining cars built in the 1930s, 1940s, and 1950s.

Schedule: Schedule varies; call for information.

Fare: Adults $8.00, senior citizens $7.00, children (3-12) $5.00, children under 3 ride free. Group rates and charters available. Additional fare for dinner train.

Locomotives: Nos. 1751 & 1752, 1957 EMD GP9s, former Grand Trunk Western/Central Vermont.

Passenger Cars: No. 5197, 1937 *Canadian Flyer* coach, former Canadian National; No. 721; No. 3370, 1949 diner, former Union Pacific.

Special Events: School field trips. Fall color tours. Ghost Train. Santa Train. Winter Snow Train. Occasional mixed-train service as freight requirements dictate throughout the year.

Notes: Cars may be chartered on scheduled runs; special trains may be chartered.

Location: U.S. 223 and Depot Street. Ten miles west of exit 5 of U.S. 23 and 20 miles northwest of Toledo.

Toledo-Ann Arbor

Contact: Dale Pape
General Manager

Mailing Address:
P.O. Box 95
Blissfield, MI 49228
Telephone: (517) 486-5979

161

JUNCTION VALLEY RAILROAD
Diesel, scheduled
14 1/8" gauge

JUNCTION VALLEY RAILROAD

Ride/Operation: The ride, more than 2 miles long, travels 22 feet down into a valley around a lake, over several bridges and trestles, through a 100-foot tunnel, playground, and a picnic area. Junction Valley Railroad is the "Largest Quarter-Size Railroad in the World." A railroad hobby shop and gift shop on premises.

Displays/Exhibits: Railroad shops; 10-stall roundhouse with turntable; seventeen railroad and six highway bridges; thirty buildings and stations; more than 865 feet of bridges and trestles; 100 foot tunnel; the only diamond-crossing trestle in the world; four miles of track; a five-track switch yard, all built to 1/4 size.

Train: Over fifty-seven freight cars all built to scale. Thirty cars are converted to haul passengers; four cabooses.

Schedule: Daily, mid May-Labor Day; Monday-Saturday, 10:00 a.m.-6:00 p.m.; Sunday, 1:00-6:00 p.m. Weekends, September-October 15, 1:00-5:00 p.m.

Fare: Adults $4.50, senior citizens $4.25, children $3.75. Group rates available. Special Events: Railroad Days: $6.25; Halloween Spook Ride, and Christmas Fantasyland Train: $5.25, no discounts-special days. Rates subject to change.

Locomotives: No. 555, MP-15; No. 1177, GP-45; No. 333, SW-1500; No. 4, Plymouth; No. 300, SW-1500 booster; No. 5000, WS-4A; No. 6000, WS-4B; No. 7000, WS-4A. All locomotives are built to 1/4 size of their models.

Special Events: Opening Day, featuring a 2,000-balloon launch. Railroad Days, June 21 & 22, July 19-20 & August 16-17. Valley of Flags, July 4. Halloween Spook Ride, October. Christmas Fantasyland Train Ride, December. Others-call for specific information.

Notes: The entire railroad, including engines, cars, bridges, trestles, tunnel, and buildings, was designed, engineered, and built by William A. Stenger.

Location: Two miles south of the Bridgeport exit off I-75; five miles west of historic Frankenmuth.

Flint

Contact: Lillian M. Stenger

Mailing Address:
7065 Dixie Highway
Bridgeport, MI 48722
Telephone: (517) 777-3480

Michigan, Clinton
R

SOUTHERN MICHIGAN RAILROAD SOCIETY
Diesel, scheduled
Standard gauge

SOUTHERN MICHIGAN RAILROAD SOCIETY

Ride/Operation: Rides are offered over two portions of the former Clinton Branch of the New York Central. Regular summer service is a 4 1/2-mile, 2-hour round trip from Clinton to Tecumseh, featuring travel across the 116-foot-long timber trestle over the River Raisin in a scenic wildlife area and across the steel bridge over Evans Creek. Fall Color Tours are 6-mile, 2-hour round trips between Tecumseh and Raisin Center, featuring an overlook of the River Raisin Valley and a spectacular crossing high above the river on a steel truss bridge.

Displays/Exhibits: An indoor museum is open during train operation.

Train: General Electric 44 ton diesel, former South Shore commuter car, gondola, cabooses.

Schedule: Summer service: June-September; lv. Clinton 11 a.m., 1 & 3 p.m.; lv. Tecumseh 12 & 2 p.m. Clinton Fall Festival: September 28-29; lv. Clinton 10 a.m., 12, 2 & 4 p.m.; lv. Tecumseh 11 a.m., 1, 3 & 5 p.m. Fall Color Tours: Weekends, October; lv. Tecumseh 11 a.m., 1:30 & 4 p.m.

Fare: Summer service and Clinton Fall Festival: Adults $7.00, senior citizens (65+) $6.00, children (2-12) $4.00, children under 2 ride free. Fall Color Tours: Adults $10.00, senior citizens (65+) $8.00, children (2-12) $6.00, children under 2 ride free.

Locomotives: No. 1, 1938 Plymouth, former Hayes Albion Corp.; Alco RS-1 diesel, former Ann Arbor (stored at Lenawee Jct.); No. 75, 1943 General Electric, former Western Maryland.

Passenger Cars: No. 1, commuter car, former Chicago, South Shore & South Bend.

Rolling Stock/Equipment: 1950 caboose No. 21692, former New York Central; 1944 caboose No. 19882, former New Haven; 1949 gondola No. 726456, former New York Central.

Special Events: Call or write for schedule.

Location: On U.S. 12 about 25 miles southwest of Ann Arbor and 45 miles northwest of Toledo, Ohio. The museum is at the corner of Clark and Division Streets. In Tecumseh, passengers board at the corner of Evans and Chicago.

ar 11 TRAIN Ann Arbor

Contact: Orcelia Davison
Publicity & Promotion

Mailing Address:
P.O. Box K
Clinton, MI 49236-0009
Business Office: (517) 456-7677
Ticket Office: (517) 423-7230

LITTLE RIVER RAILROAD
Steam, scheduled
Standard gauge

LITTLE RIVER RAILROAD

Ride/Operation: The Little River Railroad offers two round trips: a 10-mile, 80-minute ride from Coldwater to Batavia, and a 24-mile, 2½-hour ride from White Pigeon to Sturgis. Both trips run over tracks of the Michigan Southern Railroad.

Train: Combination car No. 2594, former Chicago & Alton; *Hiawatha* coaches, former Milwaukee Road; open-air cars; World War II troop car; cabooses, former Baltimore & Ohio.

Schedule: White Pigeon: May 25-July 27 & September 7-October 26, Sundays, 2:00 p.m. Coldwater: call for schedule.

Fare: Coldwater: adults $7.00, children (3-11) $4.00. White Pigeon: adults $15.00, children (3-11) $8.00. Fares vary for special events. Charters available.

Locomotives: No. 110, 1911 Baldwin 4-6-2, former Little River Railroad—the smallest standard-gauge Pacific locomotive ever built.

Special Events: Father's Day, June 15. Summer Train Robbery, July 13. Fall Train Robbery, September 7. Fall Color Runs, October 5 & 12. Ghost Train, October 26.

Contact: Terry Bloom
President

Mailing Address:
13187 SR 120
Middlebury, IN 46540
Telephone: (219) 825-9182

THE COOPERSVILLE & MARNE
RAILWAY COMPANY
Diesel, scheduled
Standard gauge

COOPERSVILLE & MARNE RAILWAY COMPANY

Ride/Operation: A 13-mile, 1½-hour round trip through western Michigan farmland, pastures, and woods on a former Grand Trunk Western route to Muskegon and Grand Haven car-ferry boats. Tracks parallel busy interstate 96 for several miles.

Train: No. 7014, former Grand Trunk Western EMD SW9, two "EL" commuter coaches, three former Canadian National heavy coaches, former GTW steel caboose.

Schedule: Saturdays, June-September. Weekends, October & December.

Fare: June-September: Adults $7.00, children $4.00. October & December: Adults $9.00, children $6.00.

Locomotives: SW9 No. 7014, former Grand Trunk Western; 4-6-0 No. 1395 and 0-6-0 No. 7456, both former Canadian National; Alco RS-1.

Rolling Stock/Equipment: 250-ton wreck crane, former Chesapeake & Ohio; several 1900-era wooden cabooses

Special Events: Great Train Robbery, September. Pumpkin Trains, October. Santa Trains, December.

Location: Western Michigan near Grand Rapids. Take exit 16 or 19 off I-96 and follow signs to downtown Coopersville.

Grand Rapids

Mailing Address:
P.O. Box 55
Coopersville, MI 49404
Telephone: (616) 837-7000

HENRY FORD MUSEUM & GREENFIELD VILLAGE RAILROAD

Steam, scheduled
Standard gauge

E.J. GULASH

Ride/Operation: The Greenfield Village Railroad offers a 2 1/2-mile, 35-minute narrated circuit of the world-famous Greenfield Village in open-air passenger cars. Rides are also now offered in an authentic 75-year old caboose. While riding you will hear interpretations of the history of the village, its occupants and the railroad.

Displays/Exhibits: The Henry Ford Museum, a general museum of American history occupying about twelve acres under one roof, contains a huge transportation collection, including the widely acclaimed "Automobile in American Life" exhibit. Greenfield Village is an eighty-one-acre outdoor museum comprising more than eighty historic structures. Also at the site are 1941 Lima 2-6-6-6 No. 1601; a 1902 Schenectady 4-4-2; an 1858 Rogers 4-4-0; an 1893 replica of the "DeWitt Clinton"; 1909 Baldwin 2-8-0, former Bessemer & Lake Erie No. 154; a 1923 Canadian Pacific snowplow; a 1924 FGE reefer; and a 1925 Detroit, Toledo & Ironton caboose.

Train: Historic steam locomotives "Edison" and "Torch Lake" (America's oldest operating locomotive) pull open-air passenger cars.

Schedule: Museum & village: Daily, 9:00 a.m.-5:00 p.m. Closed Thanksgiving & Christmas. Greenfield Village Train & Caboose Rides: Daily, April 1-October 13. Call for specifics.

Fare/Admission: Museum and village: Adults $12.50, senior citizens (62+) $11.50, children (5-12) $6.25, children under 5 free; does not include train fare. Greenfield Village Train: All-day pass, $3.00. Tickets and boarding at Main St., Suwanee Park and Smiths Creek. Caboose Rides: All-day pass $5. Boards at Smiths Creek Depot only. Prices subject to change.

Locomotives: No. 1, 1876 Ford Motor Co. 4-4-0 (rebuilt 1920s); No. 3, 1873 Mason-Fairlie 0-6-4T, former Calumet & Hecla Mining; No. 8, 1914 Baldwin 0-6-0, former Michigan Alkali Co.

Special Events: Call for specifics.

Location: One-half mile south of U.S. 12 (Michigan Avenue) between Southfield Road and Oakwood Boulevard.

Dearborn

Contact: Robert Casey
Transportation Curator

Mailing Address: P.O. Box 1970
Dearborn, MI 48121
Telephone: (313) 271-1620

166

SOCIETY FOR THE PRESERVATION OF THE
S.S. *CITY OF MILWAUKEE*
Railway display

SOCIETY FOR THE PRESERVATION OF THE S.S. CITY OF MILWAUKEE

Displays/Exhibits: This society was founded to preserve the last remaining railroad-car ferry in Betsie Bay. These ferries were an integral part of the community between 1892 and 1982, hauling railroad cars and passengers across Lake Michigan. The S.S. *City of Milwaukee* represents the classic design created by the Manitowoc Shipbuilding Company; ships of the same class served the Ann Arbor, Pere Marquette/Chesapeake & Ohio, and Grand Trunk Western railroads.

Today, the ship, coal tower, turntable, roundhouse, and marine terminal buildings remain at the site. The property adjacent to the ferry is an active lumberyard, so visitors who have not arranged a tour are asked to view the ship and artifacts from the route M-168 overlook or the Frankfort library and marina public access.

Schedule: Tours of the ship are available by special arrangement to society members. Please call or write for more information. Former railyard buildings are not currently accessible.

Admission: Society membership is $10.00 for adults and $25.00 for a family; includes tour of car ferry and newsletter.

Car Ferry: 1931 triple-expansion steamer, capacity twenty-two 50-foot railroad cars/50 passengers & crew, former Ann Arbor, former Grand Trunk Western.

Rolling Stock: Five steel boxcars and one idler flatcar, former AA.

Note: The future of the former railyard is under discussion between the Michigan Department of Transportation and the village of Elberta. Also, the former C&O railroad-car ferry S.S. *Badger,* the last steam passenger-car ferry operating on Lake Michigan, operates seasonally between Ludington, Michigan, and Manitowoc, Wisconsin. Ludington is approximately one hour south of Frankfort on U.S. 31.

Location: Elberta is across Lake Betsie from Frankfort. From Manistee, take M-22 north, and continue west on M-168 to the scenic overlook.

 P 📷 🏛 M

Contact: George P. Micka IV
Restoration Coordinator

Mailing Address:
S.P.C.M.
P.O. Box 506
Beulah, MI 49617
Telephone: (616) 780-2995

HUCKLEBERRY RAILROAD

Steam, scheduled
36" gauge

GEORGE A. FORERO, JR.

Ride/Operation: This railroad is operated in conjunction with Crossroads Village, a historic community of thirty late-nineteenth-century buildings including homes, a church, a school, a business district, and three operating mills. The *Genesee Belle,* a paddle-wheel riverboat, cruises on Mott Lake. The 8-mile, 35-minute excursion runs over a section of an original Flint and Pere Marquette branch line.

Train: Restored open- and closed-platform coaches from the Denver & Rio Grande Western, the Rio Grande Southern, and several Mexican narrow-gauge railroads.

Schedule: Daily, June 8-August 25, hourly. Weekends, September.

Admission: Adults $8.25, senior citizens $7.25, children (4-12) $5.50, children under 4 admitted free.

Locomotives: No. 2, 1920 Baldwin 4-6-0, former Alaska Railroad No. 152; No. 464, 1903 Baldwin 2-8-2, former Denver & Rio Grande Western.

Special Events: Railfan Weekend includes shop tours, photo runs, and model train exhibits. Halloween Trains. Christmas Trains. Call for dates and details.

Location: Take exit 13 (Saginaw Street) off I-475. Travel north on Saginaw to Stanley Road, east on Stanley to Bray Road, then south on Bray to the entrance.

Flint

Contact: Janet S. Weaver
Public Information Officer

Mailing Address:
5045 Stanley Road
Flint, MI 48506
Telephone: (810) 736-1700
(800) 648-PARK

TRI-CITIES HISTORICAL MUSEUM

Displays/Exhibits: The Grand Trunk Railway Depot, built in 1870, became the Tri-Cities Historical Museum in 1972. The Society has been collecting local memorabilia since its organization in 1959. Engine 1223 was one of fifteen engines built by the Lima Locomotive Works. Lima, Ohio, in 1941 for the Pere Marquette. It was moved to Grand Haven, Michigan, in August 1981 for cosmetic restoration and preservation. The ice cream social which is held once a year is a good "hands-on experience."

Schedule: By appointment.

Fare/Admission: Museum $1 donation.

Locomotives: No. 1223 Pere Marquette steam locomotive and tender, class N-1, 2-8-4, Berkshire type.

Rolling Stock/Equipment: No. 72222 Pere Marquette boxcar; No. A-986 Pere Marquette caboose; No. 77915 Grand Trunk Western caboose.

Special Events: August 14, Ice Cream Social.

Contact: Elizabeth Kammeraad
Executive Director

Mailing Address:
1N. Harbor
Grand Haven, MI 49417
Telephone: (616) 842-0700
Fax: (616) 842-3698

IRON MOUNTAIN IRON MINE
Electric, scheduled
24" gauge

IRON MOUNTAIN IRON MINE

Ride/Operation: Designated a Michigan Historical Site, the Iron Mountain Iron Mine offers guided underground tours by mine train. Visitors travel 2,600 feet into the mine to see mining demonstrations and the history of iron mining in Michigan's Upper Peninsula. Mining equipment dating from the 1870s is shown and explained.

Train: Electric locomotive, 5 cars.

Schedule: Daily, June 1-October 15, 9:00 a.m.-5:00 p.m.

Admission: Adults $6.00, children (6-12) $5.00, children under 6 admitted free. Group rates available.

Location: Nine miles east of Iron Mountain on U.S. 2.

Contact: Albert or Dennis Carollo

Mailing Address:
P.O. Box 177
Iron Mountain, MI 49801
Telephone: (906) 563-8077

MICHIGAN TRANSIT MUSEUM
Electric, diesel, scheduled
Standard gauge

WILLIAM H. HENNING

Ride/Operation: This unique train ride is a 6-mile, 40-minute trip through farmlands and a park on trackage of the Selfridge Air National Guard Base. Eastbound, the train is controlled from "el" cars, with a diesel locomotive providing electricity. Westbound, the locomotive powers the train. Located on the route is the Selfridge Military Air Museum, with more than twenty military aircraft, plus photos, models, and memorabilia. A small donation for the museum is collected with the train fare.

Displays/Exhibits: The group leases the Mt. Clemens Grand Trunk Railroad station, built in 1859, and operates it as a museum. The station is located at the Cass Avenue crossing of the Grand Trunk in Mt. Clemens.

Train: Nos. 4442 & 4450, 1924 elevated cars, former Chicago Transit Authority; diesel No. 1807. Grand Trunk Western caboose No. 77058, built in 1900, is used as a ticket office.

Schedule: Train: Last Sunday of May through last Sunday of September. Schedule subject to change. Station: Weekends, year-round, 1:00-4:00 p.m. Closed on major holidays.

Fare: Train: Adults $5.00, children (4-12) $2.50, children under 4 ride free. Air Museum: Adults $.50, children (4-12) $.25, children under 4 admitted free.

Locomotives: No. 1807, Alco S-1, former Alco plant switcher; No. 761, 1929 interurban, former Chicago, North Shore & Milwaukee; PCC No. 268, former Detroit Street Railway; No. 4040, 1954 Baldwin-Lima-Hamilton, former U.S. Air Force, RS4TC.

Location: Train departs from the Caboose Depot, 3/4 mile north of Mt. Clemens on North Gratiot Avenue. Take the North River Road exit off I-94; the museum is 3/4 of a mile west of Gratiot Avenue on Cass.

P ✳ ⌂ ▶ ◀ M ar n
TRAIN

Contact: Gary J. Michaels
Curator

Mailing Address:
P.O. Box 12
Mt. Clemens, MI 48046
Telephone: (810) 463-1863
(810) 307-5035

PROJECT 1225

Ride/Operation: Locomotive No. 1225 is exhibited periodically under steam in Michigan and elsewhere in the midwest. Several times each summer, the Engineer- and Fireman-for-an-Hour Program permits people to learn how to operate and fire the 220-ton locomotive.

Displays/Exhibits: No. 1225 is maintained in the former machine shop of the Ann Arbor Railroad at Owosso. The locomotive and tools used to repair it may be seen by visitors.

Train: Air-conditioned coaches and lounge cars.

Schedule: Exhibitions and Engineer- and Fireman-for-an-Hour: Call for dates and times. Shop: Saturdays, 10:00 a.m.-6:00 p.m., except weekends of major holidays.

Fare: Exhibitions and Engineer- and Fireman-for-an-Hour: Inquire for current tuition.

Locomotives: No. 1225, 1941 Lima 2-8-4, former Pere Marquette Railway.

Passenger Cars: Baggage car, former Chesapeake & Ohio No. 361.

Location: In yards of the Tuscola and Saginaw Bay Railway, South Oakwood Street, off highway M-71 (Corunna Avenue) in southeast Owosso.

Contact: Aarne Frobom
President

Mailing Address:
Michigan State Trust for Railway
Preservation, Inc.
P.O. Box 665
Owosso, MI 48867-0665
Telephone: (517) 725-9464

CITY OF TRAVERSE CITY
PARKS & RECREATION
Steam, scheduled
1/4 scale

CITY OF TRAVERSE CITY

Ride/Operation: No. 400, the "Spirit of Traverse City," is an oil-fired, 1/4-scale replica of a 4-4-2 steam locomotive, which takes passengers around a 4/10-mile loop at the Clinch Park Zoo and Marina on West Bay in Traverse City. The ride provides views of West Grand Traverse Bay, the marina, the beach, and the zoo, which features native Michigan wildlife and the Con Foster Museum.

Train: No. 400 pulls a train of 1/4-scale open-air cars.

Schedule: Daily, May 24-September 7 and weekends through September 21, 10:00 a.m.-4:30 p.m.

Fare: Adults $1.00, children (under 13) $.50.

Locomotives: "Spirit of Traverse City," No. 400, 1/4-scale oil-fired 4-4-2.

Passenger Cars: Three open-air cars.

Special Events: Family Fun Day, June 1, 12:00-4:00 p.m., features 25-cent rides, popcorn, and zoo admission.

Location: At Clinch Park Zoo, 100 Grandview Parkway (U.S. 31) and Cass Street.

Contact: Mr. Lauren Vaughn
Parks & Recreation Superintendent

Mailing Address:
625 Woodmere Avenue
Traverse City, MI 49686
Telephone: (616) 922-4910

Michigan, Walled Lake
R

MICHIGAN STAR CLIPPER

MICHIGAN STAR CLIPPER
DINNER TRAIN COE RAIL
Diesel, scheduled
Standard gauge

Ride/Operation: The *Star Clipper* offers a 3-hour scenic excursion throughout southeastern Michigan while passengers dine on a five-course meal reminiscent of years gone by. Live entertainment featuring Murder Mysteries or Musical Revues are performed nightly. The lunch excursion is two hours long and a three-course meal is served. On the *Star Clipper Overnight B&Bs,* passengers can relax and sleep aboard two fabulous cars that feature a 50-foot all-mahogany drawing room, a dance floor at the opposite end, and eight suites in between. The *Coe Rail Vintage Tourist Train* offers one hour rides with full commentary and optional puppet show. The newly remodeled 1884 depot offers check-in area along with a gift shop.

Train: Michigan Star Clipper Dinner Train, Star Clipper Overnight B&B's, Pasige Tavern Lounge Car, Coe Rail Vintage Tourist Train.

Schedule: *Michigan Star Clipper*: year-round; Tuesday-Thursday, Saturday, 7:00 p.m.; Friday, 7:30 p.m.; Sunday, 5:00 p.m. Mondays upon request. *Coe Rail*: April-October, Sunday, 1:00 & 2:30 p.m..

Fare: *Michigan Star Clipper*: $68.50 (food, ride, entertainment, tax). *Sleeper cars*: please call or write for information. *Coe Rail*: Adults $8.00, senior citizens (65+) & children (2-10) $7.00. Travel agent and group discounts available.

Locomotives: 1945 Whitcomb, gasoline; 1945 Alco S1; 1947 Alco S1; 1952 Alco S1.

Passenger Cars: *Michigan Star Clipper*: 1952 Pennsylvania Railroad Keystone dining cars; kitchen car; power car; 1950s-vintage stainless steel sleepers. Coe Rail: 1917 coaches, former Erie Lackawanna; 1947 tap car (lounge), former Milwaukee Road; 1920 baggage cars; 1945 box-car saloon; 1945 bay-window cabooses, former PH&D.

Special Events: Michigan Star Clipper: New Year's Eve celebration, hotel packages, corporate entertaining, fund raising events, bus tours welcome. Coe Rail: Children's birthday parties, Hobo Halloween Weekend, Santa Holiday Rides, school tours, buffet or box lunches available.

Location: On Pontiac Trail just north of Maple Road; 8 minutes north of Novi/Walled Lake exit off I-96.

Contact: J. Coe
Vice President

Mailing Address:
840 North Pontiac Trail
Walled Lake, MI 48390
Telephone: (810) 960-9440
Fax: (810) 960-9444

NORTH STAR RAIL, INC.
Steam, irregular
Standard gauge

VICTOR HAND

Ride/Operation: North Star Rail, Inc., operates day-long, steam-powered excursions over various Class I railroads.

Train: Air-conditioned coaches; most trips include deluxe, first-class cars (diners, lounges, domes, and/or observation cars).

Schedule: Varies, depending on trip. Please call or write for information.

M

Fare: Varies. Advance reservations suggested.

Special Events: Heritage Express (includes nightly fireworks and laser show with orchestra), July 4-7.

Locomotives: No. 261, 1944 Alco 4-8-4, former Milwaukee Road class S-3, leased to North Star Rail by the National Railroad Museum in Green Bay, Wisconsin.

Contact: Steve Sandberg
Chief Operating Officer

Mailing Address:
1418 Rocky Lane
St. Paul, MN 55122
Telephone: (612) 688-7320
Fax: (612) 688-7282

END-O-LINE RAILROAD PARK AND MUSEUM
Railway museum

END-O-LINE RAILROAD PARK AND MUSEUM

Ride/Operation: Rides on a manually operated turntable are given to all visitors. For the children, rides are also given on a 3½ gauge Hilfers Train. Guided tours are available.

Displays/Exhibits: A working railroad yard including a rebuilt enginehouse on its original foundation, an original four-room depot, a water tower, an 1899 section-foreman's house, and an outhouse. The turntable, built in 1901 by the American Bridge Company and still operable, is the only one left in Minnesota on its original site. The section-foreman's house will be completed in 1996. A general store and one-room schoolhouse can also be seen. A replica of the coal bunker was built in the fall of 1995 and will be used for a picnic shelter and gift shop. The enginehouse has been lengthened to its original 90 ft. It contains various exhibits and displays of railroad artifacts, photographs, memorabilia and equipment. The freight room in the depot has an HO-scale model-train layout of the railroad yards in Currie, complete with steam engine sound effects, authentic structures, and local countryside. A beautiful wrap-around mural completes the setting. A bicycle/pedestrian paved pathway connects the railroad park to Lake Shetek State Park (approximately 6 miles round trip).

Schedule: May 26-September 1, Monday-Friday, 10:00 a.m.-12:00 p.m. & 1:00-5:00 p.m.; Saturday-Sunday, 1:00-5:00 p.m. and by appointment. Last tour of the day begins at 4:00 p.m.

Admission: Adults $2.00, students $1.00, family $5.00.

Locomotives: 1923 Georgia Northern steam locomotive (restoration in progress).

Rolling Stock/Equipment: 1942 Brookville diesel switcher; 1942 Grand Trunk Western Caboose; Fairmont motor cars, Velocipede; ice cart; baggage/milk carts.

Location: Take State Highway 30 to Currie, then travel three-fourths mile north on County Road 38.

Contact: Louise Gervais
Director/Curator

Mailing Address:
440 N. Mill Street
Currie, MN 56123
Telephone: (507) 763-3708
Off season: (507) 763-3113

THE OLD DEPOT RAILROAD MUSEUM

Displays/Exhibits: A former Great Northern depot built in 1913 is filled with railroad memorabilia and pictures. This 33-foot by 100-foot country depot has two waiting rooms, an agent's office, and a large freight room, as well as a full basement. Authentic recorded sounds of steam locomotives and the clicking of the telegraph key create the realistic feel of an old small-town depot. Items displayed include lanterns, telegraph equipment, semaphores, and other signals; section crew cars, a hand pump car, and a velocipede; tools and oil cans; depot and crossing signs; buttons, badges, service pins, and caps; a large date-nail collection; and many baggage carts. Also included are children's toy trains, an HO-scale model railroad, and many railroad advertising items. Interpretation of the items is provided.

Train: Static one-half-scale train on display.

Schedule: Daily, Memorial Day-October 1, 10:00 a.m.-4:30 p.m.

Admission: Adults $2.50, children (under 12) $1.00. Babies are free.

Rolling Stock/Equipment: Two cabooses; one boxcar.

Location: 651 West Highway No. 12, 50 miles west of Minneapolis.

Contact: Howard Page
Manager

Mailing Address:
651 West Highway 12
Dassel, MN 55325
Telephone: (320) 275-3876

LAKE SUPERIOR & MISSISSIPPI RAILROAD

Minnesota, Duluth
R

Diesel, scheduled
Standard gauge

DAVE SCHAUER

Ride: A 12-mile, 1½-hour round trip that follows the scenic St. Louis River to New Duluth. The line was first built in 1870 as the Lake Superior & Mississippi Railroad and was later part of the Northern Pacific and the Burlington Northern.

Displays/Exhibits: See the listing of the Lake Superior Museum of Transportation (Minnesota, Duluth).

Train: Heavyweight coaches from the Duluth, Missabe & Iron Range; open top flatcar with seats.

Schedule: Weekends, June 14-August 31, 11:00 a.m., 2:00 p.m.

Fare: Adults $6.00, senior citizens (60+) $5.00, children (under 13) $4.00. Charter rates available.

Locomotives: No. 46, 1946 General Electric 45-ton diesel.

Passenger Cars: Two heavyweight coaches; open observation car.

Location: Six miles southwest of downtown Duluth on Grand Avenue, route 23, across from the Duluth Zoo and the Lake Superior Zoological Gardens. Train leaves from the Western Waterfront Trail; park in Western Waterfront Trail lot.

Radio Frequency: 160.380

Contact: Andrew Webb
VP Operations

Mailing Address:
506 West Michigan Street
Duluth, MN 55802
Telephone: (218) 624-7549
Fax: (218) 728-6303

**LAKE SUPERIOR
MUSEUM OF TRANSPORTATION**
Railway museum
Standard gauge

BRUCE OJARD PHOTOGRAPHY

Displays/Exhibits: A number of interesting and historic locomotives and cars, including the Great Northern's famous "William Crooks" locomotive and cars of 1861; Northern Pacific Railway #1, The "Minnetonka" built in 1870; the Soo line's first passenger diesel, FP7 No. 2500A; Duluth, Missabe & Iron Range 2-8-8-4 No. 227, displayed with revolving drive wheels and recorded sound; Great Northern No. 400, the first production-model SD45 diesel; an 1887 steam rotary snowplow; other steam, diesel, and electric engines; a Railway Post Office car; a dining-car china exhibit; freight cars; work equipment; an operating electric single-truck streetcar; and much railroadiana.

Schedule: Daily, May-September, 10:00 a.m.-5:00 p.m.; Daily, October-April, Monday-Saturday, 10:00 a.m.-5:00 p.m.; Sunday, 1:00-5:00 p.m.

Admission: Adults $5.00, children (3-11) $3.00, children under 3 admitted free, family rate $15.00. Price includes admission to adjacent Heritage and Arts Center. Subject to change.

Special Events: The museum sponsors various special excursions each year. Please call or write for details.

Location: 506 West Michigan Street, in the former Duluth Union Depot, now the St. Louis County Heritage & Arts Center; adjacent to North Shore Scenic Railroad station.

Radio Frequency: 160.38

Contact: Tom Gannon
Curator

Mailing Address:
506 West Michigan Street
Duluth, MN 55802
Telephone: (218) 733-7590

NORTH SHORE SCENIC RAILROAD

Steam, scheduled
Standard gauge

TIM SCHANDEL

Ride/Operation: Formerly the Duluth Missabe & Iron Range Railway's Lake Front Line, this railroad's twenty-six miles of track run between the Depot in downtown Duluth, along the Lake Superior waterfront, and through the residential areas and scenic woodlands of northeastern Minnesota to the Two Harbors Depot, adjacent to DM&IR's active taconite yard and ship-loading facility. The line offers 1 1/2-, 2 1/2- and 6-hour round trips with departures from Duluth and Two Harbors.

Train: Vintage diesel locomotive with open window heavy weight coaches. Steam locomotive.

Schedule: Duluth-Two Harbors, Friday and Saturday, May 3-June 9 and September 6-October 12; Wednesday-Saturday, June 12-August 31. Duluth-Lester River, daily May 4-October 15. Pizza Train/Palmers, Friday and Saturday, May 3-June 9 and September 6-October 12, Wednesday-Saturday, June 12-August 31. Formal Dinner Train/Palmers, Friday and Saturday June 1-September 7 and Saturdays September 14-October 12. Theme Dinner Train, Tuesdays June 4-August 27. Charters available. Please call for fare information and schedules.

Fare: Please call or write for information.

Special Events: Marathon train, steam excursions, boogie train, and fall color tours.

Location: Duluth: Duluth Depot, 5th Avenue West and Michigan Street; parking is at 4th Avenue West, below Michigan Street. Two Harbors: Two Harbors Depot, Lake County Historical Society, 7th and Waterfront.

Radio Frequency: 160.920

Contact: Shannon Emmons
Charter Coordinator

Mailing Address:
506 West Michigan Street
Duluth, MN 55802
Telephone: (218) 722-1273
(800) 423-1273

MINNESOTA TRANSPORTATION MUSEUM
COMO-HARRIET STREETCAR LINE

Electric, scheduled
Standard gauge

JOHN PRESTHOLDT

Ride/Operation: A 2-mile, 15-minute round trip on a restored portion of the former Twin City Rapid Transit Company's historic Como-Harriet route. Streetcars operate over a scenic line through a wooded area between Lakes Harriet and Calhoun. This is the last operating portion of the 523-mile Twin City Lines system, abandoned in 1954.

Displays/Exhibits: The Linden Hills Depot, a re-creation of the 1900 depot located at the site, houses changing historical displays about electric railways in Minnesota.

Schedule: Daily, May 23-September 1; Saturdays, Sundays & holidays, 12:30 p.m. to dusk, (5:00 p.m. in October); Monday-Friday, 6:30 p.m. to dusk. Saturdays and Sundays, May (before Memorial Day weekend), September after Labor Day, and October.

Fare: $1.00, children under 5 ride free. Chartered streetcars: $45 per half hour; please call (612) 291-7588 for charter information and reservations.

Rolling Stock: No. 10, 1912 Mesaba Railway Co. (Niles Car Co.); No. 78, 1893 DSR (Laclede Car Co.); No. 265, 1915 Duluth Street Railway (TCRT Snelling Shops, St. Paul); No. 322, 1946 TCRT PCC (St. Louis Car Co.), undergoing restoration; No. 416, 1949 TCRT PCC (St. Louis Car Co.), awaiting restoration; No. 1300, 1908 Twin City Rapid Transit.

Motor Buses: No. 103 (GM, 1962), No. 630 (Mack, 1941), No. 1303 (GM, 1954), No. 1399 (GM, 1954) operating, and No. 1488 (AM General, 1974).

Special Events: Linden Hills Neighborhood Fair, May 17-18, Linden Hills Art Party, late July/early August, both featuring multiple streetcar and motor bus operations and other events. Call or write for details.

Note: The Museum's Minnehaha Depot is located several miles east in Minnehaha Falls Park; see separate listing.

Location: The Linden Hills Depot, West 42nd Street & Queen Avenue South, at Lake Harriet in southwest Minneapolis.

♿ (depot only) ☕ P ✳ 🏛
▶ ◀ ⛩ M at ll TRAIN
🚂 St. Paul

Radio Frequency: 161.355

Contact: Louis Hoffman
General Agent

Mailing Address:
P.O. Box 17240
Nokomis Station
Minneapolis, MN 55417-0240
Telephone: (612) 228-0263
(800) 711-2591
Charter Telephone: (612) 291-7588

MINNESOTA TRANSPORTATION MUSEUM
MINNEHAHA DEPOT
Railway museum

LOUIS HOFFMAN

Displays/Exhibits: Built in 1875, the Minnehaha Depot replaced an even smaller Milwaukee Road depot on the same site. Milwaukee Road agents quickly nicknamed the depot the "Princess" because of its intricate architectural details. Until Twin City Rapid Transit Company street-cars, connected Minnehaha Falls Park to the city, as many as 13 passenger trains per day served the depot. It remained in service, primarily handling freight, for many years. Closed in 1963, the structure was donated to the Minnesota Historical Society and is staffed by volunteer members of the Minnesota Transportation Museum. Located at the south end of CP Rail System's South Minneapolis branch, once a through route to the south, the depot sees occasional freight movements and often hosts visiting private cars. Visitors may tour the depot, which appears much as it did when in service as a typical suburban station. Exhibits include telegraphy demonstrations and historic photographs of the depot and its environs.

Schedule: Sunday & holidays, May 25-September 1, 12:30-4:30 p.m.

Admission: No charge; donations welcomed.

Special Events: Annual Open House featuring refreshments and scenic trips along Minnehaha and Lake Nakomis Parkways aboard Twin City Rapid Transit Company bus No. 1399 (General Motors, 1954), May 19, 6:15-9:00 p.m. Call or write for other special events.

Note: The museum's Como-Harriet Streetcar Line is located several miles west at Lake Harriet; see separate listing.

Location: In Minnehaha Falls Park at 4926 Minnehaha Avenue.

ar ll ᵀᴿᴬⁱᴺ **M** St. Paul

Contact: Corbin S. Kidder
Stationmaster

Mailing Address:
P.O. Box 17240
Nokomis Station
Minneapolis, MN 55417-0240
Telephone: (612) 228-0263
(800) 711-2591
Stationmaster: (612) 227-5171

WESTERN MINNESOTA
STEAM THRESHER'S REUNION
Steam, scheduled

WESTERN MINNESOTA STEAM THRESHERS

Ride/Operation: The Western Minnesota Steam Threshers Reunion is a four-day show, lasting from Friday to Monday every Labor Day weekend. In operation are three railroads (full-sized, 1/4-scale, and miniature), thirty-seven steam traction engines, four hundred gas tractors, and many large stationary steam and gas engines.

Displays/Exhibits: Musical entertainment all day and evening. Free rides on a 1920 steam-operated Parker Bros. merry-go-round. Steam plowing and threshing. Morning and afternoon parades of steam and gas tractors. A complete, working horsepower farm, two sawmills, and a flour mill are in operation. An 1895 Great Northern Railway steam forging hammer stamps out souvenir plates.

Schedule: August 30-September 2, every 20 minutes, 8:00 a.m.-8:00 p.m. (train stops running at 5:00 p.m. on September 2).

Fare/Admission: Gate admission: $7 per day; $10 per season. Children under 15 admitted free. No charge for rides, exhibits, or musical entertainment.

Locomotives: No. 353, 1920 Alco 0-6-0, former Soo Line; Porter 0-4-0; Wagner & Sons 1/4-scale locomotive.

Passenger Cars: Mt. St. Helens (SPS) on display; 5 passenger cars.

Rolling Stock/Equipment: Two former Northern Pacific cabooses; various operating handcars and motor cars; track crane and miscellaneous track-maintenance equipment.

Special Events: Each June, the WMSTR hosts the "University of Rollag College of Steam Traction Engineering," which offers classroom and hands-on instruction on operating steam traction and railroad engines. Students who successfully complete this course fulfill part of the requirements needed to obtain the Minnesota Steam Traction Engineer's license.

Notes: WMSTR is an all-volunteer organization of

3,500 members. Primitive camping is available for $15 per unit for the duration of the show. Area churches serve "threshermen's" meals.

Location: Thirty-two miles southeast of Fargo, North Dakota, just off I-94.

Contact: Lynette Briden
President

Mailing Address:
2610 1st Avenue
North Fargo, ND 58102
Telephone: (701) 232-4484

TRAINS AT BANDANA SQUARE BY
TWIN CITY MODEL RAILROAD CLUB, INC.
Model railroad

LARRY VANDEN PLAS

Displays/Exhibits: Three thousand square feet of O-scale operating railroad, featuring a panorama of railroading in Minnesota during the 1940s and 1950s, when steam and diesel shared the rails. The display is located on the northeast corner of the second level in the Bandana Square shopping center, the restored Northern Pacific Como Shops that were once used to maintain passenger cars.

Schedule: Monday-Friday, 10:00 a.m.-8:00 p.m.; Saturday, 10:00 a.m.-6:00 p.m.; Sunday, 12:00-5:00 p.m.

Admission: Requested donation of $1 per person, $2 per family.

Locomotives: Displayed outside are a former Northern Pacific F9 and a former Grand Trunk Western 0-8-0.

Passenger Cars: Displayed outside is a former Chicago & North Western wooden combine.

Rolling Stock/Equipment: Boxcar, former Burlington Northern; caboose, former Chicago, Burlington & Quincy

Location: Bandana Square, 1021 Bandana Boulevard East. Second level, northeast corner. Just off Energy Park Drive between Lexington and Snelling Avenues.

St. Paul

Contact: Paul Gruetzman

Mailing Address:
Box 26, Bandana Square
1021 Bandana Boulevard East
St. Paul, MN 55108
Telephone: (612) 647-9628

STEAM PASSENGER SERVICE DIRECTORY
1997 GUEST COUPONS

ADIRONDACK SCENIC RAILROAD
Regular price: Adults $6, children $4
With coupon: Adults $5, children $3
Valid April 1997 through March 1998
Maximum discount 1 person per coupon

THE AGE OF STEAM RAILROAD MUSEUM
Regular price: Adults $3, children $1.50
With coupon: Adults $1.50, children $.75
Valid April 1997 through March 1998
Maximum discount 4 persons per coupon

ARIZONA TRAIN DEPOT
10% discount toward any purchase
Valid April 1997 through March 1998

ARKANSAS & MISSOURI RAILROAD
Regular price: Springdale trip $29/34/39; Van Buren trip $19/24/29
With coupon: Adult fare 10% discount
Valid April 1997 through March 1998
Maximum discount 4 persons per coupon

BC FOREST MUSEUM
With coupon: Group rate
Valid April 1997 through March 1998

THE B&O RAILROAD MUSEUM
Regular price: Adults $6, children $3
With coupon: Two for one admission
Valid April 1997 through March 1998

BALTIMORE STREETCAR MUSEUM
Regular price: Adults $4, children (4-11) $2
With coupon: Free admission with paid admission of equal or greater value
Valid April 1997 through March 1998
Maximum discount 1 person per coupon

BIG BEAR FARM, INC.
Regular price: Adults $5.50, children $3.50
With coupon: Adults $4.50, children $2.50
Valid April 1997 through March 1998
Maximum discount 1 person per coupon

BIG SOUTH FORK SCENIC RAILWAY, INC.
Regular price: Adults $10, children $5
With coupon: Adults $9, children $4
Valid April 1997 through March 1998
Maximum discount 6 persons per coupon

BONANZAVILLE, USA
Regular price: Adults $6, children $3, family $16
With coupon: Adults $5, children $3, family $15
Valid April 1997 through March 1998
Maximum discount unlimited

BRANSON SCENIC RAILWAY
Regular price: Adults $18.50
With coupon: Adults $16.50
Valid April 1997 through March 1998
Maximum discount 4 persons per coupon

CAMP FIVE MUSEUM FOUNDATION, INC.
Regular price: Adults $14
With coupon: Adults $13
Valid April 1997 through March 1998
Maximum discount 1 person per coupon

STEAM PASSENGER SERVICE DIRECTORY

STEAM PASSENGER SERVICE DIRECTORY

STEAM PASSENGER SERVICE DIRECTORY

STEAM PASSENGER SERVICE DIRECTORY

STEAM PASSENGER SERVICE DIRECTORY

STEAM PASSENGER SERVICE DIRECTORY

STEAM PASSENGER SERVICE DIRECTORY

STEAM PASSENGER SERVICE DIRECTORY

STEAM PASSENGER SERVICE DIRECTORY

STEAM PASSENGER SERVICE DIRECTORY

STEAM PASSENGER SERVICE DIRECTORY

STEAM PASSENGER SERVICE DIRECTORY

CAPE COD RAILROAD
Regular price: Adults $11.50, children $7.50
With coupon: Adults $9.50, children $5.50
Valid April 1997 through March 1998
Maximum discount 8 persons per coupon

CATSKILL MOUNTAIN RAILROAD CO., INC.
Regular price: Adults $6, children $2
With coupon: Adults $6, children free
Valid April 1997 through March 1998
Maximum discount 1 person per coupon

CHESAPEAKE RAILROAD
Regular price: Adults $8, children $7
With coupon: Adults $7, children $4
Valid April 1997 through March 1998
Maximum discount 2 persons per coupon

CHOO CHOO BARN
Regular price: Adults $4, children $3
With coupon: Adults $2, children $1.50
Valid April 1997 through March 1998

CLOVIS DEPOT MODEL TRAIN MUSEUM
Regular price: Adults $3, children $1
With coupon: Adults $1.50, children $.50
Valid April 1997 through March 1998
Maximum discount 6 persons per coupon

COCHRANE RAILWAY & PIONEER MUSEUM
Regular price: Adults $2, seniors $1, children $1.50
With coupon: Adults $1.50, seniors $.50, children $1
Valid April 1997 through March 1998
Maximum discount 2 persons per coupon

CONWAY SCENIC RAILROAD
With coupon: $.50 off Valley Train or $1 off Notch Train
Valid April 1997 through March 1998
Maximum discount 6 persons per coupon

CORYDON SCENIC RAILROAD
Regular price: Adults $9, children $5
With coupon: Adults $8, children $4
Valid April 1997 through March 1998
Maximum discount 1 person per coupon

CRIPPLE CREEK NARROW GAUGE RAILROAD
Regular price: Adults $7.50, children $4
With coupon: Adults $7, children $3.50
Valid April 1997 through March 1998
Maximum discount 4 persons per coupon

DANBURY RAILWAY MUSEUM
Regular price: Varies with trip
With coupon: $5 off any excursion ticket costing $25 or more
Valid April 1997 through March 1998

DELAWARE & ULSTER RAIL RIDE
Regular price: Adults $7, children $4
With coupon: Adults $6, children $3
Valid April 1997 through March 1998
Maximum discount 6 persons per coupon

THE DENNISON RAILROAD DEPOT MUSEUM
Regular price: Adults $3, seniors $2.50, children $1.75
With coupon: Adults $2, seniors $1.50, children $.75
Valid April 1997 through March 1998
Maximum discount 4 persons per coupon

STEAM PASSENGER SERVICE DIRECTORY

STEAM PASSENGER SERVICE DIRECTORY

STEAM PASSENGER SERVICE DIRECTORY

STEAM PASSENGER SERVICE DIRECTORY

STEAM PASSENGER SERVICE DIRECTORY

STEAM PASSENGER SERVICE DIRECTORY

STEAM PASSENGER SERVICE DIRECTORY

STEAM PASSENGER SERVICE DIRECTORY

STEAM PASSENGER SERVICE DIRECTORY

STEAM PASSENGER SERVICE DIRECTORY

STEAM PASSENGER SERVICE DIRECTORY

STEAM PASSENGER SERVICE DIRECTORY

STEAM PASSENGER SERVICE DIRECTORY
1997 GUEST COUPONS

FLORIDA GULF COAST RAILROAD MUSEUM
Regular price: Adults $8, children $5
With coupon: Adults $7
Valid April 1997 through March 1998
Maximum discount 4 persons per coupon

GALVESTON RAILROAD MUSEUM
Regular price: Adults $5, seniors $4.50, children $2.50
With coupon: Adults $4, seniors $3.50, children $1.50
Valid April 1997 through March 1998
Maximum discount 4 persons per coupon

GRAND CANYON RAILWAY
Regular price: Adults $49.50, children $19.50
With coupon: Adults $44.55, children (16 and under) $17.55
Coach Class Only
Valid April 1997 through March 1998
Maximum discount entire party

GREEN MOUNTAIN RAILROAD
Regular price: Adults $11, children $7
With coupon: Adults $10, children $6
Valid April 1997 through March 1998
Maximum discount 2 persons per coupon

HARPERS FERRY TOY TRAIN MUSEUM
& JOY LINE RAILROAD
Regular price: Adults $1, children $1
With coupon: Adults $.75, children $.75
Valid April 1997 through March 1998
Maximum discount 1 person per coupon

HARTMANN MODEL RAILROAD MUSEUM
Regular price: Adults $5, children $3
With coupon: Adults $4, children $2
Valid April 1997 through March 1998
Maximum discount 2 persons per coupon

HAZLET TRAIN STOP & MUSEUM
Regular price: Adults $2, children 10 and under free
With coupon: Adults $1.75
Valid April 1997 through March 1998

HISTORIC PULLMAN FOUNDATION
Regular price: Adults $4, children $2.50
With coupon: Adults $3, children $2
Valid April 1997 through March 1998
Maximum discount 4 persons per coupon

HISTORIC RAILROAD SHOPS
Regular price: Adults $2.50, children $2
With coupon: Adults $2
Valid April 1997 through March 1998
Maximum discount 2 persons per coupon

FLOYD McEACHERN
HISTORIC TRAIN MUSEUM
Regular price: Adults $3, children $2
With coupon: Adults $2.50, children $1.50
Valid April 1997 through March 1998

INDIANA TRANSPORTATION MUSEUM
With coupon: $1 off any regularly scheduled train
Valid April 1997 through March 1998
Maximum discount 8 persons per coupon

IOWA STAR CLIPPER DINNER TRAIN
Regular price: Adults $42.50
With coupon: Adults $38.25
Valid April 1997 through March 1998
Maximum discount 4 persons per coupon

STEAM PASSENGER SERVICE DIRECTORY   STEAM PASSENGER SERVICE DIRECTORY

STEAM PASSENGER SERVICE DIRECTORY   STEAM PASSENGER SERVICE DIRECTORY

STEAM PASSENGER SERVICE DIRECTORY   STEAM PASSENGER SERVICE DIRECTORY

STEAM PASSENGER SERVICE DIRECTORY   STEAM PASSENGER SERVICE DIRECTORY

STEAM PASSENGER SERVICE DIRECTORY   STEAM PASSENGER SERVICE DIRECTORY

STEAM PASSENGER SERVICE DIRECTORY   STEAM PASSENGER SERVICE DIRECTORY

IRON MOUNTAIN IRON MINE
Regular price: Adults $6, children $5
With coupon: Adults $5, children $4
Valid April 1997 through March 1998
Maximum discount 2 persons per coupon

KENTUCKY RAILWAY MUSEUM, INC.
Regular price: Adults $12.50, children $8
With coupon: Adults $10, children $6
Valid April 1997 through March 1998
Maximum discount 4 persons per coupon

LAKE SUPERIOR AND MISSISSIPPI RAILROAD
Regular price: Adults $6, seniors $5, children (under 13) $4
With coupon: Adults $5, seniors $4, children $3
Valid April 1997 through March 1998
Maximum discount 1 person per coupon

LINDEN MADISON TOWNSHIP HISTORICAL SOCIETY
Regular price: Adults $2
With coupon: Adults $1
Valid April 1997 through March 1998
Maximum discount 1 person per coupon

MAUMEE VALLEY HISTORICAL SOCIETY
Regular price: Adults $3.50, children $1.50
With coupon: Adults $3, children $1
Valid April 1997 through March 1998

McKINNEY AVENUE TRANSIT AUTHORITY
Regular price: Adults $1.50, children $1.00
With coupon: Adults $1.50, children $.50
Valid April 1997 through March 1998
Maximum discount 2 persons per coupon

MICHIGAN STAR CLIPPER DINNER TRAIN
Discount Offer: $10 off per person for a Murder Mystery
Valid on Tuesday, Wednesday, Thursday only.
Excludes holidays and month of December.
Valid April 1997 through March 1998
Maximum discount 8 persons per coupon

MONTICELLO RAILWAY MUSEUM
Regular price: Adults $5, Children $3
With coupon: Adults $4.50, Children $2.50
Valid April 1997 through March 1998
Maximum discount 4 persons per coupon

MT. HOOD RAILROAD
Regular price: Adults $21.95, Children $13.95
With coupon: One child free w/adult full fare
Valid April 1997 through March 1998
Maximum discount 1 person per coupon

MT. RAINIER SCENIC RAILROAD
Regular price: Adults $9.50, seniors $8.50, juniors $7.50, children $6.50
With coupon: Buy one admission get equal price admission free
Valid April 1997 through March 1998
Maximum discount 1 person per coupon

NATIONAL CAPITAL TROLLEY MUSEUM
Regular price: Adults $2.50, Children $2
With coupon: Free admission
Valid April 1997 through March 1998
Maximum discount 2 persons per coupon

NATIONAL RAILROAD MUSEUM
Regular price: Adults $6, Children $3
With coupon: Adults $3, Children $1.50
Valid April 1997 through March 1998

STEAM PASSENGER SERVICE DIRECTORY

STEAM PASSENGER SERVICE DIRECTORY

STEAM PASSENGER SERVICE DIRECTORY

STEAM PASSENGER SERVICE DIRECTORY

STEAM PASSENGER SERVICE DIRECTORY

STEAM PASSENGER SERVICE DIRECTORY

STEAM PASSENGER SERVICE DIRECTORY

STEAM PASSENGER SERVICE DIRECTORY

STEAM PASSENGER SERVICE DIRECTORY

STEAM PASSENGER SERVICE DIRECTORY

STEAM PASSENGER SERVICE DIRECTORY

STEAM PASSENGER SERVICE DIRECTORY

STEAM PASSENGER SERVICE DIRECTORY
1997 GUEST COUPONS

NATIONAL RAILROAD MUSEUM
AND HALL OF FAME, INC.
With coupon: 10% off
Valid April 1997 through March 1998

NEW YORK TRANSIT MUSEUM
Regular price: Adults $3, children $1.50
With coupon: Adults $1.50, children $.75
Valid April 1997 through March 1998

NORTH CAROLINA
TRANSPORTATION MUSEUM
Regular price: Adults $4/$3.50; children $3/$2.50
With coupon: Adults $3.50/$3.00 children $2.50/$2.00
Valid April 1997 through March 1998
Maximum discount 4 persons per coupon

NORTHERN PACIFIC DEPOT
RAILROAD MUSEUM
Regular price: Adults $2, seniors $1.50 children $1
With coupon: Adults $1.50, seniors $1.00, children $.50
Valid April 1997 through March 1998
Maximum discount 2 persons per coupon

NORTHWEST RAILWAY MUSEUM
Regular price: Adults $6, seniors (62 & over) $5, children $4
With coupon: Child free with one adult purchase
Valid April 1997 through March 1998
Maximum discount 1 person per coupon

NOSTALGIA STATION TOY & TRAIN MUSEUM
Regular price: Adults $3, children $1.50
With coupon: Adults $2.50, children $1.00
Valid April 1997 through March 1998
Maximum discount 4 persons per coupon

OIL CREEK & TITUSVILLE RAILROAD
Regular price: Adults $9, seniors $8, children $5
With coupon: Adults $8, seniors $7, children $4
Valid April 1997 through March 1998
Maximum discount 6 persons per coupon

OLD COLONY & FALL RIVER
RAILROAD MUSEUM
Regular price: Adults $1.50, children $.75
With coupon: Adults $1.00, children $.50
Valid April 1997 through March 1998
Maximum discount 4 persons per coupon

OLD PUEBLO TROLLEY
Regular price: Adults $1, children $.50
With coupon: Adults $.50, children $.25
Valid April 1997 through March 1998
Maximum discount 2 persons per coupon

ORANGE EMPIRE RAILWAY MUSEUM
Regular price: Adults $6, children $4
With coupon: Adults $5, children $4
Valid April 1997 through March 1998
Maximum discount 4 persons per coupon

OSCEOLA & ST. CROIX VALLEY RAILWAY
Regular price: Adults $11, children $7
With coupon: Adults $10, children $6
Valid April 1997 through March 1998
Maximum discount 4 persons per coupon

PARK LANE MODEL RAILROAD MUSEUM
Regular price: Adults $3.50, children $1.75
With coupon: Adults $2.50, children $1.25
Valid April 1997 through March 1998
Maximum discount good for entire family or group

STEAM PASSENGER SERVICE DIRECTORY

STEAM PASSENGER SERVICE DIRECTORY

STEAM PASSENGER SERVICE DIRECTORY

STEAM PASSENGER SERVICE DIRECTORY

STEAM PASSENGER SERVICE DIRECTORY

STEAM PASSENGER SERVICE DIRECTORY

STEAM PASSENGER SERVICE DIRECTORY

STEAM PASSENGER SERVICE DIRECTORY

STEAM PASSENGER SERVICE DIRECTORY

STEAM PASSENGER SERVICE DIRECTORY

STEAM PASSENGER SERVICE DIRECTORY

STEAM PASSENGER SERVICE DIRECTORY

STEAM PASSENGER SERVICE DIRECTORY
1997 GUEST COUPONS

PIKES PEAK HISTORICAL STREET RAILWAY FOUNDATION, INC.
Regular price: Adults $2, children $1
With coupon: Adults $1.50, children $.75
Valid April 1997 through March 1998
Maximum discount 1 person per coupon

PRAIRIE VILLAGE
Regular price: Adults $5, children $2
With coupon: Adults $4, children $1
Valid April 1997 through March 1998
Maximum discount 2 persons per coupon

RAILROAD MEMORIES MUSEUM
Regular price: Adults $3, children $.50
With coupon: Adults $2.50, children $.25
Valid April 1997 through March 1998
Maximum discount 2 persons per coupon

THE RAILROAD MUSEUM OF SOUTH FLORIDA, INC.
Regular price: Adults $2.50, children age 3 and under are free.
With coupon: Adults $2
Excludes Valentine, Halloween and Holiday Express trains.
Valid April 1997 through March 1998
Maximum discount 4 persons per coupon

RAILROAD & PIONEER MUSEUM
Regular price: Adults $2, senior $1, children $1
With coupon: $1 admission
Valid April 1997 through March 1998
Maximum discount unlimited

RAILSWEST RAILROAD MUSEUM & HO MODEL RAILROAD
Regular price: Adults $2.50, children $1.25
With coupon: Adults $2, children $1
Valid April 1997 through March 1998
Maximum discount 2 persons per coupon

ROARING CAMP & BIG TREES RAILROAD
Regular price: Adults $13.50, Children $9.75
With coupon: Adults $12.15, Children $8.78
Valid April 1997 through March 1998
Maximum discount 4 persons per coupon

SALAMANCA RAIL MUSEUM
With coupon: 10% discount in gift shop
Valid April 1997 through March 1998

SANTA FE DEPOT MUSEUM AND HISTORIC CENTER
Regular price: Adults $2, children $.50
With coupon: Adults $1.50, children $.25
Valid April 1997 through March 1998
Maximum discount 4 persons per coupon

SANTA FE SOUTHERN RAILWAY
Regular price: Adults $21
With coupon: Adults $19
Valid April 1997 through March 1998
Maximum discount 2 persons per coupon

SEMINOLE GULF RAILWAY
Regular price: Adults $11, children $6
With coupon: Two adult admissions $18 or two adults and two children $20 (plus tax)
Valid April 1997 through March 1998

SHORE LINE TROLLEY MUSEUM
Regular price: Adults $5, seniors $4, children $2
With coupon: Adults $4.50, seniors $3.50, children $1.50
Valid April 1997 through March 1998
Maximum discount 6 persons per coupon

STEAM PASSENGER SERVICE DIRECTORY

STEAM PASSENGER SERVICE DIRECTORY

STEAM PASSENGER SERVICE DIRECTORY

STEAM PASSENGER SERVICE DIRECTORY

STEAM PASSENGER SERVICE DIRECTORY

STEAM PASSENGER SERVICE DIRECTORY

STEAM PASSENGER SERVICE DIRECTORY

STEAM PASSENGER SERVICE DIRECTORY

STEAM PASSENGER SERVICE DIRECTORY

STEAM PASSENGER SERVICE DIRECTORY

STEAM PASSENGER SERVICE DIRECTORY

STEAM PASSENGER SERVICE DIRECTORY

STEAM PASSENGER SERVICE DIRECTORY
1997 GUEST COUPONS

SMITH FALLS RAILWAY MUSEUM
Regular price: Adults $2, children free
With coupon: Adults $1.50, children free
Valid April 1997 through March 1998
Maximum discount 1 person per coupon

SONOMA TRAIN TOWN RAILROAD
Regular price: Adults $3.50, children $2.50
With coupon: Adults $1.75, children $1.25
Valid April 1997 through March 1998
Maximum discount unlimited

STEAMTOWN NATIONAL HISTORIC SITE
With coupon: 10% off any book purchase
Valid April 1997 through March 1998
Maximum discount one purchase per coupon

TENNESSEE CENTRAL RAILWAY MUSEUM
Regular price: Adults $24, children $15
With coupon: Adults $22, children $13
Valid April 1997 through March 1998
Maximum discount 4 persons per coupon

TENNESSEE VALLEY RAILROAD
Regular price: Adults $8.50, children $4.50
With coupon: Adults $8, children $4
Valid April 1997 through March 1998
Maximum discount 6 persons per coupon

TIOGA CENTRAL RAILROAD
Regular price: Adults $10, children (6-12) $5
With coupon: Adults $9, children (6-12) $4
Valid April 1997 through March 1998
Maximum discount 10 persons per coupon

TOY TRAIN DEPOT
Regular price: Adults $2, children $1.50
With coupon: Adults $1.50, children $1
Valid April 1997 through March 1998
Maximum discount 2 persons per coupon

THE TROLLEY MUSEUM OF NEW YORK
Regular price: Adults $3, children $1
With coupon: Adults $1.50, children $.50
Valid April 1997 through March 1998
Maximum discount 8 persons per coupon

TRAINLAND USA
Regular price: Adults $3.50, children $1.50
With coupon: Adults $2.50, children $1
Valid April 1997 through March 1998
Maximum discount 4 persons per coupon

VALLEY VIEW MODEL RAILROAD
Regular price: Adults $4, children $2
With coupon: Adults $3, children $1.50
Valid April 1997 through March 1998
Maximum discount 5 persons per coupon

VIRGINIA & TRUCKEE RAILROAD
Regular price: Adults $4.50, children $2.25
With coupon: Adults $4, children $2
Valid April 1997 through March 1998
Maximum discount 6 persons per coupon

WEST COAST RAILWAY HERITAGE PARK
Regular price: Adults $5, children $4
With coupon: Adults $4, children $3
Valid April 1997 through March 1998
Maximum discount 4 persons per coupon

STEAM PASSENGER SERVICE DIRECTORY   STEAM PASSENGER SERVICE DIRECTORY

STEAM PASSENGER SERVICE DIRECTORY   STEAM PASSENGER SERVICE DIRECTORY

STEAM PASSENGER SERVICE DIRECTORY   STEAM PASSENGER SERVICE DIRECTORY

STEAM PASSENGER SERVICE DIRECTORY   STEAM PASSENGER SERVICE DIRECTORY

STEAM PASSENGER SERVICE DIRECTORY   STEAM PASSENGER SERVICE DIRECTORY

STEAM PASSENGER SERVICE DIRECTORY   STEAM PASSENGER SERVICE DIRECTORY

STEAM PASSENGER SERVICE DIRECTORY
1997 GUEST COUPONS

WEST SHORE RAIL EXCURSIONS
Regular price: Adults $7.50/$9.50, children $4.00/$5.00
With coupon: Adults $6.50/$8.50, children $3.00/$4.00
Valid April 1997 through March 1998
Maximum discount 1 person per coupon

WEST VIRGINIA NORTHERN RAILROAD
Regular price: Adults $10, seniors $8, children $5
With coupon: Adults $9, seniors $7, children $7
Valid April 1997 through March 1998
Maximum discount 4 persons per coupon

WHITEWATER VALLEY RAILROAD
Regular price: Adults $11, children $5
With coupon: Adults $10
Valid April 1997 through March 1998
Maximum discount 4 persons per coupon

WILLAMETTE SHORE TROLLEY
Regular price: Adults $5, children $3
With coupon: 10% discount on rides and purchases in gift shop
Valid April 1997 through March 1998
Maximum discount 1 family per coupon

YOLO SHORTLINE RAILROAD COMPANY
Regular price: Adults $13, children $8
With coupon: Adults $11, children $7
Valid April 1997 through March 1998
Maximum discount 8 persons per coupon

LOMITA RAILROAD MUSEUM
Regular price: Adults $1, children $.50
With coupon: Adults $.50
Valid April 1997 through March 1998
Maximum discount 1 person per coupon

MID-CONTINENT RAILWAY MUSEUM
Regular price: Adults $8, children $4.50
With coupon: Adults $7, children $3.50
Valid April 1997 through March 1998
Maximum discount 4 persons per coupon

NEW YORK & LAKE ERIE RAILROAD
Regular price: Adults $9, children $4
With coupon: Adults $8, children $3.50
Valid April 1997 through March 1998

HIGH SPRINGS STATION MUSEUM, INC.
Regular price: Adults $3, children $2
With coupon: Adults $2, children $1
Valid April 1997 through March 1998
Maximum discount 6 persons per coupon

WALKERSVILLE SOUTHERN RAILROAD
Regular price: Adults $6.50, children $3.50
With coupon: Adults $5.50, children $2.50
Valid April 1997 through March 1998
Maximum discount 4 persons per coupon

GALVESTON RAILROAD MUSEUM
Regular price: Adults $5, seniors $4.50, children $2.50
With coupon: Adults $4, seniors $3.50, children $1.50
Valid April 1997 through March 1998
Maximum discount 4 persons per coupon

HOBO RAILROAD
Regular price: Adults $8, children $5.50
With coupon: Adults $7, children $4.50
Valid April 1997 through March 1998
Maximum discount 1 person per coupon

STEAM PASSENGER SERVICE DIRECTORY

STEAM PASSENGER SERVICE DIRECTORY

STEAM PASSENGER SERVICE DIRECTORY

STEAM PASSENGER SERVICE DIRECTORY

STEAM PASSENGER SERVICE DIRECTORY

STEAM PASSENGER SERVICE DIRECTORY

STEAM PASSENGER SERVICE DIRECTORY

STEAM PASSENGER SERVICE DIRECTORY

STEAM PASSENGER SERVICE DIRECTORY

STEAM PASSENGER SERVICE DIRECTORY

STEAM PASSENGER SERVICE DIRECTORY

STEAM PASSENGER SERVICE DIRECTORY

MINNESOTA ZEPHYR LIMITED
Diesel, scheduled
Standard gauge

MINNESOTA ZEPHYR LIMITED

Ride/Operation: The *Minnesota Zephyr* dining train steeps passengers in the ambience of 1940s railroad travel. The 3 1/2-hour journey begins on the Stillwater & St. Paul Railroad, built more than 120 years ago and later acquired by the Northern Pacific Railroad. The 7-mile line first parallels the St. Croix River, then swings west through Dutchtown along scenic Brown's Creek, climbing 250 feet on grades up to 2.2 percent. The tracks pass open fields to the Oak Glen Country Club, the summit area, then head onward to Duluth Junction. The *Zephyr* stops at the junction to prepare for the return to Stillwater.

Displays/Exhibits: Stillwater Depot, which opened in 1993, features displays about the history of Stillwater and the logging and rail industry.

Train: Two 1951 diesel-electric engines: No. 788, a 1750-horsepower FP9, and No. 787, a 1500-horsepower F7; five dining cars.

Schedule: Monday-Saturday, 7:30 p.m; Sunday and afternoon trips, 12:00 p.m. Call for more information on afternoon excursions and group charters.

Fare: $56.50 for excursion and dinner. Reservations required. Call for group/charter prices.

Locomotives: FP9 No. 788, 1750-horsepower diesel; FP7 No. 787, 1500-horsepower diesel.

Passenger Cars: Two dome cars; "The Grand Dome" was built in 1938 and refurbished in 1954 by the Southern Pacific Railroad. Five dining cars; "The Northern Winds" was built in 1949.

Note: Semiformal attire requested.

Location: Follow Highway 36 east from the Twin Cities to Stillwater. Boarding for the *Zephyr* is at the Stillwater Depot at 601 North Main Street.

Contact: David L. Paradeau

Mailing Address:
601 North Main Street
P.O. Box 573
Stillwater, MN 55082
Telephone: (612) 430-3000
(800) 992-6100

LAKE COUNTY HISTORY & RAILROAD MUSEUM

Displays/Exhibits: The "3-Spot," former Duluth & Iron Range 2-6-0 No. 3, the first engine on the D&IR; a 2-8-8-4, former D&IR No. 229; a 1907 D&IR depot with exhibits relating to the early railroad, logging, and shipping history of the area. Visitors can also see the *Edna G.*, the last coal-fired tug on the Great Lakes; ore-loading docks; and Great Lakes ore boats.

Schedule: Daily, mid-May through mid-October, 9:00 a.m.-5:00 p.m.
Admission: Adults $2.00, children (7-12) $1.00, 11 and under are free.

Location: One block from the 1st Avenue shopping area. Turn off 7th Avenue (highway 61) at Waterfront Drive and head towards the lake.

Contact: Business Manager

Mailing Address:
P.O. Box 313
Two Harbors, MN 55616
Telephone: (218) 834-4898

SMOKY HILL RAILWAY
Diesel, scheduled
Standard gauge

SMOKY HILL RAILWAY

Ride/Operation: A 5-mile, 45-minute round trip on former Frisco trackage from downtown Belton, Missouri, through scenic farmland along the western Missouri high ridge. The line was constructed in 1871 by the Kansas City, Osceola & Southern; the Frisco acquired the railroad in 1921 to gain access to Kansas City. The line parallels the old Kansas City, Clinton & Springfield ("The Leaky Roof") right-of-way. The Smoky Hill Railway is approximately five miles south of the original Santa Fe Trail.

Displays/Exhibits: Two static steam locomotives; operating diesel-electric locomotive, freight and passenger cars from Midwestern railroads. A collection of refrigerator cars shows their development from all-wood to all-steel.

Train: 1956 former Baltimore and Ohio GP-9, No. 102; 1920 former Erie, Delaware & Lackawanna open-window coach, No. 4364; 1972 former Missouri Pacific wide vision cupola caboose, No. 13562.

Schedule: Weekends, May 4-October 31, train departs 2:00 p.m., tickets available 1:00 p.m. Group specials available by reservation on weekends and weekdays. Call or write for info.

Fare: Adults $5.75, senior citizens (55+) $5.25, children (under 13) $4.50, free for under 3 in parent's lap. Group rates available.

Locomotives: No. 5, 1923 Alco 2-8-0, former Okmulgee Northern; No. 1632, 1918 Baldwin "Russian" 2-10-0, former Frisco; No. 630, 1941 EMD E6, former Rock Island *Rocket*; No. 102, 1956 EMD GP9, former Baltimore Ohio.

Passenger Cars: Heavyweight business car No. 3, "Oklahoma," former Frisco; 1920 open-window coach No. 4364, former Erie-Lackawanna; 1920 heavyweight parlor car "City of Peru," former *Wabash Cannonball*; heavyweight baggage car No. 873, former Wabash; heavyweight RPO-baggage car No. 6, former Chicago Great Western; heavyweight observation-instruction car No. 80, former Santa Fe; 1940 tavern-lounge-observation car No. 55, "Hospitality"; former Kansas City Southern "Southern Belle."

Rolling Stock/Equipment: Variety of equipment including a caboose, tank, refrigerator and box cars.

Special Events: Many special events, call or write for specific information.

Location: 502 Walnut. 9 miles south on 71 Hwy. from Interchanges of I-435, I-470 and 71 Highway.

Contact: Manager of Passenger Services

Mailing Address:
502 Walnut Street
Belton, MO 64012-2516
Recorded Telephone: (816) 331-0630

STAN GAYUSKI

Ride/Operation: This railway operates a 40-mile, 1 3/4-hour round trip through the Ozark foothills over the former Missouri Pacific White River Route, now owned by the Missouri & North Arkansas Railroad. Most trips take passengers south into Arkansas, across Lake Taneycomo and two high trestles and through two tunnels. Branson, home to three theme parks and 36 theaters featuring many well-known stars, is known as the live-entertainment capital of the country.

Displays/Exhibits: The original 1906 Branson depot houses the railway's ticket office, waiting room, gift shop, and business offices.

Train: Luxury dome cars, lounge cars, and coaches, air-conditioned and heated.

Schedule: March 12-30, Wednesday-Saturday, 9:00 & 11:30 a.m., 2:00 p.m. March 31-May 24, Monday-Saturday, 9:00 & 11:30 a.m., 2:00 p.m. and Dinner Train, Saturday, 5:00 p.m. May 25-August 31, daily, 9:00 & 11:30 a.m., 2:00 & 5:00 p.m. October 1-November 1, daily, 9:00 & 11:30 a.m., 2:00 & 5:00 p.m. November 5-December 20, Wednesday-Saturday, 9:00 & 11:30 a.m., 2:00 p.m. and Dinner Train, Saturday, 5:00 p.m. Closed Thanksgiving Day.

Fare: Adults $18.50, senior citizens (55+) $17.50, student (14-18) $13.50, children (4-12) $8.75. Group rates available for parties of 15 or more; please call or write for information. Fares subject to change without notice.

Locomotives: No. 83, F9PH, BSR, former B & O Railroad; No. 4265, GP30M, BSR, former B & O Railroad.

Passenger Cars: Dome-lounge-coach "Silver Garden," dome-lounge-coach "Silver Castle," dome-lounge dining "Silver Island," all former CB&Q; tavern-lounge-observation "Westport," former Atlantic Coast Line; 60-seat coach No. 461, former Texas & Pacific; 50-seat coach "Mohave," former Santa Fe Railroad; 32-seat buffet-lounge No. 8703, renamed "City of Branson" former Pennsylvania Railroad.

Location: 206 East Main Street in historic downtown Branson, 3/4 mile east of U.S. 65. Branson is 40 miles south of Springfield.

Kansas City, St.Louis

Mailing Address:
206 East Main Street
Branson, MO 65616

Telephone:
Tickets and schedules: (417) 334-6110
(800) 2-TRAIN-2
Business info:
Sharon Thompson, (417) 336-2895

SIX FLAGS OVER MID-AMERICA
Steam, scheduled
36" gauge

SIX FLAGS OVER MID-AMERICA

Ride/Operation: The narrow-gauge Six Flags Railroad was built and first operated in 1971. It consists of one 25-ton steam locomotive, a tender, four passenger cars, and a caboose. The engine is a propane-fueled steam locomotive manufactured by Crown Metal Company.

Schedule: Runs continuously around park, stopping at two stations.

Fare/Admission: Park admission required.

Locomotive: One 25-ton narrow-gauge steam locomotive.

Passenger Cars: Open.

Rolling Stock/Equipment: One enclosed caboose.

Location: I-44 and Allentown Road, west of St. Louis.

 St. Louis

Contact: John Donnelly
Operations Supervisor

Mailing Address:
P.O. Box 60
Eureka, MO 63025
Telephone: (314) 938-5300

**Missouri, Glencoe
(Wildwood, MO)
R**

WABASH FRISCO & PACIFIC RAILWAY
"THE UNCOMMON CARRIER"

*Steam, scheduled
12" gauge*

WASHINGTON MISSOURIAN

Ride/Operation: The WF&P, founded in 1939, moved to its present location in 1961. The ride is a 2-mile, 30-minute round trip over a former Missouri Pacific right-of-way along the scenic Meramec River, upgrade through wooded areas and across three bridges. Despite its small size, the railroad is authentically operated. Standard crossing signals protect a street crossing in downtown Glencoe. Fourteen regularly scheduled departures are possible via radio-dispatched, two-train operations using three locomotives, with meets at either Bluffs, one-quarter mile out of Glencoe, or Mohan, one-half mile out. The WF&P is visited regularly by tourists from all nations. An eastward extension of an additional mile is planned.

Train: Passenger cars; wooden-benched flatcars; equal to two eight-car trains. Engine 300 re-entered service after 14 years.

Schedule: Sundays only, May 5-October 27, 11:15 a.m.-4:15 p.m.

Fare: $2.00, children under 3 ride free. No reservations accepted!

Locomotives: No. 102, 1983 Peoria, IL, 2-6-2 (coal); No. 171, 1907 Elgin, IL, 4-4-0 (coal); No. 180, 1922 4-4-0 (coal); No. 300, 1958 Alton, IL, 4-4-2 (oil); No. 350, 1959 Plainfield, IL, 4-4-4 (coal); No. 400, 1925 Shalford, United Kingdom, CPR prototype 4-6-2 (oil); No. 434, 1955 Wichita, KS, 4-6-4 (oil); No. 802, 1982 Wood River, IL, SW-11 (gasoline); No. X-41, 1945 Berkeley, Missouri, 5-horsepower 0-4-0 (gas); No. 82, 1992 rebuilt Pacific, MO, 11-horsepower "B-B" (gas); No. 5205, 1992 Bel-Ridge, MO, 22-horsepower "A" unit (gas); Alco FA style "diesel"; No. 92, 1992 rebuilt TB-11.

Passenger Cars: Seven pasenger cars plus (new in 1995) six passenger gondolas each painted and lettered as "fallen flags" of St. Louis area. The fleet of 35 cars includes 13 flats, 9 gondolas, tank, box and 2 cabooses; two vehicles were built by full-sized railroads: 1950 gondola No. 51999, former Frisco (Springfield, Missouri, shops); and 1946 aluminum hopper No. 301, former Missouri Pacific (Sedalia, Missouri, shops).

Special Events: Member's Weekend in the fall.

Note: Train operation at nearby Eureka, where the main lines of the Union Pacific and the Burlington Northern railroads parallel each other.

Location: Halfway between Eureka and Ellisville, about 25 miles west of St. Louis. Take exit 264 (Eureka) off I-44, travel 3.5 miles north on route 109 to Old State Road, and make two right turns to the depot on Washington Street-Grand Avenue.

♿ (accomodated) P ✳ ☕ 🪑 (nearby)

M ▶ ◀ 🖱 Kirkwood

Radio Frequency: 151.955

Contact: David J. Neubauer
President, Operations & Publicity
Mailing Address:
1569 Ville Angela Lane
Hazelwood, MO 63042-1630
Telephone: (recorded message)
(314) 587-3538

ST. LOUIS, IRON MOUNTAIN & SOUTHERN RAILWAY

Steam, scheduled
Standard gauge

Ride/Operation: Steam-powered train takes passengers on their choice of three different round trips over a former Missouri Pacific branch line: a 10-mile, 1 1/4-hour sightseeing trip to Gordonville; a 20-mile, 2-hour dinner trip to Dutchtown; or a 36-mile, 4-hour Murder Mystery trip to Delta with dinner catered on board.

Train: Two 1920 steel coaches, former Illinois Central; former Missouri Pacific cupola caboose; former New York Central Pullman.

Schedule: April-October: Gordonville trip: Saturday, 11:00 a.m. & 2:00 p.m.; Sunday, 1:00 p.m., Summer: add Wednesday & Friday, 1:00 p.m. Delta train: April thru October (once a month) on Saturday, 5:00 p.m. Dutchtown trip (dinner train), Saturday, 5:00 p.m. Group rates and weekday charters available. Breakfast trains and candlelight dinners also.

Fare: Adults $10.00, children (3-12) $5.00, children (2 & under) free. Dinner Train $22.00. Murder Mystery: $34.50. Air Conditioned Coach $2.00 extra.

Locomotives: No. 5, 1946 Porter 2-4-2, former Central Illinois Public Service, former Crab Orchard & Egyptian; No. 300, 1926 Alco 2-6-0, former Augusta Railway; No. 911, 1952 Baldwin-Lima-Hamilton diesel-electric, former Pittsburg Plate Glass Co.; 1949 14-inch-gauge live-steam 4-6-4.

Rolling Stock/Equipment: Open-air observation car (former piggyback car); two bay-window cabooses.

Special Events: Murder Mysteries, twice monthly. Candlelight Dinner, February 14 & 15. James Gang Robberies, twice monthly. Fall Foliage Breakfasts, October. Santa Express, November 29-30, December 7, 14 & 21. New Year's Eve Murder Mystery, December 31. Many more, call or write for specifics.

Location: Take I-55 to Exit 99, west on Hwy. 61, 4 miles to Intersection of Highway 61 & 25.

Carbondale, IL and Poplar Bluff, MO

Radio Frequencies: 160.845, 161.070

Contact: Teresa Brown
Manager

Mailing Address:
P.O. Box 244
Jackson, MO 63755
Telephone: (573) 243-1688

PATEE HOUSE MUSEUM
Railway museum

COURTESY OF PATEE HOUSE MUSEUM

Displays/Exhibits: A communications and transportation museum with exhibits including an 1860 Hannibal & St. Joseph steam locomotive and a Railway Post Office, invented by a St. Joseph postmaster to speed the mail on the Pony Express. The train is inside, beside the 1877 depot from Union Star, Missouri. Patee House, opened by John Patee in 1858 as a 140-room luxury hotel. The hotel is a National Historical Landmark, having served as a Pony Express headquarters in 1860. The museum also houses antique cars, trucks, fire trucks, telephones, radios, and furniture. Inside are the "Streets of Old St. Jo," antique buggies and wagons, and a 1920s service station.

Admission: Adults $3.00, seniors $2.50, students (under 18) $1.50.

Locomotives: Baldwin 4-4-0.

Rolling Stock/Equipment: 1960 Pacific track-maintenance motor car, former Union Pacific; 1860 Railway Post Office.

Special Events: Pony Express rerun between St. Joseph, Missouri, and Sacramento, California, the second and third weeks of June each year, in conjunction with the National Pony Express Association. Annual Jesse James Model Railroad Show, last week of June and first week of July.

Notes: Pony Express-Jesse James Weekend, 1st weekend in April, commemorates the start of the Pony Express April 3, 1860, and the death of Jesse James April 3, 1882, whose home is located next door.

Location: Five minutes from I-29, at 12th and Penn streets. Take U.S. 36 west to 10th Street exit, then travel 6 blocks north and 2 blocks east.

Contact: Gary Chilcote
Museum Director

Mailing Address:
Box 1022
St. Joseph, MO 64502
Telephone: (816) 232-8206

AMERICAN RAILWAY CABOOSE HISTORICAL
EDUCATIONAL SOCIETY, INC. (A.R.C.H.E.S.)

Cabooseum
Standard gauge

RICHARD A. EICHHORST

Displays/Exhibits: The Caboose Museum of A.R.C.H.E.S., Inc., has at least one of their twenty-five cabooses on display at any given time. While a permanent location is being planned the equipment is being stored at seven different sites in the Greater St. Louis area. A midtown St. Louis site is planned for 1997.

Focus: In addition to the interpretive center (Cabooseum) that is open to the public, A.R.C.H.E.S. is an international association with members in 31 states and Canada. The members are compiling a *Caboose Directory*, that will list the location of Cabooses in North American that are no longer in active service. Information on such locations will be appreciated. Individuals and organizations interested in Cabooses are welcome to participate.

Schedule: April 12, May 10, June 14, July 12, August 9, September 13 and October 11. Hours: 1:00-4:00 p.m. Other times by special arrangement.

Fare/Admission: Donation.

Cabooses: Alton & Southern, Baltimore & Ohio, Chesapeake & Ohio, Chicago & North Western, Chicago Great Western, Essex Terminal, Frisco, Illinois Central, Manufacturers, Norfolk & Western, Rock Island, Southern, T.R.R.A. and Union Pacific.

Special Events: Caboose Chili Cook-Off, Santa Claus Special and MetroLink, Caboose Chase Excursions and Rail Caboose Tours. These activities are sponsored by the American Association of Railroaders, Inc., as a benefit for the Cabooseum.

Location: Varies from month to month. Call or write for details.

Contact: Richard A. Eichhorst, President

Mailing Address:
P.O. Box 2772
St. Louis, MO 63116
Telephone: (314) 752-3148

MUSEUM OF TRANSPORTATION
Railway museum
Standard gauge

MUSEUM OF TRANSPORTATION

Displays/Exhibits: The Museum of Transportation has one of the largest and best collections of transportation vehicles in the world, according to John H. White, Jr., Curator Emeritus of the Smithsonian Institution. More than seventy locomotives on the grounds, from ancient 4-4-0s to the 1969 Union Pacific Centennial 6944. Collection includes the Frisco 1522 operational steam locomotive. Also passenger and freight cars, automobiles, trucks, streetcars, buses, etc.

Schedule: Daily, 9:00 a.m.-5:00 p.m. Closed Thanksgiving, Christmas, and New Year's Day.

Admission: Adults $4.00, senior citizens (65+) $1.50, children (5-12) $1.50.

Locomotives/Trolleys: Thirty-five steam locomotives including 1858 4-4-0 "Daniel Nason"; 1889 Black Diamond 2-2-2, former Reading; 4-6-0 No. 173, former Baltimore & Ohio; and 4-8-8-4 No. 4006, former Union Pacific. Twenty-eight internal-combustion locomotives, including EMD FT No.103 No. 50, former B&O; Centennial No. 6944, former UP; and gas-turbine No. 1149, former U.S. Army. Nine electric locomotives, including General Electric No. 1; No. 113, former New York Central; and P5 No. 4700, former Pennsylvania Railroad. Thirty interurbans, including an 1889 mule-drawn streetcar; test car No. 2611; No. 890, former St. Louis; and railbus No. 206, former Illinois Terminal.

Passenger Cars: Twenty-three, including parlor car, former Gulf, Mobile & Ohio; Pullman Colonial No. 94; No. A-252, former Mississippi Central; observation car No. 750, former Missouri Pacific.

Rolling Stock/Equipment: Fifty-four pieces, including poultry palace car; vinegar car No. 1634, GAT No. 96500; and composite gondola, former Chicago, Burlington & Quincy.

Location: From I-270, exit at Dougherty Ferry Road, turn west and go 1 mile to Barrett Station Road, the Museum entrance will be on the right.

Kirkwood

Contact: Wayne Schmidt
Director

Mailing Address:
3015 Barrett Station Road
St. Louis, MO 63122
Telephone: (314) 965-7998

COLLECTION OF DONALD J. WIRTH, FRANK ARDREY

Ride/Operation: Periodic mainline steam operations.

Displays/Exhibits: The 1522 is usually on display at the Museum of Transportation. During operation it is on display at overnight stops and various locations on the route of travel.

Schedule: Schedules vary and are determined by the host railroad or trip sponsor.

Fare/Admission: St. Louis Steam Train Association: free. Museum of Transportation: charges admission to view its exhibits.

Locomotives/Trolleys: Frisco 1522, the only operational Mountain type (4-8-2) steam locomotive in the United States. Built in May 1926 by Baldwin Locomotive Works, it logged over one million miles before its retirement in 1951. Restoration began in 1985 and was completed in 1988.

Rolling Stock/Equipment: A former ICRR water car; a crew car, the "Firefly," a former Milwaukee Road baggage/dorm; and the "Black Gold," a former NP baggage car, were also restored by the association.

Special Events: The 1522 pulled an excursion to the 1994 NRHS convention in Atlanta, GA; it participated in the HBO movie *Truman*; made a whistle stop tour across Iowa in 1995; appeared at Topeka, KS "Railroad Days" and has journeyed to Galesburg, IL 3 times, plus other trips.

Location: See listing for the Museum of Transportation in St. Louis, MO.

St. Louis or Kirkwood

Contact: Frank E. Willis
Membership Services

Mailing Address:
1901 Mistflower Glen Court
Chesterfield, MO 63005-4317

FRISCO RAILROAD MUSEUM
Railway museum
Standard gauge

FRISCO RAILROAD MUSEUM

Displays/Exhibits: This museum, located at station 238 on the Frisco's former Lebanon Subdivision, Eastern Division, is housed in a building originally constructed by the Frisco Railway in 1943 as a Centralized Traffic Control command center. It is the only facility in the country devoted exclusively to the preservation and display of the history and memorabilia of the Frisco Railway. The facility displays more than 2,000 items of Frisco and Frisco-related memorabilia, representing a wide range of operations, equipment, and services. In addition, it has the largest archive of historical, technical, and photographic information about the Frisco currently available to the public through its "Frisco Folks" membership program.

Schedule: Tuesday-Saturday, 10:00 a.m.-5:00 p.m.

Admission: Adults $2.00, children (under 12) $1.00. Group discounts available.

Rolling Stock/Equipment: Caboose No. 1159, boxcar No. 10055, side-door caboose No. 1156, 1551 diner-lounge "Oklahoma City" available for meetings, banquets, parties, special events. All former Frisco.

Special Events: Frisco Days, April. Christmas Open House, featuring large collection of train-related Christmas ornaments, two weeks before Christmas.

Note: Frisco steam locomotive No. 4254 is on display in a city park near the museum.

Location: At 543 East Commercial Street. Take exit 80 A/B off I-44, travel south on business 65 1.3 miles to Commercial Street (third light), then travel west 1.3 miles.

Contact: Alan Schmitt
President

Mailing Address:
543 East Commercial Street
Springfield, MO 65803
Telephone: (417) 866-SLSF (7573)
E-mail: Amunhotep@AOL.COM
Internet: http://www.crl.com/~acorley/frisco/frisco.html

WILLIAM W. KRATVILLE

Ride/Operation: Passengers take a guided, 2-1/2 mile, 30-minute trip through the zoo grounds, seeing hundreds of rare and endangered species.

Displays/Exhibits: Omaha's Henry Doorly Zoo offers the Scott Kingdoms of the Seas Aquarium. The 71,000 square foot aquarium features king penguins, sharks and thousands of fish. A zig-zag viewing tube gives visitors the sensation of walking on the ocean floor, surrounded by brightly-colored fish and menacing sharks.

The world's largest indoor rainforest grows just a seashell's toss away from the Aquarium. Tropical forests representing Asia, Africa and South America are home to 2,000 species of exotic plants and 125 species of animals.

An IMAX® 3-D Theater is opening in the spring of 1997.

Train: Weekends: No. 395-104, five open-air coaches, caboose. Weekdays: No. 119, four open-air coaches.

Schedule: Train: Daily, Memorial Day-Labor Day; weekends, April 1-May 31 and September 1-October 31; 11:00 a.m.-4:00 p.m. Zoo: Daily, year-round except Thanksgiving, Christmas and New Year's Day.

Fare/Admission: Train: Adults $2.50; children (3-11) $1.50; children under three ride free. Zoo: Admission is charged.

Locomotives: No. 395-104, 1890 Krauss 0-6-2T; No. 119, 1968 Crown 4-4-0, replica of Union Pacific 4-4-0 No. 119.

Passenger Cars: Five open-air coaches; caboose.

Rolling Stock/Equipment: Ballast maintainer; Fairmont MT14 motor car.

Special Events: Members' Day, with free train rides to zoo members. Halloween Terror Train during zoo-sponsored Halloween Party-children in costume ride free.

Location: Henry Doorly Zoo, 3701 South 10th Street.

Omaha

Contact: Cyndy T. Andrews

Mailing Address:
3701 South 10th Street
Omaha, NE 68107
Telephone: (402) 733-8401

197

UNION PACIFIC COLLECTION

Displays/Exhibits: All-new exhibits will tell the story of Union Pacific. Current exhibits include uniforms, china, model trains, and the construction of the railroad.

Schedule: Tuesday-Saturday, 10:00 a.m.-5:00 p.m.; Sunday 1:00-5:00 p.m. Closed Monday and major holidays.

Fare/Admission: Adults $3.00, seniors $2.50, children 5-12 $2.00.

Locomotives: No. 1243 Union Pacific.

Rolling Stock/Equipment: UP sleeping car National Command.

Special Events: Railroad Days.

Location: 801 South 10th Street.

  ♿ **P** ✳ 🏛 **M**

Omaha

Contact: Don Snoddy

Mailing Address: 1416 Dodge
Omaha, NE 68179
Telephone: (402) 271-3305
Fax: (402) 271-6460
E-mail: ddsnoddy@notes.up.com
Internet: http://www.uprr.com

GEORGE A. FORERO, JR.

Ride/Operation: A steam locomotive or motor car operates on weekends during the summer.

Displays/Exhibits: The museum owns more than sixty locomotives, passenger cars, and freight cars, including the largest collection of nineteenth-century railroad equipment in the country. Featured are thirty pieces from the famous Virginia & Truckee railroad, many seen in movies and on television. The museum also houses exhibits, photos, and artifacts of Nevada's railroad heritage. The state of Nevada owns an additional forty-seven pieces, stored in southern Nevada.

Schedule: Museum: Wednesday-Sunday, 8:30 a.m.-4:30 p.m. Steam train: selected weekends, May 25-September 2, plus October 19-20 and December 28-29; call or write for schedule. Motor car: weekends, May through September; call or write for schedule.

Fare/Admission: Museum: adults $2.00, children under 18 admitted free. Steam train: adults $2.50, children (6-11) $1.00, children under 6 ride free. Motor car: Adults $1.00, children (6-11) $.50, children under 6 ride free.

Locomotives: No. 25, 1905 Baldwin 4-6-0; No. 18, "Dayton," 1873 Central Pacific 4-4-0; and No. 22, "Inyo," 1875 Baldwin 4-4-0; all former V&T. No. 1, "Glenbrook," 1875 Baldwin narrow-gauge 2-6-0, former Carson & Tahoe Lumber & Fluming Co.; No. 8, 1888 Cooke 4-4-0, former Dardanelle & Russellville; No. 1, "Joe Douglass," 1882 Porter narrow gauge 0-4-2T, former Dayton, Sutro & Carson Valley.

Rolling Stock/Equipment: Coaches Nos. 3, 4, 8, 11, 12, 17 & 18, express/mail Nos. 14 & 21, caboose-coaches Nos. 9, 10 & 15, and eleven freight cars, all former V&T; French "40 & 8" boxcar; chair car No. 30, former Las Vegas & Tonopah; coaches Nos. 24 & 52, former Nevada-California-Oregon; narrow-gauge freight cars Nos. 4, 159 & 162, former Southern Pacific; baggage-mail-express No. 3, former Carson & Colorado; caboose No. 3, former Nevada Copper Belt; caboose

No. 402, former Tonopah & Tidewater; caboose No. 449, former Western Pacific; hopper No. 409, former Nevada Northern; motor car "Washoe Zephyr," former Tucson, Cornelia & Gila Bend No. 401.

Special Events: Virginia & Truckee Railroad History Symposium, October 24-26. Write or phone for current events.

Location: 2180 South Carson Street (highways 50 & 395) at the south end of town.

  P 🚌 ✳ ▶ ◀ **M**

🅰🆃 ll 🚂

Contact: Paul Lajti
Program Coordinator

Mailing Address:
Capitol Complex
Carson City, NV 89710
Telephone: (702) 687-6953

NEVADA NORTHERN RAILWAY MUSEUM
Steam, diesel, scheduled
Standard gauge

JACK SWANBERG

Ride/Operation: Keystone Route: A 14-mile, 1 1/2-hour round trip to the historic mining district of Keystone, passing downtown Ely, tunnel No. 1, the ghost town of Lane City, and Robinson Canyon. Highline Route: A 22-mile, 1 1/2-hour round trip with exciting overviews of the scenic Steptoe Valley, high in the foothills.

Displays/Exhibits: Steam, diesel, and electric locomotives; 1907 steam rotary snowplow; 1910 Jordan spreader; more than sixty pieces of antique passenger, freight, and work equipment; general offices; depot; machine shops; roundhouse.

Schedule: Museum: daily, May 25-September 1, 45-minute walking tours at 9:00 & 11:30 a.m. and 2:00 & 4:00 p.m. Steam excursions: May 25-26, June 8 & 22; July 4, 6-7, & 20, August 3-4, 17, & 31, September 1. Diesel excursions along the Highline Route depart at 5:30 p.m. Call for more information.

Fare/Admission: Museum: $2.50, children under 10 admitted free. Steam train: Adults $14.00, senior citizens & youths $12.00, children $6.00. Diesel trains: adults $10.00, senior citizens & youths $8.00, children $4.00. Group discounts and charters available.

Locomotives: No. 40, 1910 Baldwin 4-6-0, Nevada Northern Railway; No. 93, 1909 Alco 2-8-0; No. 105, Alco RS-2, and No. 109, Alco RS-3, both former Kennecott Copper Co.

Special Events: 1996 "Raildays," Labor Day weekend. Fireworks Train, July 4 (evening). Locomotive rental programs available.

Location: In eastern Nevada on U.S. 93; trains leave from the East Ely Depot at 1100 Avenue A at 11th Street East.

♿ P ☀ ☕ 📷 🚂
🎨(during Raildays) M ▶ ◀
ar ll TRAIN 🐊

Contact: Lorraine Gleave
Executive Director

Mailing Address:
P.O. Box 150040
East Ely, NV 89315
Telephone: (702) 289-2085

VIRGINIA & TRUCKEE RAILROAD CO.

Steam, scheduled
Standard gauge

VIRGINIA & TRUCKEE RAILROAD CO.

Ride/Operation: A 5-mile round trip from Virginia City to the town of Gold Hill through the heart of the historic Comstock mining region. A knowledgeable conductor gives a running commentary of the area and of the 126-year-old railroad.

Displays/Exhibits: 1888 Northwestern Pacific combine and coach; former Tonopah & Tidewater coach; former Northern Pacific caboose; No. 30, 1919 0-6-0, former Southern Pacific.

Train: Open car; two semiclosed cars.

Schedule: Daily, May 24-September 30; weekends, October; 10:30 a.m.-5:45 p.m. Cab rides available; inquire at ticket office.

Fare: Adults $4.50, children (5-12) $2.25, children under 4 ride free. All-day pass $9.00.

Locomotives: No. 29, 1916 Baldwin 2-8-0, former Longview, Portland & Northern; No. 8, 1907 Baldwin 2-6-2, former Hobart Southern.

Note: Special excursion and party trains available. Please call or write for details.

Location: At Washington and "F" Streets.

Contact: Robert C. Gray
President

Mailing Address:
P.O. Box 467
Virginia City, NV 89440
Telephone: (702) 847-0380

**HARTMANN
MODEL RAILROAD, LTD.**
Model railroad display

HARTMANN MODEL RAILROAD, LTD.

Displays/Exhibits: Housed in two buildings, each 8,000 square feet, is a railroad display for all ages. This site features many operating layouts, from G to Z scales, including a replica of Crawford Notch, New Hampshire, in the mid 1950s to early 1960s. Visitors can see several other detailed operating layouts with trains winding through tunnels, over bridges, and past miniature stations and buildings, and Thomas the Tank Engine operates by a light-sensor system. Also on display are about 5,000 model locomotives and coaches, American and European. New: Come and see our operating outdoor railroad and take a ride with us.

Schedule: Daily, 10:00 a.m.-5:00 p.m.

Admission: Adults $5.00, senior citizens $4.00, children (5-12) $3.00. Group rates available upon request.

Location: Corner Town Hall Road, Rte. 302/16 in Intervale (4 miles north of North Conway).

Contact: Roger Hartmann
President
or Nelly Hartmann
Vice President

Mailing Address:
P.O. Box 639
Jackson, NH 03846
Telephone: (603) 356-9922
Fax: (603) 356-9958

HOBO RAILROAD

Ride/Operation: A 1¼-hour train ride in a woodsy setting along the Pemigewasset River on former Boston & Maine track. On most trips passengers glimpse a variety of wildlife, including a golden eagle, ducks, a blue heron, beavers, and other small creatures. Passengers may also enjoy lunch or dinner on the train. The Hobo Picnic Lunch is a unique specialty, served in a souvenir hobo bindle stick. Fine dining is also offered on the 7:00 p.m. train aboard the "Cafe Lafayette," a restored Dome Pullman dining car.

Train: Open-platform coaches; dining car.

Schedule: Daily, May 27-late October; Wednesday-Sunday, 11:00 a.m., 1:00, 3:00, 5:00 & 7:00 p.m.; Monday & Tuesday, 11:00 a.m., 1:00, 3:00 & 5:00 p.m. As needed, mid March-May 29 & November 1-December 31; please call or write for information. Group tours available mid-March to December; call or write for more information.

Fare: Adults $8.00, children $5.50, children under 4 ride free. Food service priced separately. Reservations suggested for all trains.

Locomotives: No. 1008, 1949 Alco S-1, former Portland Terminal; No. 959, 1949 Alco S-1, former North Stratford.

Rolling Stock/Equipment: Four modified motors, former Erie & Lackawanna; modified Pullman day coach, former New York Central; two kitchen cars, former U.S. Army; several Budd cars; others.

Special Events: Easter Bunny Trains. Track Car. Fourth of July Family Party Train. Gold Panning, July & August. Halloween Specials, late October. Santa Trains, and others. Please call or write for details.

Note: Many unadvertised trains are operated. The Hobo Railroad is under the same ownership and management as the Winnipesaukee Scenic Railroad in Meredith, New Hampshire. The general office for both operations is in Lincoln.

Location: On Kancamagus Highway, in the heart of the scenic White Mountains. Take exit 32 off I-93.

Radio Frequencies: 160.47, 161.55

Contact: Eddie or Brenda Clark

Mailing Address:
P.O. Box 9
Lincoln, NH 03251
Telephone: (603) 745-2135

WHITE MOUNTAIN CENTRAL RAILROAD
Steam, scheduled
Standard gauge

GEORGE A. FORERO, JR.

Ride/Operation: A 2-mile, 30-minute ride through the scenic White Mountains, leaving from a beautiful depot at Clark's Trading Post. The train crosses a 120-foot covered bridge and climbs a 2-percent grade into the woods.

Displays/Exhibits: A facsimile of an 1890s railroad station, a wooden caboose, boxcars, and flat-cars. Other exhibits include trained bears; a fire museum; an Americana museum; a haunted house; an antique photo parlor; a 1920s-era garage; an illusion building, "Merlin's Mansion"; and much more.

Train: Climax steam locomotive; open excursion cars.

Schedule: Spring weekends, Memorial Day-June 23. Daily: June 29-Labor Day. Fall weekends only through October 14; six trains per day.

Fare: Adults $7.00, children (6-11) $6.00, children (3-5) $1.00, children under 3 ride free. Group discounts available.

Locomotives: No. 4, 1927 2-truck Heisler, former International Shoe Co.; No. 6, Climax, former Beebe River Railroad; No. 3, former East Branch & Lincoln.

Rolling Stock: Caboose; boxcar.

Location: On route 3, one mile north of North Woodstock.

Contact: W. Murray Clark
Vice President & Treasurer

Mailing Address:
Box 1
Lincoln, NH 03251
Telephone: (603) 745-8913

GEORGE A. FORERO, JR.

Ride/Operation: This line operates 1- and 2-hour excursions over former Boston & Maine track between Meredith and Lakeport. Passengers view unsurpassed scenery along the shores of New Hampshire's largest lake, Lake Winnipesaukee, in the comfort of climate-controlled coaches. Dining service is available during the summer, and the Ice Cream Parlor Car offers a make-your-own-sundae bar aboard the train. Fall foliage tours are 3-hour round trips to Plymouth.

Displays/Exhibits: An 1893 former B&M baggage car serves as the ticket office; cabooses and other rolling stock are also on exhibit.

Train: Diesel locomotives; coaches, former B&M, New Haven, and SEPTA.

Schedule: Daily, July 1-September 4; departures from Weirs at 11:00 a.m., 12:00, 1:00, 2:00, 3:00, 4:00 & 5:00 p.m.; departures from Meredith at 10:30 a.m., 12:30, 2:30 & 4:30 p.m., with a 6:30 p.m. dinner train on weekends. As needed, May 1-June 30 & September 5-October 31; please call or write for dates and information. Fall foliage: reservations required for fall foliage trips; please call or write for dates and information. Groups: please call or write for information.

Fare: One-hour trip: adults $7.50, children $6.50, children under 4 ride free. Two-hour trip: adults $7.50, children $6.50, under 4 ride free. Food service priced separately; reservations suggested for food service.

Locomotives: No. 2, 1943 44-ton General Electric, former U.S. Government; No. 1186, 1952 Alco S-3, former B&M.

Rolling Stock/Equipment: Five Budd RDC-1 coaches; 1893 baggage car, former B&M, serving as ticket office; cabooses; others.

Special Events: Track Car Weekend. Caboose Fun Trains. Others. Please call or write for details.

Note: Many unadvertised trains are operated. The Winnipesaukee Scenic Railroad is under the same ownership and management as the Hobo Railroad in Lincoln, New Hampshire. The general office for both operations is in Lincoln.

Location: In the Lakes Region of New Hampshire, with boarding at Meredith or Weirs Beach. Free parking at Meredith, just off route 3.

Radio Frequencies: 160.47, 161.55

Contact: Eddie or Brenda Clark
Mailing Address:
P.O. Box 9
Lincoln, NH 03251
Telephone:
Year-round **(603) 745-2135**
In season **(603) 279-5253**

**MOUNT WASHINGTON
RAILWAY CO.**
Steam, scheduled
4' 8" gauge (cog)

GEORGE A. FORERO, JR.

Ride/Operation: The world's first mountain-climbing railway, completed in 1869, is still 100-per-cent steam-powered. The train ascends New England's highest mountain on a breathtaking right-of-way with grades as steep as 37.41 percent. The average grade is 25 percent to the summit, elevation 6,288 feet.

Displays/Exhibits: "Old Peppersass," the world's first cog engine, on display at the Base Station; museum with historical exhibits.

Train: Open- or closed-platform coach.

Schedule: Daily, early May-October, on the hour from 8:00 a.m. Spring and fall schedules vary; call for information. Last train leaves three hours before sunset in summer. All trains are subject to cancellation because of weather conditions or lack of passengers.

Fare: Round trip: $35.00. Group rates available. Family rates and senior citizens' discounts available. Reservations recommended.

Passenger Cars: Four new wooden coaches have been built since 1990 by the Cog Railway shops.

Locomotives: Eight 0-2-2-0 cog-wheel locomotives with inclined boilers: six built by Manchester Locomotive Works, 1870-1908; No. 10, "Col. Teague," built in Mt. Washington shops, 1972; No. 8, constructed in the Cog Railway shops, placed in service in 1983.

Note: Historic Cog Railway video is available.

Location: Off U.S. route 302 east of Twin Mountain.

Contact: Charles Kenison
General Manager

Mailing Address:
Mount Washington, NH 03589
Telephone: (603) 278-5404
Advance ticket purchases:
(800) 922-8825

CONWAY SCENIC RAILROAD
Steam, scheduled
Standard gauge

LES MACDONALD

Ride/Operation: Train rides of varying duration from one hour originate at North Conway's historic 1874 Railroad Station. "Valley Train" travels south to Conway over former Boston & Maine Railroad branchline through farmlands in the Mount Washington Valley and west over former Maine Central Mountain Subdivision to Bartlett. "Notch Train" provides excursion service west from North Conway through spectacular Crawford Notch to Crawford Depot and Fabyan Station.

Displays/Exhibits: Museum of railroad memorabilia within the 123-year-old Victorian North Conway Station. Original Roundhouse and Operating Turntable highlight rail yard, where many pieces of rolling stock are displayed.

Train: "Valley Train" - restored coaches (open and closed), dining car, First Class 1898 Pullman Parlor-Observation Car. "Notch Train" refurbished coaches and Cafe Car. All equipment heated during cooler weather.

Schedule: "Valley Train" -Daily, May 17-October 26; weekends, April 19-May 11 & November 1-December 21 & November 28. Dining Car "Chocorua" available July thru late November. Please call for schedule of service. "Notch Train" - late June-October 17 (except Fridays & Sundays late June-September 10). Reservations suggested.

Fare: Valley Train: Adults from $8.00, children (4-12) from $5.50, children under 4 varies with destination. Notch Train: Adults from $31.95, children (4-12) from $16.95, under 4 from $4.95. Coach and first-class service available. Group and charter rates available on all excursions.

Locomotives: No. 7470, 1921 Grand Trunk 0-6-0, former Canadian National; No. 15, 1945 44-ton General Electric, former Maine Central; No. 1055, 1950 Alco-General Electric S-4, former Portland Terminal Co.; No. 4266, 1949 EMD F7, former Boston & Maine; No. 6505/6516, 1950 GMD FP9s, former CN/VIA Rail Canada; EMD GP7 #573, former Maine Central.

Passenger Cars: Restored wood and steel cars.

Special Events: Fall Railfan's Day, October 18. Spooky Express, October 31. "Santa Claus Express," December 6-7, 13-14, 20-21.

Location: The depot faces the village park. North Conway is on routes 16 and 302 in New Hampshire's Mount Washington Valley.

Boston, MA, or White River Jct., VT

Radio Frequency: 161.250

Contact: Russell G. Seybold
President & General Manager

Mailing Address:
P.O. Box 1947
North Conway, NH 03860
Telephone: (603) 356-5251

KLICKETY KLACK MODEL RAILROAD

Displays/Exhibits: This is the largest operating HO model railroad in New England. This railroad represents over 70,000 hours of work and is housed in a building that is 30 x 76 feet. Watch trains think for themselves as operating orders are received from the 3 color block signals; stopping on red, slowing down on yellow, or going through a green with no change of speed. This is called ATC (Automatic Train Control). Eight trains are operating simultaneously on the main lines. There are over 30 controls that you can operate. Equipment is from 1800s to present.

Schedule: July 1-September 2, Monday-Saturday, 10:00 a.m.-5:30 p.m. September 3-June 30, Thursday-Saturday, 10:00 a.m.-5:00 p.m. Closed the last week in April.

Admission: Adults $4.00, children (3-12) $3.00.

Location: At the junction of routes 28 and 109A.

Contact: Richard Parshley
Owner

Mailing Address:
P.O. Box 205
Wolfeboro Falls, NH 03896
Telephone: (603) 569-5384

NEW JERSEY MUSEUM
OF TRANSPORTATION
Steam, diesel, scheduled
36" gauge

GEORGE A. FORERO, JR.

Ride/Operation: This museum, which operates the Pine Creek Railroad at Allaire State Park, offers a 10-minute, 1 1/2-mile ride over a loop track.

Displays/Exhibits: A variety of narrow-gauge engines and cars either on display or being restored in the railroad shop. Allaire Park is the site of a restored early-1800s iron-making community.

Train: No. 502, 1902 open-platform wood coach, former Newfoundland Railway; No. 91155, 1874 wooden caboose, former Central of New Jersey; open excursion car.

Schedule: Steam: weekends & holidays, May–mid October. Diesel: weekdays, July & August. Trains run every 30 minutes from 12:00 to 5:00 p.m. Locomotives and schedules may be changed when required by operating conditions.

Fare: $2.00, children under 3 and members ride free on non-special-event days. Fares slightly higher during special events.

Locomotives: No. 6, 1927 2-truck Shay, former Ely-Thomas Lumber Co.; No. 3L, "Lady Edith," 1887 Stephenson 4-4-0T, former Cavan & Leitram Railway (Ireland); No. 26, 1920 Baldwin 2-6-2, former Surrey, Sussex & Southampton Railway; No. 1, 1942 12-ton Plymouth, former Haws Refractories; No. 40, 1940 25-ton Whitcomb, former Midvale Steel Corp.; No. 7751, 1942 25-ton General Electric, former U.S. Army; 1953 25-ton General Electric, former Kerr-McGee.

Special Events: Great Locomotive Chase/Civil War Reenactment. Railroaders' Day. *Christmas Express.* Call for dates and details.

Location: On route 524, Wall Township, Monmouth County. Take exit 98 off the Garden State Parkway and travel west, or take exit 31 off I-195 and travel east.

Contact: John P. Lyle II
General Manager

Mailing Address:
P.O. Box 622
Allaire, NJ 07727-0622
Telephone: (908) 938-5524
Fax: (908) 918-0742

NORTHLANDZ GREAT AMERICAN RAILWAY, DOLLHOUSE MUSEUM, & ART GALLERY
Model railroad display

NORTHLANDZ

Displays/Exhibits: A spectacular adventure on this one mile indoor tour through a miniature world. 135 trains and 8 miles of track are just the beginning. 25 years went into sculpting 35 foot mountains and building 40 foot bridges. Marvel at the thousands of hand crafted buildings and over 10,000 freight cars. Considered to be the world's largest miniature railway, The Great American Railway is truly unique to the world.

Schedule: Daily 9:00 a.m.-6:00 p.m.

Cost: Adults $12.75, children 2-12 $8.75, under age 2 are free.

Special events: Special events are held throughout the year. Call for information.

Location: 495 Highway 202, Flemington, New Jersey.

Contact: Steve Cohen or Greg Blair

Mailing Address:
495 Highway 202
Flemington, NJ 08822
Telephone: (908) 782-4022
Fax: (908) 782-5131

HAZLET TRAIN STOP

Displays/Exhibits: Site established in 1944. Lionel trains on display from 1916 to present with a 25' x 28' operating layout. Train sales and service of all types are available.

Schedule: November 28-January 31, Monday-Saturday, 10:00 a.m.-9:00 p.m.; Sunday, 1:00-6:00 p.m. February 1-March 31, closed Monday. April 1-September 1, closed Monday and Tuesday.

Fare/Admission: $2; children under 10 free.

Notes: Over 4500 items on display.

Location: Exit 117 Garden State Parkway. Follow Route 35 South. Second light take jug handle for right turn on Hazlet Avenue West. Cross railroad tracks then turn right on Brailley Lane.

Contact: Boyd Mason

Mailing Address:
25 Brailley Lane
Hazlet, NJ 07730
Telephone: (908) 264-7429
Fax: 908-888-7750

WHIPPANY RAILWAY MUSEUM

Railway museum
Standard gauge

STEVE HEPLER

Operation: Visit the Whippany Railway Museum, headquartered in the restored 1904 freight house of the Morristown & Erie Railway, with its outstanding collection of railroad artifacts and memorabilia. Take a leisurely stroll through a railroad yard lost in time, complete with field-stone depot; coal yard; wooden water tank and historic rail equipment. Educational and fun for all ages, the Museum also features one of the largest operating Lionel train layouts in the area, gift shop, picnic grounds, and pleasant, relaxing surroundings. New for 1997 is an exhibit on the 40th Anniversary of the demise of the New York, Ontario & Western, entitled: "Memories of the Old & Weary" as well as a display celebrating "American Railroads." The '97 Special Transportation Exhibit, "Titanic . . . 85 Years On" looks at the legends surrounding 1912 sinking of the famed luxury liner.

Schedule: Sundays, April-October, 12:00-4:00 p.m.

Admission: Adults $1.00, children (under 12) $.50.

Locomotives: Morris County Central No. 4039, an 0-6-0 built in 1942 by the American Locomotive Company; Railbus No. 10 built in 1918 by the White Motor Company for the Morristown & Erie Railroad.

Rolling Stock/Equipment: Additional equipment displayed includes a collection of assorted passenger and freight equipment from many northeast anthracite carriers, including: The Delaware & Hudson; Delaware, Lackawanna & Western; Erie; Erie-Lackawanna; and the Central Railroad Company of New Jersey. Also on display is the "Jersey Coast", a Jersey Central commuter club car, restored like a "Blue Comet" observation car.

Special Events: *Easter Bunny Express* and *Santa Claus Express* operate during holiday seasons using Morristown & Erie or historic motive power from the New Jersey Railroad & Transportation Museum Collection. Please write for details.

Location: 1 Railroad Plaza at the intersection of Route 10 West & Whippany Road in Morris County, New Jersey.

P ✳ 🚏 🍴 ▶ ◀ ar ll TRAIN

Newark, Metropark Station

Radio Frequency: 160.230
(Morristown & Erie Railway)

Contact: Joseph Krygoski
Vice President

Mailing Address:
P.O. Box 16
Whippany, NJ 07981-0016
Telephone: (201) 887-8177

TOY TRAIN DEPOT

Ride/Operation: Visitors can take a 3-mile ride through Alameda Park on a 16-inch-gauge passenger train led by an F3 diesel.

Displays/Exhibits: This museum of toy and model trains is housed in a refurbished 1898 Southern Pacific depot. Exhibits include operating layouts in N, TT, HO, S, and O gauge. The HO layout has more than twelve hundred feet of track; there are also displays of models from Z to G gauge and a 7½-inch-gauge live-steam engine.

Schedule: Wednesday-Monday, 12:00-5:00 p.m.and Wednesday-Sunday, Labor Day thru Veteran's Day, 12:00-5:00 p.m.; Train operates 12:00-4:30 p.m. Closed New Year's Day, Thanksgiving, and Christmas.

Admission: Museum: adults $2.00, children $1.50. Train: adults $2.00, children $1.50. Children under 6 must be accompanied by an adult.

Location: At the north end of Alameda Park on highway 54/70. Take U.S. 70 north from I-10 in El Paso, Texas, south from I-40 in Santa Rosa, New Mexico, or east from I-25 in Las Cruces, New Mexico.

El Paso, Texas

Contact: John Koval
President

Mailing Address:
1991 North White Sands Boulevard
Alamogordo, NM 88310
Telephone: (505) 437-2855

New Mexico, Chama
Colorado, Antonito
R

ALEX MAYES

CUMBRES & TOLTEC SCENIC RAILROAD
Steam, scheduled
36" gauge

Ride/Operation: Steam trains travel over highly scenic former Denver & Rio Grande Western narrow-gauge trackage. The 64-mile line crosses Cumbres Pass (elevation 10,015 feet) and goes through spectacular Toltec Gorge, over high bridges, and through two tunnels. Passengers may choose to ride either the *Colorado Limited* from Antonito to Osier, Colorado, via Toltec Gorge or the *New Mexico Express* from Chama, New Mexico, to Osier via Cumbres Pass or ride the full length of the lure. The two trains meet at Osier for a lunch stop, and the trains exchange locomotives for the return trip.

Train: Coaches; snack bar; souvenir-shop car; open observation car.

Schedule: Daily, May 25-mid October; lv. Chama 10:30 a.m., return 4:30 p.m.; lv. Antonito 10:00 a.m., return 5:00 p.m. Passengers are advised to dress warmly, since sudden and dramatic changes in the weather may occur.

Fare: Round trip: adults $34.00, children (under 12) $17.00. Through trips from either terminal with return by van: adults $52.00, children $27.00. Reservations recommended for all trips.

Locomotives: Nos. 463, 484, 487, 488, 489, 497, 1925 Baldwin 2-8-2s, former D&RGW.

Notes: The C&TS is a joint undertaking of the states of Colorado and New Mexico. The line is leased to Kyle Railways, Inc.

Location: Terminals at Chama, New Mexico, and Antonito, Colorado.

Contact: Joe C. Vigil
General Manager

Mailing Address:
P.O. Box 668
Antonito, CO 81120
P.O. Box 789
Chama, NM 87520
Telephone:
Antonito: (719) 376-5483
Chama: (505) 756-2151

CLOVIS DEPOT
MODEL TRAIN MUSEUM
Railroad display, museum

CLOVIS DEPOT

Displays/Exhibits Exhibits include restored Depot dorm area and dispatcher/telegraph operator
positions. Displays depict the history of the railroad in Clovis and along the "Belen Cutoff".
The model railroads tell the story of toy trains in the U.S. and Great Britain and of the history
of the railroad in Australia, Great Britain and the U.S. Southwest. Live BNSF train operations
on the mainline and in the yard can be viewed from our platform.

Ride/Operation: We provide guided tours of Depot Museum and model railroad displays including running of trains and other hands-on displays.

Schedule: Open Wednesday - Sunday, noon to 5:00
p.m.
Fare/Admission: Adults $3.00, children (12 and under)
$1.00, families (2 adults + 2 or more children) $7.00.
Rolling Stock/Equipment: Fairmont railway motor car.

Location: Located in restored AT & SF passenger depot
in Clovis at intersection of First Street and Connelly
Street. Adjacent to BNSF Mainline, two block west of
Main St. on US 60/84.

Contact:
Philip D. Williams

Mailing Address:
221 West First Street
Clovis, NM 88101
Telephone: (505) 762-0066

SANTA FE SOUTHERN RAILWAY
Diesel mixed
Standard gauge

ERICH BROCK

Ride/Operation: Mixed train 5 times a week on 18-mile former Santa Fe branch line. Train operates Santa Fe to Lamy and return. Includes 1-1/2 hour layover at the historic landmark, Legal Tender Restaurant.

Schedule: Year round: Tuesday, Thursday, Saturday, Sunday. Leaves Santa Fe depot at 10:30 a.m.; May-December, Friday evening sunset trips. Leaves one hour before sunset. Reservations required. Call for information.

Fare/Admission: Day trips: Adults $21.00, seniors (60+) $16.00, youths (age 7-13) $16.00, children 3-6 $5.00, children 2 and under are free. Soft drinks and snacks available. Evening sunset trips: $28.00 per person, includes hors d'oeuvres and soft drinks. Cash bar available.

Locomotives: GP7, No. 92, former ATSF No. 2075; GP16, No. 93, former L&N No. 1850.

Rolling Stock/Equipment: No. 1158, former CNJ Coach; No. 144, former GN Coach; No. 4014, former SP Coach; No. 1370 "Acoma," former AT&SF super-chief.

Special Events: Holiday evening trains, call for details. Private car facilities, charters, and group rates available.

Location: Santa Fe, New Mexico.

 Lamy, New Mexico

Contact: Erich Brock
Freight Agent

Mailing Address:
410 South Guadalupe St.
Santa Fe, NM 87501
Telephone: (505) 989-8600
Fax: (505) 983-7620

ARCADE & ATTICA RAILROAD
Steam, scheduled
Standard gauge

PETER SWANSON

Ride/Operation: The A&A, a common-carrier railroad that has been in existence since 1881, offers a 15-mile, 2-hour round trip over the historic trackage to Curriers.

Displays/Exhibits: Grover Cleveland's "Honeymoon Car," former New York, Ontario & Western Railway, is on display at Arcade and contains its original dishes and glassware. It may be visited on days that the passenger train operates.

Train: Open-end steel coaches and combination cars from the Delaware, Lackawanna & Western Railroad; open gondola car.

Schedule: Memorial Weekend through October: Weekends and holidays, 12:30 & 3:00 p.m.; July-August; Wednesdays, 12:30 & 3:00 p.m; Fridays,1:00 p.m.

Fare: Adults $8.50, senior citizens $7.50 children (3-11) $5.00, children under 3 ride free. Group rates available.

Locomotives: No. 14, 1917 Baldwin 4-6-0, former Escanaba & Lake Superior; No. 18, 1920 Alco (Cooke) 2-8-0, former Boyne City Railroad.

Special Events: Special fall foliage runs, Christmas trains and winter runs. Civil War Days. Children's Trains. Please call for information.

Location: In western New York, midway between Buffalo and Olean. Train departs from the Arcade depot in the center of town, at routes 39 and 98.

Contact: Linda Kempf
General Manager

Mailing Address:
278 Main Street
P.O. Box 246
Arcade, NY 14009
Telephone: (716) 496-9877

DELAWARE & ULSTER RAIL RIDE
Diesel, scheduled
Standard gauge

GEORGE A. FORERO, JR.

Ride/Operation: A 10-mile, 50-minute round trip from Arkville to Fleischmanns over the route of the historic Ulster & Delaware Railroad. Longer special trips may also operate on occasion.

Displays/Exhibits: The Arkville station and yards have been restored; in the depot are a free video show and railway exhibits.

Train: Former Pennsylvania Railroad MP-54 coaches and open cars (heated coaches subject to availability). Dining car with catering available for charter. Brill railcar may also operate.

Schedule: Weekends & Holidays, May 24-October 26 and September 6-October 26; Wednesdays-Sundays, July 2-September 1; 11:00 a.m., 1:00 & 3:00 p.m. Depot opens at 10:00 a.m. on operating days.

Fare: Adults $7.00, senior citizens $5.50, children (5-11) $4.00, children under 5 ride free.

Locomotives: D & H No. 5017, RS 36 Alco; No. 5106, 1953 Alco S-4, former Chesapeake & Ohio; No. 1012, 1954 Alco S-4, former Ford Motor Co.; M-405, 1928 J.G. Brill Co. diesel-electric railcar, former New York Central.

Rolling Stock/Equipment: Two flatcars with benches, former Cumberland & Pennsylvania; N-5 caboose, former PRR; two boxcars, former NYC; 44-ton locomotive, former Western Maryland.

Special Events: Train Robberies. Teddy Bear Runs. Tractor Pull. Antique Engine Gas-Up. Fall Foliage Runs. Halloween Train.

Location: Route 28.

Radio Frequency: 161.385

Contact: Vic Stevens
General Manager

Mailing Address:
Box 310
Stamford, NY 12167
Telephone: (914) 586-3877
(800) 225-4132

NEW YORK TRANSIT MUSEUM

Displays/Exhibits: Located in an actual 1936 subway station, this museum houses one hundred
years of transit lore and memorabilia, including eighteen vintage subway and elevated cars,
antique turnstiles, a working signal tower, a unique gift shop, and much more. The story of the
subway is the story of the city, and the New York Transit Museum offers visitors an opportunity both to discover the past and to see the present and future of public transportation in New
York City.

Schedule: Tuesdays-Sundays; Tuesday-Friday, 10:00
a.m.-4:00 p.m.; Wednesday, 10:00 a.m.-6:00 p.m.;
weekends, 12:00-5:00 p.m. Closed major holidays.

Admission: Adults $3.00, senior citizens and children
(under 17) $1.50.

Locomotives/Electric Cars: Eighteen completely
restored subway and elevated cars dating from 1903.

Rolling Stock/Equipment: Working signal tower.

Location: Corner of Boerum Place and Schermerhorn
Street, Brooklyn Heights.

Contact: Richard A. Madigan
Deputy Director

Mailing Address:
130 Livingston Street, 9th Floor
Brooklyn, NY 11201
Telephone: (718) 243-5839
Recorded Information: (718) 243-3060

MARTISCO STATION MUSEUM
CENTRAL NEW YORK CHAPTER NRHS
Railroad museum, children's ride
1-1/2" gauge

CENTRAL NEW YORK CHAPTER NRHS

Ride/Operation: The Martisco Station Museum is a brick Victorian passenger structure erected in 1870 for the New York Central & Hudson River Railroad. Located in a picturesque setting, the restored, two-story, passenger station houses a collection of railroad mementos of the local area. The adjacent ex-Pennsylvania Railroad diner houses the Chapter's collection of books and magazines. Presently, the tracks passing the station are used by the Finger Lakes Railway, five days per week.

Displays/Exhibits: A collection of railroad mementos representing the local area.

Schedule: Sundays June 1 - November 1. 2:00 p.m-5:00 p.m.

Fare/Admission: Free, donations accepted.

Locomotives: GG-1, Diesel E8 (2), Diesel FP (2), Located at NY State Fair Grounds. 0-4-0 steam narrow gauge located at Martisco.

Rolling Stock/Equipment: Several restored passenger and sleeper cars also located at NY State Fair Grounds.

Special Events: Restored E8 Diesels used on excursions on New York, Susquehanna & Western system. Contact Chapter for dates.

Location: At the end of Martisco Road off of New York State Route 175, halfway between the villages of Marcellus and Camillus.

   ♿   **P**   ✳   ☕   ◉   **M**

 Syracuse, 10 miles away

Contact: Albert Kallfelz
President

Mailing Address:
P.O. Box 229
Marcellus, NY 13108
Telephone: (315) 488-8208

CENTRAL SQUARE STATION MUSEUM
CENTRAL NEW YORK CHAPTER NRHS
Railroad display, museum

CENTRAL NEW YORK CHAPTER NRHS

Displays/Exhibits: The station houses many railfacts from the local area. A combination baggage-coach, originally a gas electric car from the Huntington & Broad Top Railroad, is being restored after being obtained from the former Rail City Museum. An 0-4-0T steam engine originally from Solvay Process quarry in Jamesville, also acquired from Rail City, is being cosmetically restored. A narrow gauge 0-4-0 from a quarry near Rochester is also on display.

Schedule: Sundays June 1 - November 1. 12:00 - 5:00 p.m.

Fare/Admission: Free, donations accepted.

Locomotives: 0-4-0T steam engine, Narrow gauge 0-4-0, 25 ton industrial switcher diesel.

Rolling Stock/Equipment: Combination baggage-coach.

Location: On Railroad Ave. just off US Route 11 to the south of the Central Square business district.

    P   ✳   ◙   M

 Syracuse, 15 miles away

Contact: Albert Kallfelz
President

Mailing Address:
P.O. Box 229
Marcellus, NY 13108
Telephone: (315) 488-8208

ALCO BROOKS RAILROAD DISPLAY

Railway display
Standard gauge

HISTORICAL SOCIETY OF DUNKIRK

Displays/Exhibits: Horatio Brooks, once superintendent of the Dunkirk Shops of the Erie Railroad, founded the Brooks Locomotive Works in 1869, when the Erie moved its shops to Hornell, New York. In 1901 the Brooks Locomotive Works became part of the American Locomotive Company, producing steam locomotives until 1929. The plant manufactured other heavy industrial and military materials until its closing in 1963. The ABRD, located at the Chautauqua County Fairgrounds since 1987, owns an original Alco-Brooks steam locomotive, a wood-sided boxcar housing displays of Chautauqua County commerce and railroads along with a gift shop, and a restored wooden caboose. Other items of interest at the site are a Nickel Plate work car, an Erie Railroad concrete telephone booth, a New York Central harp switch stand, a Pennsylvania Railroad cast-iron crossing sign, a DAV&P land line marker, and an operating crossing flasher.

Schedule: Saturdays, June 1-August 31, 1:00-3:00 p.m. (weather permitting). Daily during special events or by appointment.

Admission: Donations welcomed.

Locomotives: No. 444, 1916 Alco-Brooks 0-6-0, former Boston & Maine No. 444, former Fletcher Granite Co. (West Chelmsford, Massachusetts).

Rolling Stock/Equipment: 1907 wood-sided boxcar No. 22020, former Delaware & Hudson; 1905 wooden caboose No. 19224, former New York Central.

Special Events: Chautauqua County Antique Automobile Show & Flea Market, May 16-17. Chautauqua County Fair, July 21-27.

Location: Chautauqua County Fairgrounds, 1089 Central Avenue.

P 🚌 ✳ ► ◄ **M**

Dunkirk

Contact: Roy A. Davis
Vice President

Mailing Address:
Historical Society of Dunkirk
513 Washington Avenue
Dunkirk, NY 14048
Telephone: (716) 366-3797

NEW YORK & LAKE ERIE RAILROAD
Diesel, scheduled
Standard gauge

KEVIN ARGUE

Ride/Operation: This railroad serves freight customers and operates two excursions over former Erie Railroad trackage: the *South Dayton Flyer,* which makes a 20-mile, 2 1/2-hour round trip to South Dayton over a steep grade and through an old stone tunnel; and *The Blue Diamond,* which makes a 30-mile, 4-hour round trip to Cherry Creek, featuring a full-course dinner. Depending upon the excursion, intermediate station stops are made at South Dayton or Cherry Creek. The depot in South Dayton was featured in the motion pictures *The Natural* and *Planes, Trains and Automobiles.*

Train: Coaches, former Baltimore & Ohio; commuter cars, former Delaware, Lackawanna & Western; open-air car; dining car "City of Salamanca," former Canadian National; dining car "The Daniel Webster," rebuilt from a B&O cafe-coach by the NY&LE.

Schedule: *The Flyer:* June 14-October 19: Saturdays 1:00 p.m., Sundays 2:00 p.m.; July-August: Wednesday 12:00 p.m. *The Blue Diamond Dinner Train:* Sundays 2:00 p.m.; July-October: first Saturday of the month at 6:30 p.m. *Murder Mystery Dinner Train:* February-November, third Saturday of the month, plus Aug. 30, Oct. 16, Dec. 13 & 31. Weekday group tours scheduled for Cherry Creek and South Dayton; write or call for schedule and group rates.

Fare: *The Flyer:* adults $9.00, senior citizens $8.00, children (3-11) $4.00. *The Blue Diamond & Murder Mystery Trains:* call or write for reservations and fares.

Locomotives: No. 85, 1950 Alco S-2; No. 1013, 1965 Alco C-425, former Norfolk & Western; No. 6101, the "Charles E. Hensel"; Alco C-425, former Pennsylvania Railroad.

Special Events: Peter Cottontail Express. The Great Train Robbery. Kids' Day. Ghosts and Goblins Party. The Teddy Bears' Picnic. Santa Claus Express.

Notes: All trains except the *South Dayton Flyer* require advance reservations.

Location: Gowanda is on U.S. route 62 and state route 39, thirty miles south of Buffalo. All trains depart from 50 Commercial Street.

Contact: Dee Campbell
Director of Passenger Operations

Mailing Address:
P.O. Box 309
Gowanda, NY 14070-0309
Telephone: (716) 532-5716
Fax: (716) 532-9128

RAILROAD MUSEUM OF LONG ISLAND

Displays/Exhibits: Greenport consists of a 1890 LIong Island Rail Road freight station with exhibits depicting the development of railroad industry on Long Island. Riverhead houses a collection of vintage LIRR equipment. Pictured above is a 1907 LIRR snowplow nicknamed "Jaws III."

Schedule: Greenport: May-December, Saturday-Sunday, 12:00-5:00 p.m. or by appointment. Riverhead: Saturday, 1:00 a.m.-4:00 p.m., weather permitting.

Fare/Admission: Adults $1.00, children under 16 $.50, under 5 admitted free.

Locomotives: No. 39 LIRR 4-6-0 655 steam; No. 1556 RS-3 diesel.

Rolling Stock/Equipment: No. 200, first bilevel coach in U.S.; C-68 bay window caboose; No. 1391 electric combine; No. 7737 baggage mail.

Location: Call for information.

Contact: C. Talluto
President-Trustee

Mailing Address:
P.O. Box 726
Greenport, NY 11944
Telephone: (516) 477-0439
(516) 727-7926
E-mail: RMLIPRES@AOL

THE TROLLEY MUSEUM OF NEW YORK

Ride/Operation: This museum was established in 1955 and moved to its present location in 1983, becoming part of the Kingston Urban Cultural Park. A 2 1/2-mile, 40-minute round trip takes passengers from the foot of Broadway to Kingston Point, with stops at the museum in both directions. A gas-powered railcar operates on private right-of-way and in-street trackage along Rondout Creek to the Hudson River over part of the former Ulster & Delaware Railroad main line.

Displays/Exhibits: An exhibit hall features trolley exhibits and a theater.

Train: Railcar No. 120, 1929 gasoline-powered Brill car, former Sperry Rail Service, former Remington Arms.

Schedule: Weekends & holidays, May-October, 12:00-5:00 p.m. Last ride at 4:30 p.m. Additional dates may be scheduled; call for information. Charters available.

Fare: Adults $3.00, children $1.00. Museum: donations welcomed.

Trolleys: Whitcomb diesel-electric; seven rapid-transit cars; eleven trolleys; one interurban.

Special Events: Shad Festival, May. Fathers Day (Fathers ride free), June 15. Independence Day Run, July 4. Labor Day Run, September 1. Member's Day, October. "Fright Train", October. Santa Run, December.

Note: Adjacent to the museum are the Hudson River Maritime Museum and the Kingston Urban Cultural Center; visitors may want to schedule a boat ride along with the trolley ride, or visit the shops and restaurants. This section of Kingston is being restored to its original late-nineteenth-century appearance.

Location: In the historic Rondout Waterfront area of Kingston. Call or write for specific directions or see our world wide web page.

   P   ✳   📷   🚏   ▶   ◀   **M**

at 11 Rhinecliff

Radio Frequency: 462.175

Contact: President

Mailing Address: 89 East Strand
P.O. Box 2291
Kingston, NY 12402
Telephone: (914) 331-3399
Internet: http://www.mhrcc.org/kingston/kgntroll.html.

CATSKILL MOUNTAIN RAILROAD
Diesel, scheduled
Standard gauge

GEORGE A. FORERO, JR.

Ride/Operation: This railroad, which operates over trackage of the former Ulster & Delaware Railroad (later the Catskill Mountain branch of the New York Central), offers a 6-mile, 1-hour round trip to Phoenicia along the scenic Esopus Creek, through the heart of the beautiful Catskill Mountains. Tourists, inner-tubers, and visitors interested in canoeing or fishing may ride one way or round trip; round-trip passengers may stay at Phoenicia to visit shops and restaurants and return on a later train.

Displays/Exhibits: 1894 wooden baggage car, former Delaware & Hudson; 1937 caboose, former Lehigh Valley No. 94071.

Train: Open flatcars; wooden caboose, former Delaware & Hudson.

Schedule: Summer weekends and holidays, May 24-September 14, 11:00 a.m.-5:00 p.m.; Fall weekends and holidays, September 20-October 13, 12 noon-4:00 p.m.

Fare: Round trip: adults $6.00, children (4-11) $2.00, children under 4 ride free. One way: adults $4.00, children (4-11) $2.00, children under 4 ride free.

Locomotives: No. 1, "The Duck," 1942 Davenport 38-ton diesel-mechanical, former U.S. Air Force; No. 2, "The Goat," H.K. Porter 50-ton diesel-electric, former U.S. Navy; No. 2361, 1952 Alco RS-1, former Wisconsin Central (Soo Line).

Rolling Stock/Equipment: No. 8301, 1942 self-propelled diesel crane, former U.S. Army.

Special Events: Fall Foliage Trains and others; call for schedule.

Location: Take exit 19 (Kingston) off the New York State Thruway and travel west 22 miles on route 28 to the railroad depot in Mt. Pleasant.

Contact: Gladys Gilbert
Treasurer

Mailing Address:
P.O. Box 46
Shokan, NY 12481
Telephone: (914) 688-7400

226

MATTHEW GIARDINO

Ride/Operation: This line, operated by the Adirondack Railway Preservation Society, offers a 9-mile, 1-hour round trip and a 12-mile, 1¼-hour round trip over a section of the former Adirondack Division of the New York Central. The ride takes passengers along the Middle Branch of the Moose River through rock cuts and forests, past lakes and ponds, and through some of the most scenic areas of the Adirondack Park. Planned expansion of 52 miles to Utica (connection with Amtrak) in late 1997.

Displays/Exhibits: A small museum in the front waiting room of the century-old Thendara Station focuses primarily on the Adirondack Division and also features the New York Central and railroading in general. Adirondack Park and Forest Preserve interpretation.

Train: Six former Canadian National open-window coaches; former New York Central Pacemaker caboose; former Pennsylvania Railroad baggage/open-air car; former Pullman 12-1 sleeper, being converted to an open-air car.

Schedule: Weekends and Memorial Day, May; Saturday-Wednesday, June; Saturday-Thursday, July 1-October 31; some weekends, November; 11:30 a.m. & 2:30 p.m.

Fare: Adults $6.00, children (2-12) $4.00.

Locomotives: No. 8223, first Alco RS 3 on the New York Central; SW1 No. 705, former Louisville & Nashville.

Special Events: Mother's Day, May 11. Rail Fan Days & Father's Day,. Halloween Express, Santa Claus Special, Train Robberies. Many more special events. Call or write for details and schedules.

Note: Schedule is subject to changes or cancellations without notice.

Location: On New York route 28, 1 mile south of Old Forge and Fulton Chain of Lakes, 2 miles south of Enchanted Forest/Water Safari, 30 miles south of Adirondack Museum at Blue Mountain Lake, and 50 miles north of New York State Thruway exit 31 (Utica).

Utica

Contact: Douglas J. Ellison
Executive Director

Mailing Address:
P.O. Box 84
Thendara, NY 13472
Telephone: (315) 369-6290

TIOGA SCENIC RAILROAD
Diesel, scheduled
Standard gauge

TIOGA SCENIC RAILROAD, THOMAS TRENCANSKY

Ride/Operation: A 1 3/4-hour round trip from Owego to Newark Valley over tracks of the former Southern Central, constructed beginning in 1868 to connect southern New York with the Great Lakes. Lunch and dinner trains, as well as fall foliage and other special-event excursions may travel farther north to Berkshire.

Displays/Exhibits: Trains operate between the historic Owego and Newark Valley depots, which date from the earliest days of the Southern Central; the Owego depot, the headquarters of the SC, is completely restored. The Newark Valley depot, refurbished by the Newark Valley Historical Society, features offices and dispatch areas as they were circa 1910, in addition to historical and railroad exhibits and a model layout of the Lehigh Valley Railroad. The Bement-Billings Farmstead, a circa 1840 living museum featuring costumed interpreters demonstrating skills of that time in a home, blacksmith shop, barn, sawmill, and gristmill, can be reached via a free shuttle bus from the Newark Valley depot.

Train: GP-9; two 1920 coaches, former Delaware, Lackawanna & Western; two 1940s dinner cars, former Illinois Central.

Schedule: Weekends, May 25-October 27; lv. Owego 12:00 & 3:00 p.m.; lv. Newark Valley 1:00 & 4:00 p.m. Lunch and dinner trains: please call or write for information.

Fare: Adults $7.00, senior citizens $6.50, children (4-11) $5.00, children under 3 ride free. Lunch and dinner trains: please call or write for information. Group rates and charters available for 30 or more.

Special Events: Easter. Mother's Day. Father's Day. Fall Foliage. Halloween. Christmas. New Year's.

Location: Owego is off exit 64 of New York route 17; Newark Valley is north of Owego on route 38.

Contact: Ticket Agent

Mailing Address:
25 Delphine Street
Owego, NY 13827
Telephone: (607) 687-6786

EMPIRE STATE RAILWAY MUSEUM

Ride/Operation: First chartered in 1960, the all-volunteer Empire State Railway Museum moved to the 1899 former Ulster & Delaware depot in Phoenicia in 1984. The depot, preserved in its original condition, was added to the National Registry of Historic Places in 1995. Museum members have restored the station and are raising funds to begin restoration of four historic pieces of rolling stock: circa 1923 flatcar No. 7704 and 54-inch, wooden-sided, end-door boxcar, both former Central Vermont; 1912 four-wheel wood-bodied bobber caboose, former Pennsylvania Railroad; and 1890s express Railway Post Office car, former Boston & Maine. Visitors can board the train of the Catskill Mountain Railroad at Mt. Pleasant and ride to the museum in Phoenicia.

Displays/Exhibits: Archival photographs, films, and artifacts of the Ulster & Delaware and other regional branch lines.

Schedule: Weekends and holidays, Memorial Day-Labor Day, 11:00 a.m.-4:00 p.m.

Admission: Suggested donation: adults $3.00, senior citizens & students $2.00, children (under 12) $1.00

Rolling Stock/Equipment: Rolling stock described below is being restored in Phoenicia. No. 23, 1910 Alco 2-8-0, former Lake Superior & Ishpeming; 1915 Pullman dining car "Lion Gardiner," stored in Kingston.

Special Events: Lectures, slide shows,videos at monthly membership meetings throughout the year. Santa Claus Special. Members' picnics. Other special events.

Note: Membership includes a free copy of the *Steam Passenger Service Directory* and quarterly newsletters.

Location: Off High Street.

Mailing Address:
P.O. Box 455
Phoenicia, NY 12464
Telephone (recorded message):
(914) 688-7501

RIVERSIDE STATION

Displays/Exhibits: Nestled in the Adirondack Mountains of upstate New York along the Hudson River is the Riverside Train Depot, a former Delaware & Hudson station built in 1913, filled with railroad memorabilia and pictures. This depot replaced a smaller Adirondack Company railway station that was built in 1870. The station was restored to its original charm in 1995 and consists of a ticket agent's office, waiting room and baggage room. The baggage room is how home to a gift shop/train store. In the old waiting room you can relax and enjoy train videos that are shown continuously. In the yard there is a vintage caboose that now serves as a refreshment stand. Williams Old General Store can be seen in the background.

Schedule: June through Labor Day, 11:00 a.m.-9:00 p.m. Weekends and holidays in May, September, and October, 11:00 a.m. -7:00 p.m. Gift shop hours vary, please call first.

Admission: No charge.

Location: On State Route 8, seven miles west of I-87, the Adirondack Northway, exit 25. 30 minutes from Lake George Village.

Mailing Address:
P.O. Box 4
Riparius, NY 12862
Telephone: (518) 494-7221

ROCHESTER & GENESEE VALLEY
RAILROAD MUSEUM
Railway museum
Standard gauge

CHRISTOPHER HAUF

Ride/Operation: Track-car rides originate at the New York Museum of Transportation and operate to this museum.

Displays/Exhibits: Railroad artifacts from area railroads are housed in a restored 1900-era rural Erie Railroad station; a number of railroad cars and locomotives are on display on outdoor tracks. The combined tours and track-car ride offer a comprehensive and unique transportation experience. For further information, see the listing of the New York Museum of Transportation (New York, Rochester).

Schedule: Museum: Sundays, mid May to late October, 11:00 a.m.-5:00 p.m. Track-car rides: mid May to late October, weather permitting. Group visits by appointment.

Admission: Adults $5.00, senior citizens $4.00, students (5-15) $3.00. Includes admission to NYMT and R&GVRRM and 1.5-mile track-car ride between the museums. November through mid May, includes entry only to NYMT, and prices are lower.

Locomotives: 1946 80-ton General Electric, former Eastman Kodak No. 6; 1953 Alco RS-3, former Lehigh Valley; 1953 Alco S-4, former Nickel Plate No. 79; 1941 45-ton General Electric, former Rochester Gas & Electric; No. 1843, Fairbanks-Morse H12-44, former U.S. Army.

Rolling Stock/Equipment: 1909 70-ton hopper car No. 747803, former Pennsylvania Railroad class H-21a; baggage car No. 633 and caboose No. C-2631, both former Baltimore & Ohio; MU car No. 4628, former Delaware, Lackawanna & Western; caboose No. 19877 and flatcar, both former New York Central; 1940 sleeper-lounge "Pine Falls," former Long Island Railroad/Pennsylvania Railroad; baggage car No. 489022, former Erie-Lackawanna; Stillwell coach No. 2328, caboose No. C-254, and milk car No. 6603, all former Erie; 1958 MDT ice refrigerator car; speeder; section car; tamper; assorted maintenance-of-way equipment.

Location: Take exit 11 off Route 390 (2 miles south of New York State Thruway), travel west on Route 251 two miles to the flashing signal at East River Road, turn right, travel 1.5 miles north to the entrance of the Rochester & Genesee Valley Railroad Museum and the New York Museum of Transportation, and turn left to enter grounds.

Rochester

Contact: Michael M. Byrne
Public Relations Coordinator

Mailing Address:
49 Weiland Woods Lane
Rochester, NY 14626
Telephone: Message-(716) 533-1431
E-mail: IS000096@interramp.com
Internet: http://www.rochester.ny.us/railmuseum

ROSCOE O&W RAILWAY MUSEUM

Ride/Operation: This museum was established under the charter of the Ontario & Western Railway Historical Society in 1984 in a former Erie Railroad caboose. The O&W railway festival, first held in August of that year, has since become an annual event.

Displays/Exhibits: The museum complex consists of a restored O&W caboose, watchman's shanties, and the O&W station motif building. The museum contains displays of O&W memorabilia and other railroadiana, as well as local-history displays that show the impact of the O&W on community life, hunting, fishing, farming, tourism, and local industry. The museum is maintained and operated by members of the Roscoe NYO&W Railway Association. The Archives Center of the history of the Ontario & Western Railway is located in Middletown, NY.

Schedule: May 24-October 12: Weekends, 11:00 a.m.-3:00 p.m. Group tours with slide show available. For information contact director.

Fare: Donations welcomed.

Special Events: O&W Festival & Craft Fair, July 26-27, 10:00 a.m.-4:00 p.m. Other events are being scheduled so please contact us for further details.

Notes: For research, schedule appointment by writing to the Archives Center at O&WRHS, P.O. Box 713, MIddletown, NY 10940.

Location: Railroad Avenue.

Contact: Wilmer E. Sipple
Director & Curator
Telephone: (607) 498-4346
(607) 498-5289

Mailing Address:
P.O. Box 305
Roscoe, NY 12776-0305
Telephone: (607) 498-5500

SALAMANCA RAIL MUSEUM ASSOCIATION

Displays/Exhibits: The Rail Museum is a place where the whole family can learn the important role railroads played in the history of Salamanca and the surrounding area. For the kids, the museum grounds offer the permanent display of a box car, a crew camp car, and the chance to explore two cabooses.

Schedule: April-December, Monday-Saturday, 10:00 a.m.-5:00 p.m.; Sundays, 12:00 p.m.-5:00 p.m. April & October-December, closed Mondays. January-March, closed. Guided tours for groups are available by prior arrangement. Call for additional information.

Fare/Admission: Free, donations are appreciated.

Rolling Stock/Equipment: B&O bay window caboose, P&WVa cupola caboose, Erie 50 ft. box car, Erie crane crew car.

Location: 170 Main St. in downtown Salamanca, NY. Take exit 20 off NY Route 17, (Southern Tier Expressway) or coming south on US Route 219 to 417

West or off NY Route 353 to NY 417 East. Just follow signs.

Contact: Kenneth A. Magara
Director

Mailing Address:
170 Main Street
Salamanca, NY 14779
Telephone: (716) 945-3133

New York, Salem
R

GEORGE LERRIGO

NORTHEAST RAIL
BATTEN KILL RAILROAD
Diesel, scheduled
Standard gauge

Ride/Operation: On this line, the *Batten Kill Rambler* takes passengers on a scenic, 2-hour and 10-minute, 13-mile round trip along the Batten Kill River. An hour layover allows exploration of Shushan, NY with 2 museums. At secluded River Park, a picnic park is available by prior arrangement.

Train: Former NYC Empire State Express coaches, Budd RDC car, RS3 605 or 4116.

Schedule: Late May through October. 1996 May 21-June 26, Tuesday-Thursday 10:30 a.m; Saturday-Sunday, 10:45 a.m./1:20 p.m.; June 27-September 2, Tuesday-Thursday, 10:05 a.m.; Friday, 10:30 a.m. Saturday, 10:45 a.m./1:20 p.m. also 3:50 p.m. Sunday; September 3-October 20, Tuesday-Thursday 10:30 a.m. also 1:20 p.m. Thursday; Saturday-Sunday, 10:45 a.m./1:20 & 3:50 p.m.; July 12, 26, August 9 & 23, Fort Salem Dinner Trains 5:45 p.m. from Shushan, NY.

Fare: Adults $8.00, seniors (60+) $7.00, children (3-12) $4.00, children under 3 ride free if not occupying a seat. Charters, group rates and packages available.

Locomotives: No. 605, 1950 Alco; No. 4116, 1952 Alco still in pinstripes.

Passenger Cars: Nos. 2106 & 2108, former New York Central, No. M403, former Pennsylvania Reading Seashore Lines.

Special Events: Children's Theater at River Park. Civil War Homecoming Reenactment. Halloween Train. Santa Trains. Call or write for specific dates and times.

Location: 232 Main Street. I-87 to Route 29, at Saratoga Springs east to Salem. Left on Route 22, north to village and station.

 Saratoga Springs or Albany Rennsselear

Radio Frequency: 160.905

Contact: Karl Pingree
Administrator

Mailing Address:
1 Elbow Street
Greenwich, NY 12834
Telephone:
Operating days: (518) 854-3787
Reserv. & Schedule: (518) 692-2191
Internet: http://nyslgti.gen.ny.us/Salem

ONTARIO-MIDLAND RAIL EXCURSIONS
Diesel, scheduled
Standard gauge

CHRIS HAUF

Ride/Operation: 34 mile (RT) Fall foliage excursions on former PRR & NYC Empire State Express cars through the scenic and rural Seaway Trail near Rochester, NY.

Displays/Exhibits: Diesel powered (Alco) train rides with snacks, restrooms, souvenirs, and air conditioning. Listen to music and memories from the 1940's in cars from that era.

Schedule: Runs from Sodus to Newark NY (RT). Selected Saturdays and Sundays in the Fall at 12 noon and 2:15 p.m. Trips last approximately 2 hours. 1997 Schedule: Sunday September 21, 28 and October 5, 12, and 19. Also Saturday October 11 and 18 (tentative schedule).

Fare/Admission: Adults $10, children ages 3-15 $6.50, under 3 are free.

Locomotives: No. 40, 1962 Alco RS 36: No. 36, 1957 Alco RS1.

Rolling Stock/Equipment: 5 former NYC Empire State Express railcars (Budd), former Metro North

Special Events: First Sunday of operation children ride for $3.50, second Sunday is special music and memories from the 1940's.

Location: Sodus, take Maple St. exit south from Route 140 (approximately 30 miles east of Rochester.

Roch, 30 miles away

Contact: Bob Miner

Mailing Address: P.O. Box 1161
Webster NY 14580
Telephone: (716) 224-0581
E-mail: 000096@interramp.com
Internet: http://www.rochester.ny.us/rai/museum

JEFF ENGLISH

Displays/Exhibits: This five-hundred-foot serpentine layout occupies a 120-foot by 30-foot area and depicts actual 1950 scenes of Troy, Vermont, and the Champlain Valley. The exhibit is the largest historically accurate operating diorama of its kind, illustrating the interconnection of yesterday's smokestack industries from the gathering of raw materials in the Adirondacks and the Green Mountains, through the manufacturing processes, to the distribution of finished products to market. The exhibit thus demonstrates how Troy was such a pivotal area in the country's industrial history. Begun in 1972, the layout is approximately ninety percent completed, so visitors can see all phases of construction, from bare benchwork to finished, detailed scenes. The layout, a sophisticated historical exhibit rather than a toy-train display, is not recommended for children under twelve years old.

Schedule: Fridays, 1:00-4:00 p.m.; Saturdays, 12:00 a.m.-4:00 p.m. Closed Christmas and New Year's weeks.

Admission: $4.00, children under 5 admitted free.

Note: The Rensselaer Model Railroad Society has set up a combination gift shop/HO hobby shop to help defray the enormous costs needed to build and maintain the layout. This shop specializes in our own publications about scenery, structures, details, freight cars and operations of the steam-era world.

Location: In the basement of Davison Hall dormitory on the Rensselaer Polytechnic Institute campus. Davison Hall is opposite Troy High School on Burdett Avenue. Follow route 7 into Troy, turn south onto Burdett just east of Dunkin' Donuts, and turn right into the last parking lot.

Contact: Joe Sagmore
Visitor Coordinator

Mailing Address:
RPI Student Union
Troy, NY 12180-3590
Telephone: (518) 276-2764

DALE ROBERTS

Ride/Operation: NRHS Chapter sponsors steam and diesel excursions on the Great Smoky Mountains Railway, Sylva, NC.

Displays/Exhibits: Many types of railroad memorabilia.

Schedule: Sponsored trips on Great Smoky Mountains Railway, Saturdays, April 20 (diesel, 6-hours); September 28 (steam); and December 14 (dinner train).

Fare/Admission: For excursion fares, call Great Smoky Mountains at 1 (800) 872-4681.

Locomotives: Southern Railway No. 722, 1904 Baldwin 2-8-0. No. 722 served in and around Asheville until sale to East Tennessee and Western North Carolina Railroad. Re-purchased by Southern Railway in 1967 for use in the steam program, No. 722 is displayed in the green, gold and red livery of her excursion days.

Rolling Stock/Equipment: Southern caboose.

Location: Short McDowell St., Asheville, NC.

Contact:
Asheville Chapter NRHS, Inc.

Mailing Address:
P.O. Box 153
Asheville, NC 28802
Telephone: (704) 252-6094

TWEETSIE RAILROAD
Steam, scheduled
36" gauge

TWEETSIE RAILROAD

Ride/Operation: The Tweetsie Railroad is a theme park centered on a three-mile train ride. Visitors can enjoy the train show, live entertainment, rides, mountain crafts, and a petting zoo.

Train: Open excursion cars; wooden combine; coach.

Schedule: Daily, May 18-September 2, 9:00 a.m.-6:00 p.m.; weekends Friday-Sunday, September 3-October 31, 9:00 a.m.-6:00 p.m.

Admission: Adults $15.00, senior citizens (60+) and children $13.00, children under 4 admitted free. Group rates available. Admission includes train ride and other park attractions.

Locomotives: No. 12, 1917 Baldwin 4-6-0, former Tennessee & Western North Carolina; No. 190, 1943 Baldwin 2-8-2, former White Pass & Yukon.

Special Events: Railroaders' Day, June 17.

Location: Between Boone and Blowing Rock on U.S. 221-321. Take Mile Post 291 exit off the Blue Ridge Parkway.

Contact: Marketing Director

Mailing Address:
P.O. Box 388
Blowing Rock, NC 28605
Telephone: (704) 264-9061

MIKE DAVIS

Ride/Operation: Eight-mile round trip over four miles of the original Norfolk Southern Railway's Durham Branch.

Displays/Exhibits: U.S. Army troop sleeper houses miscellaneous railway artifacts, Southern Railway RPO, miscellaneous freight cars and motorcars.

Schedule: Open 9:00 a.m.-5:00 p.m. each Saturday. Trains run first Sunday of each month May - December at 12, 1, 2, 3, and 4 or by prior arrangement.

Fare/Admission: $5.00 adults, $3.00 children for ride; Admission to exhibits and ground is free.

Locomotives: G.E. 80 ton #71 March 1945, Whitcomb 80 Ton #75, G.E. 45 ton #67, Whitcomb 50 ton #70, Heisler #7, 80 ton 3 truck - currently under heavy restoration.

Rolling Stock/Equipment: Seaboard Air Line Caboose #5228, Aberdeen & Rockfish Caboose #308, Norfolk Southern Caboose #335, Model 15 Burro Crane. misc. freight cars.

Special Events: Santa Claus Day - first Sunday in December.

Notes: Rent-a-locomotive program for those wishing to run a locomotive, hourly rentals are available by prior arrangement

Location: Take US1 South from Raleigh NC to the New Hill Exit, (SR1011), turn left onto old US1 (SP1011), travel 2 miles to Daisy St. at the community of Bonsal, turn right onto Daisy St, travel 500 ft. - New Hope Valley Railway is on left.

M at ll

Contact: Membership Chair

Mailing Address: P.O. Box 40
New Hill, N.C. 27562
Telephone: (912) 362-5416
E-mail: EXMNOa@prodigy.com
Internet: http://prodigy.com/N/C/M/NCRRM/index.htm

239

FLOYD McEACHERN
HISTORICAL TRAIN MUSEUM
Railway museum

FLOYD MCEACHERN HISTORICAL MUSEUM

Ride/Operation: More than 3,000 articles of railroad memorabilia spanning more than 140 years of railroad history are on display at this 5,000 square foot site. "O" scale model trains operate on 1,800 feet of a beautifully landscaped layout. A video booth playing four features: "The Making of the Fugitive," "Riding on a Steam Engine #1702," "History of the Railroad," and "The Railway and the Community."

Schedule: Saturday, 8:00 a.m. - 6:00 p.m.; Sunday-Friday, 8:00 a.m. - 4:00 p.m.
Admission: Adults $3.00, children $2.00.

Location: One Front Street behind the *Great Smoky Mountains Railway* ticket office.

Contact: Floyd McEachern

Mailing Address:
P.O. Box 180
One Front Street
Dillsboro, NC 28725
Telephone: (704) 586-4085

GREAT SMOKY MOUNTAINS RAILWAY
Steam, diesel, scheduled
Standard gauge

GREAT SMOKY MOUNTAINS RAILWAY

Ride/Operation: This railway offers a choice of five scenic round-trip excursions ranging from 2½ to 7 hours over its sixty-seven miles of track from Dillsboro to Andrews. The *Great Smoky Mountains Railway* takes you through a beautiful corner of Eastern America along river gorges, across fertile valleys and through tunnels pick-axed out of a granite mountain by convict laborers.

Train: No. 1702, former U.S. Army 2-8-0; GP35s; GP7s; lightweight and heavyweight coaches; open-air cars; cabooses.

Schedule: March 31 through December 31; schedules vary with seasons. Lunch, dinner, and rail-raft trips are available. Please call or write for complete schedules.

Fare: Start at $18.00 adults and $9.00 children (under age 13). Reservations are strongly recommended.

Locomotives: No. 1702, 1942 Baldwin 2-8-0, former U.S. Army; Nos. 711 & 777, EMD GP7s; Nos. 210 & 223, EMD GP35s.

Location: Excursion trains leave from Dillsboro, Bryson City, and Andrews, North Carolina.

Contact: Malcolm G. MacNeill
President

Mailing Address:
P.O. Box 397
One Front Street
Dillsboro, NC 28725
Telephone : (704) 586-8811
(800) 872-4681

NATIONAL RAILROAD MUSEUM
AND HALL OF FAME
Railway display

NATIONAL RAILROAD MUSEUM AND HALL OF FAME

Displays/Exhibits: This museum's displays feature photographs, maps, a model-railroad layout, and four pieces of rolling stock.

Schedule: Please call or write for information.

Admission: No charge.

Rolling Stock/Equipment: Caboose No. 5241, former Seaboard Air Lines; replica of motor car.

Locomotives: Diesel engine No. 1114, former Seaboard Air Lines; replica of engine "Tornado"

Location: 2 Main Street.

Hamlet

Radio Frequency: 160.590 (CSX)

Contact: J. A. Crowell
President

Mailing Address:
2 Main Street
Hamlet, NC 28345
Telephone: (910) 582-3317

NORTH CAROLINA TRANSPORTATION MUSEUM AT HISTORIC SPENCER SHOPS

Transportation museum
Standard gauge

JIM WRINN

Ride/Operation: Steam and diesel locomotives operate April to mid December.

Displays/Exhibits: Spencer Shops was the largest railroad repair facility on the Southern Railway; more than twenty-five hundred people were employed in the fifty-seven-acre complex. The massive backshop, thirty-seven-stall roundhouse, and nine other major buildings are being restored to chronicle the history of transportation in North Carolina. Four buildings are currently open: the former Master Mechanic's Office and the Flue Shop, the 37-stall Roundhouse and Barber Junction Depot.

Train: Open and closed coaches, former Reading and former Canadian National.

Schedule: *Museum*: Daily, April 1-October 31; Monday-Saturday, 9:00 a.m.-5:00 p.m.; Sunday, 1:00-5:00 p.m., November 1-March 31; Tuesday-Saturday, 10:00 a.m.-4:00 p.m.; Sunday, 1:00-4:00 p.m. *Train*: April 1-Labor Day; Monday-Saturday, 11:00 a.m., 1:00, 2:00 & 3:00 p.m.; Sunday, 1:30, 2:30, 3:30 p.m. September-mid December: Saturday, 11:00 a.m., 1:00, 2:00 & 3:00 p.m.; Sunday, 1:30, 2:30, 3:30 p.m. Roundhouse Talk: One hour tours, 11:00 a.m. & 2:00 p.m., $1.00. Turntable Rides: Ride the 100 foot long turntable, 10:00 a.m.-4:00 p.m. every 1/2 hour, $.50.

Fare/Admission: Steam train: adults $4.00, senior citizens and children (3-12) $3.00. Diesel train: adults $3.50, senior citizens and children (3-12) $2.50. Museum: no charge.

Locomotives: No. 604, 1926 Baldwin 2-8-0, former Buffalo Creek & Gauley No. 4; No. 542, 1903 2-8-0, No. 6900, EMD E8, and No. 6133, EMD FP7, all former SR; No. 1925, 1925 Lima 3-truck Shay, former Graham County Railroad; No. 1616, AS-416 diesel, former Norfolk Southern; No. 620, EMD GP9 diesel, former Norfolk & Western.

Rolling Stock/Equipment: RPO and baggage car, both former SR; maintenance-of-way car, former NS; cabooses, former SR, former Seaboard Railway, former

NS, and former N&W; 40 & 8 boxcar.

Location: Spencer is just off I-85 about 3 miles north of Salisbury. Spencer Shops is at 411 S. Salisbury Avenue (U.S. 29-70).

Salisbury

Contact: Kelly Wrinn
Programs Specialist

Mailing Address:
411 S. Salisbury Avenue
P.O. Box 165
Spencer, NC 28159
Telephone: (704) 636-2889

WILMINGTON RAILROAD MUSEUM
Railway museum

CHARLES KERNAN

Displays/Exhibits: Maintenance-of-way exhibits, dining-car china, timetables, safety awards, labor exhibit, photos, O-scale exhibit, and extensive HO-model history exhibit. Displays primarily represent the Atlantic Coast Line Railroad, but others are featured.

Schedule: Monday-Sunday; Monday-Saturday, 10:00 a.m.-5:00 p.m.; Sunday, 1:00-5:00 p.m. Closed Mondays November 1-March 31.

Admission: Adults $2.00, children (6-11) $1.00, children under 6 admitted free.

Locomotives: 1910 Baldwin 4-6-0.

Rolling Stock/Equipment: Boxcar, former Richmond, Fredericksburg & Potomac; caboose, former ACL; caboose, former Norfolk & Western; motor cars.

Location: 501 Nutt Street.

&. (limited)

Contact: Brian C. Collins
Executive Director

Mailing Address:
501 Nutt Street
Wilmington, NC 28401
Telephone: (910) 763-2634

BONANZAVILLE, U.S.A.
Railway display
Standard gauge

BONANZAVILLE, U.S.A.

Displays/Exhibits: Bonanzaville, U.S.A., a pioneer village, museum, and interpretive center, includes more than forty buildings (mostly original). At the Railroad Complex is the former Embden, North Dakota, depot, which has been completely refurbished to its turn-of-the-century appearance. Also at the site is former Northern Pacific 4-4-0, No. 684, the only remaining locomotive of the first eleven purchased when the NP began operations. Visitors can also see a caboose, passenger coaches, and a railroad snowplow. A second station, from Kathryn, North Dakota, is the headquarters for the Spud Valley Railroad Club. The station agent's former living quarters have been transformed by the club into a model-train complex that shows the Fargo-Moorhead area in the 1950s, including the Union Stockyards, the Northern Pacific Depot, Dilworth, and many other buildings along Front Street (now Main Avenue).

Schedule: Late May-late October, daily; please call for schedule. November-April: museum only; 9:00 a.m.-5:00 p.m.

Admission: Please call for information.

Location: On U.S. highway 10. Travel west from I-29 exit 65; travel east from I-94 exit 343.

    ♿ **P** ✼ 兔 **M** Fargo

Campground adjacent

Contact: Dr. Laura French
Executive Director

Mailing Address:
P.O. Box 719
West Fargo, ND 58078
Telephone: (701) 282-2822
Information: (800) 700-5317
Fax: (701) 282-7606

QUAKER SQUARE
Model railroad display
O gauge

QUAKER SQUARE

Displays/Exhibits: These model railroad displays are built around and inside of three original Broadway Limited train cars that were built in 1937. One LGB layout is displayed inside a 1937 Pullman car.

Schedule: Daily except Thanksgiving, Christmas, and New Year's.

Fare/Admission: Free.

Locomotives: LGB displays.

Rolling Stock/Equipment: Several steam locomotives and cars.

Location: Heart of downtown Akron. Corner of Mill and Broadway Streets.

Contact: Roy Bain
Advertising Director

Mailing Address:
135 S. Broadway
Akron, OH 44308
Telephone: (330) 253-5970
Fax: (330) 253-7021

MAD RIVER & NKP RAILROAD SOCIETY
Railway museum
Standard gauge

DENNIS BRANDAL

Displays/Exhibits: A depiction of small-town railroading, including buildings, rolling stock, loco-motives, and many items pertaining to everyday railroad life, with many hands-on items. Cars contain exhibits and photographs about railroad history; depots and other structures appear as they did in use; and several passenger and freights trains are on display. On loan from the B&O Museum in Baltimore is the wooden scale-model replica of the Mad River & Lake Erie's "Sandusky," the first locomotive to operate in Ohio and reportedly the first to have a whistle.

Schedule: Daily, May 30-September 5; weekends, May, September & October; 1:00-5:00 p.m.

Admission: Adults $2.00, children $1.00.

Locomotives/Trolleys: Lake Shore electric interurban under restroration; Alco RSD 12 No. 329 and EMD GP30 No. 900, both former Nickel Plate; EMD F7A No. 671, former Wabash; Fairbanks-Morse H12-44 No. 740, former Milwaukee Road; Brooks 0-6-0 No. 1190, former Buffalo, Rochester & Pittsburgh; Porter fireless 0-6-0 No. 7, former Cleveland Electric Illuminating.

Passenger Cars: Former Chicago, Burlington & Quincy "Silver Dome," the first dome car built in the U.S.; coach No. 105, former NKP; diner, former Seaboard Air Lines; sleeper "Tiger River," former Southern; RPO, former Pennsylvania Railroad; Pullman sleeper "Donizetti"; coach No. 618, former Milwaukee Road; two baggage cars, former Wabash and former Louisville & Nashville.

Rolling Stock/Equipment: Cabooses, freight cars, track speeders, and specialty equipment such as former New York Central wedge snowplow, former NKP dy-namometer car, former N&W 200-ton wreck crane, and more.

Special Events: The society sponsors main-line excur-sions and common-carrier trips; please call or write for information. Annual Flea Market.

Note: Many pieces of railroad-related highway equip-ment are on display or under restoration.

Location: 253 Southwest Street, two blocks from downtown.

Contact: Dennis J. Brandal
Curator

Mailing Address:
233 York Street
Bellevue, OH 44811-1377
Telephone: (419) 483-2222

DALE W. BROWN

Displays/Exhibits: Founded in 1938, this club has an exhibit in Cincinnati Union Terminal's former Control Tower A, the former operating and dispatching center for terminal operations from 1933 to 1973. The tower, which overlooks the busy Norfork Southern and CSX yards and main lines and the former Southern Railway bridge to Kentucky, has been restored by CRRC members as their display and meeting location. Displays include the former track-diagram board, with lights showing track occupancy and the location of switches; the dispatcher's desk; the train starting board; and railroadiana, headlights, bells, whistles, lanterns, and photos related to Cincinnati railroading. The club has an extensive library and photo collection in its archives at the tower.

Schedule: Saturdays, Memorial Day to Labor Day, 10:00 a.m.-5:00 p.m.; Sundays 12:00 p.m. -5:00 p.m. Third Sunday of the month, October-June, 12:00-4:00 p.m.

Admission: No charge. Parking is $3.00 per day in Union Terminal lot.

Locomotives/Trolleys: Curvedside car No. 2435, former Cincinnati Street Railway, is on display at the south ramp of the terminal.

Special Events: August 9: *Summerail 97*, 1:00-10:00 p.m. Multi-media sync-sound slide shows, $12. *Summerail Railroadiana Show & Sale*, 10:00 a.m.-5p.m., free. Both shows at Cincinnati Union Terminal's Rotunda.

Notes: Amtrak Station is at the Museum center.

Location: 1301 Western Avenue at Ezzard Charles Drive. Take exit 1H or 1G off I-75.

Cincinnati

Contact: Dale W. Brown
Trustee and Librarian

Mailing Address:
P.O. Box 14157
Cincinnati, OH 45250-0157
Telephone: (513) 651-RAIL (7245)
Internet: http://www.rrhistorical.com/crrc

PAUL W. PRESCOTT

Displays/Exhibits: The Conneaut station, built by the Lake Shore & Michigan Southern in 1900, is adjacent to Conrail (former New York Central) tracks. Inside are extensive displays of timetables, passes, lanterns, old photos, builder's plates, telegraph instruments, and models of locomotives, cars, and structures. An HO-scale model railroad operates during regular hours. On display outside are a train, section cars, track equipment, and a ball signal. On the station platform are baggage trucks, hand carts, and old trunks. A stready parade of Conrail trains passes the station.

Schedule: Daily, Memorial Day through Labor Day, 12:00-5:00 p.m.

Admission: Donations welcomed.

Locomotives/Trolleys: No. 755, 1944 Lima 2-8-4, former Nickel Plate.

Rolling Stock/Equipment: A 90-ton hopper car and a wooden caboose, both former Bessemer & Lake Erie.

Location: In the old New York Central station at Depot and Mill streets, north of U.S. 20 and I-90. Blue-and-white locomotive signs point the way to the museum.

Mailing Address:
P.O. Box 643
Conneaut, OH 44030
Telephone: (216) 599-7878

PATRICIA PORTER

Ride/Operation: Twice a month, the Carillon Park Rail and Steam Society, an auxiliary organization of Carillon Historical Park, operates a scale-model layout at the western edge of this outdoor historical museum. Associate members and their families may ride (membership is $5).

Displays/Exhibits: Rail-related exhibits include an 1835 Baltimore & Ohio "grasshopper" locomotive; a 1903 Barney and Smith wood-bodied passenger car; a 1904 G.C. Kuhlman Co. interurban; a 1903 J.G. Brill summer trolley; an H.K. Porter locomotive; 0-6-0 No. 6721, former New York Central; a Baltimore & Ohio caboose; a 1909 Lima fireless locomotive; the 1894 Bowling Green, Ohio, train depot; and a 1907 railroad watchtower. Inside the depot is original equipment as well as a model of the "Cincinnati," the first locomotive to enter Dayton, in 1851.

Schedule: May-August: Tuesday-Saturday, 10:00 a.m.-6:00 p.m.; Sunday 1:00-6:00 p.m.; September-October: Tuesday-Saturday, 10:00 a.m.-5:00 p.m.; Sunday 1:00-5:00 p.m. Closed Monday except Labor Day (open 1:00-5:00 pm.)

Admission: Adults $2.00, children (ages 6-17) $1.00, children under 6 admitted free. Present your Carillon Park membership for free admission. Free parking. No pets.

Location: Take exit 51 off I-75; travel east on Edwin C. Moses Boulevard, then turn right onto Stewart Street, right onto Patterson Boulevard, and right onto Carillon Boulevard. Park entrance is on the left.

Contact: Mary Mathews
Executive Director

Mailing Address:
2001 South Patterson Boulevard
Dayton, OH 45409-2023
Telephone: (937) 293-2841
Fax: (937) 293-5798

THE DENNISON RAILROAD
DEPOT MUSEUM
Steam, diesel, scheduled
Railway museum

RUSTY FOX

Ride/Operation: This museum sponsors excursions ranging from 1-hour to all-day trips, through an arrangement with the Columbus & Ohio River Railroad in Coshocton.

Displays/Exhibits: Restored 1873 Pennsylvania Railroad station, once the site of a World War II canteen that served more than one million GIs. The depot was part of a complex begun in the mid-1860s by the Pittsburgh, Cincinnati & St. Louis Railroad; at its peak, the Dennison yards and shops employed three thousand workers. Depot restaurant includes a "Canteen Restaurant" with a unique 1940s themed atmosphere and family dining; Exhibit includes a large N-scale layout of Dennison during its heyday; original waiting rooms (men's and women's) filled with railroad displays; a ticket booth; a baggage room; a Railway Express building and office; a 1950 former Norfolk & Western caboose; a 1920 tank car with engine and caboose and a 1946 "Thermos Bottle" engine.

Train: Steam locomotive No. 1551, 1912 Montreal Locomotive Works, former Canadian National; historic passenger coaches. Diesel excursions are also offered.

Schedule: Museum: Tuesday-Saturday, 10:00 a.m.-5:00 p.m.; Sunday, 11:00 a.m.-5:00 p.m.

Fare/Admission: Museum: adults $3.00, senior citizens $2.50, students $1.75, children under 7 admitted free. Excursions: fare varies; 1-hour rides are generally $7.00 for adults and $5.00 for students. Please call or write for more specific information.

Special Events & Excursions: Railroad Festival, third week of May. Santa Ride, December 8.

Canteen Restaurant Hours: Tuesday-Thursday, 11:00 a.m.-7:00 p.m., Friday-Saturday, 11:00 a.m.-8:00 p.m., Sunday, 11:00 a.m.-5:00 p.m.

Location: 400 Center Street where routes 36, 250 and 800 meet, 18 miles east of I-77.

Contact: Wendy Zucal
Museum Director

Mailing Address:
P.O. Box 11
400 Center Street
Dennison, OH 44621
Telephone: (614) 922-6776

ASHTABULA, CARSON & JEFFERSON SCENIC LINE

Ride/Operation: A 12-mile, 1-hour round trip over the last remaining portion of the New York Central's Ashtabula-to-Pittsburgh "High Grade" passenger mainline. The train travels through scenic woodlands and farmland between the quaint village of Jefferson to Carson, a staging yard for Conrail's coal & iron-ore operations in historic Ashtabula Harbor.

Train: Air-conditioned coach, former Erie No. 1022; baggage cars, former Lackawanna Nos. 200 and 201; open-window coach, former Long Island Railroad No. 7133; caboose, former Nickel Plate No. 425.

Schedule: Weekends, June 21-October 26; 12:30, 2:00 & 3:30 p.m. Reservations required in October. Charters available May 1-November 1.

Fare: Adults $7.00, senior citizens $6.00, children $5.00.

Locomotives: No. 107, 1950 Alco S-2 diesel, former Nickel Plate and Fairport, Painesville & Eastern; No. 518, 1951 Alco S-2 diesel, former Erie and former Centerior Energy plant switcher (Ashtabula).

Special Events: Halloween train, featuring haunted baggage car. Dinner/Mystery trains. Write for details and run dates. Reservations required.

Notes: All passenger operations conducted by AC & J Scenic Line, Incorporated.

Location: In northeastern Ohio, accessible from I-90 and I-80 via State Route 11. Trains depart at Jefferson Street, two blocks east of State Route 46 in Jefferson.

Cleveland & Erie, Pennsylvania

Contact: Frank Rueter
General Manager

Mailing Address:
P.O. Box 222
Jefferson, OH 44047-0222
Telephone: (216) 576-6346

I&O SCENIC RAILWAY

Ride/Operation: A working, common-carrier freight and passenger railroad, this line offers a 12-mile, 1-hour round trip through the rolling hills of southwest Ohio over a former Pennsylvania Railroad branch line.

Train: Four electric commuter cars built in 1930 for the Delaware, Lackawanna & Western Railroad; open gondola car.

Schedule: April 6-December 22.

Fare: Adults $9.00, senior citizens $8.00, children $5.00.

Locomotives: No. 55, 1950 EMD GP7, former Chesapeake & Ohio.

Special Events: Golden Lamb Sunday dinner packages. Mystery Dinner Tours. Train Rides with Santa.

Location: In southwestern Ohio, between Dayton and Cincinnati. Take I-71 or I-75 to Lebanon and follow the signs to the station on South Broadway.

P 🚌 ✳ ☕ ▶ ◀

🚂 **TRAIN** Cincinnati

Radio Frequency: 161.385

Contact: Passenger Service Representative

Mailing Address:
198 South Broadway
Lebanon, OH 45036
Telephone: (513) 398-8584

MAUMEE VALLEY HISTORICAL SOCIETY

Operation: The depot is part of a five building museum complex. Guided tours cover the entire complex.

Displays/Exhibits: Depot and caboose are authentically furnished. Railroad memorabilia on display.

Schedule: Wednesday-Sunday, 1:00-4:00 p.m.

Rolling Stock/Equipment: Caboose and baggage car.

Location: The museum is on River Road in downtown Maumee and can be reached easily from U.S. Routes 20 and 24.

Contact: Judy Walrod
Special Events Coordinator

Mailing Address:
1031 River Road
Maumee, OH 43537
Telephone: (419) 893-9602
Fax: (419) 893-3108

HOCKING VALLEY SCENIC RAILWAY
Steam, scheduled
Standard gauge

HOCKING VALLEY SCENIC RAILWAY

Ride/Operation: This historic railroad offers a 12-mile round trip to Haydenville and a 25-mile round trip to Logan with a visit to an 1860s settlers' village at Robbin's Crossing. The train operates over a former Chesapeake & Ohio route that was once a part of the original Hocking Valley Railway, listed on the National Register of Historic Places. Special trains include the Canal Winchester 100-mile round trip Steam Specials; please call or write for information.

Train: Coaches, former Rock Island and former Baltimore & Ohio; open-air car.

Schedule: Weekends and holidays, May 25-October 31. Haydenville train: 12:00 p.m. Logan train: 2:30 p.m.

Fare: Haydenville: adults $6.50, children (2-11) $4.00. Logan: adults $9.50, children (2-11) $6.50.

Locomotives: No. 33, 1916 Baldwin 2-8-0; No. 5833, 1952 EMD GP7, former Chesapeake & Ohio; No. 7318, 1942 General Electric; No. 3, 1920 Baldwin 0-6-0.

Special Events: Santa Claus Trains only Logan train in operation call for dates and details. Canal Winchester Steam Specials; please call or write for information.

Location: On route 33 in southeastern Ohio, 60 miles southeast of Columbus.

Contact: Passenger Agent

Mailing Address:
P.O. Box 427
Nelsonville, OH 45764
Telephone (weekdays): (513) 335-0382
Weekends during operating season:
(614) 753-9531

BUCKEYE CENTRAL SCENIC RAILROAD
Diesel, scheduled
Standard gauge

BUCKEYE CENTRAL SCENIC RAILROAD

Ride/Operation: A 12-mile round trip over part of the former Shawnee Branch of the Baltimore & Ohio Railroad, through Licking County to Heath. The train winds its way through the countryside, passing over two trestles and a long steel bridge over the Licking River.

Displays/Exhibits: Station built just after the Civil War; railroad memorabilia.

Train: Passenger cars, a gondola, and cabooses.

Schedule: Weekends, May 25-October 15, 1:00 & 3:00 p.m. Charters available May 15-October 31.

Fare: Adults $6.00, children (2-11) $5.00, children under 2 ride free when accompanied by an adult.

Locomotives: No. 8599, 1948 Electro-Motive SW1, former Penn Central Railroad.

Rolling Stock/Equipment: Seven passenger cars, two circa 1910, three 1958, one 1941, and one 1956; 1941 gondola; three cabooses, former Norfolk & Western, former Chesapeake & Ohio, 1941 former Pere Marquette.

Special Events: Halloween Nite Train Rides. Santa Specials. Train Robberies. Hobo Parties. Please call for schedules.

Location: National Road is located on U.S. Route 40, 3 1/2 miles east of Hebron or 1 1/2 miles west of Jacksontown, with easy access from I-70. Use either the Rt. 79 N. exit to Rt. 40 (turn right) or the Rt. 13 N. exit to Rt. 40 (turn left).

Contact: Robert H. Miller
President

Mailing Address:
P.O. Box 242
Newark, OH 43055
Telephone: (614) 366-2029

TROLLEYVILLE U.S.A.

Ride/Operation: A 2 ½-mile ride over a scenic residential and park route; optional carbarn tour to view Trolleyville's complete collection.

Displays/Exhibits: Rare photos, streetcar memorabilia, and novelties in the ticket office; Harry Christiansen Library (by appointment); restored Baltimore & Ohio depot from Berea, Ohio, housing the Morris Stone collection of O-gauge traction equipment, along with an operating O-gauge layout, under wire.

Schedule: Weekends & holidays, May 4-November 24; 12:00-5:00 p.m.; Wednesday & Friday, May 22-September 27; 10:00 a.m.-3:00 p.m.

Fare: Adults $4.00, senior citizens $3.60, children (3-11) $2.00, children under 3 ride free.

Trolleys: Two Brill Veracruz open summer trolleys; three wooden and five steel heavyweight interurbans, former Chicago Aurora & Elgin; two lightweight interurbans, former Aurora, Elgin & Fox River; city cars, former Cleveland, Pittsburgh, Cincinnati, Shaker Heights, and Blackpool, England; Dallas double-ended PCC; three box motors from Iowa and Michigan; others.

Rolling Stock/Equipment: 1968 boxcar, former Chesapeake & Ohio; 1965 boxcar, former Pennsylvania Railroad; 1914 caboose, former Norfolk & Western; 1875 four-wheel caboose, former New York & Ontario.

Special Events: Moonlight Rides. Popsicle Fridays. Train Shows. Murder Trains. Bus Tours. Halloween Party. Flea Market. Trolleys on Parade. Festival of Lights. Please call or write for information.

Location: At 7100 Columbia Road (state route 252-S), east of exit 9 of the Ohio Turnpike. Off I-480, two miles south of Great Northern Mall. Six miles west of the Bagley Road exit of I-71, and one mile north on Columbia Road.

Cleveland

Contact: Cliff Perry
General Manager

Mailing Address:
7100 Columbia Road
Olmsted Township, OH 44138
Telephone: (216) 235-4725
Fax: (216) 235-6556

ORRVILLE RAILROAD
HERITAGE SOCIETY
Diesel, irregular
Standard gauge

Ride/Operation: Diesel powered main line excursions.

Displays/Exhibits: Former Pennsylvania Railroad depot, now a museum.

Schedule: Open May-September. Trains run on Excursion Days May 3-4 & September 20.

Fare/Admission: No charge.

Special Events: Depot Days, June 14-15. Christmas at the Depot, November 28-29.

Location: Orrville is on Ohio Route 57 three miles north of U.S. 30 to Orrville or 16 miles south of I-76. Museum is three blocks west of State Route 57 at Depot and Market Streets.

Contact: Roger Scott or Bob Cutting

Mailing Address:
P.O. Box 11
Orrville, OH 44667
Telephone: (330) 683-2426

CEDAR POINT
AMUSEMENT PARK/RESORT
Steam, scheduled
Standard gauge

DAN FEIDIT

Ride/Operation: Six operating steam locomotives that travel a scenic 1-mile ride through the amusement park.

Display/Exhibit: The wolds's largest amusement ride park with 56 rides, inclusing 12 roller coasters.

Schedule: Open May through October; trains operate daily through the operating season and depart every 10 minutes

Fare/Admission: Call for details.

Location: Midway between Cleveland and Toledo Ohio, Exit 7 from the Ohio Turnpike to U.S. Route 250 North into Sandusky and follow the signs

 Sandusky, 4 miles away

Contact:
Cedar Point Marketing

Mailing Address:
P.O. Box 5006
Sandusky, OH 44871-5006
Telephone: (419) 627-2350
Fax: (419) 627-2200
Internet: http://www.cedarpoint.com

OHIO CENTRAL RAILROAD
Steam, diesel, scheduled
Standard gauge

DOYLE YODER

Ride/Operation: The Ohio Central, a 70-mile-long working railroad, operates the diesel- and steam-powered Sugarcreek Service, a 1-hour round trip over former Wheeling & Lake Erie trackage in the Amish country known as the "Switzerland of Ohio."

Train: Passenger coaches, former Burlington, former Grand Trunk, and former Lackawanna.

Schedule: Monday-Saturday, May 2-October 26, 11:00 a.m., 12:30, 2:00 & 3:30 p.m. Extra trains added, Saturdays, July, August & October, 5:00 p.m.

Fare: Adults $7.00, children (3-12) $4.00, children under 3 ride free.

Locomotives: No. 1551, 1912 Montreal 4-6-0, former Canadian National; No. 13, 1920 Alco 2-8-0, former Buffalo Creek & Gauley; No. 12, 1950 Alco S-1, former Timken Roller Bearing; No. 6325, 1942 Alco 4-8-4, former Grand Trunk Western.

Special Events: Swiss Festival, September 27-28.

Location: Ohio Central Station, 111 Factory Street.

Contact: Laura Jacobson
Manager

Mailing Address:
P.O. Box 427
Sugarcreek, OH 44681
Telephone: (330) 852-4676

Ohio, Waterville and Grand Rapids
D-R

TOLEDO, LAKE ERIE &
WESTERN RAILWAY
Diesel, scheduled
Standard gauge

GEORGE A. FORERO, JR.

Ride/Operation: A 20-mile, 2-hour round trip over a portion of the former Clover Leaf Division of the Nickel Plate Road. The train travels through villages, fields, and woodlands and over a 900-foot-long bridge over the Maumee River and the old Miami & Erie Canal.

Displays/Exhibits: Cars that are not part of the train; World War II troop sleeper; freight cars; maintenance-of-way equipment.

Train: Electric commuter cars, former New York Central and former Lackawanna; coaches, former Baltimore & Ohio and NYC; parlor car; Pullman car; cabooses.

Schedule: Sundays and holidays, May 6-October 29; Waterville round trip, 1:00 & 4:00 p.m.; Grand Rapids round trip, 2:30 p.m.; one-way trip, 5:30 p.m. Tuesdays and Thursdays, May 29-September 4; Waterville round trip, 10:30 a.m. & 1:30 p.m.; Grand Rapids round trip, 11:45 a.m.; one-way trip, 2:45 p.m. Saturdays, Waterville round trip, 11:30 a..m., 2:00 & 4:30 p.m.; Grand Rapids round trip 12:45 & 3:15 p.m.; one-way trip, 5:45 p.m. Charters may be scheduled any time.

Fare: Round trip: adults $8.00, senior citizens $7.00, children (3-12) $4.50. One-way fare and group rates available. Caboose and parlor-car seats available on some trains for $1.00 extra each way per person.

Locomotives: No. 5109, 1948 Alco S-4, former Chesapeake & Ohio; No. 112, 1946 Alco S-2, former U.S. Steel; No. 202, 1920 Baldwin 0-6-0, former Detroit Edison Co.; No. 1, 1941 44-ton Whitcomb, former Ann Arbor Railroad; No. 15, 1908 Porter 0-6-0T, former Brooklyn Eastern District Terminal.

Note: Stopovers are permitted at each terminal.

Location: Waterville Depot: take U.S. 24 to state route 64 north and turn right on Sixth Street. Grand Rapids: take state route 65 to Mill Street, then travel south on Mill Street one block.

P 🚌 ✳ 🏕 TRA͟I͟N **M**
🛤 Toledo

Contact: Kim Duryea
Charter Director

Mailing Address:
P.O. Box 168
Waterville, OH 43566
Telephone:
Waterville Depot: (419) 878-2177

MAHONING VALLEY
RAILROAD HERITAGE ASSOCIATION
Railway display

BRUCE LIGHTCAP

Ride/Operation: This organization was founded in 1985 to establish an operating railroad museum and to preserve the railroading heritage of greater Youngstown and Warren, Ohio. It focuses on the railroads that served the area, including the Pennsylvania, the New York Central, the Erie, and the Baltimore & Ohio, and in the specialized breed of railroading used by the steel industry. The organization is planning construction of a regional rail museum to be located on the west side of Youngstown.

Displays/Exhibits: Former YS&T No. 301 is on public display at the Canfield Fairgrounds with a Youngstown & Southern wooden caboose. No. 301 is in the Western Reserve Village, a re-creation of a pioneer village comprising historic buildings that have been moved to the fairgrounds, which includes the former Erie station from Canfield, Ohio, and a crossing watchman's tower. Other equipment owned by the organization is in storage and can be toured by prior arrangement.

Schedule: Rolling stock can be seen only by prior arrangement. YS&T No. 301 can be visited every day from dawn to dark and during the Canfield fair in early September. Call for a guided tour of rolling stock or locomotive.

Admission: No charge, except during fair days or special events. Fair: $4.00 per person.

Locomotives: 1915 Baldwin 0-6-0 No. 301, former Youngstown Sheet & Tube Co.

Passenger Cars: No. 454017 and No. 3617, troop sleepers converted to camp cars, former Delaware, Lackawanna & Western; No. 6519, Railway Post Office, former PRR.

Rolling Stock/Equipment: Pugh-type hot-metal cars and slag car, former Youngstown Sheet & Tube Co.; N5c cabin car, former PRR; caboose; A-6 Fairmont motor car, former Bessemer & Lake Erie; Pollock Co. hot metal car; transfer caboose, former Pittsburgh & Lake Erie; Blast Furnace Larry car #9, Sharon Steel Co.

Location: At the Canfield Fairgrounds, south of Canfield, Ohio.

Youngstown

Contact: J. Richard Rowlands
Historian

Mailing Address:
P.O. Box 3055
Youngstown, OH 44511
Telephone: (330) 568-0328

LANCE CHESTER

Displays/Exhibits: This museum, housed in a 1926-27 former Santa Fe freight house, has one of the largest collections of railroad artifacts in the Midwest. Memorabilia pertaining to all railroad professions can be found here: one room is devoted to more than 400 pieces of dining-car china; another holds a library that includes many books as well as postcards, railroad money, and items of local history. The former loading dock, now enclosed, contains HO- and N-gauge model-railroad layouts. Enid was known as the railroad hub of Oklahoma; 10 main tracks radiated outward from it. All rolling stock has been returned to its original color and lettering.

Schedule: Tuesdays-Fridays, 1:00-4:00 p.m.; Saturdays, 10:00 a.m.-1:00 p.m. Also by appointment.

Admission: Donations welcomed.

Locomotives: No. 1519, former St.Louis-San Francisco 4-8-2; No. VMCX1, 50-ton General Electric class BB switcher, former Vulcan Chemicals.

Passenger Cars: No. 968186MWX, 86-foot RPO/combination car, former Chicago, Burlington & Quincy.

Rolling Stock/Equipment: Cabooses No. 25323, former Union Pacific; No. 1281, former Frisco; No. 132, former Missouri-Kansas-Texas; No. 1139, former Northern Pacific; No. 12433, former Burlington Northern; and No. 999567, former Santa Fe. No. CONX50004,1928 automobile boxcar, former Santa Fe/Continental Oil Co.; No. CONX190, 3-dome tank car, former COC; tank car No. PSPX 16397; flatcar No. 105288, former "Frisco", two section cars; Herbard shop mule; White trackmobile.

Special Events: Model-railroad swap meets each year. Annual Christmas Party.

Location: Thirty miles west of I-35 in north-central Oklahoma, on U.S. routes 60, 81, 64 & 412. The museum is 6 blocks northwest of the downtown Enid square.

Contact: Robert E. Chester
Editor/Vice President

Mailing Address:
702 North Washington
Enid, OK 73701
Telephone: (405) 233-3051

HUGO HERITAGE RAILROAD
Diesel, scheduled
Standard gauge

CHOCTAW COUNTY HISTORICAL SOCIETY

Ride/Operation: This operation offers a 2 1/2-hour round trip from Hugo (Circus City, U.S.A.) to points north and south, including Paris, Texas.

Displays/Exhibits: A museum located in the former 1915 Frisco depot, the largest one left on Frisco's southwest lines. Displays include an HO-gauge model railroad on a mountain layout, railroad artifacts, turn-of-the-century memorabilia, rare photographs, and a working Harvey House restaurant.

Train: Climate-controlled coaches pulled by the Kiamichi Railroad's engines on the Kiamichi right-of-way.

Schedule: Saturdays, April-November, 2:00 p.m.

Fare/Admission: Train: adults $15.00, children (4-12) $10.00. Museum: no charge. Group specials available.

Passenger Cars: Two 1940s coaches: No. 1001, "Kiamichi Country," former Norfolk & Western; No. 1002, "Circus City U.S.A."

Rolling Stock/Equipment: Baggage car No. 372, former Frisco (stored); circa 1950 Railway Express truck; Kiamichi No. SL1, 1949 F-7A, former Kansas City Southern No. 70-A.

Special Events: Railroad Days, Fall Color Runs. Call for dates and details.

Note: The Hugo Heritage Railroad is now being operated by Little Dixie Community Action Agency.

Location: 300 Block West Jackson.

Contact: Nita Pence
Manager

Mailing Address:
502 West Duke
Hugo, OK 74743
Telephone: (405) 326-6630
Toll free: 1-888-RR Depot
Fax: (405) 326-2305

WAYNOKA HISTORICAL SOCIETY

Ride/Operation: Museum is housed in the former Santa Fe Depot, next door to the Harvey House. Buildings are to be restored with over $500,000; architects currently working on plans. Located on BNSF main line from Chicago to Los Angeles - many trains daily.

Displays/Exhibits: Railroad memorabilia; Transcontinental Air Transport exhibit; German prisoner-of-war paintings; local history; Harvey House display, railways Ice Plant display; John Holbird mural.

Schedule: Weekends 2:00-4:00 p.m. and by appointment. Call (405) 824-1886 or 824-5871.

Fare/Admission: Free

Location: 2 blocks west of US 281 at West end of Waynoka Street.

 P **M**

Contact: Sandi Olson

Mailing Address:
P.O.Box 193
Waynoka, OK 73860
Telephone: (405) 824-1886 or 824-5871
Fax: (405) 824-7331

YUKON'S BEST RAILROAD MUSEUM
Railway museum

HUGH SCOTT

Displays/Exhibits: This museum contains an extensive display of railroad antiques and artifacts. Emphasis is placed on the Rock Island Line, but many other railroads are represented.

Schedule: Please call or write for information.

Admission: No charge.

Rolling Stock/Equipment: Boxcar No. 5542 and caboose No. 17039, both former Rock Island; caboose No. 13724, former Missouri Pacific; caboose No. 25865, former Union Pacific.

Location: Third and Main streets.

Contact: John A. Knuppel
Curator

Mailing Address:
1020 West Oak Street
Yukon, OK 73099
Telephone: (405) 354-5079

SUMPTER VALLEY RAILROAD RESTORATION

Ride/Operation: A 10-mile round trip takes passengers through a wildlife area to the city of Sumpter. Views include the rugged Elkhorn Mountains, beautiful Sumpter Valley, and dredge tailings left from gold-mining days.

Displays/Exhibits: Original SVR boxcars and stock cars, old boilers, and an original SVR 2-8-2 steam locomotive. Members are also establishing an SVR museum at the Sumpter depot, which they hope to open to the public this season.

Train: Two-truck, 40-ton Heisler; plans also call for operation of an original SVR 2-8-2 this summer.

Schedule: Weekends and holidays, May 28-September 30.

Fare: Round trip: adults $8.00, children $6.00, family $20.00. One way: adults $5.00, children $4.00, family $13.00.

Passenger Cars: Original SVR 1890s Pullman coach; two open-air cars; open-sided boxcar.

Rolling Stock/Equipment: Original SVR-built caboose; six hopper cars; two flatcars; tank car.

Special Events: Founders' Day Celebration. Moonlight Dinner Rides, three times a year.

Location: In the Blue Mountains of eastern Oregon.

Take I-84 to Baker City, then take highway 7 along the Powder River to Railroad Park.

Baker City

Contact: Ron Brinton
President

Mailing Address:
P.O. Box 389
Baker City, OR 97814
Telephone: (503) 894-2268

OREGON ELECTRIC RAILWAY MUSEUM
Electric, scheduled
Standard gauge

STEVE MORGAN

Ride/Operation: A 1-mile ride through fields in the mid-Willamette Valley.

Displays/Exhibits: Streetcars, artifacts and photographs of Portland area cars.

Schedule: 1996-Weekends and holidays, from last weekend in July through October 31. 1997-Weekends and holidays, May 1-October 31.

Admission: Will be posted. Call for information.

Trolleys: Nos. 503 & 506, 1904 Brill semi-convertible, Portland; No. 1067, 1908 Co. Shops, wooden interurban, Portland Railway Light & Power; Nos. 1118 & 1159, 1947 St. Louis, PCC-St. Louis/San Francisco; No. 1187, 1908 New S. Wales, open Car, Sydney; No. 1191, 1912, C. G. Kuhlman, baggage car/RPO, Mt. Hood Railway & Power; No. 1304, 1911/1946 Westminster Shops, interurban, British Columbia Elec. Rwy.; No. 1318, 1923 St. Louis, L. A. Railways open/closed narrow gauge; No. 1445, 1898, McGuire sweeper East Side Railways No. 102/Port. Traction No. 1445.

Locomotives: Nos. 251 & 254, GE 25-ton electric; No. 351, GE 35-ton electrics, former Anaconda Copper Co.; No. 401, Baldwin/Westinghouse 40-ton electric; 1942 GE 25-ton diesel.

Rolling Stock/Equipment: 2 flat cars, U.S. Navy/BN; BN camp car; and GN caboose.

Location: The museum has been relocated to 3995 Brooklake Road NE, Brooks, Oregon just west of I-5 at Western Antique Power, Inc.

P ✳ 🚻 ▶ ◀ **M** aт n

 Portland and Salem

Contact: Greg Bonn
Museum Director

Mailing Address:
Oregon Electric Railway
Historical Society
P.O. Box 308
Lake Oswego, OR 97034
Telephone: (503) 222-2226

MOUNT HOOD RAILROAD

Ride/Operation: A 44-mile, 4-hour round trip to Parkdale, following the Hood River up a 3-percent grade to a switchback and climbing through forests to an upper valley carpeted with fruit orchards. The ride offers unparalleled views of Mount Hood and Mount Adams.

Train: Pullman heavyweight coaches; concession car; newly refurbished caboose.

Schedule: January-March, charter tours; April 5-6, 12-13, 10:00 a.m.; April 16-June, Wednesday-Saturday, 10:00 a.m. & Saturday-Sunday, 3:00 p.m.; July-August, Tuesday-Sunday, 10:00 a.m. & Saturday-Sunday 3:00 p.m.; September-October, Wednesday-Sunday, 10:00 a.m. & Saturday-Sunday, 3:00 p.m.; November, weekends, 3:00 p.m.; December, weekends, 10:00 a.m. Four hour round trip.

Fare: Adults $21.95, senior citizens (60+) $18.95, children (2-11) $13.95, infants free.

Locomotives: Nos. 88 and 89, EMD GP9s.

Special Events: Fruit Blossom Special, April 19-20. Mother's Day Special, May 11. Train Robbery, May 17-18, June 14-15, July 19-20, August 16-17 & September 20-21. Mexican Fiesta Special, August 30-31. Hood River Harvest Festival, October 18-19. Halloween Spook Train, October 25-26. Thanksgiving Holiday Special, November 29. Annual Christmas Tree Trains, December 6-7, 13-14, & 20-21. Reservations required.

Note: The Mount Hood Railroad depot, constructed in 1911 and recently restored, has been designated a National Historic Site.

Location: Hood River is 63 miles east of Portland on I-84. The railroad is in the heart of the Columbia River Gorge National Scenic Area, only a few minutes from Bonneville Dam and Multnomah Falls.

Hood River and Bingen

Contact: Diane Martin-Langley
Marketing Director

Mailing Address:
110 Railroad Avenue
Hood River, OR 97031
Telephone: (503) 386-3556

SAMTRAK
Diesel, irregular
Standard gauge

SAMTRAK

Ride/Operation: Traveling over the former Portland Traction Company's interurban right-of way along the Willamette River, this line offers a 1-hour round trip between two of Portland's most popular attractions: the Oregon Museum of Science & Industry; and the historic Oaks Amusement Park, dating from 1905. Passengers may stop to visit these sites at either end and return on a later train.

Train: "Little Toot," 1942 diesel-electric and a 45-ton diesel electric; tank car converted to passenger car; former Simpson Timber Company logging caboose.

Schedule: May-June, weekends only 11:00 a.m.-4:00 p.m. July-August, Wednesday-Sunday, 11:00 a.m.-5:00 p.m. September, Friday-Sunday, 11:00 a.m.-4:00 p.m. October, Saturday-Sunday, 12:00-4:00 p.m. (1st 2 weekends). Operates on Monday holidays. Schedule varies; please call or write for information.

Fare: Adults $4.00, children (1-4) $1.50, children under 1 ride free. Caboose cupola seats $1.00 extra.

Locomotives: The line's freight operations use No. 100, SW-1, former Portland Traction Co.; No. 5100, 70-ton, former Southern Pacific; No. 602, SW-8, former Oregon, Pacific & Eastern.

Rolling Stock/Equipment: Various pieces of work equipment are stored at the freight headquarters.

Special Events: Annual "Oktoberfest" at Oaks Amusement Park, September 19-21; passengers are shuttled to the park at no charge.

Location: Boarding locations are at Spokane Street, under east end of Sellwood Bridge; at Oaks Amusement Park; and at the Oregon Museum of Science & Industry, 1945 SE Water Avenue.

P   Portland

Radio Frequency: 160.575

Contact: Donna Samuels
Director, Passenger Operations

Mailing Address:
P.O. Box 22548
Portland, OR 97222
Telephone: (503) 653-2380

WASHINGTON PARK & ZOO RAILWAY
Steam, diesel, scheduled
30" gauge

GEORGE BAETJER/WASHINGTON PARK & ZOO RAILWAY

Ride/Operation: A 4-mile round trip around the zoo and through forested hills to Washington Park, passing the elephant enclosure for a close-up view of the zoo's world-famous pachyderm herd and overlooking the Alaska Tundra exhibit. The stop at Washington Park station offers a panoramic view of Mount Hood, the city of Portland, and Mount St. Helens, and passengers may obtain a stopover pass there to visit the Rose Test Gardens and the Japanese Garden, located nearby.

Train: Streamlined cars and open coaches; two trains are wheelchair-accessible. The train is one of the last registered Postal Railway Stations in the United States.

Schedule: Daily from mid March until end of September. Zoo loop trip: daily, March 15-May 23, weather permitting. Full round trip: daily, May 24-September 30. Trains depart at frequent intervals.

Fare/Admission: Full round trip: adults $2.75, senior citizens and children (3-11) $2.00, children under 3 ride free. Zoo loop trip: adults $1.75, senior citizens and children (3-11) $1.25, children under 3 ride free. Zoo admission is required to ride railway.

Locomotives: 4-4-0 No. 1, replica of Virginia & Truckee "Reno"; *Zooliner,* replica of General Motors *Aerotrain;* diesel-powered *Oregon Express*; diesel powered switcher and fire train.

Rolling Stock/Equipment: One work train.

Location: 4001 S.W. Canyon Road.

Portland

Radio Frequency: 151.655

Contact: Mark Dillon
Retail Manager

Mailing Address:
4001 S.W. Canyon Road
Portland, OR 97221
Telephone: (503) 226-1561
Fax: (503) 226-6836

WILLAMETTE SHORE TROLLEY
Electric, scheduled
Standard gauge

STEVE MORGAN

Ride/Operation: Trolleys operate along the former Portland, Eugene & Western "Red Electric" rail line, 6-3/4 miles between Portland and Lake Oswego along the Willamette River. The Portland terminus is located at RiverPlace, a former industrial area. It then heads south on private right-of-way until traversing Moody Avenue for five city blocks. Then back on private right-of-way passing through condominium projects, skirting two beautiful riverside parks, and crossing three high trestles beside the river. Penetrating Elk Rock via a curved quarter mile tunnel, it then runs parallel to the Portland & Western main line before ending at the old SP depot in Lake Oswego.

Schedule: Friday-Sunday, March-May; Daily (except Monday), June-Labor Day; Friday-Sunday, Labor Day-New Year's Day; Saturday-Sunday, January-February, weather permitting, call for schedule. Departs Lake Oswego at 10:00 a.m., noon, 2:00 p.m. and 4:00 p.m. Departs Portland at 11:00 a.m., 1:00 p.m., 3:00 p.m. and 5:00 p.m. (one way).

Fare: Adults $5.00, children (3-12) $3.00, children under 3 free, with adult. Charters available by special arrangement.

Trolleys: The 1932 Brill Master unit, formerly Portland Traction 4012, has been renumbered to 813, its former city line number. The car is referred to locally as the "Broadway Car."

Note: The Willamette Shore Trolley is now being operated by the Oregon Electric Railway Historical Society.

Location: Lake Oswego, 311 N. State St. Between "A" Avenue and Foothills Rd. in the old SP Depot. Portland, 2611 SW Moody Avenue at Sheridan St.

Portland

Contact: Roy E. Bonn
General Manager

Mailing Address:
Oregon Electric Railway
Historical Society
P.O. Box 308
Lake Oswego, OR 97034
Telephone: (503) 222-2226

ALTOONA RAILROADERS MEMORIAL MUSEUM
Railway museum
Standard gauge

Displays/Exhibits: Altoona built the Pennsylvania Railroad, and the Pennsylvania Railroad built Altoona. More than sixty-seven hundred steam locomotives were built and maintained in the Altoona shops; peak railroad employment in Altoona was nearly eighteen thousand. The Altoona Railroaders Memorial Museum is dedicated to the memory of the men and women of the PRR, telling stories of the people who laid the track, built the locomotives, and guided trains across the Allegheny Ridge. Various exhibits and special programs are featured throughout the year; currently, guests can view an interactive exhibit about women in railroading. In the spring of 1997, the Altoona Railroaders Memorial Museum will move into the former PRR Master Mechanics Building. In this historic structure, visitors will be able to experience what it was like to live and work in a community that was a company - the Pennsylvania Railroad. Food and beverages are available on site during summer hours.

Schedule: Summer hours: daily, April 7-October 26, 10:00 a.m.-6:00 p.m. Winter hours: (Beginning October 27, 1996) Tuesday-Sunday, 10:00 a.m.-5:00 p.m. Closed Monday.

Admission: Adults $3.50, senior citizens (over 62) $3.00, children (3-12) $2.00. Call for group rates and school packages.

Locomotives: The Juniata-built K4s, No. 1361 is currently undergoing restoration. GG1, No. 4913, is on display along with 1918 Vulcan 0-4-0T switcher *Nancy*, and two diesel locomotives.

Passenger Cars: The *Loretto*, private rail car of Charles M. Schwab; dining car; two coaches; three sleeping cars; two other private rail cars and other equipment.

Rolling Stock/Equipment: Express refrigerator car.

Location: Downtown Altoona. Take the 17th Street exit off Interstate 99 (former Route 220).

Altoona

Contact: Peter D. Barton
Executive Director

Mailing Address:
1300 Ninth Avenue
Altoona, PA 16602
Telephone: (814) 946-0834

HORSESHOE CURVE
NATIONAL HISTORIC LANDMARK
Railway display

RAILROADER'S MEMORIAL MUSEUM

Displays/Exhibits: When Altoona's Horseshoe Curve opened in 1854, it revolutionized rail travel and cleared the way for westward expansion. The Curve's story is now told at the modern, interpretive Visitor Center, located in a picturesque setting. A seven-minute film describes the role of Pennsylvania transportation in America's move to the West; guests may ride to track elevation aboard a single-track funicular or walk the 194 stairs. Horseshoe Curve is located on Conrail's busy East-West Main Line, with more than fifty trains passing each day. Trains climbing or descending the 1.8-percent grade can be viewed and photographed safely from the trackside park.

Schedule: Summer hours: daily, April 7-October 26, 9:30 a.m.-7:00 p.m. Winter hours: (beginning October 27), Tuesday-Sunday, 10:00 a.m.-4:30 p.m. Closed Monday.

Admission: Adults $3.50, senior (over 62) $3.00, child (3-12) $1.50. Call for group rates and school packages.

Locomotives: Former Pennsylvania Railroad GP9, No. 7048, is on display at track elevation.

Location: Kittanning Point Road, State Route 4008. Follow Heritage Route signs.

Altoona

Contact: Peter D. Barton
Executive Director

Mailing Address:
1300 Ninth Avenue
Altoona, PA 16602
Telephone: (814) 941-7960

PIONEER TUNNEL COAL MINE & STEAM TRAIN
Steam, scheduled
Narrow gauge

PIONEER TUNNEL COAL MINE & STEAM TRAIN

Ride/Operation: Scenic ride along the Mahanoy Mountain behind an old-fashioned steam locomotive of the 0-4-0 type built in 1927 by the Vulcan Iron Works of Wilkes Barre, PA. Miner-guides tell the story of Strip-mining, bootlegging and the Centralia Mine Fire.

Displays/Exhibits: Also available is a tour of a real anthracite coal mine in open mine cars pulled by a battery operated mine motor. Miner-guides show and tell the fascinating story of anthracite coal mining.

Schedule: Call for details.

Fare/Admission: Call for details.

Locomotives: A spare "Lokie" of the 0-4-0 type also built by the Vulcan Iron Works is presently being restored and fitted with a new boiler by the Benson Mountain Co. of Rhode Island.

Rolling Stock/Equipment: 2 battery powered mine locomotives.

Special Events: 5th annual "Pioneer Day" - August 23, 1997. In addition to regular coal mine tours and steam train rides, many special events are held in community park adjacent to Pioneer Tunnel. Large craft fair, live music, ethnic foods, activities for children and more.

Location: From Interstate 81 - Take exit 36W (Frackville). Follow Rt. 61 north to Ashland.

Harrisburg, 65 miles away

Contact:
Kathy Lattis

Mailing Address:
19th & Oak Streets
Ashland, PA 17921
Telephone: (717) 874-3850
(717) 875-3301

275

AVONDALE RAILROAD CENTER
Railway museum
Standard gauge

BRIAN R. WOODCOCK

Displays/Exhibits: This museum is located in historic Chester County, Pennsylvania, on the former Pennsylvania Railroad Octoraro Branch, extending from Chadds Ford, Pennsylvania, to the Maryland state line. The display consists of four former PRR passenger cars and a former Atlanta, Birmingham & Atlantic Baldwin steam locomotive. Iron Horse Antiques is an antique shop located inside the train, and nearby is a former Pomeroy & Newark Railroad freight station (the only surviving structure of this line) and the original Avondale former PRR passenger station.

Schedule: Display: daily. Iron Horse Antiques: Wednesday-Sunday, 10:00 a.m.-5:00 p.m.

Admission: No charge.

Locomotives: 1907 Baldwin slope-back steam locomotive.

Rolling Stock/Equipment: Four MP-54 passenger cars.

Special Events: Seasonal events. Please call or write for information.

Note: Other area attractions include Longwood Gardens, the Brandywine River Museum, the Brandywine Battlefield, the Hagley Museum, the Winterthur Museum, the Delaware Natural History Museum, and the Delaware Art Museum. A local airport features rides in restored vintage aircraft.

Location: On U.S. 1 and route 41, two miles off the U.S. 1 bypass, six miles from Longwood Gardens and twelve miles from Wilmington, Delaware.

Wilmington, Delaware

Contact: Brian Woodcock

Mailing Address:
State and Pomeroy Streets
P.O. Box 809
Avondale, PA 19311

BELLEFONTE HISTORICAL RAILROAD
Diesel, scheduled
Standard gauge

W.M. RUMBERGER

Ride/Operation: Scheduled and special trips over the 60-mile Nittany & Bald Eagle Railroad to Lemont, Vail (Tyrone), and Mill Hall. Regular service includes stopovers at Lemont, Bellefonte, Curtin Village, and Julian Glider Port. Fall foliage and railfan runs cover up to 120 miles; all-inclusive restaurant runs to Tyrone are also offered.

Displays/Exhibits: The Bellefonte Station, a restored former Pennsylvania Railroad structure built in 1888, houses an operating N-gauge layout of the Bellefonte-Curtin Village route, as well as historical photos and memorabilia of area railroading. A snowplow and caboose under restoration are displayed beside the station.

Train: No. 9167, 1952 RDC-1, and 1962 No. 1953; air-conditioned passenger cars. Can be configured for meal service.

Schedule: Weekends and holidays, May 30-September 5, 1:00, 2:15, & 4:00 p.m. Destinations vary. Charters are available any time, year-round. Tyrone restaurant runs: last Friday of the month, January-October.

Fare: Varies depending on destination. Minimum: adults $5.00, children (2-11) $2.00.

Special Events: Spring, fall, and Christmas runs.

Location: Central Pennsylvania, a short distance from I-80.

Contact: W. M. Rumberger

Mailing Address:
The Train Station
Bellefonte, PA 16823
Telephone: (814) 355-0311

ALLEGHENY PORTAGE RAILROAD
NATIONAL HISTORIC SITE
Railway display
Standard gauge

ALLEGHENY PORTAGE RAILROAD

Displays/Exhibits: This site was established in 1964 to commemorate the first railroad to cross the Allegheny Mountains, in 1834. The Portage Railroad, considered a technological wonder of its day, played a role in opening the interior of the United States to trade and settlement. Today's park, covering fifteen hundred acres, preserves remains of this railroad and reveals its interesting story. The visitor center features a twenty-minute motion picture and exhibits that help tell the story of the railroad. A new feature is the Engine House 6 Exhibit Building, which protects the remains of the original engine house and includes a full-sized model of a stationary steam engine. The Lemon House, a tavern during the days of the railroad, is being restored to its nineteenth-century appearance and will open in the spring of 1997.

Schedule: Visitor Center: daily, May 29-September 4, 9:00 a.m.-6:00 p.m.; daily, September 5-May 26, 9:00 a.m.-5:00 p.m. Closed Christmas Day. Ranger-guided Train Tours: Thursday-Saturday, June-mid October.

Admission: Please call the Visitor Center for current information.

Locomotives: A full-sized model of the 1837 steam locomotive "Lafayette" is on display in the Visitor Center.

Location: Off the Gallitzin exit of U.S. 22, between Altoona and Cresson.

 Altoona

Contact: Superintendent

Mailing Address:
P.O. Box 189
Cresson, PA 16630
Telephone: (814) 886-6150

GETTYSBURG RAILROAD
Steam/diesel, scheduled
Standard gauge

REGINA RUKSTELIS

Ride/Operation: This railroad operates over a former Reading Company branch line. The regular ride is a 16-mile, 1½-hour round trip to Biglerville; special 50-mile, 5-hour dinner trips are made on selected dates to Mt. Holly Springs.

Train: Open-side excursion cars; steel coaches; double-deck open car.

Schedule: Biglerville: weekends, April, 1:00 & 3:00 p.m. Thursday-Sunday, May 1-June 30; Thursday-Friday, 10:00 a.m. & 12:30 p.m.; weekends, 1:00 & 3:00 p.m. Daily, July 1-August 31; weekdays, 11:00 a.m. & 1:00 p.m.; weekends, 11:00 a.m., 1:00 & 3:00 p.m. Thursday-Sunday, September 1-October 30; Thursday-Friday, 11:00 a.m. & 1:00 p.m.; weekends, 11:00 a.m., 1:00 & 3:00 p.m. Also September 1, 11:00 a.m. & 1:00 p.m. Mt. Holly Springs: May 3, 2:00 p.m. (Apple Blossom Trip); June 20, 6:00 p.m. (Summer's Eve Trip); July 19, 5:00 p.m. (Hobo Special); August 15, 6:00 p.m. (Moonlight Trip); September 27, 2:00 p.m. (Fall Harvest Trip). Reservations suggested for these trips.

Fare: Biglerville: adults $8.00, seniors (65+) $7.50, children (3-12) $4.00. Mt. Holly: adults $18.00, seniors (65+) $16.00, children (3-12) $10.00. Special Events: adults $9.00, senior $8.50, children (3-12) $5.00.

Locomotives: No. 76, 1920 Baldwin 2-8-0, former Mississippian Railway; No. 1278, 1948 Canadian 4-6-2, former Canadian Pacific; No. 70 RS36 Alco; No. 39 GP9, former Western Maryland.

Special Events: Easter Bunny Train, April 6, 1:00 & 3:00 p.m. Civil War Train Raids; July 4-5, 11:00 a.m. & 1:30 p.m.; September 20-21, 1:00 p.m. & 3:30 p.m.

Lincoln Train, August 2-3, 1:00 & 3:00 p.m. Fall Foliage Trips, October 4, 11, 12, 18 & 19, 10:00 a.m. Halloween Train, October 25-26, 1:00 & 3:00 p.m. Christmas Train, December 6-7 & 13-14, 1:00 & 3:00 p.m.

Location: At the former Reading Station on Washington Street in the center of Gettysburg.

Contact: Station Master

Mailing Address:
Passenger Service
106 North Washington Street
Gettysburg, PA 17325
Telephone: (717) 334-6932

SHENANGO PYMATUNING RAILWAY
HISTORICAL SOCIETY
Railroad display, museum

SHENANGO PYMATUNING RAILWAY HISTORICAL SOCIETY

Display/Exhibit: Greenville Railroad Park has two tracks of equipment displays, two museum buildings, and assorted other items such as signals, mileposts and similar railroad memorabilia. It is located along the former Jersey City-Chicago mainline of the Erie Railroad now operated by Conrail. Museums contain railroad artifacts, photographs and other materials with great emphasis on the Bessemer & Lake Erie, which was headquartered in Greenville.

Schedule: May & September: Weekends. June through August: Afternoons, except Mondays. Special arrangements can be made for tour groups.

Fare/Admission: Donation, except for Kids Party Caboose which has fixed rental price.

Locomotives: Baldwin 1936 0-10-2, world's largest two-cylinder steam switcher built as Union Railroad 304 and subsequently sold and finally operated as Duluth, Missabe & Iron Range 604 (described in November 1989 TRAINS magazine).

Rolling Stock/Equipment: Bessemer & Lake Erie taconite-pellet ore car; B&LE steel cupola caboose 1985; Union Pacific mainline cupola caboose 25437, Wheeling & Lake Erie cupola caboose 207 (converted for use as a place for children's parties); Pittsburg & Shawmut Fairmont track motor car.

Location: Greenville Railroad Park is at 314 Main Street. Exit 1 off I-80 to PA Route 18 north 17 miles through downtown Greenville or exit 34 off I-79 to PA Route 358 west 14 miles to Greenville. Park is directly on Route 358 and just off Route 18.

Contact: F. N. Houser
National Director

Mailing Address: 314 Main Street
Greenville, PA 16125-2615
Telephone: (412) 588-4009

HOWARD J. WALTON

Ride/Operation: A half-mile ride (eventually to be a one-mile loop) on a two-foot-gauge railroad through forest and pasture, where deer and other animals roam.

Displays/Exhibits: Steam engines, gas engines, precision models, coal-mining equipment, an antique reciprocating-saw display, antique tractors, and other mechanical antiques, as well as a former Delaware & Hudson battery-powered coal-mine locomotive, a 1920 wooden Central Vermont caboose, and other railroad artifacts. Also located here is a performing-bear show, a game farm, and a museum.

Train: 1922 Krauss 24-inch-gauge 0-4-0; 1936 Whitcomb gas locomotive; 1948 Brookville gas locomotive; open cars with bench seats, made from narrow-gauge flatcars.

Schedule: May 1-July 4, weekends, 12:00-5:00 p.m.; July 5-October 31, Thursdays-Sundays, 12:00-6:00 p.m. Bear shows are at 1:00, 2:00, 3:00 & 4:00 p.m.; train runs before and after bear shows.

Fare: Adults $5.50, children (3-12) $3.50, children under 3 admitted free. Ticket includes park admission and railroad fare.

Rolling Stock/Equipment: 1934 D&O passenger car; work cars; ballast hopper car; handcar; others.

Special Events: Halloween Pumpkin Special, last two weeks of October. Christmas Week Special.

Location: Eight miles north of Honesdale. Take route 6 west through Honesdale to route 170 north, then follow signs for Big Bear Farm and the Ponderosa Pines Campground.

Contact: A. E. Burr
Manager

Mailing Address:
RD 3, Box 1352
Honesdale, PA 18431
Telephone: (717) 253-1794

STOURBRIDGE LINE RAIL EXCURSIONS
Diesel, scheduled
Standard gauge

GEORGE A. FORERO, JR.

Ride/Operation: A 50-mile round trip from Honesdale to Hawley and Lackawaxen, through scenic Wayne and Pike Counties along the Lackawaxen River, closely following the route of the old Delaware & Hudson Canal.

Displays/Exhibits: Former gravity-railroad coach on display on Hawley; a replica of the "Stourbridge Lion" and a gravity-railroad coach on display in Honesdale.

Train: 1940s BL2; five 1940s coaches, former Jersey Central, completely refurbished.

Schedule: Weekend Special Events, March 30-December 14.

Fare: Fares vary depending on type of excursion; see events listed below.

Locomotives: No. 54, 1949 EMD BL2, former Bangor & Aroostook.

Special Events: Bunny Train, $10. Great Train Robbery, $12. Dinner Theatre, $40. Bavarian Festival, $26. Fall Foliage, $11 & $17.50. Halloween, $10. Santa Express, $10. Call for dates and times.

Location: Northeastern Pennsylvania, about 24 miles from Scranton.

Contact: Annetta DeYoung
Executive Director

Mailing Address:
742 Main Street
Honesdale, PA 18431
Telephone: (717) 253-1960

RAIL TOURS, INC.

Ride/Operation: This line offers a 40-minute round trip to Nesquehoning and a 1¾-hour round trip to Lake Hauto and a 2½ hour roundtrip to Hometown Trestle. In October, 33-mile, 2 3/4-hour Flaming Foliage Rambles are made to Haucks, passing over scenic Hometown Trestle. All trips operate over a former Central of New Jersey branch.

Displays/Exhibits: An exhibit inside the Jim Thorpe depot features mining artifacts and other items of local history.

Schedule: 40-minute trip: weekends and holidays. May 10-September 1, 12:00, 1:00, 2:00 p.m.; weekends, September 6-28, 12:00, 1:00, 2:00 & 3:00 p.m. 1¾-hour trip: Sundays & holidays, May 25-September 1, 3:00 p.m. 2½ hour trip: Saturdays, May 24-August 30, 3:00 p.m. Flaming Foliage Rambles: October 5, 11-13, 18-19, 10:00 a.m. & 2:15 p.m.; October 17, 2:15 p.m.; October 6 & 25-26, 1:15 p.m.

Fare: 40-minute trip: Adults $5.00, children (2-11) $3.00, children under 2 ride free. 1¾-hour trip: Adults $8.00, children (2-11) $4.00, children under 2 ride free. 2½ hour trip: Adults $10.00, children (2-11) $5.00, children under 2 ride free. Flaming Foliage Rambles: Adults $14.00, children (2-11) $7.00, children under 2 ride free.

Locomotives: 1913 D-10 4-6-0 No. 1098, former Canadian Pacific; 1937 SW900 EMD No. 11, former Maryland & Pennsylvania No. 83.

Passenger Cars: Coaches, former Reading, former Septa and former Central of New Jersey.

Rolling Stock/Equipment: Various wood and steel cabooses; former CNJ freight cars.

Location: At the former Central of New Jersey depot along U.S. 209 in downtown Jim Thorpe, 26 miles north of Allentown. Take the Lehighton/Mahoning Valley exit (No. 34) off the Northeast Extension of the Pennsylvania Turnpike (Route 9) and travel six miles on U.S. Route 209 south to Jim Thorpe.

Contact: John Eline
Sales and Customer Service

Mailing Address:
P.O. Box 285
Jim Thorpe, PA 18229
Telephone: (717) 325-4606

WANAMAKER, KEMPTON & SOUTHERN, INC.

Steam, scheduled

WANAMAKER, KEMPTON & SOUTHERN, INC.

Standard gauge

Ride/Operation: A 6-mile, 40-minute round trip through scenic Pennsylvania Dutch country over part of the former Reading Company's Schuylkill & Lehigh branch. The steam train is supplemented by a unique gasoline-engine trolley, the "Berksy."

Displays/Exhibits: Restored stations relocated from Joanna and Catasauqua, Pennsylvania; original circa 1874 Wanamaker station; operating HO-gauge model layout (on steam Sundays).

Train: Open-window coaches; open gondola; caboose.

Schedule: May-October, Sundays; June & September, first and third Saturdays; July, August & October, Saturdays. 1:00, 2:00, 3:00, & 4:00 p.m.

Fare: Adults $4.50, children (3-11) $2.50, children 2 and under ride free.

Locomotives: No. 2, 1920 Porter 0-4-0T, former Colorado Fuel & Iron; No. 65, 1930 Porter 0-6-0T, former Safe Harbor Water Power; No. 35, 1927 Mack/SWMRR gas-electric switcher; No. 20, 1935 Whitcomb gas-mechanical switcher; No. 602, 1944 Whitcomb diesel-electric.

Passenger Cars: Coaches Nos. 1494 & 1474 and combine No. 408, all former Reading Company; coach No. 582, former Lackawanna.

Rolling Stock/Equipment: Assorted freight cars and caboose, former Lehigh & New England; steel and wood cabooses, former Reading.

Special Events: Mother's Day Special, May 11. Father's Day Special, June 15. Sandman Special, June 21. Kids' Fun Weekend, August 2-3. Harvest Moon Special, September 19-20. Halloween Train, October 25-26. Santa Claus Special, December 6-7.

Location: Depot is located at Kempton on routes 143 or 737, a short distance north of I-78. The site is about 20 miles west of Allentown and 30 miles north of Reading.

Contact: Linda Hartman
Vice President, Advertising

Mailing Address:
P.O. Box 24
Kempton, PA 19529
Telephone: (610) 756-6469

READING COMPANY
TECHNICAL & HISTORICAL SOCIETY
Railway museum
Standard gauge

Displays/Exhibits: Working LEMTU car, built for locomotive-engineer training; working stands for first- and second-generation diesels; working two-thirds-sized replica of a Reading A5A 0-4-0 switcher; museum car with many artifacts and working signals; rolling stock; gift shop in baggage car.

Schedule: Weekends, May-October, 12:00-5:00 p.m.

Admission: Donations welcomed.

Locomotives: No. 103, NW2, fully restored; No. 5513, GP30; No. 5308, Alco C-630; No. 900, FP7; No. 6300, U30C; No. 5204, Alco C424; No. 3640, GP35; other locomotives in the yard or to be delivered.

Passenger Cars: Two baggage cars; No. 863, MU car; Blueliners Nos. 9111, 9113, 9118 & 9131; Nos. 9152 & 9162, last RDCs built; ten passenger cars, former Reading.

Rolling Stock/Equipment: Boxcars, gondolas, covered hopper, cabooses.

Special Events: Annual Train Meet, First Sunday of October.

Note: GP30 No. 5513 was featured at EMD's fiftieth anniversary celebration of the FT diesel locomotive at LaGrange, Illinois.

Location: Wall Street, at the railroad.

P 🚌 ✳ 📷 ▶ ◀ **M**

Contact: Public Relations
Chairperson

Mailing Address:
Box 15143
Reading, PA 19612-5143
Telephone: (610) 372-5513

REUBEN S. BROUSE

Ride/Operation: This operation offers two narrated rides. The Lewisburg & Buffalo Creek Railroad is a 1 1/2-hour round trip over the former Reading Railroad through Victorian Lewisburg, past Bucknell University, and along the Susquehanna River and the cliffs of the Buffalo Mountains to the village of Winfield. The West Shore Railroad is a 2 1/2-hour round trip over the former Reading & Pennsylvania Railroad through the scenic Amish and Mennonite farms of the Buffalo Valley to Victorian Mifflinburg. A dinner train is available on Wednesdays during summer and fall.

Displays/Exhibits: Delta Place Station displays engines, passenger cars, a dining car, several cabooses, a train station, and scales.

Train: Steel coaches; cabooses; dining car.

Schedule: Weekends, April 5-June 15 & September 6-October 26; April-May, 2:00 p.m.; June-October, 11:30 a.m. & 2:00 p.m. Tuesday-Sunday, June 17-August 31, 11:30 a.m. & 2:00 p.m. Dinner Train: Wednesdays, June-October; June-September, 6:00 p.m.; October, 5:30 p.m. First Saturday of the month, May-October, 6:00 p.m. Reservations required for dinner train 48 hours in advance of trip. Railroad is closed on Mondays.

Admission: Lewisburg & Buffalo Creek: adults $7.50, senior citizens $6.50, children (3-11) $4.00. West Shore: adults $9.50, senior citizens $8.50, children (3-11) $5.00. Dinner train: Wednesday, $25.00; Saturday, $30.00. Group rates available on public excursions.

Locomotives: No. 9425, 1950 EMD SW1 & No. 2233, 1963 EMD GP30, both former PRR.

Passenger Cars: 1916 steel coaches, former Erie-Lackawanna; 1915 dining car, former Jersey Central; 1926 club car, former PRR.

Rolling Stock/Equipment: Cabooses, former PRR, Erie/Lackawanna, Reading, and Santa Fe.

Special Events: Easter Bunny Express. School Field Trips. Mother's Day Dinner Train. Father's Day Dinner Train. Entertainment Dinner Trains. Railcar Show. Antique Machinery Show. Fall Foliage Excursion. Haunted Train Rides. Santa Claus Express.

Location: Delta Place Station, on route 15 two miles north of Lewisburg.

Radio Frequency: 164.55

Contact: Dennis W. Confer
General Manager

Mailing Address:
RR 3, Box 154
Route 15 North
Lewisburg, PA 17837
Telephone: (717) 524-4337

Pennsylvania, Marienville
R

KNOX & KANE RAILROAD
Steam, diesel, scheduled
Standard gauge

GEORGE A. FORERO, JR.

Ride/Operation: This line offers one round trip each operating day to Kane and the Kinzua Bridge over a former Baltimore & Ohio branch line. Passengers may board at Marienville for a 96-mile, 8-hour trip or at Kane for a 32-mile, 3½ hour trip. The 2,053-foot-long, 301-foot-high Kinzua Bridge, built in 1882 to span the Kinzua Creek Valley, was at the time the highest bridge in the world. It is on the National Register of Historic Places and is a National Historic Civil Engineering Landmark.

Train: Steel coaches; open cars; two snack and souvenir cars.

Schedule: Friday-Sunday, June & September; Tuesday-Sunday, July & August; Wednesday-Sunday, beginning of October; weekends, October 15-16 & 22-23; lv. Marienville 8:30 a.m., lv. Kane 10:45 a.m.

Fare: From Marienville: adults $20.00, children $13.00. From Kane: adults $14.00, children $8.00. Advance reservations suggested. Box lunches available by advance order, $3.75.

Locomotives: No. 38, 1927 Baldwin 2-8-0, former Huntington & Broad Top Mountain; No. 44, Alco diesel; No. 58, Chinese 2-8-2 built in 1989; Porter Switcher No. 1.

Location: In northwestern Pennsylvania, about 20 miles north of I-80.

Mailing Address:
P.O. Box 422
Marienville, PA 16239
Telephone: (814) 927-6621

MIDDLETOWN & HUMMELSTOWN RAILROAD
Diesel, scheduled
Standard gauge

MIDDLETOWN & HUMMELSTOWN RAILROAD

Ride/Operation: An 11-mile, 1.25 hour round trip over a former Reading Company branch line. The train travels on the towpath of the historic Union Canal along scenic Swatara Creek as a narrator describes the points of interest along the line. Trains are normally powered by a 65-ton diesel electric locomotive. On the return trip, a musician plays and leads a sing-along.

Displays/Exhibits: The yard adjacent to the station is home to over 30 pieces of railroad rolling stock. It includes freight cars, passenger cars, streetcars, and diesel, steam and electric locomotives.

Schedule: Saturdays, June-August & October; Sundays, June-October; Tuesday-Friday, July-August. Also Memorial Day weekend and Labor Day. Call or write for train schedule.

Fare/Admission: Adults $6.00, children (3-11) $3.00, under age 3 ride free. Write for special event fares or group rates.

Locomotives/Trolleys: No. 1, 1941 General Electric, former U.S. Army; No. 2, 1955 General Electric, former Standard Slag and Stone; No. 1016, 1969 Alco T-6, former Newburgh & South Shore; No. 91, 1910 Canadian Locomotive Co. 2-6-0, former Canadian National; PST Nos. 77 & 86, 1932 Brill; PST No. C-121, 1923 Brill Snowsweeper; No. 66, 1948 General Electric Steeplecab, former Kansas City Public Service No. 2; No. 2104, 1947 St. Louis Car Co. PCC.

Rolling Stock/Equipment: Coaches, 1916/1920 Pullman, former Lackawanna; Pennsylvania Railroad baggage car; several freight cars including a wooden boxcar with link and pin couplers.

Special Events: Easter Bunny Express, Railfan Day, Uncle Sam Visits, July 4. Caverns Picnic. Dinner Trains Santa Ride. and New Year Eve Special. Reservations required for dinner trains and some special events. Call for dates and details.

Location: On Race Street in Middletown, 6½ blocks south of PA Route 230. Twenty minutes from Hershey and Harrisburg.

Middletown

Contact: Wendell J. Dillinger
President

Mailing Address:
136 Brown Street
Middletown, PA 17057
Telephone: (717) 944-4435

NORTHERN CENTRAL RAILWAY
Diesel, scheduled
Standard gauge

CHARLES WEBB

Ride/Operation: The Northern Central Railway Co. has assembled a fleet of heritage railcars to make up its "Liberty Limited" dinner train. Food is prepared on board and live entertainment provided to take passengers back in time to the era of legendary rail travel.

Schedule: Ticket office is open daily 8:30 a.m.-4:30 p.m. Trains run on weekends and holidays.

Fare: $34.99 and up.

Locomotives: Former Alco RSD5. Former C&NW FP7.

Rolling Stock/Equipment: Luxury observation car "Northern Lights"; Pullman "Imperial Sands"; Pullman "Catalpa Falls"; Budd "New Freedom" diner; Pullman kitchens "Bras D'or Lake"; Pullman "Glen Rock" diner; Pullman "York" dance car; St Louis "Stewartstown" power car.

Special Events: Murder Mystery Trains, Comedy Trains, Magic Trains, Dinner and Brunch Trains, Holiday Trains, Caboose Charters.

Location: 3.1 miles west of I-83, exit 1 on Pennsylvania Route 851. One block south of 851.

 Baltimore, 20 miles away

Contact: Ken Bitten

Mailing Address:
117 N. Front Street
New Freedom, PA 17349
Telephone: (717) 235-5609
Internet: http://www.classic rail.com/ncry

289

NEW HOPE & IVYLAND RAILROAD
Steam, diesel, scheduled
Standard gauge

NEW HOPE & IVYLAND RAILROAD

Ride/Operation: This line offers a 9-mile, 50-minute round trip from the historic 1891 New Hope depot to Lahaska over the former Reading Railroad. The narrated excursion takes passengers along the Delaware Canal, across the famous "Perils of Pauline" trestle, past a farmhouse that was used in the Underground Railroad, and through the rolling hills and valleys of Bucks County. Dinner, brunch, and wine-and-cheese trains operate year round.

Train: 1920s former Reading steel coaches; air-conditioned parlor cars with snacks and beverages sold on board; air-conditioned dining cars.

Schedule: Weekends year-round. Daily, mid April-November. Dinner, brunch, and wine-and-cheese trains, weekends. Number of trips per day varies with the seasons; please call or write for information.

Fare/Admission: Adults, $7.95, senior citizens $6.95, children 2-11 $3.95, children under 2 $1.00.

Locomotives: No. 40, 1925 Baldwin 2-8-0, former Lancaster & Chester; No. 3028, 1946 Alco 4-8-4, former National de Mexico; No. 1513, 1949 Alco RSC-2, former Seaboard Air Line; No. 9423, 1950 EMD SW1, former Pennsylvania.

Special Events: Fireworks Express, July 4. Fall Foliage Trips. Haunted Halloween Trains, 2 weeks before Halloween. Santa Claus Express, Thanksgiving through Christmas.

Location: West Bridge Street, route 179. Convenient access from I-95, routes 202 and 611, and the Pennsylvania Turnpike.

New York, Philadelphia, Princeton, Trenton

Contact: Irene Rumbas
Group Coordinator

Mailing Address:
P.O. Box 634
New Hope, PA 18938
Telephone: (215) 862-2332
Fax: (215) 862-2150

LAKE SHORE RAILWAY
HISTORICAL SOCIETY, INC.
Railway museum
Standard gauge

VINCENT MOSKALCZYK

Displays/Exhibits: At this site, the restored former New York Central passenger station built by the Lake Shore & Michigan Southern Railway in 1899 houses extensive displays, including a Heisler demonstration model built in 1915. Other items include a 1908 wooden Bessemer & Lake Erie boxcar, three generations of refrigerator cars, a Whitcomb switcher, a fireless Heisler steam locomotive, the first New York Central U25B diesel, a former South Shore "Little Joe" electric built by the nearby General Electric plant, standard sleepers, a baggage car, an operational diner, and an 1890 Lake Shore & Michigan Southern wooden business car. The museum is adjacent to Conrail (former New York Central) and Norfolk Southern (former Nickel Plate) main lines.

Schedule: Daily, May 3-18; Wednesdays-Sundays and holidays, May 24-September 1; weekends, September 7-October 27; 1:00-5:00 p.m.

Admission: No charge; donations welcomed.

Special Events: Christmas at the Station, December 6 & 13, 10:00a.m.-5 p.m. and December 7 & 14, noon-5 p.m.

Location: At Wall and Robinson Streets. Fifteen miles east of Erie, the site is two miles north of exit 11 off I-90 and 3 blocks south of U.S. 20.

Erie

Contact: James C. Caldwell

Mailing Address:
P.O. Box 571
North East, PA 16428-0571
Telephone: (814) 825-2724
Weekdays (814) 875-6643

BRANDYWINE SCENIC RAILWAY
Diesel, scheduled
Standard gauge

ANTHONY DIYENNA

Ride/Operation: A fifteen-mile/twenty-mile, 1 hour or 1½ hour round trip, operating both north-bound and southbound from the Northbrook Depot through the Brandywine River Valley on the ex-Reading Railroad's Wilmington & Northern branch. The railroad line passes through scenic rolling countryside past well-known historical and cultural sites including the Brandywine River Museum, Winterthur Museum and Gardens, the Wyeth estate and the village of Chadds Ford.

Train: 1924 Pullman-built steel open-window coaches, former Delaware, Lackawanna & Western; 1971 steel bay-window caboose, former Baltimore & Ohio.

Schedule: Saturdays and Sundays, March 22-December 21, depart 11:00 a.m., 12:30, 2:00 and 3:30 p.m. Special Events depart 11:00 a.m., 1:00 & 3:00 p.m. "Rails-to-the-River" combination train and canoe trips, May-September, depart 9:30 a.m. and 12:30 p.m. weekends.

Admission: Adults $8.00, seniors 55+ $7.00, children (2-12) $6.00. Special Events: Adults $10.00, seniors 55+ $9.00, children 2-12 $8.00. Group rates and caboose rental rates available upon request.

Special Events: Spring Thaw, April 5-6 & 12-13. Bunny Trail Express, March 22-23, 29-30. Fall Foliage Spectaculars, October 4-5, 11-12, 18-19 & 25-26. North Pole Express, November 28-30 & December 6-7, 13-14 & 20-21. Private charters available year round.

Location: On Northbrook Road one mile north of PA Route 842, six miles west of West Chester.

Wilmington, DE , 12 miles away
Paoli, PA, 6 miles away

Contact: David L. Hope
Director of Operations

Mailing Address:
1505 Grant Road
West Chester, PA 19382-7725
Telephone: (610) 793-4433
Fax: (610) 793-5144

THE FRANKLIN INSTITUTE
SCIENCE MUSEUM
Model railroad display, railroad display
Standard gauge

Displays/Exhibits: The centerpiece of Railroad Hall is a Baldwin Locomotive Works No. 60000, a 3-cylinder 4-10-2 built in 1926 and moved to the Franklin Institute in 1933. Two other locomotives share the room: Reading's Rocket of 1838 and a Reading 4-4-0 built in 1842. New to the exhibit is a G gauge model railroad which viewers can operate; it includes full-size signals actuated by the trains and a video hookup between the locomotive and a monitor in a half-size cab.

The remainder of the museum collection covers the larger subject of U.S. industrial technology and science. There are models, films and quizzes on videodiscs, and a giant walk-through heart. The Franklin Institute is at 20th Street and The Parkway in downtown Philadelphia, within walking distance of Suburban Station.

Schedule: 9:30 a.m.-5:00 p.m. daily.
Fare/Admission: $9.50 adults, $8.50 children (4-11), under 4, free.

Location: Center city Philadelphia.

  ♿   **P**   ✳   ☕   🚻   🍴

M   30th Street, 1/4 mile away

Contact: Elaine Wilner

Mailing Address:
222 N. 20th Street
Philadelphia, PA 19103
Telephone: (215) 448-1176
For Museum information: (215) 448-1200
Fax: (215) 448-1235
E-mail: ewilner@fi.edu
Internet: http://fi.edu

READING BLUE MOUNTAIN & NORTHERN RAILROAD CO.

Steam, diesel, irregular
Standard gauge

CHARLES J. RIEDMILLER

Ride/Operation: Train excursions over the main lines and branches including the Lehigh Line which is isolated in the Lehigh River Gorge and considered to be one of the most scenic areas in Pennsylvania.

Displays/Exhibits: Locomotives nos. 425 and 2102 may be seen at corporate headquarters in Port Clinton and are occasionally on display at Steamtown National Historic Site in Scranton, Pennsylvania, as a traveling educational display. The Reading Company Technical and Historical Society's collection of vintage Reading Company diesel locomotives and rolling stock may be visited on the RBMN's Pennsy branch in Leesport.

Schedule: Varies. Please call or write for current information.

Fare/Admission: Varies. Please call or write for current information.

Locomotives: No. 425, Baldwin 4-6-2, former Gulf, Mobile & Ohio; no. 2102, 1945 Reading Co. Shops 4-8-4, former Reading Company; nos. 5706 and 5898, 1952 EMD E8a's, former Pennsylvania Railroad; nos. 9166 and 9168, Budd Company RDCs, formerly SEPTA.

Rolling Stock/Equipment: Coaches, former DL&W; vista dome, air-conditioned coach; occasional caboose.

Special Events: Spring, summer, fall excursion. Please call or write for current information.

Location: Corporate offices and shops are located on Route 61, which is three miles north of exit 9B off I-78. Near Hamburg, Pennsylvania.

Contact: Ed Teahl

Mailing Address:
P.O. Box 218
Port Clinton, PA 19549
Telephone: (610) 562-2102
Fax: (610) 562-0596

JOHN J. HILTON

Ride/Operation: The East Broad Top Railroad, chartered in 1856, is the last operating narrow-gauge railroad east of the Mississippi. The road hauled coal, freight, mail, express, and passengers for more than eighty years. Today the East Broad Top offers passengers a 10-mile, 50-minute ride through the beautiful Aughwick Valley with its own preserved locomotives; the ride takes passengers from the historic depot at Rockhill Furnace to the picnic grove, where the train is turned. The railroad is a Registered National Historic Landmark.

Displays/Exhibits: Railroad yard with shops, operating roundhouse, and turntable. EBT freight cars, cabooses, work equipment, and a gas-electric car can be seen.

Train: Wooden coaches; parlor cars; open cars.

Schedule: Weekends, June through October 13.

Admission: Adults $9.00, children $6.00.

Locomotives: No. 12, 1911 Baldwin 2-8-2; No. 14, 1912 Baldwin 2-8-2; No. 15, 1914 Baldwin 2-8-2; No. 17, 1918 Baldwin 2-8-2; all original East Broad Top Railroad.

Special Events: Fall Spectacular, Columbus Day Weekend.

Note: Dates, times, and fares are subject to change; please call or write for latest information.

Location: At Rockhill Furnace, adjacent to Orbisonia on route 522. Take the Fort Littleton or Willow Hill exit off the Pennsylvania Turnpike.

Contact: Joe Kovalchick
President

Mailing Address:
Rockhill Furnace, PA 17249
Telephone: (814) 447-3011

JOEL SALOMON

Ride/Operation: A nonprofit, educational museum incorporated in 1962, the Rockhill Trolley Museum is composed of volunteers who preserve, restore, and maintain a collection of two dozen electric rail vehicles, about twelve of which are in operating condition. Trolleys operate over dual-gauge trackage on the former Shade Gap Branch of the East Broad Top Railroad for a 2-mile, 20-minute round trip. Standard-gauge streetcars meet narrow-gauge steam trains. Walking tours are offered.

Displays/Exhibits: A small building at the site houses some artifacts, a few hands-on exhibits, and a collection of photographs of one hundred years of transit history.

Schedule: Weekends and holidays, May-October, 11:30 a.m.-4:30 p.m.

Fare: Adults $3.00, children (2-12) $1.00 if accompanied by an adult. Group rates by arrangement. Special fares during Fall Spectacular.

Locomotives/Trolleys: No. 163, 1924 Brill curveside car, former York Railways (Pennsylvania); No. 172, 1929 "Toonerville" type, former Porto, Portugal; No. 249, 1904 double-truck Brill semi-convertible; No. 311, 1923 double-truck Birney, former Johnstown, Pennsylvania; No. 315, 1909 Kuhlman, former Chicago, Aurora & Elgin interurban; No. 1875, 1912 St. Louis Car Co., summer car from Rio de Janeiro; No. 205, Philadelphia "Bullet" car. Liberty Liner *Independence Hall* (former *Electroliner* No. 803-804) operates by arrangement.

Rolling Stock/Equipment: Work car No. 402 and 1915 snowplow, both former Philadelphia & Western; 1898 snow sweeper; PCC car, former Washington, D.C.; 1910 snow sweeper, former Scranton, Pennsylvania; 1930 dropside work car; Philadelphia subway/bridge car No. 1009 (under restoration); Johnstown No. 355 (under restoration). Other cars in storage.

Special Events: Fall Spectacular, Columbus Weekend: all operable trolleys run, food service aboard

Independence Hall, and full-course dinner served Saturday night. Santa's Trolley, December 14.

Note: Since the museum relies on volunteers, operations are sometimes limited to 1 or 2 cars.

Location: On U.S. 522, 20 miles north of exit 13 of the Pennsylvania Turnpike. Adjacent to East Broad Top Railroad in Rockhill Furnace.

Contact: Sam Kuhn
Head of Operations

Mailing Address:
460 Paul Avenue
Chambersburg, PA 17201
Telephone: (717) 263-3943

LAUREL HIGHLANDS RAILROAD
Steam, scheduled

APPALACHIAN RAILROAD

Ride/Operation: The Laurel Highlands Railroad offers scheduled one-hour round-trip journeys visiting various cities along 62 miles of trackage from the former Pennsylvania and Baltimore & Ohio Railroads.

Displays/Exhibits: The Youngwood Railroad Historical Society maintains a museum in the Youngwood Railroad Station which includes many railroad artifacts and displays.

Schedule: May through October (weekends). Trains depart 11:00 a.m., 12:30 p.m. (2-hour trip) and 3:00 p.m. Saturdays and 11:00 a.m., 1:00 p.m. & 3:00 p.m. Sundays from the Scottdale platform. Call or write for the exact departure locations on the dates you would like to travel.

Fare: Adults $7.50 ($12.00), children (5-12) $5.00 ($7.00), children under 5 ride free.

Locomotives: 1934 H.K. Porter 2-4-0 (originally from the Connellsville area), 1942 Whitcomb 80-ton center cab, 1943 GE 25-ton switcher.

Passenger Cars: Three 1926 Jersey Central coaches, 1910 D&RGW Pullman coach.

Special Events: Coal & Coke Festival, Scottdale. Glass Festival, Mt. Pleasant. Italian Festival, Uniontown. Train Robberies. Halloween. Santa Trains.

Notes: Nearby attractions include the world famous Falling Waters home of Frank Lloyd Wright, The Seven Springs Ski Resort, and the Linden Hall Mansion.

Location: The Laurel Highlands Railroad is located in southwestern Pennsylvania just a few miles southeast of Pittsburgh with easy access from I-70, US 40 and US 119.

Connersville, Greensburg, PA

Contact: John Buckwalter
Business Manager

Mailing Address:
P.O. Box 70
Belpre, OH 45714
Telephone: (412) 626-8330
Fax: (304) 422-2805

STEAMTOWN NATIONAL HISTORIC SITE
Railway museum
Standard gauge

NPS PHOTO: KEN GANZ

Ride/Operation: A 27-mile round-trip steam excursion will operate between Scranton and Moscow, Pennsylvania, beginning Memorial Day weekend through the first weekend of November.

Displays/Exhibits: The site's visitor facilities include two museums, a theater, a visitor center, restored portions of the roundhouse, and a bookstore. Roundhouse tours, locomotive shop tours, preservation shop tours, and various additional programs will be offered. Many locomotives and cars are on display in the buildings and in the historic Delaware, Lackawanna & Western Railroad yards.

Train: A five- to ten-car passenger train, powered by either former Canadian Pacific 4-6-2 No. 2317, former Canadian National 2-8-2 No. 3254, or visiting locomotives are used for the main excursion. Yard duties are performed with Baldwin 0-6-0 No. 26.

Schedule: Daily, 9:00 a.m.-5:00 p.m. Closed Thanksgiving, Christmas, and New Year's Day.

Admission: Park: Adults $6.00, senior citizens (62+) $5.00, children (5-15) $2.00, children (4 and under) free. Excursion: adults $10.00, senior citizens (62+) $8.00, children (under 16) $5.00. Call for group rates.

Locomotives: Many steam locomotives; three operate.

Passenger Cars: Electric trailers; suburban and day coaches; combines; business car; troop sleeper.

Rolling Stock/Equipment: Railway Post Office car, boxcars, cabooses, gondolas, hoppers, snowplows, baggage cars, and tank car.

Location: Entrance is off West Lackawanna Avenue

Contact: Superintendent

Mailing Address:
150 South Washington Avenue
Scranton, PA 18503
Telephone: (717) 340-5200

ROADSIDE AMERICA
Model railroad

ROADSIDE AMERICA

Displays/Exhibits: Roadside America, an idea born in June 1903, is a childhood dream realized. From day to day and almost without interruption, this indoor miniature village has grown to be the largest and most beautiful of its type. More than sixty years in the making by Laurence Gieringer, it is housed in a new, modern, comfortable, air-conditioned building and covers more than eight thousand square feet of space. The display includes 2,570 feet of track for trains and trolleys and 250 railroad cars. O-gauge trains and trolleys run among the villages.

Schedule: July 1-September 5; weekdays, 9:00 a.m.-6:30 p.m.; weekends, 9:00 a.m.-7:00 p.m. September 6-June 30: weekdays, 10:00 a.m.-5:00 p.m.; weekends, 10:00 a.m.-6:00 p.m.

Admission: Adults $4.00, senior citizens $3.75, children $1.50.

Location: Take exit 8 off I-78 between Allentown and Harrisburg.

  ♿   P   ✳

Contact: Alberta Bernecker

Mailing Address:
P.O. Box 2
Shartlesville, PA 19554
Telephone: (215) 488-6241

STEWARTSTOWN RAILROAD
Diesel, scheduled
Standard gauge

RAY MCFADDEN

Ride/Operation: A 1¾-hour, 15-mile round trip between Stewartstown and New Freedom, Pennsylvania, whose station was on Lincoln's route to Gettysburg. These rural excursions operate over a railroad opened more than a century ago.

Displays/Exhibits: Stewartstown Station Depot, waiting room, ticket window, and office have been virtually unchanged since construction in 1914. The Stewartstown Station and other structures along the line have been placed on the National Register of Historic Places.

Schedule: Sundays & holidays, May through September, 1:00 & 3:00 p.m. Countryside Excursions: Saturdays & Sundays in October, Noon., 1:30 & 3:00 p.m. Autumn Rail Rambles. Fall Foliage Specials, Sundays (first three only). November, 1:00 & 3:00 p.m.

Fare: Adults $6.00, seniors $5.00, children $3.00, under 3 free unless occupying a seat.

Locomotives: No. 9, 1943 Plymouth 35-ton ML-8, former U.S. Army, No. 10, 1949 GE 44-ton diesel, former Coudersport & Port Allegheny D-1.

Rolling Stock/Equipment: Former Reading Company and Central Railroad of New Jersey all steel, open-window coaches.

Special Events: Easter Bunny Hops. North Pole Express. Brunch Specials. Halloween Haunted Train.

Notes: Ticket sales limited to capacity of train. Tickets are sold on a first-come first-serve basis except special trains which are by reservation.

Location: Fifteen miles south of York, Pennsylvania and forty miles north of Baltimore, Maryland. Take Exit 1 off of I-83 and travel four miles east on Pennsylvania Route 851.

 Baltimore, MD

Contact: George M. Hart
Treasurer

Mailing Address:
P.O. Box 155
Stewartstown, PA 17363
Telephone: (717) 993-2936

CHOO CHOO BARN
Model railroad display
O gauge

JOHN HERR

Displays/Exhibits: A fantastic model railroad exhibit of Lancaster County, Pennsylvania. Seventeen operating trains, 135 moving figures and vehicles and incredibly detailed hand-crafted scenery make this O gauge display a Lancaster County favorite. The adjacent Strasburg Train Shop is a model railroader's paradise. Thousands of detail items are available for the layout builder. "Thomas' Trackside Station," a Shining Time Station store, has over 500 Thomas the Tank Engine and Friends items.

Schedule: Daily: April, May, September-December, 10:00 a.m.-5:00 p.m. June-August, 10:00 a.m.-6:00 p.m.

Fare: Adults $4.00, children ages 5-12 $2.00, under 5 free. Groups with 15+: Adults $2.75, children ages 5-12 $1.25. Price includes tour escort and driver.

Special Events: Canned Food FridaysDonate a canned food item for free admission. Call for dates and times.

Location: From Lancaster follow Rt. 30 East to Rt. 896. Take Rt. 896 South approximately 3 miles to traffic light in Strasburg. Go left and follow Rt. 741 East. Choo Choo Barn is ½ mile outside of town or right.

Contact: Thomas G. Groff

Mailing Address:
P.O. Box 130
Strasburg, PA 17579
Telephone: (717) 687-7911
Fax: (717) 687-6529
Internet: www.800padutch.com/chochoo.html

301

THE NATIONAL TOY TRAIN MUSEUM
Model railroad museum
Toy trains and accessories

Displays/Exhibits: Housed in a beautiful replica of a Victorian railroad station, this museum has one of the finest collections in the world of toy trains, dating from 1880 to the present. The collection includes items from such manufacturers as Ives, Lionel, American Flyer, LGB, and Marklin. Five operating layouts feature O-, S-, G-, HO-, and standard-gauge trains. A video on train subjects plays continuously.

Schedule: Daily, May 1-October 31; weekends and special holiday dates, April, November & December; 10:00 a.m.-5:00 p.m.

Admission: Adults $3.00, senior citizens (65+) $2.75, children (5-12) $1.50. Group discounts available.

Location: 300 Paradise Lane. From the Strasburg sta-tion, travel east on route 741, turn north onto Paradise Lane, and go past the Red Caboose Motel.

Lancaster

Contact: Thelma Rapp

Mailing Address:
P.O. Box 248
Strasburg, PA 17579
Telephone: (717) 687-8976

RAILROAD MUSEUM OF PENNSYLVANIA
Railway museum

RAILROAD MUSEUM OF PENNSYLVANIA

Displays/Exhibits: The Railroad Museum of Pennsylvania was established by the commonwealth of Pennsylvania to collect, preserve, and interpret the history of railroading in the state. The museum displays one of the world's finest collections of steam, electric, and diesel-electric locomotives, passenger and freight cars, and related memorabilia. The 90,000-square-foot building covers six tracks, which exhibit equipment dating from 1825 to 1992. In the extensive yard (open during summer months, weather permitting) are more than twenty-five additional locomotives and cars. Interpretive exhibits help tell the story of railroading in Pennsylvania.

Schedule: Daily, May 1-October 31; Tuesday-Sunday, November 1-April 30; Monday-Saturday, 9:00 a.m.-5:00 p.m.; Sunday, 12:00-5:00 p.m. Closed on certain holidays.

Admission: Adults $6.00, senior citizens $5.00, youths (6-12) $4.00, children under 6 free.

Locomotives: Indoors: the Pennsylvania Railroad Historical Collection, including K4s 4-6-2 No. 3750; L1s 2-8-2 No. 520; G-5 4-6-0 No. 5741; H3 2-8-0 No. 1187; B1 electric switcher; and GG1 electric No. 4935. Also the "Tahoe," 1875 Baldwin 2-6-0, and all three major classes of logging locomotive: Shay, Heisler, and Climax. Outdoors: E-44 electric, former Pennsylvania Railroad; GG1 No. 4800; Baldwin S-12 diesel switcher; others.

Rolling Stock/Equipment: 1855 wooden combine, former Cumberland Valley; 1895 combine No. 4639, former PRR; early PRR coaches and express, baggage, and mail cars; Pullman "Lotos Club"; business car No. 203, former Western Maryland; P70 coach, former PRR; 1950s-era freight train.

Special Events: Charter Day, March. Reading Weekend, July. Circus Days, August. Railroad Art Show, September. Halloween Haunt, October. Christmas Program, "Home for the Holidays," December. Please write for schedules.

Location: On Pennsylvania route 741 opposite the Strasburg Rail Road.

Lancaster

Contact: Robert L. Emerson
Director

Mailing Address:
Box 15
Strasburg, PA 17579
Telephone: (717) 687-8628

STRASBURG RAIL ROAD
Steam, scheduled
Standard gauge

JOHN E. HELBOK

Ride/Operation: A 9-mile, 45-minute round trip from Strasburg to Paradise. Train travels through lush farmlands and turns around adjacent to the Amtrak main line.

Displays/Exhibits: The Strasburg Rail Road, one of the oldest and busiest steam tourist railroads in the country, displays a large collection of historic cars and locomotives.

Train: Open-platform wooden combine and coaches; "Hello Dolly" open observation car; first-class service including food and beverages aboard parlor "Marian." Lunch served on full-service diner "Lee Brenner" on hourly trains.

Schedule: Daily, April-October. Number of trips per day varies with the season, from four to fourteen. During July and August two trains operate, providing service every half-hour. Complete timetables are sent upon request. Dinner Train Service: Thursday-Sunday, July-August, 7:00 p.m.; weekends, September-October and May-June. Call for reservations and information.

Fare: Adults $7.50, children $4.00. Group rates available. Parlor car: adults $12.00, children $6.00. Dining car (ride only): adults $8.50, children $5.00.

Locomotives: No. 31, 1908 Baldwin 0-6-0 & No. 89, 1910 Canadian 2-6-0, former Canadian National; No. 90, 1924 Baldwin 2-10-0, former Great Western; No. 475, 1906 Baldwin 4-8-0, former Norfolk & Western; No. 972, 1912 Montreal, former Canadian Pacific.

Special Events: Easter Bunny Trains, Easter weekend. Halloween Ghost Trains, October 25. Santa Claus Trains, weekends, November 29-December 14.

Location: On Route 741 in Pennsylvania Dutch country, a short distance from Lancaster.

Lancaster

Radio Frequency: 161.235

Contact: G. Fred Bartels
President

Mailing Address:
P.O. Box 96
Strasburg, PA 17579
Telephone: (717) 687-7522
E-mail: srrtrain@prolog.net
Internet: http://padutch.welcome.com/srr.html

OIL CREEK & TITUSVILLE RAILROAD
Diesel, scheduled
Standard gauge

BEVERLY SNYDER

Ride/Operation: A 27-mile, 2½-hour round trip over former Pennsylvania Railroad trackage through the Oil Creek valley, birthplace of the oil industry. The train makes its way through Oil Creek State Park, passing Petroleum Centre and Drake Well Park. Oil Creek State Park has picnic facilities, bicycle rentals, hiking trails, and a bike trail on the original (circa 1860) right-of-way of the Oil Creek Railroad. Drake Well Park has a working, steam-operated replica of the world's first oil well, plus the Drake Well Museum. The railroad is sponsored by the Oil Creek Railway Historical Society.

Train: Open-window coaches, former Delaware, Lackawanna & Western; *Wabash Cannon Ball* coach No. 1399; RPO; open car.

Schedule: School Runs, Tuesday-Thursday, May 13-15 & 20-22; lv. Perry Street 11:15 p.m.; lv. Drake Well 11:30 p.m.; lv. Rynd Farm 12:30 p.m. (12:30 p.m. trip is one-way). Wednesday-Sunday, July, August & October 2-20. Wednesday-Friday, lv. Perry Street 2:00 p.m.; lv. Drake Well 2:15 p.m.; lv. Rynd Farm 3:30 p.m. (3:30 p.m. trip is one-way). Weekends, lv. Perry Street 11:45 a.m. & 3:15 p.m.; lv. Drake Well 12:00 & 3:30 p.m.; lv. Rynd Farm 1:15 & 4:30 p.m. (4:30 p.m. trip is one-way). Passengers may board at any of the three sites. Fall School Runs October 1, 2, 8, 9, lv. Perry Street 10:45 a.m.; lv. Drake Well 11:00 a.m.; lv. Rynd Farm 12:15 p.m. (12:15 p.m. trip is one-way).

Fare: Adults $9.00, senior citizens $8.00, children (3-17) $5.00. One-way, group, car-rental, and train-rental rates available. Box lunches available with advance notice.

Locomotives: No. 75, 1947 Alco S-2, former South Buffalo Railway.

Special Events: Peter Cottontail Express, March 22, 2:00 p.m. Murder Mystery Dinner Train, July 12 & 26, August 30, September 13 & 27, 6:45 p.m. Moonlight Honky Tonk Excursion, August 9, 6:00 p.m. Haunted Train Excursion, October 25, 6:00 p.m. Santa Train Excursion, December 13-14, 2:00 p.m. Passengers may board special-event trains in Perry Street only.

Location: Easily accessible from I-79 and I-80. Trains depart from station at 409 South Perry Street in Titusville and at Rynd Farm, 3½ miles north of Oil City on Route 8.

Mailing Address:
P.O. Box 68
Oil City, PA 16301
Telephone: (814) 676-1733

PENNSYLVANIA TROLLEY MUSEUM
Electric, scheduled
5' 2 1/2" gauge, standard gauge

SCOTT R. BECKER

Ride/Operation: A 3½-mile round trip along a portion of the former Pittsburgh Railways Washington-to-Pittsburgh interurban line and up the scenic Arden Valley, along a former coal-mine railroad, to our new Arden Loop.

Displays/Exhibits: Trolleys from Pittsburgh, Philadelphia, Johnstown, Boston, New Orleans, and western Pennsylvania. In the museum's Visitors Education Center is the exhibit "Working Under Wires." Also on display are a 1930 Baldwin-Westinghouse diesel, a Bessemer & Lake Erie combine, and wooden trolley shelters from the Pittsburgh Railways; the Pittsburgh, Harmony, Butler & New Castle Railway; and the Pittsburgh & Butler Street Railway.

Schedule: Weekends, April-December; 11:00 a.m.-5:00 p.m. Daily, Memorial Day-Labor Day, 11:00 a.m.-5:00 p.m.

Fare: Adults $5.00, senior citizens $4.00, children (2-11) $3.00. Group rates available with advance reservation.

Locomotives/Trolleys: No. 3756, double-truck steel car, former Pittsburgh; No. 5326, double-truck steel car, former Philadelphia Rapid Transit; No. 832, double-truck steel car, former New Orleans; Nos. 66 & 73, double-truck center-door cars, former Philadelphia Suburban Transit; three other Philadelphia cars; No. 1711, Pittsburgh Railways PCC car.

Location: Two miles from downtown on North Main Street Extension; take exit 8 off I-79. The site is on the former broad-gauge main line of the Pittsburgh-Washington interurban.

Contact: Scott R. Becker
Executive Director

Mailing Address:
1 Museum Road
Washington, PA 15301
Telephone: (412) 228-9256
Fax: (412) 228-9675
Internet: http://www.pa-trolley.org

TIOGA CENTRAL RAILROAD
Diesel, scheduled
Standard gauge

RICHARD L. STOVING

Displays/Exhibits: Ticket office is former Grand Trunk business car built in 1894.

Ride/Operation: 24-mile roundtrip excusions Wellsboro Junction to Tioga, PA.

Schedule: May 10 - October 19: Saturday and Sunday, 11:00 a.m., 1:00 p.m. and 3:00 p.m. June 7-October 18, Saturday evening dinner train departing Wellsboro Junction 5:30 p.m. No reservations on excursions. Reservations required on dinner trains.

Fare/Admission: Excursions: adult $10, seniors (60+ $9, children 6-12 $5. Dinner $28 all ages, deposit required.

Locomotives: Alco RS3, RS1, S2

Rolling Stock/Equipment: 1930s era office PRR & CNR.

Special Events: Wellsboro Rail Days, October 25-26. Special railfan trips including run to Corning, N.Y.

Location: Three miles north of Wellsboro, PA, on state route 287. Wellsboro is on U.S. 6.

Contact: Richard L. Stoving
TCRR

Mailing Address:
P.O. Box 269
Wellsboro, PA 16901
Telephone: (717) 624-0990

LYCOMING COUNTY HISTORICAL SOCIETY & MUSEUM

History museum
Toy trains

TERRY WILD STUDIO

Displays/Exhibits: The Shempp toy-train collection is one of the finest in the country. More than 337 complete trains, one hundred individual engines (twelve are one-of-a-kind), and two working model layouts are on display. Exhibit includes items in L, TT, N, OO, HO, O, and 1 gauges; Lionel, American Flyer, Marx, Ives, and American Model Train Company pieces; an American Flyer Mayflower; a copper-and-gold-finished GG1; and American Flyer S-gauge displays.

Schedule: May 1-October 31: Tuesday-Friday, 9:30 a.m.-4:00 p.m.; Saturday, 11:00 a.m.-4:00 p.m.; Sunday, 1:00-4:00 p.m. November 1-April 30: Tuesday-Friday, 9:30 a.m.-4:00 p.m.; Saturday, 11:00 a.m.-4:00 p.m. Closed major holidays.
Admission: Adult $3.50; seniors, AARP & AAA $3.00; children $1.50.

Location: 858 West Fourth Street.

M

Contact: Sandra B. Rife
Executive Director

Mailing Address:
858 West Fourth Street
Williamsport, PA 17701-5824
Telephone: (717) 326-3326

OLD COLONY & NEWPORT
SCENIC RAILWAY
Diesel, scheduled

GEORGE A. FORERO, JR.

Ride/Operation: The Old Colony & Newport Railway was established in 1863 to bring passengers from Boston, Massachusetts, to steamboats operating for New York and other parts of the eastern United States. After several mergers with other railroad companies, the OC&N reappeared in 1979 as one of the most scenic railways in New England. Passengers can take a 3-hour, 21-mile or a 1-hour, 10-mile round trip; the 3-hour ride includes a 1-hour stop at Green Animals Topiary Gardens (admission is extra; passengers may stay aboard the train if they choose). Both rides take passengers along picturesque Narragansett Bay and feature views of the Newport Naval Base, colorful ships sailing in the bay, and the beautiful rocky beaches that follow the 130-year-old right-of-way.

Train: 1912 open-platform coach, former Boston & Maine; 1884 open-platform parlor car, former Intercolonial Railway; P70 heavyweight coach.

Schedule: Three-hour trip: May 4-November 16, Sundays & holidays, 12:30 p.m. One-hour trip: July 2-September 2; Wednesdays, Thursdays & Saturdays, 11:00 a.m., 12:30 & 2:15 p.m.

Fare: Three-hour trip: coach, adults $6.00, senior citizens $5.00, children (under 15) $4.00; parlor car, $9.00. One-hour trip: coach, adults $5.00, senior citizens $4.00, children (under 15) $3.00; parlor car, $7.00.

Locomotives: No. 84, 1945 45-ton General Electric; No. 64, 1942 45-ton General Electric.

Rolling Stock: 1938 steel caboose, former Pennsylvania Railroad.

Special Events: Environmental guided trips. Fall Foliage trips. Christmas in Newport. Please call or write for schedules and fares.

Note: Historic buildings, gift shops, restaurants, and yachting centers are within walking distance.

Location: 19 America's Cup Avenue, next to the Newport Gateway and Visitor's Center in the heart of downtown Newport.

P 🚌 ✳ (nearby) 🍴 (nearby)

📷 ▶ ◀ M TRAIN

Providence

Radio Frequency: 160.395

Contact: Donald Elbert
Executive Director

Mailing Address:
P.O. Box 343
Newport, RI 02840
Telephone: (401) 849-0546
Charters: (401) 624-6951

MATT CONRAD

Ride/Operation: This museum offers a 6-mile, 45-minute round trip between Rockton and Greenbrier on a portion of the Museum's 12-mile long rail line, which was originally operated by the Rockton-Rion Railway. As track rebuilding progresses, the trip will be extended; please write for further details.

Displays/Exhibits: Founded in 1973, the museum features exhibits in some of its pieces of rolling stock. Guided tours, which include the interior of the former Seaboard office car "Norfolk" dining car no. 3157 and Railway Post Office car no. 27 are also given.

Train: Consists of former Canadian National commuter coaches; open-air cars, former Southern Railway and Strategic Air Command; cabooses, former Nickel Plate; Southern and Seaboard Coast Line.

Schedule: May 3-October 18, first and third Saturday of the month. 9:30 a.m.-3:30 p.m. Please write for information on charter trips.

Fare/Admission: Adults $4.50, children (2-12) $2.75, infants in arms ride free. Open-air car $1.00 added to above fares. Site tour: donations accepted.

Locomotives: No. 44, 1927 Baldwin 4-6-0, former Hampton & Branchville; No. 76, 1949 45-ton Porter diesel, and No. 82, 1941 45-ton General Electric, both former U.S. Army Transportation Corps; No. 33, 1946 44-ton General Electric, former Pennsylvania Railroad; No. 4, 1946 25-ton General Electric, former Tarmac/Lone Star Corporation.

Passenger Cars: 1910 office car "Norfolk", former Seaboard Air Lines; 1926 Pullman "Bizet"; 1927 RPO car; lightweight coach. 1940 lightweight coach "South Carolina," former Southern Railway.

Rolling Stock/Equipment: Two baggage cars, former Southern; assorted boxcars; 1946 express refrigerator car, former SAL; tank cars; flatcars; dump cars; cabooses; maintenance-of-way equipment; motor cars; gang cars.

Special Events: Easter Bunny Train, March 30. Railfan Weekend, April 19-20. Motor and Gang Car Day, July 19. Train Ride with Santa Claus, November 29, 30, December 6.

Note: The museum is recruiting volunteers. Please write for details.

Location: 230 Industrial Park Road, Winnsboro, SC 29180. Two miles south of Winnsboro, at the junction of highway 34 and U.S. 321, a short distance from I-77. The site is about 25 miles north of Columbia.

Columbia

Contact: President/Superintendent

Mailing Address:
P.O. Box 7246
Columbia, SC 29202-7246
Telephone: (800) 968-5909
(Olde English Historical District Office
M-F, 9:00 a.m.-5:00 p.m.)
For More Information: (803) 796-8540
(704) 393-0335

BLACK HILLS CENTRAL RAILROAD
Steam, scheduled
Standard gauge

MICHAEL A. EAGLESON

Ride/Operation: A 20-mile, 2-hour round trip between Hill City and Keystone Junction, through forests and mountains near Mount Rushmore National Monument, over a four-percent ruling grade that was once part of the Burlington Railroad. This year marks the thirty-ninth year of operation of the Black Hills Central Railroad. The ticket terminal and a gift shop are located in a former Chicago, Burlington & Quincy station; a snack bar is located at the terminus.

Train: Vintage coaches; half-open coaches; open observation cars.

Schedule: Mid May-September; Monday-Friday, lv. Hill City 8:00 & 10:15 a.m. and 1:30 & 3:45 p.m., lv. Keystone 9:00 & 11:15 a.m. and 2:30 & 4:45 p.m. (4:45 trip is one-way); weekends, lv. Hill City 10:15 a.m., 1:30 & 3:45 p.m., lv. Keystone 11:15 a.m., 2:30 & 4:45 p.m. (4:45 trip is one-way). July-August, evening runs added. Early spring and fall, reduced schedule. Please call for more information.

Fare: Adults $14.00, children (4-14) $9.00, children under 4 ride free when not occupying a seat. Prices include tax and are subject to change.

Locomotives: No. 7, 1919 Baldwin 2-6-2, former Prescott & Northwestern; No. 104, 1926 Baldwin 2-6-2, former Peninsula Terminal Railroad.

Note: No. 7 and some of its cars have appeared in "Gunsmoke," the Disney film *Scandalous John,* and the television movie *Orphan Train.*

Location: In the western part of South Dakota, near Mt. Rushmore National Monument.

Contact: Robert Warder
President

Mailing Address:
P.O. Box 1880
Hill City, SD 57745
Telephone: (605) 574-2222
Fax: (605) 574-4915

PRAIRIE VILLAGE
Steam, irregular
Standard gauge, 24" gauge

DAVE SANFORD

Ride/Operation: Prairie Village is a collection of turn-of-the-century buildings assembled from area towns. There are many steam traction engines on display, along with gas tractors and all types of farm equipment. Passengers may take a two-mile ride around the grounds; part of the loop is from the original Milwaukee line that ran from Pipestone, Minnesota, to Wessington Springs, South Dakota. One-third of a mile of 24-inch-gauge track surrounds the old Wentworth, South Dakota, depot.

Displays/Exhibits: Junius, South Dakota, depot; former Chicago & North Western turntable from Sioux Falls, South Dakota (scheduled to be installed in 1995); chapel car "Emmanuel;" Russell snowplow; tank car; two former REA/Santa Fe express refrigerator cars; track tamper; motorized way cars.

Train: No. 29, 0-6-0, and No. 11, 0-4-0; former REA/Santa Fe express refrigerator car converted to coach; 1909 former C&NW combination coach/baggage car No. 7403 (with original seats and lights); coaches, former Deadwood Central; former Illinois Central caboose.

Schedule: Village Museum: daily, Memorial Day to Labor Day. Train: Every Sunday and during Fall Jamboree.

Fare/Admission: Museum: $5.00. Two-mile ride: $3.00. One-third-mile ride: $1.00 Fall Jamboree: $5.00.

Locomotives: No. 29, 1944 Lima 0-6-0, former Army, former Bay City Terminal, former Iron & Steel Processing, former Duluth & Northeastern; No. 11, Alco 0-4-0T, former Cadillac & Lake City, former Deadwood Central; No. 5, 1927 Orenstein & Koppel 0-4-0T used in Germany until after World War II.

Special Events: Railroad Days, mid June. Prairie Village Fall Jamboree, August 22-24.

Location: Two miles west of Madison. From Sioux Falls, take I-29 north to the Madison/Coleman exit, then travel west on highway 34.

Contact: Bill Nolan

Mailing Address:
Prairie Village
P.O. Box 256
Madison, SD 57042-0256
Telephone: (605) 256-3644

Train information: P.O. Box 302
Madison, SD 57042-0302
Telephone: (605) 256-6177

WHETSTONE VALLEY EXPRESS
Diesel, scheduled
Standard gauge

WHETSTONE VALLEY EXPRESS

Ride/Operation: A 20-mile, 2½-hour round trip from Milbank to Corona over a former Milwaukee Road branch. Dinner is available. The train is operated by the common-carrier Sisseton Milbank Railroad in conjunction with the Whetstone Valley Railroad Historical Society.

Displays/Exhibits: Railroad museum-1911 depot. During annual Trainfair operating model railroads, antiques, slide shows, videos and collectibles, located in National Guard Armory. Free shuttle between armory and depot.

Schedule: Excursion and charters operate May 1-through October.

Fare/Admission: Adults $12.00, children $6.00. Reservations required for "Dinner In the Diner."

Locomotives: No. 627, 1954 EMD SW1200 former Milwaukee Road; No. 561, 1953 EMD SW1200, former Santa Fe.

Passenger Cars: No. 2705, 1934 combine, and 1940 caboose, both former Milwaukee. No. 993, 1911 coach; No. 2111, 1913 coach; and No. 756, 1911 diner; all former Soo line. No. 992298 1974 Milwaukee Road caboose.

Special Events: Trainfair, August 9-10. Model train railroad memorabilia, slide shows.

Note: Train robberies occur on every train, conductors dress in uniform, and hobos ride the rails.

Location: In northeastern South Dakota, 126 miles north of Sioux Falls, 180 miles west of Minneapolis, Minnesota, and 126 miles south of Fargo, North Dakota.

Fargo, North Dakota

Contact: Neil Bagaus
Director of Passenger Operations

Mailing Address:
Whetstone Valley Express
P.O. Box 631
Milbank, SD 57252
Telephone: (800) 675-6656
Fax: (605) 432-9463

CHATTANOOGA CHOO-CHOO

Ride/Operation: Opened in 1909 as the Southern Railway's Terminal Station, this depot welcomed thousands of travelers during the golden age of railroads. Today, the restored station is the heart of the Chattanooga Choo Choo Holiday Inn, a thirty-acre complex with a full range of entertainment. Forty-eight passenger cars are part of the 360-room hotel; three passenger cars serve as a bar, formal restaurant, and meeting/banquet room. A 1924 former New Orleans trolley takes passengers on tours of the historic property.

Displays/Exhibits: Terminal Station, listed on the National Register of Historic Places; HO-gauge model railroad, 174 feet long and 33 feet wide, featuring 3,000 feet of track, 150 switches, 120 locomotives, 1,000 freight cars, 80 passenger cars, and 320 structures. On display in the formal gardens, a former train yard, is a former Cincinnati Southern steam locomotive.

Schedule: Call for hours of operation.
Fare: Trolley: $.50. Model Railroad: adults $2.00, children $1.00.

Location: 1400 Market Street.

Contact: Julie Dodson
Director of Marketing

Mailing Address:
1400 Market Street
Chattanooga, TN 37402
Telephone: (800) 872-2529
(423) 266-5000

TENNESSEE VALLEY RAILROAD
Steam, scheduled
Standard gauge

STEVEN R. FREER

Ride/Operation: A 6-mile, 45-minute round trip, much on original ET&G roadbed, across Chicka-mauga Creek and Tunnel Boulevard and through 986-foot-long Missionary Ridge Tunnel to East Chattanooga Depot, where a shop, turntable, displays, and active steam-locomotive repair shop are located.

Displays/Exhibits: Tour of caboose, display car, theater car, diner, Pullmans, and various steam and diesel locomotives; Grand Junction Depot; large gift shop; audio-visual show; outside exhibits.

Train: Heavyweight coaches with adjustable windows; air-conditioned lightweight coaches Nos. 661 & 907, former Central of Georgia; diner No. 3158.

Schedule: Daily, May, September & October, 10:00 a.m.- 2:00 p.m; daily, June-August, 10:00 a.m.-5:00 p.m.; Saturdays, April-November, 10:00 a.m.-5:00 p.m.; Sundays, April-November, 12:00-5:00 p.m.; lv. East Chattanooga 10:30 & 11:40 a.m., 12:55, 2:20, 3:35 & 4;35 p.m.; lv. Grand Junction 11:00 a.m., 12:15, 1:35, 2:45, 4:00 & 5:00 p.m. (5:00 p.m. train is one-way). *Downtown Arrow* service to Chattanooga Choo-Choo hotel complex; weekends, June-August, with food service and extra-fare seating. Schedules subject to change.

Fare: Regular fare: adults $8.50, children (3-12) $4.50. *Downtown Arrow:* adults $13.50, children (3-12) $9.50. Group rates and charters available.

Locomotives: No. 610, 1952 Baldwin 2-8-0, and Nos. 8669 & 8677, Alco RSD-1 diesels, former U.S. Army; No. 349, 1891 Baldwin 4-4-0, former Central of Georgia; No. 509, 1910 Baldwin 4-6-0, former Louisiana & Arkansas; No. 630, 1904 Alco 2-8-0, and No. 4501, 1911 Baldwin 2-8-2, both former Southern Railway; No. 913, Alco RS-1, former Hartford & Slocomb; No. 36, Baldwin VO1000, former U.S. Air Force; ACT-1, DOT experimental electric train; No. 6914, EMD E8, former Southern Railway; No. 1829, EMD GP7L, former U.S. Army.

Special Events: North Georgia Specials, some powered by steam locomotive No. 4501. Others. Please call or write for information.

Location: 4119 Cromwell Road, near the Jersey Pike exit of Tennessee highway 153 and 1 1/2 miles west of the I-75/highway 153 interchange (exit 4).

Radio Frequency: 160.425

Contact: Robert M. Soule
President

Mailing Address:
4119 Cromwell Road
Chattanooga, TN 37421-2119
Telephone: (423) 894-8028
Fax: (423) 894-8029

COWAN RAILROAD MUSEUM
Railway museum

COWAN RAILROAD MUSEUM

Displays/Exhibits: The former station is now a museum housing a re-creation of a turn-of-the-century telegraph operator's office, various artifacts, and an HO-scale model of the Cowan Pusher District. Nearby the CSX line from Nashville to Chattanooga (once Nashville, Chattanooga & St. Louis, later Louisville & Nashville) climbs over Cumberland Mountain south of Cowan. The grades are steep enough to require helpers in each direction; they are added to southbound trains at Cowan.

Train: Steam locomotive, flatcar, caboose.

Schedule: Thursday-Saturday, May-October, 10:00 a.m.-4:00 p.m. Sunday, May-October, 1:00-4:00 p.m.

Admission: No charge, donations welcomed.

Note: Food is available in Cowan; lodging can be found in Winchester, seven miles west.

Location: Take exit 135 off I-24; 12 miles west on U.S. 41A and 64 and about 15 miles north of the Alabama border.

 P M

Contact: Howard Coulson
President

Mailing Address:
P.O. Box 53
Cowan, TN 37318
Telephone: (615) 967-7365

SOUTHERN APPALACHIA RAILWAY MUSEUM

Railway museum
Standard gauge

SOUTHERN APPALACHIA RAILWAY MUSEUM

Ride/Operation: This museum, a nonprofit corporation, is dedicated to the preservation of rail equipment pertinent to the region. Although a permanent site has not been established, members continue an ongoing effort to restore and maintain equipment. Once restored, the equipment is available for lease to individuals or organizations.

Displays/Exhibits: Coaches; combine; RPO; sleepers; collection of railroad artwork and artifacts.

Schedule: Weekends, by appointment. Only escorted visits are available, because of ongoing restoration.

Admission: Donations welcomed.

Rolling Stock: Boxcar, former Boston & Maine; caboose No. 6487, former Louisville & Nashville; coach No. 664, "Fort Oglethorpe," 1947 Budd, former Central of Georgia; sleeper-lounge "General Beauregard," 1942 Pullman, former Illinois Central; baggage cars No. 1608, 1926 Pullman, and No. 1625, 1928 Pullman, both former Atlantic Coast Line; coach No. 619, 1947 Milwaukee, former "Roanoke Valley," 1949 Pullman; 22-seat combine No. 720, 1914 Pullman; coaches Nos. 826 and 827, 1949 Budd, No. 1075, 1922 Pullman, and No. 846, 1958 Pullman; and RPO No. 34, 1928 American Car & Foundry; all former Southern.

Note: The museum welcomes new members.

Location: Middlebrook Industrial Park.

Contact: John E. Humphrey

Mailing Address:
P.O. Box 5870
Knoxville, TN 37928
Telephone: (615) 691-4147

BROADWAY DINNER TRAIN
Diesel, scheduled
Standard gauge

BROADWAY DINNER TRAIN

Display/Exhibit: Each car is unique, some dating back as far as 1939. We have plaques in each car designating which railroad(s) that particular car once ran on, and any other pertinent information or specifications on each car.

Ride/Operation: 2-1/2 hour rail excursion through middle Tennessee. A four course meal is served each Thursday, Friday and Saturday evening. Five entrees to choose from. Live entainment nightly featuring Nashville singer/songwriter.

Schedule: Open 52 weeks per year. Regularly scheduled excursions each Thursday, Friday and Saturday boarding at 6:30 for 7:00 p.m. departure . Dining on train while in the depot Monday - Wednesday 5:00 p.m. - 10:00 p.m. from an expanded menu. No charge for admission on stationary train. Closed Sunday.

Fare/Admission: $46.95 adult, $30.00 children 12 and under on rolling excursion. No charge for admission on stationary train. Closed Sunday.

Locomotives: 2 EMD E8 locomotives No.5764 and 6802. Powered by Cummins diesel generator situated in restored RPO Post Office Car.

Rolling Stock/Equipment:

Special Events: Murder mystries, children's excursions; call for schedule. We cater to corporate and tour groups.

Location: In Nashville - I40 to exit 209B, Broadway Demonbreun exit. Head toward middle of downtown, where Broadway will dead end into Riverfront Park. Train is to the right of park, behind Nashville Thermal Transfer plant.

Contact:
Dwayne Johnson
General Manager

Mailing Address:
108 First Avenue South
Nashville, TN 37201
Telephone: (615) 254-8000
1-800-254-5855
Fax: (615) 254-5855

TENNESSEE CENTRAL RAILWAY MUSEUM

Diesel, irregular
Standard gauge

STEVEN D. JOHNSON

Ride/Operation: Our excursion train trips are designed to provide the general public with the chance to experience traditional American passenger train travel during the post-WWII years. The museum operates trips each year between Nashville & Watertown, TN; and Columbia, TN & Lawrenceburg, TN.

Displays/Exhibits: Our display consists of the rolling stock we have acquired over the past six years. We have restored a former Family Lines caboose to use as an Operation LifeSaver caboose. We have two former Amtrak, nee ATSF 4700 Budd series stainless steel coaches, TCRX 4711 & 4719, plus former Amtrak nee PRR 3119 buffet diner lounge in operable condition and available for display. Our motive power roster is made up of a former U.S. Army SW8 2038 and a former U.S. Army Plymouth 10-tonner.

Schedule: Museum: 9:00 a.m.-3 p.m. or by appointment. Trains: varies, call for information.

Fare/Admission: Museum: no charge. Trains: Adults, $24.00 regular seats, $49.00 dome seats; children $15.00 regular seats. Group rates available.

Locomotives: No. 52 EMD SW8 TCRX, No. 1062 Plymouth 10-tonner

Passenger Cars: TC 102 Pullman-Standard TC Ry business car; TCRX 4711 & 4719 former Amtrak nee ATSF 48-seat Budd stainless steel coaches; TCRX 3119 former Amtrak nee PRR buffet diner lounge used in Congressional service; NERR 9400 former Amtrak nee NP dome coach owned by Nashville & Eastern RR but in TCRM's custody; TCRX 1354 power car former Amtrak 54' baggage car; TCRX 1365 commissary car former Amtrak baggage car; 10 cabooses.

Location: I-40, Broadway exit 209, east on Broadway to 1st Avenue South. Site is just east of the Broadway Dinner Train concrete platform in downtown Nashville.

Contact: Robert E. Hultman

Mailing Address:
1305 Chestnut Drive
Brentwood, TN 37027-7828
Telephone: (615) 833-5158
Leave message: (615) 781-0262
E-mail: jtdavis@usit.net

DOLLYWOOD ENTERTAINMENT PARK

Steam, scheduled
Narrow gauge

RICHARDS & SOUTHERN

Ride/Operation: The *Dollywood Express,* located in the Village area of Dollywood, takes visitors on a 5-mile journey through this scenic park, known as "the friendliest town in the Smokies." As passengers ride on the authentic, coal-fired steam train, they can catch a glimpse of the different areas of Dollywood: Daydream Ridge, Rivertown Junction, The Village, Craftsman's Valley, Country Fair, Showstreet, Jukebox Junction and the Dollywood Boulevard. The *Dollywood Express* also takes visitors through replicas of a typical turn-of-the-century mountain village and logging community. During Christmas Festivals, the train is decorated with lights and features a special Christmas message for visitors.

Train: The train has been part of the park since June 1, 1961, when the park was known as Rebel Railroad. It has been known as the *Dollywood Express* since May 1986, when the park became Dollywood. The Dollywood Express, with seven open-air passenger cars, is pulled by ninety-ton 2-8-2 Baldwin steam locomotives.

Schedule: One 30-minute ride is offered every hour during park operating hours.

Fare/Admission: Train fare is included with Dollywood admission: adults $25.99 + tax, senior citizens (60+) $21.99 + tax, children (4-11) $17.99 + tax. Group rates available for groups of 20 or more.

Locomotives: "Klondike Katie," 1943 Baldwin 2-8-2, former U.S. Army No. 192; "Cinderella," 1939 Baldwin 2-8-2, former U.S. Army No. 70.

Passenger Cars: Seven open-air passenger cars.

Special Events: Annual Fall Festival, October. Smoky Mountain Christmas Festival, mid November-December. School field trips.

Location: Please call for specific directions.

Contact: Ellen Long
Publicist

Mailing Address:
1020 Dollywood Lane
Pigeon Forge, TN 37863-4101
Telephone: (423) 428-9488

COLLECTION OF LITTLE RIVER RAILROAD AND LUMBER CO. MUSEUM

Displays/Exhibits: The museum is located on the original site of the Little River Lumber Company sawmill, housed in the original Walland Depot which was moved to this site. The Little River Company logged huge tracts in what is now the Great Smoky Mountains National Park. Inside exhibits include over 200 vintage photos with text describing logging and railroad operations in detail, a history of trainwrecks, and the full locomotive roster. The Little River was known for its innovative locomotives, including the first 2-4-4-2 and the smallest Pacific ever built. Outside, Shay No. 2147 is displayed along with a vintage wood caboose and assorted logging and milling equipment.

Schedule: Daily: June-August, October. Weekends: April, May, September. 10:00 a.m.-5:00 p.m., Sunday 2:00-6:00 p.m. Closed November-March.

Admission: Free, donation appreciated.

Locomotives: Little River Shay No. 2147.

Passenger Cars: Vintage wooden caboose, portable steam engine, sawmill equipment.

Special Events: Spring Fest, first weekend in May. Old Timer's Day, last weekend in September.

Notes: The museum underwent a major renovation in 1996 with all new exhibits. A new building, a replica of the Elkmont Post Office, is being built for 1997 and will house an expanded museum gift shop. Two-year memberships are $21.47.

Location: Museum is located on Highway 321 in Townsend, near the west entrance to the Great Smoky Mountains National Park; approximately 18 miles east of Maryville, 15 miles southwest of Pigeon Forge.

Contact: Sandy Headrick

Mailing Address:
P.O. Box 211
Townsend, TN 37882
Telephone: (423) 448-2211
Fax: (423) 448-2312
E-mail: hmmotel@ix.netcom.com
Internet: http://thesmokies.com/features/commerce/we091996/index.htm

AUSTIN & TEXAS CENTRAL RAILROAD
Steam, scheduled
Standard gauge

GEORGE A. FORERO, JR.

Ride/Operation: A 66-mile round trip through the scenic Texas hill country, two hours each way, over the former Southern Pacific route built in 1881.

Train: Southern Pacific Mikado No. 786, steam-era coaches, and air conditioned sleeper lounge cars.

Schedule: Hill Country Flyer runs March-December, Saturdays and Sundays. Twilight Flyer runs a two hour evening excursion first Satuday each month.

Fare: Coach: adults $24.00, children (under 13) $10.00. Air-conditioned lounge car: adults $38.00, children (under 13) $10.00. One-way fares, senior-citizen and group discounts available.

Locomotives: Southern Pacific Mikado No. 786, built by Alco 1916.

Passenger Cars: Six P70 coaches built for the Pennsylvania Railroad in the 1920s, streamlined Nickel Plate, Missouri Pacific and Santa Fe sleeper-lounge cars.

Special Events: Wildflower Trains in spring. Special Christmas season scheudule. Special charters available.

Location: Five miles northwest of Austin in Cedar Park (intersection of U.S. 183 and Farm Road 1431).

Radio Frequency: 160.550

Contact: Arden Brands
Executive Director

Mailing Address:
Box 1632
Austin, TX 78767-1632
Reservations: (512) 477-8468
Office/Administration: (512) 477-6377

AGE OF STEAM RAILROAD MUSEUM
Railway museum
Standard gauge

BOB LAPRELLE

Displays/Exhibits: Operated by the Southwest Railroad Historical Society since 1963, this museum offers a nostalgic journey back to the days of steam locomotives and name passenger trains, featuring some of the world's largest steam, diesel-electric, and electric locomotives. A superlative collection of heavyweight passenger equipment includes meticulously restored dining car "Goliad," former Missouri-Kansas-Texas; business car "Texland," former Fort Worth & Denver; and parlor-club car No. 3231, former Santa Fe. Other exhibits include chair and Pullman cars, vintage freight cars and cabooses, Dallas's oldest surviving train station, and many railroad artifacts. Come blow the steam locomotive whistles and enjoy one of the nation's foremost railroad collections. Former Santa Fe "doodlebug" M-160 and former Western Railroad VO-1000 No. 1107 operate periodically within the museum site. Also on display is Santa Fe Tower 19, a Texas landmark interlocking tower built in 1903.

Schedule: Wednesday-Sunday, 10:00 a.m.-5:00 p.m.

Admission: Adults $3.00, children (under 13) $1.50.

Locomotives/Trolleys: "Big Boy" No. 4018, 1942 Alco 4-8-8-4 & "Centennial" No. 6913, EMD DDA40X, both former Union Pacific; No. 1625, 1918 Alco 2-10-0, former Eagle-Picher Mining Co.; No. 4501, 1942 Baldwin 4-8-4, former Frisco; No. 7, 1923 Baldwin 0-6-0, former Dallas Union Terminal Co.; No. 4903, Pennsylvania RR GG1 electric; M-160, diesel-electric "Doodlebug," former Santa Fe; No. 1107, Baldwin VO-1000 diesel-electric, former Western Railroad Co., former Colorado & Wyoming; No. 115, 1956 Fairbanks-Morse H12-44, former Southern Pacific No. 2379.

Special Events: Open daily during State Fair of Texas, October, 10:00 a.m.-6:00 p.m.

Location: Two miles east of downtown at 1105 Washington Street, on the north side of the State Fair of Texas grounds at Fair Park. From I-30 eastbound, take exit 47A to Parry Avenue, turn left and travel 3 blocks to the entrance. From I-30 westbound, take exit 47A right onto Exposition Avenue, then turn left on Parry Avenue.

Dallas

Contact: Bob LaPrelle
Executive Director

Mailing Address:
P.O. Box 153259
Dallas, TX 75315-3259
Telephone: (214) 428-0101

McKINNEY AVENUE TRANSIT AUTHORITY
Electric, scheduled
Standard gauge

JIM CUMBIE/MCKINNEY AVENUE TRANSIT AUTHORITY

Ride/Operation: A 2⅘mile, 30-minute round trip in restored vintage streetcars between the downtown Arts District and the shops, galleries, and restaurants of McKinney Avenue. More than half of the route (along McKinney and Cole Avenues) is original Dallas Railway & Terminal trackage, a line that began service in 1890. The system is operated with volunteer labor by the nonprofit McKinney Avenue Transit Authority. Federal, city, and private funds have been pledged and active planning is underway to extend the route northward to Cityplace at Bowen and US 75, and westward to the West End Historic District.

Displays/Exhibits: Carbarn tours are available upon request.

Schedule: Daily; Sunday-Thursday, 10:00 a.m.-10:00 p.m.; Friday-Saturday, 10:00 a.m.-midnight. Frequency of service varies from 15 to 30 minutes, depending on the number of cars in service.

Fare: Round trip: adults $1.50, children $1.00, senior citizens $ .50. Passes and tokens are also sold. Charters available. Free transfers to and from DART's Hop-A-Bus and Dallasites downtown circulator routes.

Trolleys: In operation, four closed streetcars: No. 122, "Rosie," 1906 single-truck Brill, former Oporto, Portugal; No. 186, ("The Green Dragon"), 1913 Stone and Webster "turtle roof," and Birney No. 636, ("Petunia"), both former Dallas, Texas; No. 369, ("Matilda"), Australia W-2 class. Under restoration: former North Texas Traction Interurban No. 332. In storage, operable: former Toronto PCCs 4613 and 4614. In storage and awaiting restoration are former Dallas rebuilt Peter Witt No. 754 and former Dallas Stone and Webster cars Nos. 183, 189, and 323.

Special Events: Couples-only Love Trolleys, on or near Feb. 14. Free rides for Moms and Dads on their holidays. Free cake served on board and special activities

during weekend closest to annual anniversary of start-up date.

Location: Two main terminals: McKinney Plaza on McKinney Avenue between Bowen and Hall, one-half mile west of North Central Expressway (U.S. 75); and St. Paul by Ross, 2 blocks south of Woodall Rodgers Freeway (Spur 366) in the Arts District. More than 20 additional stops are along the route.

Dallas

Mailing Address:
3153 Oak Grove Avenue
Dallas, TX 75204
Telephone: (214) 855-0006
Fax: (214) 855-5250

GEORGE A. FORERO, JR.

Ride/Operation: Round trip daily from Grapevine's Historic District along 21 miles of the old Cotton Belt Railroad (1888) to Fort Worth's Historic Stockyards.

Ten mile round trip over Fort Worth & Western Railroad freight line through Ft. Worth following the Chisholm Trail route. Stockyards Station is the largest train station in the Southwest.

Displays/Exhibits: Grapevine's Historic District, Fort Worth's Historic Stockyards. Turntables at both depot locations.

Train: Fully restored 1896 Cooke 4-6-0; four open-window passenger coaches; two open-air touring coaches.

Schedule: Daily. Please call or write for timetable.

Fare: Grapevine to Stockyards: Adults $19.95, children (3-12) $9.95. 10-mile round trip in Ft. Worth: Adults $10.00, children (3-12) $5.50.

Locomotives: No. 2248, 1896 Cooke 4-6-0.

Special Events: Chisholm Trail Days, June. Pioneer Days, September. Round Trips to Granbury.

Location: Cotton Belt Depot: 707 S. Main St., Grapevine, TX. Stockyards Station Depot: 140 East Exchange Avenue in the Stockyards, Ft. Worth, TX.

Fort Worth

Mailing Address:
140 East Exchange Avenue
Fort Worth, TX 76106
Telephone: (817) 625-RAIL (7245)
(800) 952-5717
Fax: (817) 740-1119

THE CENTER FOR TRANSPORTATION & COMMERCE, THE GALVESTON RAILROAD MUSEUM

Railway museum, standard gauge

JIM CRUZ

Ride/Operation: Steam Engine 555 takes passengers on excursions on selected dates during the year. Terminal for the "Texas Limited" charter excursion train between Houston and Galveston. (Train yarded in facility when not in use.)

Displays/Exhibits: This museum, located on five acres surrounding the former Santa Fe Union Station, displays the largest rail collection in the Southwest, including steam and diesel locomotives and passenger and freight cars. Spectacular sound and light shows present the history of Galveston, which was served by the passenger trains of the Santa Fe, the Rock Island, the Southern Pacific, the Burlington, and the Katy. The People's Gallery depicts "A Moment Frozen in Time," where ghosts of travelers past await boarding calls in the restored 1930s art deco depot. A working HO-gauge model of the port of Galveston provides an overview of the port.

Schedule: Daily, 10:00 a.m.-5:00 p.m. Closed Thanksgiving and Christmas.

Admission: Adults $5.00, senior citizens $4.50, children $2.50. Group discounts.

Locomotives: Operable engines include No. 555, former Magma Arizona No. 5, 1922 Alco 2-8-0, former Southern Pacific 1303, 1949 EMD NW2. Static displays include No. 410, 1947 Fairbanks Morse H-20-44, former Southwestern Portland Cement, ex-ACY & N&W; No. 1, 1929 Baldwin 2-6-2, former Waco, Beaumont, Trinity & Sabine; No. 314, 1894 Cooke 4-6-0, and No. 100, 1955 Budd RDC, both former SP; others.

Rolling Stock/Equipment: 1929 Pullman Private Car, "Anacapa," 1928 PRR Business Car. "Martin W. Clement," former PRR "Pennsylvania " (this car equipped & maintained for Amtrak operation). Santa Fe Superintendent's car No. 403, various Pullman sleepers, dining car, RPO and others. Lunch on former SOU 3305 and CBQ 302 ("Silver Hours") dining cars. Four baggage cars house railroad history exhibits, numerous, vintage freight equipment - including cabooses and

UTLX 83699, "the largest tank car (type) ever built," and ex-CRIP "hook" with tender and tool car.

Location: 123 Rosenberg; free parking off 26th and Santa Fe Place. Galveston Trolley stop.

Houston

Contact: John K. Dundee
Executive Director

Mailing Address:
123 Rosenberg
Galveston, TX 77550
Telephone: (409) 765-5700

GULF COAST RAILROAD MUSEUM
Gulf Coast Chapter, National Railway Historical Society
Railway museum

DAVID M. SEE

Displays/Exhibits: This museum, located near the Southern Pacific's Sunset Route in northeastern Houston, features historic locomotives and passenger and freight cars of regional significance, many in operable condition. The recently completed visitor center is housed in former Santa Fe 1928 end-door baggage-express car No. 1890, which also contains a collection of railroad artifacts.

Schedule: March 22-November 2, Saturdays, 11:00 a.m.-4:00 p.m. Sundays , 1:00 p.m.-4:00 p.m. Group tours available at other times by appointment.

Admission: Adults $3.00, children (under 13) $1.50.

Locomotives: No. 14, 1949 Alco, former Houston Belt & Terminal; No. 510, 1949 Baldwin DS 44-750, former Texas Mexican.

Passenger Cars: Streamlined sleeper "Verde Valley," 1942 Pullman, former Santa Fe; all-stainless chair car "New Braunfels," 1955 Pullman, former Missouri-Kansas-Texas, built for the *Texas Special;* tavern-lounge-observation "Good Cheer," 1940 Pullman, former Kansas City Southern, built for the streamlined *Southern Belle;* 1947 streamlined parlor car "Alton," former Gulf, Mobile & Ohio; streamlined baggage-RPO No. 3401, 1938 Budd, former Santa Fe; heavy-weight baggage car No. 50, 1915 Barney & Smith, former Spokane, Portland & Seattle.

Rolling Stock/Equipment: Caboose No. 6, 1949 MKT (Denison) shops, former MKT; 1979 bay-window caboose No. 4696, former Southern Pacific; 1927 riveted steel tank car No. 2198, former Cities Service Oil.

Special Events: National Model Railroad Month Open House, November, features layouts from area model

railroad clubs in the museum's cars. Occasional main-line steam and diesel excursions as fund-raisers. Various local railroad-related tours and day trips.

Location: 7390 Mesa Drive, about 1 1/2 miles north of McCarty Road (U.S. highway 90) off North Loop 610.

Contact: Museum Director

Mailing Address:
P.O. Box 457
Houston, TX 77001-0457
Telephone: (713) 631-6612

TEXAS LIMITED
Steam, scheduled
Standard gauge

TEXAS LIMITED

Ride/Operation: This excursion train travels on a charter basis from Houston to historic Galveston Island, with a stop at League City Park in the NASA/Clear Lake area.

Displays/Exhibits: The Galveston terminal is the historic Center for Transportation and Commerce, which includes a large collection of locomotives, cars, and other railroad artifacts. NASA, Space Center Houston, and the Gulf Greyhound Park are located in League City-NASA/Clear Lake.

Schedule: Until further notice, operation is limited to private charters. Regular schedule will resume at a future date and time to be announced.

Fare: Please call or write for information.

Locomotives: Two EMD F7s.

Passenger Cars: Seven restored passenger cars from the 1930s, 1940s, and 1950s.

Location: Houston Eureka Station, 567 T.C. Jester.

Contact: April Smith

Mailing Address:
3131 West Alabama Street
Suite 309
Houston, TX 77098
Telephone: (713) 522-0574

TEXAS STATE RAILROAD
Steam, scheduled
Standard gauge

GEORGE A. FORERO, JR.

Ride/Operation: A 4-hour, 50-mile round trip over a major segment of the original Texas State Railroad, built in 1896. Two trains make simultaneous round trips through the rolling pine and hardwood forest of East Texas. Victorian-style depots are located in Rusk and Palestine.

Train: Two combines (1914 & 1923 AT&SF), seven commuter coaches (1920s Chicago, Rock Island & Pacific). Three open observation coaches (1910 I&GN, 1920 Pennsylvania Railroad and 1920 Erie Lackawanna).

Schedule: Weekends, March-May, August-October; Thursday-Sunday, June-July; first three Saturdays, November. Leave Rusk for Palestine 11:00 a.m., return 3:00 p.m. Leave Palestine for Rusk 11:00 a.m., return 3:00 p.m.

Fare: Round trip: adults $18.00, children (3-12) $11.00, children under 3 ride free. One way: adults $12.00, children (3-12) $7.00; children under 3 ride free. June, July & August all tickets discounted $2.00.

Locomotives: No. 201, 1901 Cooke 4-6-0, former Texas & Pacific No. 316; No. 300, 1917 Baldwin 2-8-0, former Texas Southeastern No. 28; No. 400, 1917 Baldwin 2-8-2, former Magma Arizona No. 7; No. 500, 1911 Baldwin 4-6-2, former Santa Fe No. 1316; No. 610, 1927 Lima 2-10-4, former Texas & Pacific No. 610.

Special Events: Dogwood Rail Excursions, Easter Sunrise Drama, Great Texas Train Race, Starlight Runs, WWII Living History Encampments, Civil War Re-enactments, Texas Ranger Living Histories, Photography Workshop, Motor Car Weekends, Murder on the Disoriented Express, Steam Restoration Shop Tours, Texas & Pacific/Engine 610 Tours, Old West Round-up. Many more, call for specific dates and times.

Location: Rusk Depot is 2½ miles west of Rusk on U.S. 84; Palestine Depot is 4 miles east of Palestine on U.S. 84.

Contact: Curtis Pruett
Complex Manager

Mailing Address:
P.O. Box 39
Rusk, TX 77785
Telephone: (903) 683-2561
In Texas: (800) 442-8951

ography

TEXAS TRANSPORTATION MUSEUM
Railway museum

TEXAS TRANSPORTATION MUSEUM

Ride/Operation: Passengers enjoy a one-third-mile caboose ride on the "Longhorn & Western Railroad" behind a 60-ton diesel. The track is being extended one mile.

Displays/Exhibits: Santa Fe business car No. 404; heavyweight Pullman "McKeever"; Missouri Pacific transfer caboose; Union Pacific caboose; Southern Pacific station from Converse, Texas, with railroad displays and pictures; G-gauge garden railroad; 5,000 square foot display building with 100 foot long HO model railroad; transportation toy display; fire trucks; antique automobiles and carriages; technology display.

Train: One locomotive; one or two cabooses. Steam operates if available; Motor-car rides available at other times during regular hours.

Schedule: Museum: Thursday, Saturday & Sundays, 9:00 a.m.-4:00 p.m. Train: Sundays, 1:00-3:00 p.m.; train departs every 30 minutes.

Fare/Admission: Suggested donation: adults $3.00, children and students $1.00. Includes admission and all rides.

Locomotives: No. 6, 1911 Baldwin 2-8-0, former Moscow, Camden & San Augustine; No. 1, 1925 Baldwin 0-4-0T, former Comal Power Company; No. 7071, 1942 44-ton General Electric switcher, former U.S. Air Force; No. 4035, 1952 Baldwin RS-4 60-ton switcher, former U.S. Army.

Special Events: Every Sunday, all divisions of the museum operating as much equipment as possible. With advance reservation, the museum is available for groups with train rides.

Location: At Wetmore and Wurzback Parkway north of San Antonio International Airport in McAllister Park, 11731 Wetmore Road.

P M

San Antonio

Contact: Jared Davis
Special Events Coordinator

Mailing Address:
11731 Wetmore Road
San Antonio, TX 78247-3606
Telephone: (210) 490-3554

RAILROAD AND PIONEER MUSEUM
Railway museum

FRED M. SPRINGER

Displays/Exhibits: Early Santa Fe and Missouri-Kansas-Texas station equipment and furniture, including a working telegraph for train orders, as well as segregated waiting rooms. The museum houses a large collection of railroad artifacts and displays of woodworking, ranching, farming, blacksmithing, and local history. Also displayed is a large collection of railroad timetables and passes, photographs, and papers from around the world.

Schedule: Tuesday-Friday, 1:00-4:00 p.m.; Saturday, 10:00 a.m.-4:00 p.m.

Admission: Adults $2.00, senior citizens and children $1.00, children under 5 admitted free.

Locomotives: No. 3423, 1921 Baldwin 4-6-2, former Santa Fe; No. 2301, 1937 Alco, the oldest surviving Santa Fe diesel.

Rolling Stock/Equipment: Steel caboose No. 1556, former Gulf, Colorado & Santa Fe; three section cars; steel caboose No. 140, former MKT; handcar, caboose, and boxcar, all former Missouri Pacific; World War II Pullman troop sleeper; an MKT (Glover Glade) Pullman sleeper (1917).

Special Events: Texas Train Festival, third weekend in September, includes model train show, one-eighth-gauge operating models, full-sized Santa Fe operating equipment, living history demonstrations, and arts and crafts. Special exhibits.

Note: The museum has acquired the former MKT Temple depot, the last mission-style 1912 MKT depot in Texas, and is planning to restore it and open it as a railroad research center. Just recently, the museum acquired the Temple Santa Fe (Southern Div. Headquarters Depot) built in 1910.

Location: 710 Jack Baskin (31st Street and Avenue H). Temple is in central Texas, between Austin and Waco; take the Avenue H exit off I-35.

Contact: Mary Irving
Director

Mailing Address:
P.O. Box 5126
Temple, TX 76505
Telephone: (817) 778-6873

Utah, Heber City
R

HEBER VALLEY RAILROAD
Steam, diesel, scheduled
Standard gauge

STEVEN W. BELMONT

Ride/Operation: A 32-mile, 3½-hour round trip through the high mountain meadows of the Heber Valley, across rivers and streams and into the deep canyon of the Provo River to Vivian Park.

Displays: Various freight cars, maintenance-of-way equipment, and related machinery. The railroad is operated by the Heber Valley Railroad Authority, a nonprofit organization formed jointly by Heber City, Wasatch County, and the state of Utah. During 1994, repairs were completed to former Union Pacific No. 618, one of the first standard-gauge steam locomotives in the U.S. to be removed from static display and placed in operation on a tourist railroad.

Train: Former Lackawanna commuter coaches; former Louisville & Nashville heavyweight; former Union Pacific combination car; former UP steel caboose or former Kennecott Copper caboose; various "mountain observation" cars.

Schedule: Daily, May 26-September 30; weekends, February 3-March 31, May 4-26, October 5-27. Please call or write for complete schedule.

Fare: Adults $16.00, seniors $14.00, children (12 & under) $10.00, children (2 years & under) not occupying a seat ride free.

Locomotives: No. 618, 1907 Baldwin 2-8-0, and No. 1011, 1940 EMD NW2, both former UP; No. 1218, 1953 Davenport 44-ton diesel, 1813, 1952, EMD MRS-1, both former U.S. Army.

Note: Trains will be operated by either No. 1011 or No. 1813 when No. 618 is having monthly service or an annual inspection performed.

Location: Heber City Depot, 450 South 600 West. Heber City is 46 miles east of Salt Lake City on U.S. 40.

Salt Lake City

Radio Frequency: 150.995

Contact: Gloria Montgomery
Executive Director

Mailing Address:
P.O. Box 609
Heber City, UT 84032
Telephone: (801) 654-5601

OGDEN UNION STATION

Displays/Exhibits: The model railways are done in realistic scenes behind glass enclosures. The classic cars are in roped off area. Gems and Minerals are in glass case with descriptions of what they are. Browning guns are in separate classifications behind glass.

Ride/Operation: Ogden Union Station is composed of four indoor museums, model railroad, classic cars, Browning firearms Natural History - there is also an art gallery. Outside are three actual locomotives.

Schedule: Monday - Saturday 10:00 a.m. - 5:00 p.m. Sundays 11:00 a..m. - 3:00 p.m. Memorial Day to Labor Day.

Fare/Admission: $2.00 adults, $1.50 senior citizens (65+) $1.00 children 3-12, under 3 free. Special group rates are available.

Locomotives: The Spencer S. Eccles center is our rolling stock. The most powerful locomotive built is a gas turbine called "Big Blow." Also The Centennial is the largest diesel produced.

Special Events: Hof Winterfest January 17-18 or 24-25 (tentative). Hostler Model Railroad Fair March 8-9. Gem & Mineral Show March 14, 15, 16. Homier Tool Show, March 27, 28, 29. Railfest May 9-10. Cowboy Poetry July 17. Christmas Tree Express December 5-6.

Location: 2501 Wall Ave., Ogden, Utah 84401

Contact:
Evelyn Moritz

Mailing Address:
2501 Wall Avenue
Ogden, UT 84401
Telephone: (801) 629-8535
Fax: (801) 629-8555

GOLDEN SPIKE NATIONAL HISTORIC SITE

Displays/Exhibits: This is the spot where the famous Golden Spike ceremony was held on May 10, 1869, completing the nation's first transcontinental railroad. Exact operating replicas of the original locomotives are on display; these locomotives run to the Last Spike Site on their own power each morning (from April to the second weekend in October) and return to the engine-house in late afternoon. In the Visitor Center are color movies and many exhibits. Park rangers are on hand to explain the importance of the railroad and the significance of the ceremony of 1869.

Schedule: Daily; May 26-September 1, 8:00 a.m.-6:00 p.m.; September 7-May 25, 8:00 a.m.-4:30 p.m. Closed Thanksgiving, Christmas, and New Year's Day.

Admission: $4.00 per car, $2.00 per adult (17-61).

Locomotives: Full-sized operating replicas of Union Pacific 4-4-0 No. 119 and Central Pacific 4-4-0 No. 60, the "Jupiter."

Special Events: Annual Celebration, May 10, features re-enactments. Annual Railroader's Festival, August 9, includes games, contests, and re-enactments. Annual Railroader's Film Festival & Winter Steam Demonstration, December 26-28. No entrance fees for special events. Many more events, call for specifics.

Note: Ranger Talks, Big Fill Walk, self-guided auto tours, locomotive demonstrations, and other activities are available. Check the activities board in the Visitor Center.

Location: 32 miles west of Brigham City, Utah via hwy. 13 and 83 through Corinne.

Contact: Rick Wilson
Chief Ranger

Mailing Address:
P.O. Box 897
Brigham City, UT 84302
Telephone: (801) 471-2209

JEFF TERRY

Ride/Operation: This group sponsors excursions powered by historic Union Pacific steam and diesel locomotives over the UP's lines; most trips feature one or more photo stops. A highlight is a trip from Denver to the Pacific Northwest in September and October to celebrate the 50th anniversary of the inaugural of the streamliner *City of Portland*. Those interested can travel on one or several segments of the trip, which includes layovers at major cities such as Laramie, Wyoming; Boise, Idaho; Spokane, Washington; and Portland, Oregon. This trip features travel over the Granger cutoff, which has not seen passenger service in 20 years; a ride along the Snake River, crossing it on 3,900-foot-long Joso Bridge; rare mileage on the Montana Division from Pocatello, Idaho, to Butte, Montana; and the Columbia River Gorge.

Schedule: Excursions this year are scheduled to run in Iowa, Illinois, Missouri and Arkansas. Please call or write for information.

Fare: Varies depending on trip. Reservations required; please call or write for ticket information and availability.

Locomotives: No. 3985, 1943 Alco 4-6-6-4, largest operating steam locomotive in the world; No. 844, 1944 Alco 4-8-4, last steam locomotive purchased by the UP; Nos. 951, 963B & 949, 1955 EMD A-B-A E9s; No. 6936, DD40AX, largest diesel built; all currently UP.

Passenger Cars: Original UP streamliner fleet cars, rebuilt to current standards.

Note: The Pacific Limited Group is responsible for ticket sales, advertising, staffing, and the safe operation of excursions. All railroad equipment and locomotive crews are provided by the Union Pacific Railroad. The PLG is made up of the Central Coast Chapter, NRHS; the Promontory Chapter, NRHS; the Union Pacific Historical Society; and the Feather River Rail Society.

Mailing Address:
P.O. Box 27081
Salt Lake City, UT 84119
Telephone: (801) 355-5871

GREEN MOUNTAIN RAILROAD
GREEN MOUNTAIN FLYER
Diesel, scheduled
Standard gauge

GREEN MOUNTAIN RAILROAD

Ride/Operation: A 26-mile, 2-hour round trip from Bellows Falls to Chester. Ludlow foliage specials feature a 6-hour round trip. The former Rutland Railroad trackage goes through three river valleys, offering many scenic highlights. The Green Mountain Railroad is a working freight line.

Train: Restored open-window coaches, former Rutland Railroad and Jersey Central.

Schedule: Summer: June 17-18 & 24-25; July 1-September 4, Tuesday-Sunday. Fall: September 16-October 15, daily. Ludlow Trip: September 30, October 1, 7, 8, 14 & 15. Rutland Limited, September 7.

Fare: Round trip: adults $10.00, children $6.00, children under 3 not occupying a seat ride free. One way: adults $6.00, children $4.00. Please call or write for schedules and fares for special-event trains.

Locomotives: Alco RS-1 No. 405, former Rutland; EMD GP9 No. 1849, former Burlington Northern; EMD GP9 No. 1850, former Chesapeake & Ohio; EMD GP9 No. 1848, former Bangor & Aroostook; EMD GP9R No. 1851, former Norfolk Southern.

Note: Tickets are sold at Bellows Falls Union Station, on all trains, and in Chester at Cummings Hardware.

Special Events: Valentine's Day, Sugar on Snow, March, Easter Bunny, Mother's Day, Memorial Day, May and Santa Express. Call for dates and details.

Location: The railroad station is located on Depot Street at the junction of the Green Mountain and Boston & Maine railroads. Take exit 5 or 6 off I-91. Bellows Falls is in southern Vermont, on the New Hampshire border.

Bellows Falls

Contact: Barbara Adams

Mailing Address:
P.O. Box 498
Bellows Falls, VT 05101
Telephone: (802) 463-3069

JOHN E. HELBOK

Displays/Exhibits: This museum displays an extensive and internationally renowned collection of Americana housed in thirty-seven historic buildings on a forty-five-acre site. The railroad exhibit features the restored 1890 Shelburne depot with a Central Vermont steam locomotive and the private car "Grand Isle." Nearby is former Woodstock Railroad steam inspection car "Gertie Buck." There is also a wooden replica of Baldwin's "Old Ironsides" of 1832 and a collection of railroad memorabilia. Other exhibits at the museum include a 220-foot sidewheel steamer, the *Ticonderoga*, which was moved overland from Lake Champlain, and collections of antiques, quilts, carriages, art, decoys, and tools.

Schedule: Daily, late May-late October, 10:00 a.m.-5:00 p.m. Guided tours: late October-late May, 1:00 p.m.

Admission: Admission ticket valid for two consecutive days (daily season only). Group rates available for groups of 15 or more.

Locomotives: No. 220, 1915 Alco 4-6-0, former Central Vermont.

Note: Limited handicapped accessibility.

Location: On U.S. route 7, seven miles south of Burlington.

P M

Contact: Collections Department

Mailing Address:
P.O. Box 10
Shelburne, VT 05482
Telephone: (802) 985-3346
Fax: (802) 985-2331

SGT. MALCOLM WILLIAMS

Displays/Exhibits: This military-history museum displays items of transportation dating from 1776 to the present. Inside the fifteen-thousand-square-foot museum are dioramas and exhibits; on five acres outside are rail rolling stock, trucks, jeeps, amphibious marine craft, helicopters, aircraft, and an experimental hovercraft.

Schedule: Daily, 9:00 a.m.-4:30 p.m. Closed Mondays and all federal holidays.

Admission: No charge.

Locomotives: No. 607, Lima 2-8-0; narrow-gauge Vulcan 0-6-0; MRS-1, 120-ton diesel electric.

Passenger Cars: U.S. Army medical ambulance car; Berlin duty train sleeper.

Rolling Stock/Equipment: Caboose, Jordan spreader, snowplow, steam crane, tank car, World War II ammunition car, flatcar, all former U.S. Army; German caboose (from Berlin duty train) and tank car.

Location: Off I-64 at route 105 and Fort Eustis Boulevard (exit 250A), 20 miles south of Williamsburg.

Williamsburg or Newport News

Contact: Barbara Bower

Mailing Address:
Building 300
Besson Hall
Fort Eustis, VA 23604-5260
Telephone: (757) 878-1115

OLD DOMINION RAILWAY MUSEUM

Displays/Exhibits: This museum's collection includes a caboose, freight equipment, and track-maintenance equipment; a Richmond, Fredericksburg & Potomac baggage car contains exhibits on telegraphy, passenger depots, the Railway Express Agency and railroad workers.

Schedule: Weekends; Saturday, 11:00 a.m.-4:00 p.m.; Sunday, 1:00-4:00 p.m.

Admission: Donations requested.

Locomotives: Porter saddletank 0-4-0.

Rolling Stock/Equipment: 1959 boxcar and 1969 caboose, both former Seaboard; 1937 baggage car, former RF&P; track-inspection car.

Special Events: Floodwall Guided Walking Tours, second Sunday of each month. Children's Day, mid-September.

Note: The museum is a public-service project of the Old Dominion Chapter of the National Railway Historical Society.

Location: 102 Hull Street, near the downtown tourist area, adjacent to the former Southern Railway Hull Street station and the Richmond Floodwall Promenade.

P 🚌 ✳ 📷 M ar n

Richmond

Contact: Michael P. Bonner
Director

Mailing Address:
P.O. Box 8583
Richmond, VA 23226
Telephone: (804) 233-6237

VIRGINIA MUSEUM OF TRANSPORTATION
Railway museum
Standard gauge

VIRGINIA MUSEUM OF TRANSPORTATION, INC.
RESOURCE LIBRARY & ARCHIVES

Displays/Exhibits: Founded in 1963 as the Roanoke Transportation Museum, Inc., the VMT was designated as the official transportation museum of the commonwealth of Virginia in 1983, in recognition of the quality and diversity of its collection. On exhibit at the site, a 1917 former Norfolk & Western freight station, are a number of steam, diesel, and electric locomotives and an extensive collection of passenger cars, freight cars, cabooses, trolleys, and memorabilia. Other displays include a PCC car from Washington, D.C.; a former N&W dynamometer car; the first N&W diesel; a former Illinois Terminal Railroad business car; antique automobiles and trucks; and former N&W class J 4-8-4 No. 611.

Schedule: March-December: daily. January-February: Tuesday-Sunday. Monday-Saturday, 10:00 a.m.-5:00 p.m.; Sunday, 12:00-5:00 p.m. Closed some holidays.

Admission: Adults $5.00, senior citizens $4.00, youths (3-18) $3.00, (all admissions taxed) children under 3 free. Group rates are available.

Locomotives/Trolleys: No. 611, J Class 4-8-4, former Norfolk & Western; No. 4, 1910 Baldwin class SA 0-8-0, former Virginian Railway; No. 6, 1897 Baldwin class G-1 2-8-0, former N&W; No. 763, 1944 Lima class S-2 2-8-4, former Nickel Plate; No. 1, Celanese 0400 fireless locomotive; many diesels, City of Roanoke trolley, and D.C. Transit trolley.

Rolling Stock/Equipment: IT Presidential Business car, N&W Safety Car No. 418, N&W Dynamometer Car, Southern "Glen Summit" sleeping car, Southern "Lake Pearl" sleeping car, N&W Class PG passenger car.

Special Events: The Resource Library & Archives sponsors monthly Transportation Heritage lectures, and quarterly bus tours to transportation sites. Spring Railfair, Fall "Roanoke Railway Festival", monthly exhibits on transportation and many children's hands-on exhibits. Exhibit of miniature traveling circus.

Location: 303 Norfolk Avenue, S.W.

♿ (partially)   P   🚌   ☀   📷

🍴   ►   ◄   **M**

 Lynchburg and Clifton Forge, VA

Contact: Katherine F. Houck
Executive Director

Mailing Address:
303 Norfolk Ave., S.W.
Roanoke, VA 24016
Telephone: (703) 342-5670
Fax: (703) 342-6898

THOMAS THOMPSON JR.

Ride/Operation: This railway offers a 3/4-mile scenic train ride from the historic Great Northern Depot to downtown Anacortes along the city's waterfront and tree-lined parkways. In operation since 1986, this family-owned tourist line is one of the world's smallest narrow-gauge passenger railroads (as distinguished from a miniature railway). Turntables at each end of the line rotate the locomotive for its return trip. Limited cab rides are allowed.

Displays/Exhibits: Railroad artifacts and photographs in the depot; Tangley air calliope.

Train: Maine/Wales-style narrow-gauge train of four passenger cars, pulled by a Forney-type steam locomotive. The cars, acclaimed for their beauty and luxurious comfort, feature cherry-wood interiors, red velvet cushions, plush carpeting, and a marble fireplace.

Schedule: Weekends and holidays, June 14-September 1; frequent departures, 12:00-4:30 p.m.

Fare: $1.00.

Locomotives: Forney-type steam locomotive, rebuilt from a 1909 H.K. Porter compressed-air 0-4-0 mining locomotive, fueled with fir bark.

Passenger Cars: One observation-parlor car, two roofed open summer cars, one baggage-parlor car. Includes seven steel flatcars formerly used at the Asarco Smelter in Tacoma.

Rolling Stock/Equipment: Includes seven steel flatcars formerly used at the Asarco Smelter in Tacoma and one gondola (wood-sided for ballast service).

Special Events: Anacortes Arts and Crafts Festival, August 2, 3.

Note: Nearby attractions include an adjacent maritime museum, an art gallery in depot, and the ferry to the San Juan Islands.

Location: 7th Street and R Avenue. Take R Avenue exit to narrow gauge railway crossing, turn right.

P 🚌 ✳ 📷   🪑 ▶ ◀

🏛 TRAIN   Seattle, Everett,
Mt. Vernon-Burlington

Contact: Thomas G. Thompson, Jr.
President

Mailing Address:
387 Campbell Lake Road
Anacortes, WA 98221
Telephone: (360) 293-2634
Internet: http://www.teleport.com/~eshoms/pages/ary.htm

341

REMLINGER FARMS NARROW GAUGE RAILROAD
Steam, scheduled
24" gauge

ROBERT W. MRE

Ride/Operation: A one-mile dog bone loop through the grounds of Remlinger Farms. The ride features a one hundred foot curved tunnel, two percent grade up along the Tolt River.

Display/Exhibit: Old farm machinery, a G gauge outdoor railroad and an animal petting farm.

Schedule: Mid April-Christmas: weekends, 12:00-4:00 p.m. June-August: Monday-Friday, 11:30 a.m.-3:00 p.m., weekends 11:00 a.m.-5:00 p.m. October: daily, call for details.

Fare/Admission: $2.00, under age 1 are free. Cab rides, $3.00.

Locomotives: One Crown 4-4-0 modified.

Rolling Stock/Equipment: Three covered excursion cars.

Special Events: Call for information.

Location: Carnation is located 25 miles east of Seattle.

Contact: Robert W. Mre

Mailing Address:
Remlinger Farms
32610 NE 32nd
Carnation, WA 98014
Telephone: (206) 333-4135

Washington, Chehalis
R

CHEHALIS-CENTRALIA
RAILROAD ASSOCIATION
Steam, scheduled
Standard gauge

Ride/Operation: A 12-mile, 1¾-hour round trip over ex-Weyerhaeuser trackage (former Milwaukee Road) between South Chehalis and Millburn, under contract with the Mt. Rainier Scenic Railroad. An extended trip to Ruth (nine miles west of Chehalis), offered on Saturdays, passes through scenic rural farmlands and a river valley. Selected Saturdays feature dinner train on the 5:00 p.m. trip. Call for information.

Displays/Exhibits: Restored Union Pacific C-5 cabooses serve as the ticket office and gift shop.

Train: Two open-window heavyweight coaches, former UP; open-air observation car.

Schedule: Weekends and holidays, May 24-September 1; lv. Chehalis 1:00 & 3:00 p.m. Ruth trip: Saturdays; lv. Chehalis 5:00 p.m.

Fare: Round trip: adults $7.00, children (3-16) $5.00. Ruth trip: adults $11.00, children $9.00.

Locomotives: No. 15, 1916 Baldwin 90-ton 2-8-2, former Cowlitz, Chehalis & Cascade, former Puget Sound & Cascade No. 200. This engine had been displayed for thirty years in a local park; restoration was completed in 1989 by Mt. Rainier Scenic Railroad shop and volunteers from Lewis County.

Rolling Stock/Equipment: Z-frame 40-foot wood boxcar used as shop/supply car, former Milwaukee; steel 40-foot boxcar used as movable billboard, former Burlington Northern, former Chicago, Burlington & Quincy.

Location: Midway between Seattle, Washington, and Portland, Oregon. Chehalis: On Main Street; I-5 to exit 77. Turn west to first street south (Riverside Road). Proceed 1/4 mile to Sylvenus Street. Turn left one block to railroad tracks.

Centralia

Radio Frequencies: 161.385, 160.635

Contact: Harold Borovec

Mailing Address:
1945 South Market Boulevard
Chehalis, WA 98532
Telephone: (206) 748-9593

DAYTON HISTORICAL DEPOT SOCIETY

Displays/Exhibits: The Dayton Depot is the oldest depot in Washington state and it is the only depot in Washington with the agent's quarters still intact, including kitchen, bedroom and bathroom decor.

Schedule: Tuesday-Saturday, 10:00 a.m.-5:00 p.m.
Fare: $1.00
Rolling Stock/Equipment: Caboose display in restoration phase.
Special Events: Depot Days, arts & crafts exhibits on the depot grounds. Hometown Christmas, arts & crafts exhibits inside the depot. Call for dates.

Location: 222 Commercial Street, Dayton, WA.

 Pendleton, Oregon

Contact: Ginny Butler

Mailing Address:
P.O. Box 1881
Dayton, WA 99328
Telephone: (509) 382-2026

MT. RAINIER SCENIC RAILROAD
Steam, scheduled
Standard gauge

J. S. DAVID WILKIE

Ride/Operation: A 14-mile, 1 1/2-hour round trip over a secluded right-of-way, over former Milwaukee Road trackage, on the south slope of Mt. Rainier. The train goes through farms, forests, and tree farms, over rivers and creeks, up hills and down. There is a 20-minute lay-over at Mineral Lake. Passengers may stay there to visit or picnic and return on a later train. The *Cascadian Dinner Train* makes a 4-hour round trip to Eatonville (26-mile trip), and offers a five-course prime rib dinner, prepared and served aboard a restored Union Pacific dining car and lounge/observation car.

Displays/Exhibits: No. 10, 1912 Heisler, 3-truck, former Pickering Lumber Co., the first successful Heisler built.

Train: Steam power on all runs; closed coaches with bench seats; open-air cars.

Schedule: Daily, June 15-Labor Day; weekends, Memorial Day-end of September; 11:00 a.m., 1:15 & 3:30 p.m. Dinner train: spring and fall, 1:00 p.m.; summer, 5:30 p.m.

Fare: Adults $9.50, senior citizens $8.50, juniors (12-17) $7.50, children (under 12) $6.50. Dinner train: $55.00, reservations required.

Locomotives: Operable: No. 5, 1924 Porter 2-8-2, former Port of Grays Harbor; No. 10, 1928 Climax 3-truck, former Hillcrest Lumber Co.; No. 11, 1929 Lima, 3-truck Pacific Coast Shay, former Pickering Lumber Co.; No. 17, 1929 Alco 2-8-2T, former Hammond Lumber Co.; No. 30, 1940 Alco S-1, former NPT Co.; No. 41, 1941 Alco RSD-1, former Dept. of Transportation; No. 42, 1942 Alco S-1, former U.S. Army; and more.

Passenger Cars: Two former SP commuter coaches; open-air car; dining car; lounge/observation car, former Alaska Railroad, and former BC Rail (CP) coaches.

Rolling Stock/Equipment: Log trains, work trains, freight trains.

Special Events: Christmas Train, first three weekends in December. Railfan Photo Specials, spring or fall weddings, charters, movies, commercials.

Location: On highway 7, 42 miles southeast of Tacoma.

Tacoma

Radio Freqency: 161.385, 160.635

Contact: Jack Anderson
General Manager

Mailing Address:
P.O. Box 921
Elbe, WA 98330
Telephone: (360) 569-2588
Fax: (360) 569-2438

KING COUNTY DEPARTMENT OF
TRANSPORTATION-TRANSIT DIVISION
("METRO TRANSIT")
Scheduled, electric/600 volt, standard gauge

Ride/Operation: Two 1927 Australian streetcars began service along Elliott Bay from Pier 70 to Main Street in May 1982. The streetcars were brought from Melbourne, Australia, thanks to the enthusiasm and support of Seattle City Councilmember George Benson, a long-time supporter of public transportation. Three more streetcars joined the fleet in June 1990 to help provide frequent service when the streetcars began traveling beyond the waterfront into the International District. Tasmanian mahogany and white ash woodwork capture the elegance of travel in a bygone era. The streetcars can accommodate 52 seated passengers and 40 standing riders on the 2.1 mile ride.

Displays/Exhibits: Maintenance building has wheel-chair accessible ramp to viewing windows, typically one or more cars visible, located at Pier 70 terminal (North).

Schedule: Operates daily, summer (every 20 minutes), 9:00 a.m.-midnight; winter 10:00 a.m.-7:00 p.m. Closed Thanksgiving, Christmas and New Year's Day. Call for specific station timetable.

Fare: $.85 off peak, $1.10 peak (6:00-9:00 a.m./3:00-6:00 p.m. weekdays). All passes, permits and transfers are accepted.

Trolleys: 6 streetcars (5 in service) - (1) 1925 Class W-2 train, (4) 1928 Class W-2 trains and (1) 1930 Class W-2 train.

Stations (9): Jackson Street, Occidental Park, Washington Street, Madison Street, University Street, Pike Street, Bell Street, Vine Street, & Broad Street.

Location: Downtown Seattle waterfront.

 Seattle (1 block from streetcar track)

Contact: Friendly Streetcar Conductor

Telephone: (206) 684-2046 (voice)
(206) 689-3413 (TTY)
Metro's Rider Information: (206) 553-3000
Community Transit: 1-800-562-1375
Pierce Transit: 1-800-562-8109

Washington, Snoqualmie
D-R

PUGET SOUND RAILWAY HISTORICAL ASSOCIATION

PUGET SOUND RAILWAY
HISTORICAL ASSOCIATION
Diesel, scheduled
Standard gauge

Ride/Operation: This group offers a ride between Snoqualmie and North Bend.

Displays/Exhibits: The 1890 Snoqualmie depot houses the Northwest Railway Museum.

Train: Wood and steel heavyweight passenger cars pulled by Alco or Fairbanks-Morse diesel locomotives.

Schedule: Weekends, May 26-September 27; Sundays, May-October. Open Memorial Day, July 4, and Labor Day. Depot open Thursday-Monday, 10:00 a.m.-5:00 p.m..

Fare/Admission: Train: adults $6.00, senior citizens $5.00, children $4.00. Museum: no charge.

Locomotives: No. 201, Alco RSD-4, former Kennecott Copper Corp.; No. 1, Fairbanks-Morse H12-44, former Weyerhaeuser Timber Co.; No. 7320, General Electric 45-ton diesel switcher, former U.S. Navy.

Rolling Stock/Equipment: Miscellaneous pieces.

Special Events: Santa Train, November 29-30, December 6-7, & 13-14.

Location: 38625 S. E. King Street, Snoqualmie.

Contact: Richard R. Anderson

Mailing Address:
P.O. Box 459
Snoqualmie, WA 98065
Telephone: (206) 746-4025

YAKIMA VALLEY RAIL AND STEAM MUSEUM
Diesel, scheduled
Standard gauge

ERIC NELSON

Ride/Operation: This museum operates freight and passenger service on the former Northern Pacific White Swan branch line. Passenger excursions are 20-mile round trips from Harrah to White Swan.

Displays/Exhibits: The 1911 former NP railroad depot in Toppenish serves as the museum and gift shop. The freight house has been converted to an engine house, where steam locomotive No. 1364 is being restored. The former NP section foreman's house is adjacent to the depot.

Train: Pending completion of the steam-locomotive restoration, the two former Pennsylvania Railroad heavyweight cars are pulled by a diesel.

Schedule: Train: April-October; Saturdays & Sundays, 1:00 p.m. Museum: daily, summer; weekends, winter.

Fare/Admission: Train: adults $5.00, children $3.00, family $20.00. Museum: adults $2.00, senior citizens & children (under 18) $1.00. Charters available.

Locomotives: No. 1364, 1902 Baldwin 4-6-0, former NP; No. B-2070, 1953 120-ton Alco, former U.S. Army.

Passenger Cars: Two 1920s P70 heavyweights, former PRR; No. 588, 1947 coach, former NP; combine, former New Haven.

Location: 10 Asotin Avenue.

Contact: Douglas Shearer
Public Relations

Mailing Address:
P.O. Box 889
Toppenish, WA 98948
Telephone:
Museum: (509) 865-1911
Chamber of Commerce: (509) 865-3262

DAVID WILKE

Ride/Operation: A 7-mile, 1½-hour round trip over a former Northern Pacific branch line originally constructed as the Bellingham Bay & Eastern Railroad in 1902. The train climbs a 2.3-percent grade along highway 9, then heads through a tunnel, along Mirror Lake, and through a forest inhabited by beavers. Passengers may also tour the steam locomotive and ride an old hand-pump car.

Displays/Exhibits: Varies; business car "Madison River," former NP; 1923 Shell Oil Co. tank car; 1900-1923 boxcars, former Great Northern; handcar; track motor car; cabooses (wooden, former NP; steel, former Spokane, Portland & Seattle).

Train: Steam locomotive; 86-seat coach, originally Pullman parlor car "Dunlop"; coffee-shop coach; 88-seat coach, originally Pullman parlor car "Clearview."

Schedule: Nonreserved trains and motor-car rides: Saturdays and Tuesdays, July 2-August 31; trains, 11:00 a.m. & 1:00 p.m.; motor cars, 3:15 p.m. Special trains, by reservation only: October 26, December 7, 14 & 21. Please call or write for weekday schedules.

Fare: Trains: Adults $10.00, children (2-17) $5.00. Motor-car rides: $1.50. Charters on regularly scheduled trains: business car or 32-seat coach, $250; 86-seat coach, $600. Please call or write for special charter prices.

Locomotive: No. 1070, 1907 Alco (Manchester) 0-6-0, former NP.

Passenger Cars: Coach No. 627, originally 1910 Pullman parlor car "Dunlop"; 1912 coach No. 634, Pullman "Clearview"; coffee-shop coach No. 1681, originally 1925 Pullman coach; 1926 Pullman business car "Madison River," built for the *North Coast Limited;* and baggage car; all former Northern Pacific.

Special Events: Autumn Train, October 26. Santa Claus Train, December 7, 14 & 21, including live music. Reservations required.

Location: 10½ miles north of Sedro Woolley on highway 9.

 Seattle or Everett

Mailing Address:
Box 91
Acme, WA 98220
Telephone: (360) 595-2218

YAKIMA ELECTRIC RAILWAY MUSEUM
Electric, scheduled
Standard gauge

DENNIS L. DILLEY

Ride/Operation: A 90-minute round trip through city streets, past orchards, and along the Naches River and the shoulder of Yakima Ridge through Selah Gap, over a route established by the former Yakima Valley Transportation Company in 1907.

Schedule: First weekend in May-mid-October and weekends and holidays: Lv. Yakima 10:00 a.m., 12:00, 2:00 & 4:00 p.m.; lv. Selah 11:00 a.m., 1:00 & 3:00 p.m. Fridays, July-August, 7:00 p.m. Please call to confirm the Friday evening trip.

Fare: Adults $4.00, senior citizens $3.50 and children (6-12) $2.50, children under 6 free with adult ticket. Family rate $12.00. Charters available.

Locomotives/Trolleys: Line Car "A," 1909 Niles 26-ton boxcab converted to line-car use in 1922 (in continuous service since 1909); freight motor No. 298, General Electric 50-ton steeple-cab; Nos. 21 & 22, 1930 double-truck Brill Master Units that originally operated in Yakima from 1930 to 1947; Nos. 1776 & 1976, single-truck Brill cars from Oporto, Portugal (the same type that operated in Yakima from 1907-1929); others.

Note: Guided tours of the Car Barn Museum are available during public-ride hours by request; donations are welcomed.

Location: Passengers may board at the shop of the Yakima Electric Railway Museum at 3rd Avenue and Pine or at the Selah Terminal.

P * ⛪ ▶ ◀ M ar n

Contact: General Manager

Mailing Address:
P.O. Box 649
Yakima, WA 98907-0649
Telephone: (509) 575-1700

JOHN HELBOK

Ride/Operation: This railroad, a reconstruction of a logging railroad that saw sixty years of service, features two switchbacks and climbs grades as steep as eleven percent, providing overlooks and panoramas of mountain scenery. Passengers may choose either a 22-mile, 4½-hour round trip to the top of Bald Knob (elevation 4,842 feet) or an 8-mile, 1½-hour round trip to Whittaker Station.

Displays/Exhibits: Modern steam-locomotive shop, open on weekdays.

Train: Restored logging cars converted for passenger use.

Schedule: Daily, May 25-September 2; weekends, September 6-October 27. Bald Knob: Tuesday-Sunday, 12:00 p.m. Whittaker: daily, 11:00 a.m., 1:00 & 3:00 p.m. Dinner train: Reservations required. Please call or write for information.

Fare: Bald Knob: adults $13.00, children $7.00. Whittaker: adults $9.00, children $5.00. Dinner train: adults $25.00, children $15.00. Special group rates available, Tuesday-Friday. Charter rates available upon request. Prices include admission to museums and historical presentation.

Locomotives: No. 2, 1928 Lima 3-truck Shay; No. 4, 1922 Lima 3-truck Shay; No. 5, 1905 Lima 3-truck Shay; No. 6, 1929 3-truck Heisler; No. 6, 1945 Lima 162-ton 3-truck Shay, former Western Maryland No. 6; No. 7, 1921 Lima 3-truck Shay; No. 8, 1919 3-truck Climax; No. 612, 1943 Baldwin 2-8-0; No. 20, 1941 45-ton General Electric.

Special Events: Fall Color Runs, October.

Note: Reservations are accepted.

White Sulphur Springs

Radio Frequency: 31.98

Contact: Superintendent

Mailing Address:
P.O. Box 107
Cass, WV 24927
Telephone: (304) 456-4300
(800) CALL-WVA

HARPERS FERRY TOY TRAIN MUSEUM
& JOY LINE RAILROAD

Railway museum
16" gauge

HARPERS FERRY TOY TRAIN MUSEUM & JOY LINE RAILROAD

Ride/Operation: Passengers ride around the 1,780 feet of track aboard a 1953 waist-high train, traveling over a trestle and past an authentic railroad station brought to Harpers Ferry from Hagerstown, Maryland. The museum houses pre-World War II toy trains.

Displays/Exhibits: Two full-sized section cars; railroad tools.

Train: Two 1953 amusement-park trains.

Schedule: Weekends, April-November.

Fare/Admission: $1.00.

Locomotives: F-7; steam-type Miniature Train Company locomotive; gas-powered shop-made locomotive.

Passenger Cars: Four 12-person cars.

Rolling Stock/Equipment: Four flatcars; stock car; caboose; snowplow.

Location: One mile west of Harpers Ferry National Park, on Bakerton Road.

P ✳ 🍺 📷 🛒 🔔

Harpers Ferry

Contact: Christian Wallich
General Manager

Mailing Address:
Route 3, Box 315
Harpers Ferry, WV 25425
Telephone: (304) 535-2291
(304) 535-2521

WEST VIRGINIA
NORTHERN RAILROAD
Diesel, scheduled; future steam
Standard gauge

BOB ROBINSON

Ride/Operation: A three-hour, 21.4 mile, narrated round trip from Kingwood to the CSX interchange at Tunnelton, West Virginia. The train travels over the coal shipping route of the more than century old West Virginia Northern Railroad. To reach Tunnelton, the train proceeds through a switchback, then a double switchback, to climb 401 feet through woods to reach the 2,120 foot summit. After following the ridge through open fields and historic coal mining towns, the train eases down a long, winding 416 foot descent to 30 degree Marion Curve where the cars clear a rock outcropping by a mere foot. Ruling grade is 4.77 percent. Two locomotive run-arounds are performed. The trip passes scenic overviews and occasionally stops at yard sales and flea markets. There is a half hour layover at Tunnelton.

Displays/Exhibits: Early century water tank; former B&O office car No. 900 (under restoration by private owner); various Maintenance of Way equipment; former B&O depot (being restored as a museum by Tunnelton Historical Society).

Train: Various combinations of three closed coaches, an open-window coach, an open air car, and two cabooses. Occasionally, long consists are pulled with two MU'ed diesel-electric locomotives.

Schedule: Weekends & holidays, mid-May to October 31, 11:00 a.m. & 3:00 p.m.; weekdays, in October only, noon. Train charters (25 or more) and speeder car runs (2 fares minimum) can be scheduled anytime all year.

Fare: Adults and teens $10.00, seniors 62+ $8.00, children (3-12) $5.00. Group rates available.

Locomotives: WVN No. 50, 1946 EMD NW2 with SW1200 modifications; WVN No. 52, rare 1960 EMD SW1200 with factory installed dynamic brake (50 and 52 can be MU'ed); No. 17, 1941 Vulcan Iron Works 0-4-0T, formerly Carbon Limestone, ex-New York Shipbuilding (No. 17 is being restored for future steam service).

Special Events: October Fall Leaf Specials (all month). Preston County Buckwheat Festival runs last weekend September beginning Thursday. Northern Nightmare Express (Halloween). Santa Claus Runs. Call for other events, (Flea Market Specials, Civil War Battle re-enactments, etc.)

Notes: Pre-civil war B&O tunnel nearby; rafting on Cheat River.

Location: North central West Virginia, take Route 7 or Route 26 to Kingwood, turn on Sisler Street at west edge of town.

Connellsville, PA

Radio Frequency: 161.250

Contact: Dennie Arnold
Agent

Mailing Address: P.O. Box 424
Kingwood, WV 26537
Telephone: (304) 329-3333
Fax: (304) 329-6482

POTOMAC EAGLE

Ride/Operation: Diesel-powered, open-window coach trains take passengers on a 3-hour, 15-minute round trip through the beautiful South Branch Trough. Riding the rails along the clear waters of the Potomac River's South Branch, passengers can watch for American bald eagles (seen on ninety percent of Potomac tours during the 1996 season) that have made this remote region their home.

Train: Open-window coaches; open-top sightseeing car; temperature-controlled lounge car/dining car offering First Class Service (luxury lounge/dinner seating and luncheon).

Schedule: May 3-June14: Saturdays, 1:00 p.m. June 21 - Aug. 31, 1p.m. Saturday and Sunday. September 6-28: weekends; Saturdays, 10:00 a.m. & 2:00 p.m.; Sundays, 1:00 p.m. September 29-October 31: daily; Monday-Friday, 1:00 p.m.; weekends, 10:00 a.m & 2:00 p.m. All-day round trip, Romney to Petersburg: April 26, May 31, June 28, July 26, August 21, September 27, October 24-25; depart 9:00 a.m., return 5:30 p.m.

Fare: May-September: adults $18, senior citizens (60+) $16, children (3-12) $10, children under 3 ride free. Classic Club $38. Season pass coach; $80 adult, $50 child. Adults $20, senior citizens (60+) $18, children (3-12) $12, children under 3 ride free, Classic Club $44. All-day round trip: adults $38, senior citizens (60+) $35, children (3-12) $15, Classic Club $70.

Locomotives: GP9s, former Baltimore & Ohio; F-units, former CSX.

Passenger Cars: 1920s open-window coaches, former Canadian National; 1950-era lounge car, former Chesapeake & Ohio.

Special Events: Spring Mountain Festival, April 26. Trough Excursion to Sycamore Bridge, May 18. Railfan Day, May 13. Memorial Day, May 27, coach $10. Ronald McDonald Days, August 9-10. Labor Day, September 2, coach $10. Hampshire Heritage Days, September 6-9. Hardy Heritage Weekend, September 27. Fall Railfan Special, October 4.

Location: Route 28, one mile north of Romney.

Cumberland, Maryland

Contact: Janet Corbitt
Passenger Agent

Mailing Address:
P.O. Box 657
Romney, WV 26757
Telephone: (304) 422-6069
(800) 22-EAGLE

EAST TROY ELECTRIC RAILROAD
WISCONSIN TROLLEY MUSEUM
Electric, scheduled
Standard gauge

SCOTT STANKOVSKY

Ride/Operation: This museum offers the longest ride of its type in the country; trolleys take passengers on a 10-mile round trip over original trackage of the famed Milwaukee Electric Railway & Light Company. This line, completed in 1907, is the last remnant of a network of more than two hundred miles of interurban trackage that used to serve southeastern Wisconsin.

Displays/Exhibits: An extensive collection of Milwaukee Electric photos and artifacts. Cars undergoing restoration include former Chicago North Shore & Milwaukee No. 228 and former WP&L No. 26, LaCrosse Birney No. 12, MER&L No. 800.

Schedule: Weekends, May 24-October 26.

Admission: Adults $8.00, children (4-11) $4.00.

Trolleys: Chicago South Shore & South Bend 9, 11, and 30; Diners No. 24 Beverly Shores and No. 25 Ravenswood; open car No. 21; Chicago Transit Authority 4420; Duluth-Superior 253; Philadelphia (SEPTA) PCC 2185; Toronto PCC 4617.

Rolling Stock/Equipment: Milwaukee Electric crane L6, freight locomotives L8, L9, and line car D23.

Special Events: Railfan Weekend, May 3-4. Dinner Trains, Mother's Day, Father's Day, Octoberfest, Sweetest Day and to be announced Jazz and Birthday Trains. Model Railroad Swap Meet, Sept. 27-28.

Location: 2002 Church Street, East Troy. East Troy is 30 miles southwest of Milwaukee. Take the highway 20 exit off I-43 in East Troy, head west to County highway ES, travel south on ES to Church Street, and turn right.

P   🚌   ✳ 🧍   🚉 🍴   **M**
at 11   TRAIN

Contact: Paul Averdung
Mailing Address:
P.O. Box 556
Waukesha, WI 53187
Telephone:
Operating Hours: (414) 642-3263
All Other Times/Group &
Party Reservations: (414) 548-3837

CHIPPEWA VALLEY
RAILROAD ASSOCIATION
Steam, diesel
16" gauge

CHIPPEWA VALLEY RAILROAD

Ride/Operation: 16" gauge, ½ mile ride through the woods of Carson Park, Eau Claire, Wisconsin.

Displays/Exhibits: Depot, roundhouse, turntable, Soo Line Pacific No. 2719, 4-6-2, Alco 1923, National Register, Standard G, under restoration; Chicago & Northwestern interlocking tower (last operating tower in Wisconsin).

Schedule: Sundays, Memorial Day through Labor Day.

Fare: Adults $1.00, children $ .50.

Locomotives: Two 4-4-0 steam locomotives [(1) Crown, (1) Chippewa Valley Railroad/Sandley]; one miniature train G-16 diesel. Soo line No. 2719, 4-6-2, standard display.

Rolling Stock/Equipment: Variety of coaches including (2) wooden Sandley coaches.

Location: Carson Park Drive, Carson Park, Eau Claire.

Tomah, WI or Minneapolis, MN

Contact: David G. Peterson

Mailing Address:
P.O. Box 925
Eau Claire, WI 54702
Telephone: (715) 835-7500
(715) 835-1411
E-mail: steam@discover-net.net

NATIONAL RAILROAD MUSEUM

Ride/Operation: Visitors to this museum can take a 20-minute train ride in vintage equipment, enjoy the "Rails to America" theater show, and embark on guided or self-guided tours of the equipment displays. On the train, the uniformed conductor talks about hobo history, the museum, and local points of interest. "Rails to America" is a 20-minute, 9-projector multimedia show that presents an outline of railroad history.

Displays/Exhibits: Established in 1958, this museum holds more than seventy historic locomotives and railroad cars, as well as railroad memorabilia, archives, a research library, and a 30- by 70-foot model-railroad display.

Schedule: Museum: daily, 9:00 a.m.-5:00 p.m. Train: May 1-October 15. Guided tours: May 29-September 4. Closed Easter, Thanksgiving, Christmas, and New Year's Day.

Fare/Admission: May 1-October 15: adults $6.00, senior citizens $5.00, students (6-15) $3.00, children under 6 admitted free, family rate $16.00. October 16-April 30: Half-price. Group rates available.

Locomotives: No. 4017, 4-8-8-4, former Union Pacific; No. 24, 2-8-0, former Lake Superior & Ishpeming; No. 2718, 4-6-2, former Soo Line; No. 2736, 2-8-4, former Chesapeake & Ohio; No. 5017, 2-10-4, former Santa Fe; No. 506, 2-10-2, former Duluth, Missabe & Iron Range; No. 101, 2-8-0 "General Pershing," former U.S. Army; No. 29, Pullman 0-4-0; No. 5, Shay; No. 315, Alco C-430, former Green Bay & Western; No. 38A, E9, former Milwaukee; *Aerotrain* No. 2, former Rock Island; GP30 No. 715, former Wisconsin Central; No. 706, Fairbanks-Morse H-10-44; others.

Passenger Cars: General Eisenhower's WWII Command Train "Bayonet"; observation car "Silver Spirit," former Chicago, Burlington & Quincy; sleeper "Poplar River," former Great Northern; dome diner No. 8003, former UP; No. 2330, Railway Post Office, former CB&Q; others.

Special Events: Boxcar Willie Concert, March 17. Antique Auto Show, Memorial Day weekend. Railfest. Thomas the Tank and Friends Event. Railroad Memorabilia Show & Auction. Football Train. Haunted Train. Christmas Train/Breakfast with Santa Claus Train. Special Dinner Train charters. And much more. call for more information on dates and events.

Location: 2285 South Broadway, Take highway 172 to Ashland Avenue (business highway 41); travel north to Cormier Avenue and east three blocks.

Contact: Ralph Justen

Mailing Address:
2285 South Broadway
Green Bay, WI 54304
Telephone: (414) 437-7623

CAMP FIVE MUSEUM
FOUNDATION, INC.

Logging museum
Steam, scheduled

CAMP FIVE MUSEUM FOUNDATION, INC.

Ride/Operation: Camp Five offers visitors a unique mix of history, steam railroading, and ecology. Visitors ride the *Lumberjack Special* steam train to the museum complex; once there, take a guided surrey tour through beautiful forests managed on a perpetual-cycle basis. A hayrack/pontoon ride on the Rat River is also an optional offer.

Displays/Exhibits: Logging museum with an early-transportation wing and an active blacksmith shop; half-hour steam engine video; nature center with northern Wisconsin wildlife diorama; petting corral; large outdoor display of logging artifacts.

Schedule: Daily, June 16-August 24, 11:00 a.m., 12:00, 1:00 & 2:00 p.m. Heritage Celebration, August 2-4. Fall Color Tours, September 27 & October 4 trains at 11:00 a.m. & 1:00 p.m. The Hayrack/Pontoon Trip thru a Natural Wildlife Refuge, Adult $2.50, Children (4-12) $1.25, under three are free.

Fare/Admission: Adults $14.00, Students (13-17) $9.00, children (4-12) $4.75, family $38.00. Group discounts available, call for more information.

Locomotive: 1916 Vulcan 2-6-2.

Passenger Cars: Cupola cabooses.

Special Events: Heritage Celebration, August 9, 10. Featuring a rendezvous, early Americana skills and crafts, blacksmith, old-time music, plus much more.

Location: West of Laona on U.S. Highway 8.

Contact: Mary R. Connor
Executive Director

Mailing Address:
RFD #1
Laona, WI 54541
Telephone: (715) 674-3414
(800) 774-3414

Wisconsin, North Freedom
D-R

WILLIAM RAIA

MID-CONTINENT RAILWAY
HISTORICAL SOCIETY

Steam, scheduled
Standard gauge

Ride/Operation: Mid-Continent, which has operated steam trains at North Freedom since 1963, is dedicated to preserving turn-of-the-century railroading. Its line and equipment are historic, all a part of the "golden age of railroading." The 7-mile, 50-minute "Experience 1900" round trip takes passengers on a former Chicago & North Western branch line built in 1903 to serve iron mines. Trains depart from a restored 1894 C&NW depot.

Displays/Exhibits: The museum is nationally known for its wooden passenger and freight cars; restored equipment is displayed in the coach shed. The collection also includes locomotives, snowplows (including a 1912 steam rotary), and steam wreckers. Artifact and photography exhibits are in the depot and the coach shed.

Train: Open-platform cars from the Delaware, Lackawanna & Western; freight or mixed trains often run for special events.

Schedule: Daily, May 20-September 2; weekends, May 4-May 19 & September 7-October 20; 10:30 a.m., 12:30, 2:00 & 3:30 p.m. Specials days & times for school groups scheduled in May & September.

Fare: Adults $8.00, senior citizens $7.00, children (3-15) $4.50, family (2 adults, 2 or more children) $22.00. Group discounts available. Higher fares may apply at some special events.

Locomotives: No. 1385, 1907 Alco 4-6-0, former C&NW; No. 2, 1912 Baldwin 2-8-2, former Saginaw Timber; No. 9, 1884 Baldwin 2-6-0, former Dardanelle & Russellville; No. 1, 1913 Montreal 4-6-0, former Western Coal & Coke Co.; No. 2645, 1900 Brooks 4-6-0, former Soo (Wisconsin Central); No. 440, 1901 Baldwin 2-8-0, former Union Pacific; No. 49, 1929 Alco 2-8-0, former Kewaunee, Green Bay & Western; No. 31, 1925 EMC gas-electric car, former Montana Western; No. 988, 1947 Alco RSC-2, former Milwaukee Road.

Special Events: Autumn Color, October 5-6 & 12-13.

Santa Express, November 30-December 1. Snow Train '97, February 14-16, 1997.

Location: In Sauk County, seven miles west of Baraboo. Follow route 136 west to PF, then turn south to North Freedom. The depot is one-half mile west of the four-way stop in North Freedom.

Contact: Don Meyer
General Manager

Mailing Address: P.O. Box 358
North Freedom, WI 53951-0358
Telephone: (608) 522-4261
(800) 930-1385
Internet: http//:www.mcrwy.com

359

Wisconsin, North Lake
D-R

KETTLE MORAINE RAILWAY
Steam, scheduled
Standard gauge

DONALD M. MURPHY

Ride/Operation: A leisurely, nostalgic, 8-mile round trip over a former Milwaukee Road branch line. The train departs from the 1889 depot in North Lake, travels up 2-percent grades and through two moraine cuts, and crosses the Oconomowoc River on a 125-foot timber trestle.

Displays/Exhibits: No. 1000, EMD gas-electric car, former Chicago Great Western; restored 1889 railroad depot.

Train: Steel coaches; combination car; "hobo car"; caboose.

Schedule: Sundays First Sunday in June through third Sunday in October & Labor Day, 12:30, 2:00 & 3:30 p.m. Rain or Shine. Extra 11:00 a.m. trip the first three Sundays in October (Fall Colors), plus the first three Saturdays in October, 12:30, 2:00 & 3:30 p.m. Subject to change when necessary to meet operating conditions.

Fare: Adults $7.50, children (3-11) $4.00, children under 3 ride free when not occupying a seat. Charter and group rates available.

Locomotives: No. 9, 1901 Baldwin 2-6-2, former McCloud River; No. 3, 1917 65-ton Heisler, former Craig Mountain Railroad; No. 3, 1943 Davenport gas-powered 0-4-0 switcher, former Heil Co. & U.S. Air Force.

Special Events: Please call or write for schedule.

Location: North Lake is at the junction of Highways VV (formerly 74) and 83, northwest of Milwaukee. The site is on route 83, 9 miles north of exit 287 off I-94, south of Holy Hill, south of Hartford, and north of Hartland.

Milwaukee

Contact: Richard M. Hinebaugh
President

Mailing Address:
Box 247
North Lake, WI 53064
Telephone: (414) 782-8074

OSCEOLA & ST. CROIX VALLEY RAILWAY
MINNESOTA TRANSPORTATION MUSEUM

Steam, diesel, scheduled
Standard gauge

MORT JORGENSON

Ride/Operation: Enjoy the scenic St. Croix River Valley on a 90-minute round trip between Osceola, Wisconsin, and Marine-on-St. Croix, Minnesota. A 45-minute round trip through rural Wisconsin between Osceola and Dresser.

Displays/Exhibits: See the restored Osceola Historical Depot featuring exhibits about railroading and the Osceola area. U.S. Railway Post Office exhibits aboard Northern Pacific Triple combine No. 1102.

Schedule: Weekends, May 24-October 26, along with Memorial Day, May 26; July 4; and Labor Day, September 1. Charters are available throughout the season on Thursdays. Trains depart Osceola between 11:00 a.m. and 3:45 p.m.

Fare: Osceola to Marine-on-St.-Croix: adults $11.00, children (5-15) $7.00, children under 5 free. Osceola to Dresser: adults $7.00, children (5-15) $4.00, children under 5 free. All taxes included.

Locomotives: Northern Pacific No. 328, 1907 Alco 4-6-0; Northern Pacific No. 105, 1957 SW1200; Minnesota Transportation Museum No. 102, 1948 NW2.

Passenger Cars: Northern Pacific triple combine No. 1102, Great Northern Empire Builder coach No. 1213, Great Northern coaches No. 1096 and 1097, Lackawanna coach No. 2232, Rock Island Coaches No. 2604 and 2608.

Note: The OSV is a nonprofit organization of the Minnesota Transportation Museum, the Osceola Historical Society, and local communities. The Museum provides equipment and operating crews. Trains operate on Wisconsin Central track between Withrow, Minnesota and Amery, Wisconsin under a trackage rights agreement.

Location: The Osceola Depot is on Depot Road, just off state highway 35. Osceola is on the Minnesota/Wisconsin border, about an hour northeast of the Twin Cities.

St. Paul

Contact: Todd Rust
General Superintendent

Mailing Address:
P.O. Box 17240
Nokomis Station
Minneapolis, MN 55417-0240
Telephone: (612) 228-0263
(800) 711-2591

PARK LANE MODEL RAILROAD MUSEUM
Model railroad museum

PARK LANE MODEL RAILROAD MUSEUM

Displays/Exhibits: This museum features a collection of more than two thousand models of all ages, ranging from tiny Z gauge through N, HO, S, O, and Buddy L gauges. Several operating model railroad layouts can also be seen.

Schedule: Daily, mid May-mid September; Monday-Saturday, 10:00 a.m.-5:00 p.m; Sunday, 10:00 a.m.-3:00 p.m.

Admission: Adults $3.50, children (6-12) $1.75, children under 6 admitted free with paying adult.

Note: The museum is located 11 miles from the Circus World Museum in Baraboo and 20 miles from the Mid-Continent Railway Museum in North Freedom.

Location: In the Wisconsin Dells area, near exit 89 of I-90 and I-94. The museum is at the intersection of state route 23 and Herwig Road.

Contact: Alexander Zmuda
Director

Mailing Address:
S-2083 Herwig Road
Reedsburg, WI 53959
Telephone: (608) 254-8050

J. P. PERKINS

Display/Exhibit: Eight rooms of display in the old C&NW depot and numerous items outside on the adjoining track. Each room represents a different facet of the railroad industry with many items dating back well into the 1800s. There is a display of two G gauge models on an elevated track, one diesel, on site.

Ride/Operation: We are a self supporting museum, non-profit corporation and staffed by volunteers.

Schedule: Memorial Day weekend-Labor Day weekend, 10:00 a.m.-5:00 p.m.

Fare/Admission: Adults $3.00, children 6-12, $.50, under age six are free.

Rolling Stock/Equipment: In larger track type items, we have an 1896 track inspector's bicycle, a velocipede, 1860 4-man handcar, gas Fairmont motor car and a hand-operated crane. Most significant though, we feel, is the fact every aspect of railroading is covered by this collection. Stewardess uniform, C&NW band uniform, chair from Pres. Coolidge's rail car, very old Roomette from Pullman car, Korean steam gauge from WWI engine, old pictures, posters, original art, and of course the brass bells, steam whistles, head lights, Mars light and timetable dating back to 1896.

Special Events: Fund raisers on Spooner's Rodeo days and other special city days.

Notes: In our Spooner room, dedicaled to the rail workers of the Spooner area, we have a memorial board and also a sponsor board and we encourage and greatly appreciate those who contribute to these in order for the museum to continue to grow.

Location: Located in the old C&NW Depot on Front St. in downtown Spooner. One block E of main downtown inlersection, (behind Post Office and parking lot) or one block E of Hwy 70 & 63 stop light, then north on Front Street.

Contact: Betty Jo Brown

Mailing Address:
N8425 Island Lake
Spooner. WI 54801
Telephone: (715) 635-3325

RIVERSIDE & GREAT NORTHERN RAILWAY

Steam, scheduled

GEORGE A. FORERO, JR.

15" gauge

Ride/Operation: Elmer and Norman Sandley purchased the right-of-way of the former LaCrosse & Milwaukee Railroad (1854-1902) in 1952 and operated the 15-inch-gauge Riverside & Great Northern Railway from 1954 to 1982. The R&GN is now being restored by the Riverside & Great Northern Preservation Society, Inc., with two of the original locomotives operating on a 3-mile round trip through scenic rock cuts and wooded areas. The Canadian Pacific (former Milwaukee Road) main line, which parallels the R&GN right-of-way, sees frequent operations.

Displays/Exhibits: Sandley Light Rail Equipment Works being restored; gift and hobby shop and museum in car shop building. A 1920s style lunchroom is in the station.

Schedule: Daily: Memorial Day-Labor Day; 10:00 a.m.-5:30 p.m. Weekends: Mid May, September through mid October, 10:00 a.m.-4:00 p.m.

Fare/Admission: Train: adults $5.00, senior $4.00, children (4-15) $3.00, family maximum $14.00. Museum: no charge.

Locomotives: No. 82, 1957 4-4-0, former Milwaukee County Zoo; vertical-boilered "Tom Thumb"; No. 95, SW style diesel.

Passenger Cars: Five 12-passenger cars.

Rolling Stock/Equipment: Several 4-wheel work-train cars; 8-wheel ballast hopper.

Special Events: Please call or write for information.

Location: One mile north of Wisconsin Dells. Take U.S. 12 north from Crossroads to county road A and travel to the Canadian Pacific overpass; depot is on the east side of the Canadian Pacific tracks. Or take Stand Rock Road from Broadway west of the Canadian Pacific Wisconsin River bridge and travel one mile north to the Canadian Pacific overpass on county road A.

    P   🚌   ✳ **M**

Wisconsin Dells

Contact: Bill Koster

Mailing Address:
N115 County Road N
Wisconsin Dells, WI 53965
Telephone: (608) 254-6367

364

WYOMING TRANSPORTATION MUSEUM AND LEARNING CENTER

Transportation museum

WYOMING TRANSPORTATION MUSEUM AND LEARNING CENTER

Displays/Exhibits: Transportation displays housed in the historic Union Pacific depot.

Schedule: Depot is currently under construction; call for a personal tour or for information.

Location: 15th Street and Capitol Avenue.

Contact: Janet L. Cowley
Executive Director

Mailing Address:
P.O. Box 704
Cheyenne, WY 82003
Telephone: (307) 637-DEPO (3376)
Fax: (307) 634-9349

HERITAGE PARK HISTORICAL VILLAGE

Ride/Operation: With more than one hundred restored buildings and exhibits assembled from many parts of western Canada, Heritage Park is an authentic living memorial to pre-1914 western settlement. A visit begins with a 7-minute streetcar ride from the Fourteenth Street entrance over a winding route to the park's main gate. Inside, a steam train operates continuously on a 20-minute schedule.

Displays/Exhibits: Original stations from Bowell, Laggan, Midnapore, and Shepard; water tank; sand tower; six-stall roundhouse; railway car shop; single-track engine shed; No. 76, 1882 business car, used at Last Spike ceremonies on completion of the Canadian Pacific Railway, November 7, 1885; No. 100, 1901 private car, former Dominion of Canada No. 100 (Prime Minister's car); No. 5, 1902 business car "Pacific"; No. 141, 1907 suburban coach; Canadian Pacific wooden colonist cars, coaches; freight cars; work equipment.

Train: Two 1885 open-platform coaches; former Canadian National observation car No. 15097.

Schedule: Daily, May 18-September 2, 9:00 a.m.-5:00 p.m. Weekends and holidays, September 7-October 14, 9:00 a.m.-5:00 p.m.

Admission: Adults $10.00, children $6.00 (includes free pancake breakfast served from 9:00 a.m. to 10:00 a.m. daily).

Fare: Train $2.00 per person, or pay $6.00 per person and receive unlimited rides including antique midway, S. S. Moyie Sternwheeler boat and horse-drawn wagon rides. Streetcar $ .50.

Locomotives/Trolleys: No. 2023, 1942 Alco 0-6-0, former U.S. Army No. 4012 (operating); No. 2024, 1944 Lima 0-6-0, former U.S. Army No. 4078 (operating); No. 5931, 1949 Montreal 2-10-4, former Canadian Pacific No. 5934; No. 4, 1905 Angus Shops 0-6-0, former CP No. 2144; No. 7019, 1944 Alco S-2, former CP; double-truck closed cars Nos. 14 & 15, 1910 Ottawa Car, former Calgary Municipal.

Location: In southwest Calgary at Heritage Drive and 14th Street S.W. - just 20 minutes from downtown Calgary, easy access via city transit system.

Contact: Rick Smith
General Manager

Mailing Address:
1900 Heritage Drive S.W.
Calgary, AB T2V 2X3
Telephone: (403) 259-1900

FORT EDMONTON PARK

Ride/Operation: Nestled in Edmonton's river valley, Fort Edmonton Park is brought to life by costumed staff reenacting life as it was in Edmonton from its fur-trading days of the 1840s through its development into a bustling city of the 1920s. The train takes visitors from the present day through four historical eras.

Displays/Exhibits: More than seventy period buildings staffed with historical interpreters dressed in period costumes.

Schedule: Daily, May 18-September 1; Sundays, September; train runs continuously.

Fare: Adults $6.50, senior citizens and youths (13-16) $5.00, children (6-12) $3.25, family $19.50. Prices include tax and train ride. May vary in 1997.

Locomotives: No. 107, 1919 Baldwin 2-6-2, former Oakdale & Gull Railway (restored to a 1905 appearance).

Passenger Cars: Three passenger cars.

Special Events: Please call or write for calendar.

Location: Whitemud Freeway and Fox Drive, 10 minutes from downtown.

Mailing Address:
P.O. Box 2359
Edmonton, AB T5J 2R7
Telephone: (403) 496-8787

ALBERTA PRAIRIE RAILWAY EXCURSIONS

Steam, scheduled
Standard gauge

ALBERTA PRAIRIE RAILWAY EXCURSIONS

Ride: Round-trip tours of several varieties are featured from Stettler to a combination of rural lineside communities: Meeting Creek, Donalda, Big Valley, Rumsey, Rowley, Castor, Halkirk and Morrin. Excursions are operated on a former Canadian National branch line through picturesque parkland and prairies in central Alberta and on a former Canadian Pacific branch line past Stettler to Castor. All excursions include full-course roast-beef buffet dinner and on-board entertainment and commentary.

Displays/Exhibits: Restored railway stations, community museums, historical sites, and curio shops.

Train: 1920 Baldwin 2-8-0; coaches, from various dates; vintage diesel power on selected trips.

Schedule: Weekends and selected weekdays, late May-August. Weekends, September-mid October. Dinner trains selected dates November to April.

Fare: Adults $55.00, senior citizens $51.00, students $38.00, children $29.50.

Locomotives: No. 41, 1920 Baldwin 2-8-0, former Jonesboro Lake City & Eastern No. 41, former Frisco No. 77, former Mississippian No. 77, former Huntsville Depot No. 9.

Passenger Cars: Two 1925 Pullman coaches, former Erie Lackawanna lightweight self-propelled coaches; 1920 and 1931 heavyweight sleepers, former Canadian Pacific; 1930s day coaches, 1919 combination coach/baggage, four 1920s-era day coaches, four 1950s-era day coaches, open-air observation car, caboose, all former Canadian National.

Special Events: Murder Mysteries. Canada Day Special. Train Robberies. Overnight Camp-out. Casino Train. Railfan. Family Specials. Entertainment is featured on selected routes and in selected communities.

Location: Stettler is a 2½-hour drive on main highways from both Edmonton and Calgary.

Contact: R. C. Willis
General Manager

Mailing Address:
Postal Bag 800
Stettler, AB T0C 2L0
Telephone: (403) 742-2811
Fax: (403) 742-2844

CANADIAN MUSEUM OF RAIL TRAVEL
Railway museum
Standard gauge

WALTER LANZ

Ride/Operation: This static display portrays the elegant lifestyle aboard trains of the past. Plans call for five complete train sets, under cover, by 1998. Several pieces for these future consists are now in storage.

Displays/Exhibits: The centerpiece is an entire set of the Canadian Pacific Railway's 1929 "flag train," the *Trans-Canada Limited,* featuring restored inlaid woods, brass fixtures, plush upholstery, and wool carpets; cars include solarium-lounge "River Rouge"; day parlor No. 6751; sleepers "Rutherglen," "Glencassie," and "Somerset"; dining car "Argyle"; and baggage-sleeper No. 4489. Also on display are 1928 business car "British Columbia"; former CPR baggage car No. 4481, containing an operating HO-gauge model railway; 1927 former CPR executive night car "Strathcona"; modernized sleeper "Redvers," former *Soo-Spokane Train DeLuxe*; 1907 observation-library-buffet-sleeper "Curzon." The 1900-era Elko Station is the visitor center and gift shop. The dining car is often open for tea, coffee, and light refreshments.

Schedule: Daily; summer, 8:00 a.m.-8:00 p.m.; winter, Tuesday-Saturday, 12:00 noon-5:00 p.m.; Shoulder seasons, daily 10:00 a.m.-6:00 p.m.

Admission: Various categories; Grand Tour tickets strongly recommended. Large groups and bus tours should make advance arrangements.

Special Events: School Programs, September-May; ask about the overnight option for out-of-town classes. Special Railway Gala Christmas Dinners, early December, feature gourmet dining and lodging aboard the restored cars. Bus tours and other groups can book luncheons, dinners, or the museum's famous tea and scones service during their stop.

Location: 1 Van Horne Street (downtown on highway 3/95), Cranbrook.

P   ✻   ☕   ❶   🛉
📷 M   ar n

Contact: Mark McDonald
Associate Director

Mailing Address:
Box 400
Cranbrook, BC V1C 4H9
Telephone: (604) 489-3918
Fax: (604) 489-5744
E-mail: camal@cyberlink.bc.ca

BRITISH COLUMBIA FOREST MUSEUM
Steam, scheduled
36" gauge

Ride/Operation: A 1½-mile steam-train ride through forested areas and over a long, curved, wooden trestle, passing a logging camp and historic machinery.

Displays/Exhibits: Standard-gauge Shay and Climax locomotives; railroad equipment, including log cars and engines; logging museum on the site of the first community building in the Cowichan Valley (1863).

Train: Steel open-platform coaches; open cars.

Schedule: Museum, May-September, 9:30 a.m.-6:00 p.m. (Museum open for visits & self-guided tours from April-May & September-October at off-season admission rates).

Fare/Admission: Adults $7.00, senior citizens and students (13-18) $6.00, children (5-12) $4.00, children under 5 admitted free, family day pass (2 adults and up to 3 children) $25.00. Includes train ride and admission to park. Family membership $45 (10 family visits/year). Corporate membership $250. Group rates available. Fares subject to change. Prices do not include 7% GST.

Locomotives: No. 1, 1921 Lima 2-truck Shay; No. 9, 1925 class B 45-ton 2-truck Climax; No. 24, 1900 Vulcan 12-ton side-tank 0-4-0T; No. 25, Vulcan 18-ton saddletank 0-4-0T; No. 22, 1926 Plymouth gas locomotive; No. 26, 10-ton Plymouth; No. 27, 8-wheeled logging crew speeder; No. 1, narrow-gauge diesel, former White Pass & Yukon.

Rolling Stock/Equipment: Rail cars; tank cars; track crew car; dump cars; flatcar; jiggers; other construction/industrial equipment.

Special Events: National Forestry Week, May 4-10. Classic Tractors of Vancouver Island Picnic, June 15. Fords & Friends Picnic, July 13. Celebration of Steam, August 9-10.

Location: On Vancouver Island, on highway 1 about one mile north of Duncan and 55 minutes from Victoria.

Contact: Mike Osborn
Manager

Mailing Address:
R.R. #4
2892 Drinkwater Rd.
Duncan, BC V9L 3W8
Telephone: (604) 746-1251
Fax: (604) 746-1487

FORT STEELE RAILWAY

Ride/Operation: Passengers enjoy a 2-mile, 25-minute ride through the grounds of Fort Steele Heritage Town. The double-loop track climbs to the Kootenay River Lookout where riders disembark to enjoy the majestic scenery. The conductor gives a brief talk on local history and railroading before the train returns to the station.

Displays/Exhibits: Fort Steele is a collection of over 60 original and reconstructed buildings on the original townsite. Live steam train, living history street, actors, live variety stage show, horse farming demonstrations, blacksmith, general store, and historic gardens.

Schedule: Daily, end of June through first Monday in September, 10:00 a.m.-5:00 p.m. Train leaves from the shed-roofed station.

Fare/Admission: Family $10.00, adults $4.00, senior citizens $3.00, children (6-16) $2.00, children under 6 ride free.

Locomotives: No. 115 "Robert E. Swanson," 1934 Lima 3-truck Pacific Coast Shay; 1895 Sharp, Stewart 0-4-4T "Dunrobin," built for the Duke of Sutherland in Scotland; No. 1077, 1923 Montreal Locomotive Works.

Notes: Be sure to walk through the shops if open.

Location: Fort Steele Heritage Town is in eastern British Columbia. Fort Steele is located 16 km northeast of Cranbrook on Route 93-95 and is on the Crow's Nest Pass line of the Canadian Pacific Railway.

Contact: Ross Wimmer
General Manager

Mailing Address:
9851 Highway 93/95
Fort Steele, BC V0B 1N0
Telephone: (604) 489-2051
Fax: (604) 489-2624
Internet: http://www. islandnet.com/~bcma/museums/fsht/intro.html

BC RAIL, LTD.

Ride/Operation: BC Rail offers a spectacular 80-mile, six-hour round trip to Squamish including a two-hour stopover there. Heading the train is no. 2860, a stainless-steel-jacketed "Royal Hudson"; resplendent in polished maroon and black, it makes a fine sight at the head of its tuscan-red passenger train. The highly scenic route takes passengers along the coast of Howe Sound where they view the island-dotted sea on one side and coastal mountains on the other. Passage available in standard class or parlor class (a restored vintage dining car). Train-boat option also available.

Schedule: Wednesday-Sunday & holiday Mondays: May 31-September 21. Boarding begins at 9:00 a.m. and seating is on first come-first served basis. NOTE: No service June 4, 5 & September 17, 18.

Fare/Admission: Adults $45.00, seniors/youth $39.50, children $12.50, under age 5 are free. Parlor class $86.25. Adult train-boat $77.57, senior/youth $65.54, children $21.40, under age 5 are free. Reservations are required by telephone using Visa or Mastercard.

Locomotives: No. 2860, 1940 Montreal 4-6-4, former Canadian Pacific No. 3716, 1912 Montreal 2-8-0, former CP.

Rolling Stock/Equipment: Power car, 11 coaches, 2 cafe lounge cars, 1 parlor car.

Special Events: Jingle Bell Express, December 14-15.

Location: 1311 West First Street, North Vancouver. The station is located at the foot of Pemberton Street, a 20 minute drive from downtown Vancouver.

Vancouver, 8 miles away

Contact: Jean Cullen
Marketing

Mailing Address:
P.O. Box 8770
Vancouver, BC V6B 4X6
Telephone: (604) 631-3500
800-663-8238
Fax: (604) 984-5505
E-mail: PASSINFO@bcrail.com
Internet: OURWORLD.COMPUSERVE.COM/homepages/bcrail_TPO

WESTERN VANCOUVER ISLAND
INDUSTRIAL HERITAGE SOCIETY
Steam, scheduled
Standard gauge

Ride/Operation: A 3-mile round trip along the industrial waterfront.

Displays/Exhibits: Restored CP Rail station; 1947 Hayes logging truck; Fairmont speeder; other restoration work in progress.

Schedule: Weekends and statutory holidays, July 1-September 4, 11:00 a.m.-4:00 p.m., on the hour.

Fare: Adults $3.00, children $2.00.

Locomotives: No. 2, "Two Spot," 1912 Lima 42-ton 2-truck Shay; No. 7, 1928 Baldwin 90-ton 2-8-2 ST; No. 11, 1942 General Electric 45-ton diesel-electric; No. 1, 1928 Westminster Iron Works Buda gas switcher; No. 8427, Montreal Locomotive Works/Alco RS-3 diesel.

Rolling Stock/Equipment: Two modified cabooses, former Canadian National; early 1900s Victoria Lumber & Manufacturing Co. crew car.

Special Events: Santa Claus Run.

Location: The restored CP Rail station at Harbour Quay in Port Alberni on Vancouver Island. The Alberni Valley is a one-hour drive from Nanaimo, the B.C. Ferry terminal to the mainland.

Contact: Hugh Grist
Treasurer

Mailing Address:
"The Station"
3100 Kingsway Avenue
Port Alberni, BC V9Y 3B1
Telephone: (604) 723-2118
Work phone: (604) 724-7501

PRINCE GEORGE RAILWAY & FORESTRY MUSEUM
Railway museum
Standard gauge

Displays/Exhibits: This museum houses a large collection of railway buildings, rolling stock, and equipment, complemented by the Fire Hall, housing a 1929 Reo fire truck, a 1948 fire truck, and a horse-drawn fire sleigh. The pioneer building contains a large telephone display and an operating telegraph system. A turn-of-the-century bunkhouse shows how the Yelanka, a local ethnic group, lived while working on the railway. Logging displays include a 1930 band saw, a 1950 gang saw, and several pieces of logging road equipment.

Schedule: May-September, daily 9:30 a.m.-5:00 p.m.

Admission: Adults $2.50, senior citizens & children $1.00, family (up to 4) $5.00, $1 per ride.

Locomotives: No. 1520, 1906 4-6-0, and No. 9169, EMD F7A, both former Canadian National; No. 586, RS-10, former BC Rail; No. 101, 44-ton General Electric, and 65-ton Atlas diesel, both former U.S. Navy; and many more, write for specifics.

Passenger Cars: 1913 business car "Nechako," former GTP; "Endeavour," former BC Rail; sleeper; coach; combine and many more, write for specifics.

Rolling Stock/Equipment: Head-end power car from *American Freedom Train;* baggage car; road repair car; 1903 snowplow; operating 1913 100-ton steam wrecking crane; boxcars; cabooses; tank cars; work cars; operating 89 foot turntable, and many more, write for specifics.

Special Events: Steam Days will be held on the third Sunday of each month during the season.

Location: 850 River Road, just north of Canadian National yards, close to downtown, and adjacent to Cottonwood Island Nature Park.

Vancouver

Contact: Roy Smith

Mailing Address:
Central British Columbia Railway &
Forest Industry Museum Society
P.O. Box 2408
Prince George, BC V2N 2S6
Telephone: (604) 563-7351

KWINITSA RAILWAY
STATION MUSEUM
Railway museum

KWINITSA RAILWAY STATION MUSEUM

Display/Exhibit: The Kwinitsa Railway Station Museum is housed in an authentic 1912 Grand Trunk Pacific Railway station and several rooms are restored to their original state, including the telegrapher's office and living quarters, and the bunkroom for the section crew. This award winning museum also features exhibits chronicling the early history of Prince Rupert and its role as the terminus of the Grand Trunk Railway. Videos depicting railway construction in 1911 and the operation of this and similar stations along the Skeena River complement the exhibits. In the old waiting room a small gift shop offers books on the railway and souvenirs. The scenic ocean front location and the adjacent park make this an excellent place to visit.

Schedule: Daily, 9:00 a.m.-12:00 p.m. and 1:00-5:00 p.m. Beginning of June until the first weekend of September.

Fare/Admission: Donations welcomed.

Location: On the Prince Rupert's scenic waterfront at the western terminus of the CNR and Highway 16.

Contact: Susan Marsden
Curator

Mailing Address:
P.O. Box 669
Prince Rupert, BC V8J 3S1
Telephone: (604) 624-3207
(604) 627-1915

WEST COAST RAILWAY
HERITAGE PARK
Railway displays

GRANT FERGUSON

Displays/Exhibits: This site offers a static display of more than 60 locomotives and pieces of rolling stock as well as artifacts related to the railway history of British Columbia. Features of the display include 1890 former Canadian Pacific business car "British Columbia"; former Pacific Great Eastern RSC-3 No. 561; former PGE interurban sleeper "Clinton"; museum display car "Cowichan River"; and 2-6-2 No. 2, the first steam locomotive on the PGE.

Schedule: Daily, May 1-October 31, 10:00 a.m.-5:00 p.m.

Admission: Adults $5.00, children (under 13) $4.00, family (2 adults with children under 13) $12.00. Minirail $1 extra.

Locomotives: No. 551, 65-ton, former PGE; No. 53, former CP; No. 960, former B.C. Electric; 2-8-2 No. 16, former Comox Logging & Railway; Nos. 4069 & 4459, both former CP; others.

Passenger Cars: "Bell Island" sleeper No. 2183, former CP; colonist car No. 2514 and observation No. 598, both former CP; cafe-observations Nos. 1090 & 1057, both former Great Northern; diner "Dunraven," former Canadian National.

Rolling Stock/Equipment: Snowplow No. 55365, former CN; Jordan spreader No. 402846 and steam crane No. 414330, both former CP; cabooses Nos. 1817 & 1821, former PGE; transfer caboose, former GN; others.

Note: Guided tours of the park can be arranged at any time of the year for tour groups and trade associations.

Location: 33547 Government Road. Located 1/2 mile (1 km) west of Highway 99. Take Centennial Way approximately 2 miles (3 km) north of McDonald's on Highway 99 in Squamish. Look for the West Coast Railway Heritage Park directional signs.

Contact: Site Manager

Mailing Address:
P.O. Box 2387
Squamish, BC V0N 3G0
Telephone: (604) 898-9336
Toll free: (800) 722-1233

ROCKY MOUNTAINEER RAILTOURS
Electric, scheduled
Standard gauge

ROCKY MOUNTAINEER RAILTOUR

Ride/Operation: Rocky Mountaineer Railtours is a two-day, all daylight train tour operating between May and October. Beginning in Vancouver, Calgary, Banff or Jasper, the train travels east- and westbound through the spectacular scenery of British Columbia, Alberta and the Canadian Rockies. All *GoldLeaf Dome* and *Signature Service* guests enjoy two days onboard the Rocky Mountaineer, overnight accommodations in Kamloops, breakfast and lunch daily with exemplary service and magnificent views. This tour can be combined with a variety of Independent Package Tours and Customized Group Programs.

Train: Five locomotives; six baggage cars; 37 coaches; four bi-level dome coaches; one parlour coach, steam-generating unit.

Schedule: May 1-29 & October 2-16 (Value Season): Departs *alternating* Sundays, Tuesdays & Thursdays. June 1-September 30 (Regular Season): departs *every* Sunday, Tuesday & Thursday.

Fare: *Signature Service* fares begin at $371 during Value Season and $449 during Regular Season. *GoldLeaf Dome Coach Service* fares begin at $761 during Value Season and $839 during Regular Season. All prices, based on double occupancy, are in U.S. dollars and do not include 7% GST.

Locomotives: Nos. 800, 804, 805, 806, and 807 General Motors GP40-2 locomotives.

Passenger Cars: Seventeen Dayniter 44seat coaches, 1954 Canadian Car and Foundry, rebuilt 1972 and 1985-88, twenty cafe coaches, 48-seat No. 5749, 1949 Pullman, four 72-seat bi-level dome coaches, 1995, 1996 Rader Railcar.

Contact: Eric Belanger

Mailing Address:
1150 Station Street, 1st Floor
Vancouver, BC V6A 2X7
Telephone: (604) 606-7200
Canada & USA: 1 (800) 665-7245
Reservations Fax: (604) 606-7250
E-mail: rkymtn@fleethouse.com

ROYAL HUDSON STEAM TRAIN

Ride/Operation: The Royal Hudson Steam Train Society and Harbour Cruises Ltd. team up to offer a boat-and-train excursion between Vancouver and Squamish, about 40 miles — boat in one direction and train in the other, and there is also the option of riding the train both ways.

Train: The train uses BC Rail tracks along the shore of Howe Sound. The line was opened in 1956 by the Pacific Great Eastern (BC Rail's original name), extending PGE's line south from its long-time terminal at Squamish to Vancouver. BC Rail operates regular passenger trains on its scenic line to Lillooet and Prince George. The train that carried King George VI and Queen Elizabeth from Quebec to Vancouver in 1939 was pulled by Hudson No. 2850, which was adorned with cast-metal replicas of crowns on its running board skirting. After the trip, with Royal assent, CPR applied crowns to all 45 of its semistreamlined Hudsons and designated them "Royal Hudsons."

Schedule: 1 steam (Canadian Pacific 4-6-4 No. 2860) Air-conditioned coaches, snack car May 31-September 17, 1995, Wednesday-Sunday (daily July 1-Labor Day), boat leaves Vancouver 9:30 a.m., train leaves North Vancouver 10 a.m. Train returns to North Vancouver 4:00 p.m., shuttle bus arrives Vancouver 4:30; boat arrives Vancouver 4:30, shuttle bus arrives North Vancouver 5:00 p.m.

Fare/Admission: Train round trip: Adults $45.00, seniors 65+ $29.50, youths (age 12-18) $39.50, children 5-11 $12.50, under age 5 are free. Train and boat: Adults $70.50, youths and seniors $61.25, children $20, under age 5 are free. Credit cards accepted. Group discounts available. Tickets are available through travel agents, the Vancouver Travel Information Centre, and Harbour Ferries.

Locomotives: Motive power is Royal Hudson No. 2860, built by Montreal Locomotive Works in 1940 for Canadian Pacific.

Notes: There is a snack bar on the train, and a buffet brunch or a salmon dinner is available on the boat.
Location: The boat departs from the north foot of Denman Street in Vancouver, between the Westin Bayshore Hotel and Stanley Park. The train departs from 1311 West 1st Street in North Vancouver, across the harbor from Vancouver. At the end of the trip shuttle buses return you to your starting point.

Mailing Address:
Harbour CruisesLtd.
No. 1–North Foot of Denman Street
Vancouver, BC V6G 2W9
Telephone: (604) 688-7246
Outside Vancouver: (800) 663-1500

D. SHORES/THE VINTAGE LOCOMOTIVE SOCIETY, INC.

Ride/Operation: A 36-mile, 2-hour round trip to Grosse Isle over the Oakpoint Subdivision of the Canadian National Railways. Vintage wooden cars are pulled by a beautiful American Standard locomotive that was in service on the Canadian Pacific from 1882 to 1918.

Displays/Exhibits: On display in the city of Winnipeg are former Canadian National 2-8-0 No. 2747 and 4-8-2 No. 6043.

Train: Wood combination car; four wood coaches.

Schedule: Sundays, June-September, 11:00 a.m. & 3:00 p.m.

Admission: Adults $13.00, senior citizens and youths (12-17) $11.00, children (2-11) $7.00, children under 2 not occupying a seat ride free. Fares and schedules subject to change without notice.

Locomotives: No. 3, 1882 Dübs & Co. (Glasgow) 4-4-0, former Canadian Pacific, former City of Winnipeg Hydro.

Passenger Cars: Coaches, former Keeweenaw Central, former Canadian Northern, former CP; business car, former CP (awaiting restoration).

Rolling Stock/Equipment: Boxcars; bunk car; caboose; flatcar.

Location: Train departs from the CN St. James Station near 1661 Portage Avenue, just west of St. James Street.

Contact: K. G. Younger
Treasurer

Mailing Address:
The Vintage Locomotive Society, Inc.
P.O. Box 33021
RPO Polo Park
Winnipeg, MB R3G 3N4
Telephone: (204) 832-5259

THE RAILWAY MUSEUM OF MANITOBA

Display/Exhibit: See the Railway Museum of Manitoba and take a step back in time to the days when Canada was young and the railroad began linking east to west over virgin prairie. See the equipment that carried freight across country enroute to Europe or the Orient. The Railway Museum of Manitoba offers a window to the past when people lined up for two city blocks waiting to buy tickets for the Beach Trains. See where Winnipeg relives her glory days as the transportation hub of the continent. Exhibits include the "Countess of Dufferin," the first steam engine in western Canada, a 1922 Mack AB railbus owned by Winnipeg Hydro still in working order, and an electric locomotive from the Hudson Bay Mining & Smelting Company. Examples of modern freight trains thunder along the CN mainline a few yards away and passenger trains stop on the next track over.

Schedule: May-Labor Day: Thursday-Monday 12:00-6:00 p.m. Weekends, holidays and remaining year: 12:00-4:00 p.m.
Fare/Admission: Donation.

Location: The museum is located in the heart of downtown Winnipeg in the VIA Rail Station, 123 Main Street, Tracks 1 and 2.

Mailing Address:
Midwest Rail Association
Box 1855
Winnipeg, MB R3C 3R1
Telephone: (204) 942-4632

SALEM & HILLSBOROUGH
RAILROAD
Steam, diesel, scheduled
Railway display

BOB MITCHELL

Operation: This operation, a project of the New Brunswick Division of the Canadian Railroad Historical Association, features a museum, static display, and gift shop. On September 16, 1994, a fire destroyed the railroad's shops and offices, as well as considerable rolling stock. However, the line still features its 1-hour, 10-mile excursions, 3½-hour, 22-mile dinner excursions, and chartered excursions.

Schedule: Museum: Daily, June 23-September 2, 10:00 a.m.-8:00 p.m. Train: June 8-October 19.

Fares/Admission: Train: Adults $6.75, seniors $6.00, children (6-12) $3.50, under 6 free, family pass $20.00. Gift Shop & Museum: $1.00. Dinner Runs: $22.00. Fall Foliage: Adults $10.00, seniors $9.00, children (6-12) $5.00, under 6 free, family pass $30.00.

Locomotives: No. 29, 1897 4-4-0, former Canadian Pacific (damaged in fire); No. 1009, 1912 4-6-0, and No. 8245, 1958 MLW MS-10p, and No. 1754, 1975 RSC14 (rebuilt 1959 RS 18), all former Canadian National.

Passenger Cars: Coaches dating from 1911 to 1942.

Rolling Stock/Equipment: Cabooses; double-ended snowplow; 1920 Jordan spreader; 100-ton 1913 steam wreck crane; 1921 tank car; others.

Special Events: Transportation Day, Father's Day, Canada Day, Homecoming Day, Fall Foliage Train, 1 hr. Sunday Excursions, 1:30 and 3:00 p.m. Dinner Trains. Call for dates, specific menu and departure times.

Location: On highway 114, on the way to The Rocks Provincial Park and Fundy National Park, 12 miles south of Moncton.

VIAMoncton

Radio Frequency: 172.305

Contact: E. F. Bowes
Director

Mailing Address:
P.O. Box 70
Hillsborough, NB E0A 1XO
Summer: (506) 734-3195
Off-season: (506) 734-3100

SYDNEY & LOUISBOURG
RAILWAY MUSEUM
Railway museum

SYDNEY & LOUISBURG RAILWAY MUSEUM

Displays/Exhibits: This museum, located in the original 1895 Louisbourg railway station, features exhibits describing the history of the S&L, railway technology, and local and marine history. Several model trains are included, and a model of the complete S&L line. Outside, visitors can see the restored original freight shed, rolling stock, and the "roundhouse," which houses some of the rolling stock in the winter and a display of memorial quilts.

Schedule: Daily; June 1-June 30 & September 1-mid October, 9:00 a.m.-5:00 p.m.; July 1-August 31, 9:00 a.m.-7:00 p.m. Other times by appointment. Bus and school tours welcome.

Admission: No charge; donations welcomed.

Passenger Cars: 1881 passenger car; 1914 passenger car.

Rolling Stock/Equipment: Caboose; tank car; freight car; small handcar; maintenance equipment.

Special Events: Craft fairs, concerts, display of memorial quilts, roundhouse. Annual Reunion, second Sunday in September each year.

Location: Main Street, at the entrance of town. Louisbourg is 22 miles from Sydney on highway 22.

Contact: Bill Bussey
President

Mailing Address:
P.O. Box 225
Louisbourg, NS B0A 1M0
Telephone: (902) 733-2720

TOWN OF CLINTON

Displays/Exhibits: The town of Clinton is proud to be a part of Canada's heritage of education. Situated within Sloman Memorial Park is an Ontario Department of Education school car. Car no. 15089, which was originally an 80 foot dining car, is admired by residents of and visitors to Clinton. Designed to reach settlers throughout Ontario's wilderness, the school traveled throughout the interior providing education to both parents and children. In 1926, a total of seven train-car schools covered an area of 4500 miles, ranging from the Ontario-Manitoba border to the outskirts of Sudbury. The Sloman School Car on Wheels exhibits the original classroom set-up of desks, books, puzzles and the usual teaching devices of a functioning classroom.

Schedule: Victoria Day weekend-Labor Day. Thursdays & Fridays, 2:00 p.m.-5:00 p.m.; Saturdays, Sundays and holidays, 1:00 p.m.-5:00 p.m. Other times by appointment.

Admission: No charge.

Passenger Cars: Car No. 15089, former dining car.

Location: The school on wheels is located at the junction of Ontario Highways No. 4 and No. 8. It is 45 miles (72km) from London, 58 miles (93km) from Kitchener-Waterloo, and 115 miles (185km) from Detroit, Michigan.

Contact: Margaret Sloman

Mailing Address:
P.O. Box 488
Clinton, ON N0M 1L0
Telephone: (519) 482-3027

COCHRANE RAILWAY
& PIONEER MUSEUM
Railway museum

COCHRANE RAILWAY & PIONEER MUSEUM

Displays/Exhibits: This museum preserves a three-dimensional picture of the pioneer railway and homesteading days, as a tribute to the men and women who opened northern Ontario, an empire bigger than the territories of many United Nations members. A model train display aboard a former Canadian National coach introduces the main railway exhibits, which include a telegraph operator's corner, a ticket office, a document display, an insulator collection, and uniforms. There is also a large, varied display of photographs. Many of the pictures are from the large collection assembled by the Rev. W. L. L. Lawrence around 1912, for which the museum is now trustee. Also, in Train "Tim" Horton Memorial Museum great hockey artifacts are displayed.

Schedule: June 29-September 1, daily, 11:00 a.m.-7:00 p.m. Open Monday-Wednesday & Friday-Sunday. Closed Thursday.

Admission: Adults $2.00, seniors $1.00, families $4.00, student/children $1.50. Group fees $25 per group or $1 per person.

Locomotives: No. 137, 2-8-0, former Temiskaming & Northern Ontario.

Passenger Cars: Caboose and three coaches, former CN.

Rolling Stock/Equipment: Interpretive car.

Special Events: Museum Days, two days in August; free hot dogs and soda served. Please call or write for specific dates.

Note: Lodging and a restaurant are available at Union Station, adjacent to the museum.

Location: 210 Railway Street, northeast of Cochrane Union Station.

Contact: Paul Latondress
Museum Curator

Mailing Address:
P.O. Box 490
Cochrane, ON P0L 1C0
Telephone: (705) 272-4361

FORT ERIE RAILROAD MUSEUM

Displays/Exhibits: This museum displays railroad-related exhibits in two train stations, one built in 1910 and another built in 1873; also on display are maintenance-of-way equipment, a steam engine, a caboose, and a fireless engine.

Schedule: Daily, May 23-September 5, 9:00 a.m.-5:00 p.m. Weekends, September 6-October 8, 9:00 a.m.-5:00 p.m. Subject to change; please call or write to confirm.

Admission: Adults $2.00, children $.50. Includes admission to the town's two other museums, the Fort Erie Historical Museum and the Ridgeway Battlefield Museum.

Locomotive: No. 6218, former Canadian National 4-8-4; Porter fireless locomotive.

Location: Central Avenue, near Gilmore Road.

Contact: Jane Davies
Curator

Mailing Address:
P.O. Box 339
Ridgeway, ON L0S 1N0
Telephone: (905) 894-5322

KOMOKA RAILWAY MUSEUM
Railway museum
Standard gauge

JOHN KANAKOS

Displays/Exhibits: Housed in Komoka's former Grand Trunk station, which was built in 1880 and was moved to its present site across the tracks when purchased in 1974, this museum preserves the railroad history of Ontario. Many railroad items are available for close examination, such as telegraph keys, spike hammers, spike pullers, switch lanterns, steam gauges, a railroad safe, and a baggage sleigh; there are also Fairmont motor cars and a three-wheel velocipede. The museum's pride is a 1913 Shay steam logging locomotive, now undergoing restoration in its own building. When restored, a pre-1939 steel-sided baggage car will house a model railroad display and a theater for multimedia presentations. Visitors may also view the tiny (8-foot by 9-foot) Longwoods flagstop station, and researchers are welcome to browse the extensive library of books, photos, and newspaper clippings.

Schedule: June 1-September 30: Tuesday and Thursday, 7:00-9:00 p.m.; Saturday, 9:00 a.m.-12:00 p.m.; Sunday, 1:00-4:00 p.m. Group tours and off-peak visits may be arranged in advance.

Admission: $2.00 donation.

Special Events: Day trips to other local railroad museums. Pancake breakfast, held in conjunction with the annual Thames Valley Central Modular Railroad Club's model railroad flea market, mid April. Toy Miniatures Flea Market and Show, October. Handcar rides.

Location: 133 Queen Street, adjacent to the Komoka Community Center. Komoka is 10 minutes west of London and halfway between Detroit and Toronto.

Contact: Ronald Davis
Curator

Mailing Address:
P.O. Box 22
133 Queen Street
Komoka, ON N0L 1R0
Telephone: (519) 657-1912

HALTON COUNTY RADIAL RAILWAY

Ride/Operation: Located on the right-of-way of the former Toronto Suburban Railway, Canada's first operating railway museum offers a 2-mile ride through scenic woodlands. Two loops are in service.

Displays/Exhibits: Many pieces of electric-railway rolling stock from lines in Ontario, ranging from early wooden cars to PCC cars from Toronto. Also on display are a line car, a crane car, a sweeper, an electric locomotive, a caboose, and boxcars.

Schedule: Weekends and holidays, May, September, and October; Wednesday-Sunday, June; daily, July-August; 10:00 a.m.-5:00 p.m. Night Shows 6:30-9:30 p.m.

Fare: Adults $6.50, senior citizens (65+) $5.50, youth (3-18) $4.50, family rate (1 adult or senior & up to 4 youth or 2 adults or seniors & up to 3 youth) $17.50. Night shows: adults $4.50, senior citizens $3.75, youth (3-18) $3.00. Different rates apply on special-event days. Medium Group Rate (6-19 in group): Adults $5.50, senior citizens (65+) $4.75, youth (3-18) $3.75. Charters and group tours available for groups of 20 or more during the week with advance reservation: adults $4.75, senior citizens $4.25, youth (3-18) $3.00. Prices include tax.

Trolleys: No. 327, 1893 4-wheel open car (rebuilt 1933); No. 55, 1915 Preston single-truck closed car; No. 2890, 1923 small Peter Witt, Ottawa; No. 2424, 1921 large Peter Witt; and No. 4000, 1938 PCC; all former Toronto Transportation Commission. No. 107, 1912 Montreal & Southern Counties interurban; No. 1326, 1910 Toronto Railway Co.; No. 8, 1915 Jewett Car Co. heavy interurban, former London & Port Stanley; No. 732, trolley coach, former Hamilton Street Railways.

Special Events: Summer Extravaganza/Yard & Craft Sale, June 23. Happy 75th Birthday T.T.C., July 21.

Night Show & Corn Roast, August 17. Fall Cavalcade of Color, September 28-29. Christmas Fiesta (10:00 a.m.-4:00 pm.), December 1. Christmas Night Shows, December 7 & 14.

Location: 13,629 Guelph Line, Milton. Take exit 312 (Guelph Line) off highway 401 and travel north nine miles (15km).

Contact: Joan Johns
Curator

Mailing Address:
RR #2
Rockwood, ON N0B 2K0
Telephone: (519) 856-9802

HERITAGE RAILWAY COMPANY

Steam, diesel, scheduled
Narrow gauge

HERITAGE RAILWAY COMPANY

Displays/Exhibits: CPR caboose used as ticket office and open to public.

Ride/Operation: Two locomotives. One diesel (G16), one steam. Railway operated by volunteers; most have railway backgrounds.

Schedule: May-October.

Fare/Admission: $1.00, children under 3 are free.

Locomotives: No. 6412 steam, Crown Corp., 4-4-0. No. 6512 diesel, F7.

Rolling Stock/Equipment: Five steel open passenger coaches.

Special Events: Heritage Festival and Airshow (over Lake Nipissing) on August 1 holiday weekend. Non-profit.

Notes: Adjacent boat ride on catamaran.

Location: 230 Memorial Drive at lakefront and beside CPR mainline.

Contact: Parks Department
City of North Bay

Mailing Address:
200 McIntyre Street East
North Bay, ON P1B 8H8
Telephone: (705) 474-0400

ANTHONY SCULLION

Displays/Exhibits: This museum features all types of transportation from Canada's earliest days to the present, along with many other types of exhibits relating to science and technology. There are four steam locomotives on display in the huge Railroad Hall; the cabs of some are accessible, and sound effects give the feeling of live locomotives. The engines are meticulously restored, with polished rods and lighted number boards and class lights. The scene is enhanced by station benches, platform lights, signs, and memorabilia.

Schedule: May 1-Labor Day: daily, 9:00 a.m.-6:00 p.m.; Friday, 9:00 a.m.-9:00 p.m. Labor Day-April 30: Tuesday-Sunday, 9:00 a.m.-5:00 p.m. Closed Mondays except statutory holidays. Closed Christmas Day.

Admission: Adults $6.00, seniors citizens and students $5.00, children (6-15) $2.00, children under 6 admitted free, family rate (2 adults and children under age 16) $12.00, groups of 15 or more (without a guide) $2.50 per person, school groups (children's tours) $1.50 per person. Tour leader and bus driver admitted free.

Locomotives: No. 6400, 1936 Montreal 4-8-4, former Canadian National, displayed at the 1939 New York World's Fair. No. 926, 1912 4-6-0; No. 2858, 1938 Montreal "Royal Hudson" 4-6-4; No. 3100, 1928 Montreal 4-8-4; all former Canadian Pacific.

Passenger Cars: 1892 business car "Terra Nova," former Newfoundland Railway.

Location: At 1867 St. Laurent Boulevard in southeast Ottawa.

Contact: Jean-Guy Monette
Public Relations Officer

Mailing Address:
1867 St. Laurent Blvd.
P.O. Box 9724
Ottawa, ON K1G 5A3
Telephone: (613) 991-3044

PORT STANLEY TERMINAL RAIL
Diesel, scheduled
Standard gauge

AL HOWLETT

Ride/Operation: Three different rides all from the station in Port Stanley, on the harbor next to the lift bridge. Trains pass over two bridges and northward for up to 7 miles through the Kettle Creek Valley. Port Stanley is a commercial fishing village on the north shore of Lake Erie.

Displays/Exhibits: Equipment includes cabooses; heavyweight coaches; open coaches; baggage cars; boxcars; flatcars; hopper cars; a snowplow; tank cars; Burro Cranes; and more. Ticket office and displays are in the former London & Port Stanley station.

Train: Open excursion cars; cabooses, former Canadian National, modified into enclosed coaches; standard coaches, former VIA. The "Little Red Caboose" can be chartered for birthday parties and other events with advance reservation.

Schedule: Union & Whites: January to April, Sunday; May-June, Saturday & Sunday; July-August, daily; September-October, Saturday & Sunday; November-December, Sunday. St. Thomas Parkside: May-June, Sunday; July-August, daily; September-October, Sunday.

Fare: Union & Whites: Adults $8.00, children 2-12 $4.00, seniors $7.00. St. Thomas Parkside: Adult $11.00, children 2-12 $5.50, seniors $10.00. Fares do not include GST tax. For group and charter rates call Shirley Liggett at (519) 672-7953.

Locomotives: No. L-1, 1952 25-ton General Electric; No. L-2, 1950 Canadian Locomotive Co.; and No. L-5, "Albert," 1947 50-ton Whitcomb; all former Consolidated Sand & Gravel Co., Paris, Ontario; General Electric 44-ton "Winnie."

Special Events: Easter Bunny, April. Wild Flowers, May. Santa Claus Trains, December.

Note: This site offers fair exchange on U.S. funds. Mastercard & VISA are accepted.

Location: On highway 4 south of London, about 20 minutes from highway 401.

Contact: Al Howlett
Marketing

Mailing Address:
309 Bridge Street
Port Stanley, ON N5L 1C5
Telephone: (519) 782-3730
Fax: (519) 782-4385
Internet: http://www.mgl.ca/~saries/pstr.html

ALGOMA CENTRAL RAILWAY INC.
Scheduled
Standard gauge

ELMER KARS

Ride/Operation: Operate both tour trains and regular passenger service. Tour trains take you on a one-day wilderness excursion to Agawa Canyon Wilderness Park. Regular passenger train provides service to Hearst, Ontario as well as access to a variety of wilderness lodges.

Schedule: Passenger service operates year round. Agawa Canyon train tour operates daily June through mid-October. Snow train operates Saturday and Sunday, January through mid-March.

Fare: Contact Passenger Sales for specific fares.

Locomotives: F9s (refurbished); 1950s VIA coaches (refurbished).

Notes: We also operate 2 private cars "Agawa" and "Michipicoten" on a rental basis - groups of 8-12.

Location: Depot is located in downtown Sault Ste. Marie, five minutes from the International Bridge. Sault Ste. Marie is one hour north of the Mackinac Bridge.

Contact: Passenger Sales

Mailing Address: P.O. Box 130
129 Bay Street
Sault Ste. Marie, ON P6A 6Y2
Telephone: (705) 946-7300
Toll-free: (800) 242-9287
Fax: (705) 541-2989

SMITHS FALLS RAILWAY MUSEUM

Ride/Operation: The museum features a Canadian Northern railway station restored to its former elegance. Exhibits depict railroad history in Canada and Smith Falls. A ride in the Wickham Inspection Car will take you to see the drawbridge overlooking the Rideau Canal. Enjoy such special events as model railroad displays, telegraphers, blacksmiths, and hand-car rides.

Displays/Exhibits: 1914 former Canadian Northern station, now a national historic site; agent's bay; railroad and artifacts display in Main Waiting Room. Train display includes a diesel locomotive, coaches, and a caboose; other displays include steam locomotive No. 1112, former Canadian Northern; a 1947 Cadillac railcar; a 1913 dental car; Wickham inspection cars, work cars, ballast cars, and assorted freight equipment.

Schedule: May-October, 10:00 a.m.-4:00 p.m.

Fare: Adults $2.00, seniors $1.50, children under 13 admitted free.

Locomotives: No. 6591 MLW S-3, former Canadian Pacific; former CN 4-6-0 No. 1112, undergoing restoration.

Passenger Cars: No. 23, Crossen 1896, former CRHA #23, CP #23, Quebec Central; No. 101, CC&F 1920 coach, former CN #5019; No. 102 CC&F 1923 coach, former CN #5032; No. 104 CC&F 1923 coach, former CN #5042; No. 105 CC&F 1924 coach, former CN #4997, 5079; No. 5802 CC&F 1923 coach, former RVDX #103, CN #5802; No. 23, former CN; No. M-26, former CP. More not listed.

Rolling Stock/Equipment: No. 77137 Grand Trunk Railroad caboose 1891 (r/b 1922), former CRHA #77137, GTW #77137; No. 437183 1945 CP caboose; No. 437169 1945 CP caboose; No. 22 1934 tank car, former Canada Starch #CSTX22; No. 376541 Otis-Hart 1929 dump car, former CP #376589; No. 404266 autobox, former CP boxcar #404266; No. 404177 1912 boxcar, former CP #404177, 173884. More not listed.

Location: 90 William Street West; signs in town indicate museum location. From Ottawa, take highway 15 south; from Kingston, take highway 15 north; from Brockville, take highway 29 north.

Contact: Julia Brady
Curator

Mailing Address:
P.O. Box 962
Smiths Falls, ON K7A 5A5
Telephone: (613) 283-5696
Fax: (613) 283-5696
E-mail: can-sfrmc@immedia.ca

SOUTH SIMCOE RAILWAY

Ride/Operation: An 8-mile, 50-minute round trip over a scenic portion of the former Canadian National line from Hamilton to Allandale. Former Canadian Pacific No. 136, an 1883 4-4-0, or former CP No. 1057, a 1912 4-6-0, hauls 1920s-vintage cars.

Train: Former Canadian Pacific 82-seat steel day coach and 32-seat steel combine; former Toronto, Hamilton & Buffalo 74-seat steel coach.

Schedule: May, June & November: Weekends 10:30, 11:30 a.m., 1:00, 2:00, 3:00 p.m. July-October: Wednesday-Friday, 10:30, 11:30 a.m., 1:00, 2:00 & 3:00 p.m.; weekends, add 4:00 p.m. December 6-21: Weekends 10:00, 11:30 a.m., 1:30 & 3:00 p.m.

Fare: Adults $9.00, senior citizens $8.00, students (12-18) $8.00, children (3-11) $5.50. Family ticket (2 adults and up to 3 children) $22.00. Baggage car parties for up to 20, including personalized cake, $110. Charters, movie/photo shoots, call for details.

Locomotives: 1883 4-4-0 No. 136, 1959 diesel-hydraulic No. 22, ; and 1912 4-6-0 No. 1057, all former CP; diesel switcher No. 10, former Pilkington Glass.

Passenger Cars: Nine cars from the 1920s, undergoing or awaiting restoration.

Rolling Stock/Equipment: A variety of vintage freight equipment in various stages of restoration.

Location: On Simcoe County Road 10, 2-1/2 miles north of Highway 9, between Highways 50 & 27. From Highway 400, take Highway 9 west to the second set of traffic lights (Simcoe Road 10). Head north to the only traffic lights in town and turn left.

Radio Frequency: 172.95

Contact: Karen Smith
Office Manager

Mailing Address:
P.O. Box 186
Tottenham, ON L0G 1W0
Telephone: (905) 936-5815

Ontario, Uxbridge and Stouffville
M-D-R

YORK DURHAM HERITAGE RAILWAY
Diesel, scheduled
Standard gauge

JOHN SKINNER, EAGLE VISION PHOTOGRAPHY

Displays/Exhibits: See the newly restored 90-year old Uxbridge Station with the unique "witch's hat" design. Inside the station is the railway's gift shop and museum. Displays include old photos and railway memorabilia.

Ride/Operation: The tourist train winds 20 km (12.2 mi) through the rolling Oak Ridges Moraine and some of the most scenic terrain in Ontario. The railway offers passengers an entertaining, nostalgic, exciting, and scenic trip between Stouffville and Uxbridge.

Schedule: Victoria Day weekend through Canadian Thanksgiving. Trains run weekends and holidays, 3 times daily.

Fare/Admission: Adults $15, seniors 60+ $10, children 4-12 $8, under age 3 free.

Locomotives: No. 3612 Alco 1956 diesel; no. 1310 Alco 1951 diesel; no. 201 50T(7040) 1950.

Rolling Stock/Equipment: No. 1462 passenger coach; no. 3209 & 3232 cafe cars; no. 4960 Pullman car; no. 4977 coach; no. 15041 rules car.

Special Events: Stouffville Strawberry Festival, July 1.

Location: Uxbridge Station is located on Railway Lane off Brock Street in Uxbridge. From downtown Toronto take the Don Valley Parkway to 404, exit east on Stouffville side road. Stouffville Station is located on this road which turns into Main Street in Stouffville. Approximately 35 minutes from Toronto.

Contact:
Carol Ann Ross

Mailing Address:
P.O. Box 462
Stouffville, ON L4A 7Z7
Telephone: (905) 852-3696
Fax: (905) 462-0099 (call first)
E-mail: quelch.c@sympatico.ca

BARBARA WHITE

Displays/Exhibits: The museum has exhibits that interpret the development and operation of railroads on Prince Edward Island. The exhibits include a map of actual rail coverage and styles of stations structures; many original papers and certificates; baggage room displays a storage workshop with lots of rare pieces of equipment. The station has three rooms: men's waiting room (main gallery); office (original equipment & furniture and many papers and timetables); ladies waiting room; baggage room, now storage workshop.

Ride/Operation: Historic station telling railway history through pictures, artifacts, equipment, stories and museum and site itself.

Schedule: Open mid-June; no rides.

Fare/Admission: $1.50 for adults, under 12 free.

Special Events: Mid July on site Strawberry Fair; lots of entertainment, strawberries and ice cream, door prizes, games for children, great social time.

Location: Route 16A 26 km east of Souris, Prince Edward Island, Canada.

Contact: Prince Edward Island Museum

Mailing Address:
2 Kent Street
Charlottetown Prince Edward Island
C1A 1M6
Telephone: (902) 368-6600
Fax: (902) 368-6608

HULL-CHELSEA-WAKEFIELD
STEAM TRAIN
Steam, diesel, scheduled
Standard gauge

HULL-CHELSEA-WAKEFIELD

Ride/Operation: This line offers a 36-mile, 5-hour round trip through the Gatineau Hills, Chelsea, and Farm Point with a 2-hour stop at the picturesque village of Wakefield in the Gatineau Valley. A tour guide on each coach gives the history of the line, the train, and the region. In Wakefield, passengers can watch the engine being turned on the hand-powered turntable and filled at the water tower.

Train: 1907 Swedish steam engine; nine 1940 open-window coaches, one with a snack bar.

Schedule: Weekends, May; Tuesdays, Wednesdays & weekends, June, September & October; daily, July-August; 1:30 p.m.

Fare: Adults $23.00, senior citizens $21.00, students $20.00, children $11.00; one-way $19.50. Taxes not included. Group rates and charters available.

Locomotives: No. 909, 2-8-0; No. 244, 1962 General Motors.

Special Events: Sunset Train, every Friday in July & August, 6:30 p.m.

Location: Minutes from the Canadian Parliament Building in Ottawa and neighbor to the New Hull Casino.

Contact: Andre Groulx
Sales/Marketing

Mailing Address:
165 Deveault Street
Hull, PQ J8Z 1S7
Telephone: (819) 778-7246
(800) 871-7246
Fax: (819) 778-5007

CANADIAN RAILWAY MUSEUM

Display/Exhibit: The largest railway museum in Canada, the CRM owns a collection of more than 130 pieces of rolling stock, including steam and diesel locomotives, passenger and freight cars, street cars and interurbans.

Ride/Operation: A 1½ mile ride through the museum grounds. Streetcar operates daily; train operates Sunday and holidays.

Train: No. 30, 70-ton General Electric, former Canadian National; No. 1002, MSW S-3, former Port of Montreal; No. 20, MLW RS2, former Roberval & Saguenay; No. 1959, Montreal Tramways streecar; No. 3, Montreal Tramways open observation car; "John Molson," operating replica of an 1850s steam locomotive.

Schedule: Daily May 4 - September 1. Weekends: September 6-October 19, 9:00 a m. - 5:00 p.m.

Fare/Admission: Adults $5.75, senior citizens (60+) $.75, students $3.25, children $2.75, family rate (2 parents and up to 3 children) $14.50, children under 5 admitted free. Group discounts available for 20 or more people. Reservations required.

Locomotives: Included are the oldest existing Canadian-built steam locomotives, former Canadian Pacific No. 144; No. 77, the oldest surviving diesel-electric; the "Rocket," the first electric streetcar to operate in Montreal, in 1892.

Rolling Stock/Equipment: First class coach, former CP; business car "Saskatchewan."

Location: Thirty minutes from downtown Montreal on Route 209, one mile south of Route 132.

Contact:
Ms. Marie-Claude Reid
Director

Mailing Address:
120 St. Perre Street
Saint-Constant, PQ J5A 2G9
Telephone: (514) 632-2410

RUSTY RELICS MUSEUM
Railway museum
Standard gauge

RUSTY RELICS MUSEUM

Displays/Exhibits: This museum, which is primarily a museum of pioneer days in Saskatchewan, is housed in a former Canadian National Railway station. A 1943 Canadian Pacific caboose and a CN motor car are on display outside; a former CN tool shed, containing railroad tools, is located in the yard. A new attraction is a 1905 one-room country school, complete with artifacts and an outside storage shed that shelters the pioneer agricultural equipment. The museum, which is located near the Moose Mountain Provincial Park and White Bear Lake, serves as Carlyle's tourist information center.

Schedule: Daily, June-September, or by appointment.

Admission: Adults $2.00, students $1.00, preschool children admitted free.

Location: At Railway Avenue and 3rd Street West. Carlyle is in southeast Saskatchewan about 60 miles north of the U.S. border and 40 miles west of the Manitoba border.

Contact: Delores Cutler
Administrator

Mailing Address:
Box 840
Carlyle, SK S0C 0R0
Telephone: (306) 453-2266
Off-season: (306) 453-2987

WESTERN DEVELOPMENT MUSEUM

Display/Exhibit: Transportation displays covering land (buggies, wagons, snowplanes, cars, trucks), rail (steam, diesel, CPR station), water: (boats), air: (early planes and gliders; British Commonwealth Air Training Program, Including an Ansom MKI and Snowbirds Gallery, as well as an outdoor Shortline Steam locomotive.

Schedule: Daily, 9:00 a.m.-6:00 p.m. A steam operated short line train runs Saturdays, Sundays and holidays, weather permiting, from May holiday weekend to September holiday weekend 11:00 a.m.-4:30 p.m

Fare/Admission: Museum: Adults $4.50, seniors/ students $3.50, children $1.50, Train: $1.00 per person.

Locomotives: Steam locomotive built by Montreal locomotive works 1913 (CPR 4-6-2) CPR Diesel locomotive Engine 6553 built by Montreal Locomotive works 1956. Electric trolley bus built by Canadian Car & Foundry, purchased in 1951; 1929 streetcar double truck built by Ottawa Preston.

RollingStock/Equipment: 1931 LaSalle; 1911 Rauch & Lang; 1955 Crown Victoria; 1927 Citroen Half-track; 1903 Ford Model A Runabout; 1911 Hupmobile; 1928 Whippet, 1907 Russell; 1919 White Truck; Linn tractor. Many other cars of various makes & models spanning 1906-1986.

Location: Junction of Highways 1 and 2, north end of Moose Jaw.

Contact:
Lyn Johnston

Mailing Address:
Box 185, 50 Diefenbaker Drive
Moose Jaw, SK S6H 4N8
Telephone: (306) 693-5989
Fax: 306-691-0511

A

Abilene & Smoky Valley Railroad 129
Adrian & Blissfield Railroad 161
Adirondack Scenic Railroad 227
Age of Steam Railroad Museum 323
Alaska Railroad 3
Alberta Prairie Railway Excursions 368
Alco Brooks Railroad Display 222
Algoma Central Railway Inc. 391
Allegheny Portage Railroad
    National Historic Site 278
Altoona Railroaders Memorial Museum 273
American Railway Caboose Historical Educational
    Society, Inc. (A.R.C.H.E.S) 193
Anacortes Railway 341
Arizona Railway Museum, The 7
Arizona Train Depot 9
Arcade & Attica Railroad 217
Arkansas & Missouri Railroad 18
Asheville Chapter, National
    Railway Historical Society, Inc. 237
Ashtabula, Carson & Jefferson Scenic Line 252
Austin & Texas Central Railroad 322
Avondale Railroad Center 276
Avondale Railroad Center Delaware Project 79

B

BC Rail, Ltd 377
B&O Railroad Museum 147
Baltimore Streetcar Museum 148
Bay Area Electric Railroad Association
    Western Railway Museum 49
Belfast and Moosehead Lake Railroad 146
Bellefonte Historical Railroad 277
Berkshire Scenic Railway 159
Big Bear Farm 281
Big South Fork Scenic Railway 137
Billy Jones Wildcat Railroad 39
Black Hills Central Railroad 311
Bluegrass Railroad Museum 138
Bonanzaville, U.S.A. .245
Boone & Scenic Valley Railroad,
    Iowa Railroad Historical Society 120
Boothbay Railway Village 141
Brandywine Scenic Railway 292
Branson Scenic Railway 188
British Columbia Forest Museum 370
Broadway Dinner Train 318
Buckeye Central Scenic Railroad 256

C

California State Railroad Museum 50
California State Railroad Museum.
    Sacramento Southern Railroad 51

Camp Five Museum Foundation, Inc. 358
Canadian Museum of Rail Travel 397
Canadian Railway Museum 369
Cape Cod Railroad 158
Carillon Historical Park 250
Carthage, Knightstown & Shirley Railroad 115
Cass Scenic Railroad State Park 351
Catskill Mountain Railroad 226
Cedar Point Amusement Park/Resort 259
Center For Transportation & Commerce,
    The Galveston Railroad Museum 326
Central Florida Railroad Museum
    Central FL Chapter NRHS 90
Central Square Station Museum
    Central New York Chapter, NRHS 221
Chattanooga Choo Choo 314
Chehalis-Centralia Railroad Association 343
Chesapeake Beach Railway Museum 149
Chesapeake Railroad .152
Children's Museum of Indianapolis, The 114
Chippewa Valley Railroad Association 356
Choo Choo Barn 301
Cincinnati Railroad Club 248
City of Traverse City Parks & Recreation 173
Clovis Depot Model Train Museum 215
Cochrane Railway & Pioneer Museum 384
Colorado Railroad Museum 67
Conneaut Railroad Museum 249
Connecticut Antique Machinery Association, Inc. .76
Connecticut Trolley Museum 74
Conway Scenic Railroad 206
Coopersville & Marne Railway Company, The . .165
Corydon Scenic Railroad 109
Cowan Railroad Museum 316
Cripple Creek Narrow Gauge Railroad 60
Cumbres & Toltec Scenic Railroad 214

D

Dansbury Railway Museum 72
Danville Junction Chapter, NRHS 104
Dayton Historical Depot Society 344
Delaware & Ulster Rail Ride 218
Dennison Railroad Depot Musuem, The 251
Descanso, Alpine & Pacific Railway 19
Dequincy Railroad Museum 139
Dollywood Entertainment Park 320
Durango & Silverton Narrow-Gauge Railroad 64

E

East Broad Top Railroad 295
East Troy Electric Railroad,
    Wisconsin Trolley Museum 355
Ellicott City B&O Railroad Station Museum 151
Elmira Railway Museum 395

Empire State Railway Museum 229
End-O-Line Railroad Park and Museum 176
Eureka Springs & North Arkansas Railway 14

F

Fillmore & Western Railway 28
Florida Central 82
Florida Gulf Coast Railroad Museum, Inc. 89
Floyd McEachern Historical Train Museum 240
Folsom Valley Railway
    Div. of Golden Spike Enterprises 30
Forney Historic Transportation Museum 61
Fort Collins Municipal Railway 65
Fort Edmonton Park 367
Fort Erie Railroad Museum 385
Fort Fairfield Railroad Museum 142
Fort Madison, Farmington & Western Railroad . .124
Fort Smith Trolley Museum 16
Fort Steele Railway 371
Fort Wayne Railroad Historical Society 111
Franklin Institute Science Museum 293
Fox River Trolley Museum 105
French Lick, West Baden
    & Southern Railway 112
Frisco Railroad Museum 82

G

Gadsden-Pacific Division
    Toy Train Operating Museum, Ltd. 10
Galesburg Railroad Museum 101
Georgetown Loop Railroad 66
Gettysburg Railroad 279
Gold Coast Railroad Museum 86
Golden Gate Live Steamers, Inc. 20
Golden Spike National Historic Site 334
Grand Canyon Railway 12
Great Plains Transporation, The 131
Great Smoky Mountains Railway 241
Green Mountain Railroad/
    Green Mountain Flyer 336
Gulf Coast Railroad Museum 327

H

Halton County Radial Railway 387
Hardin Southern Railroad 133
Harpers Ferry Toy Train Museum
    & Joy Line Railroad 352
Hartmann Model Railroad 207
Hawaiian Railway Society 94
Hazlet Train Stop 211
Henry Ford Museum &
    Greenfield Village Railroad 166
Henry Morrison Flagler Museum 88
Heber Valley Railroad .332

Heritage Park Historical Village 366
Heritage Railway Company 388
Hesston Steam Museum 113
High Springs Station Museum 85
Historic Pullman Foundation 98
Historic Railroad Shops 93
Hobo Railroad 202
Hocking Valley Scenic Railway 255
Hoosier Valley Railroad Museum 118
Horseshoe Curve National
    Historic Landmark 274
Huckleberry Railroad .168
Hugo Heritage Railroad 264
Hull-Chelsea-Wakefield Steam Train 396
Huntsville Depot 2

I

I&O Scenic Railway 253
Iowa Star Clipper Dinner Train 128
Iron Mountain Iron Mine 170
Illinois Railway Museum 106
Indiana Transportation Museum 117
Irvine Park Railroad 43

J

Junction Valley Railroad 162

K

Kelley Park Trolley 54
Kennesaw Civil War Museum 92
Kentucky Central Railway 135
Kentucky Railway Museum 134
Kettle Moraine Railway 360
King County Dept. of Transportation
    Transit Div. (Metro Transit) 346
Klickety Klack Model Railroad 208
Komoka Railway Museum 386
Knott's Berry Farm 23
Knox & Kane Railroad 287
Kwinista Railway Station Museum 375

L

Lahaina, Kaanapali & Pacific Railroad 95
Lake County History & Railroad Museum 186
Lake Shore Railway
    Historical Society, Inc. 291
Lake Superior & Mississippi Railroad 178
Lake Superior Museum of Transportation 179
Lake Whatcom Railway 349
Laurel Highlands Railroad 297
Laws Railroad Museum & Historical Site 22
Leadville Colorado & Southern Railroad 69
Linden Railroad Museum 116
Little River Railroad 164

Little River Railroad
   and Lumber Company 321
Lomita Railroad Museum 36
Lowell National Historical Park 160
Lycoming County Historical
   Society & Museum 308

M

Mad River & NKP Railroad Society 247
Mahoning Valley Railroad
   Heritage Association 262
Maine Narrow Gauge Railroad
   Company and Museum 145
Manitou & Pike's Peak Railway 70
Martisco Station Museum Central
   New York Chapter NRHS 220
Mason City & Clear Lake Electrical
   Railway Historical Society 121
Maumee Valley Historical Society 254
McCloud Railway Company 40
McKinney Avenue Transit Authority 324
Michigan Transit Museum 171
Michigan Star Clipper
   Dinner Train Coe Rail 174
Mid-Continent Railway
   Historical Society 359
Midland Railway 130
Middletown & Hummelstown Railroad 288
Midwest Central Railroad 126
Midwest Electric Railway 127
Minnesota Transporation Museum
   Como-Harriet Streetcar Line 181
Minnesota Transporation Museum
   Minnehaha Depot .182
Minnesota Zephyr Limited 185
Monticello Railway Museum 102
Mount Hood Railroad .269
Mt. Rainier Scenic Railroad 345
Mount Washington Railway Co. 205
Museum of Alaska Transportation & Industry 5
Museum of Science and Industry 99
Museum of Transportation 194

N

Napa Valley Wine Train 42
National Capital Trolley Museum 155
National Historic Argo Gold Mill 68
National Museum of Science & Technology 389
National New York Central Railroad Museum . . .110
National Railroad Museum 357
National Railroad Museum and Hall of Fame . . .242
National Toy Train Museum, The 302
Nevada Northern Railway Museum 200
Nevada State Railroad Museum 199

New Hope & Ivyland Railroad 290
New Hope Valley Railway 239
New Jersey Museum of Transportation 209
New York & Lake Erie Railroad 223
New York Transit Musuem 219
Niles Canyon Railway 32
North Alabama Railroad Museum 1
North Carolina Transportation
   Museum at Historic Spencer Shops 243
Northeast Rail Batten Kill Railroad 234
Northlandz Great American Railway, Dollhouse
   Museum & Art Gallery 210
North Shore Scenic Railroad 180
North Star Rail, Inc. 175
Northern Central Railway 289
Northern Counties Logging Museum 25
Northern Pacific Depot Railroad Museum 97
Nostalgia Station Toy and Train Museum 136

O

Ohio Central Railroad .260
Ogden Union Station 333
Oil Creek & Titusville Railroad 305
Old Colony & Fall River Railroad Museum 157
Old Colony & Newport Scenic Railway 309
Old Depot Railroad Museum, The 177
Old Dominion Railway Museum 339
Old Pueblo Trolley 11
Old Wakarusa Railroad 119
Omaha Zoo Railroad 197
Ontario & Western Roscoe,
   O&W Railway Museum 232
Ontario-Midland Rail Excursions 235
Orange Empire Railway Museum 45
Oregon Electric Railway Museum 268
Orland, Newville & Pacific Railroad 44
Orrville Railroad Heritage Society 258
Osceola & St. Croix Valley Railway
   Minnesota Transportation Museum 361

P

Pacific Limited Group .335
Park Lane Model Railroad Museum 362
Patee House Museum 192
Pennsylvania Trolley Museum 306
Pike's Peak Historical Street
   Railway Foundation, Inc. 59
Pioneer Tunnel Coal Mine & Steam Train 275
Platte Valley Trolley 62
Portola Railroad Museum 47
Port Stanley Terminal Rail 390
Potomac Eagle 354
Poway-Midland Railroad 48
Prairie Dog Central 380

Prairie Village 312
Prince George Railway & Forestry Museum 374
Project 1225 172
Puget Sound Railway Historical Association 347

Q

Quaker Square 246
Queen Anne's Railroad .80

R

Railroad and Pioneer Museum 331
Railroad Memories Museum 363
Railroad Museum of Long Island 224
Railroad Museum of Oklahoma 263
Railroad Museum of New England 77
Railroad Museum of Pennsylvania 303
Railroad Museum of South Florida 83
Railswest Railroad Museum 123
Rail Tours, Inc. 283
Railtown 1897/Sierra Railway Company 35
Railway Museum of Manitoba, The 379
Railway Exposition Company 132
Rayville Railroad Museum 103
Reader Railroad 17
Reading, Blue Mountain & Northern Railroad . . .294
Reading Company
    Technical & Historical Society 285
Redwood Valley Railway Corp. 21
Remlinger Farms Narrow Gauge Railroad 342
Rensselaer Model Railroad Exhibit 236
Riverside & Great Northern Railway 364
Riverside Train Depot .230
Roadside America 299
Roaring Camp & Big Trees
    Narrow Gauge Railroad 26
Rockhill Trolley Museum 296
Rocky Mountaineer Railtours 373
Rochester & Genesee Valley Railroad Museum . .231
Royal Hudson Steam Train 378
Rusty Relics Museum .398

S

Salamanca Rail Musuem 233
Salem & Hillsborough Railroad 381
Samtrak 270
San Diego Model Railroad Museum 52
San Diego Railroad Museum 24
Sandy River Railroad Museum
    Division Philips Historical Society 144
San Francisco Municipal Railway 53
San Pedro & Southwestern Railroad 6
Santa Cruz, Big Trees & Pacific Railway 27
Santa Fe Depot Museum & Historic Center 125
Santa Fe Southern Railway 216

Seashore Trolley Museum 143
Seminole Gulf Railway .84
Shasta Sunset Dinner Train 41
Shelburne Museum 337
Shenango Pymatuning Railway
    Historical Society 280
Shore Line Trolley Museum 73
Silver Creek Stephenson Railroad 100
Silverwood Central Railway 96
Six Flags Over Mid-America 189
Ski Train, The 63
Skunk Train, The California Western Railroad . . .31
Sloman School Car on Wheels 383
Smiths Falls Railway Museum Corp. 392
Smithsonian Institution .78
Smoky Hill Railway 187
Society for the Preservation of
    Charter Railroad Resources 33
Society for the Preservation of the
    S.S. City of Milwaukee 167
Sonora Short Line Railway 56
South Carolina Railroad Museum 310
South Coast Railroad Museum 34
South Simcoe Railway .393
Southeastern Railway Museum 91
Southern Appalachian Railway Museum 317
Southern Michigan Railroad Society 163
Southern California Chapter Railway
    & Locomotive Historical Society 46
St. Louis, Iron Mountain & Southern Railway . . .191
St. Louis Steam Train Association 195
Steamtown National Historic Site 298
Stewartstown Railroad .300
Stourbridge Line Rail Excursions 282
Strasburg Rail Road 304
Sunrise Optimist of Sedalia . . . .
Sydney & Louisburg Railway Museum 382

T

Tarantula Train 325
Tennessee Central Railway Museum (TCRM) 319
Tennessee Valley Railroad 315
Texas Limited 328
Texas State Railroad 329
Texas Transportation Museum 330
Tiny Town Railroad 71
Tioga Central Railroad .307
Tioga Scenic Railroad .228
Toledo, Lake Erie & Western Railway 261
Toy Train Depot 213
Trainland U.S.A. 122
Trains at Bandana Square by Twin City
    Model Railroad Club, Inc 184
Train Town 55

Travel Town Museum 37
Travel Town Museum/Crystal Springs
   & Cahuenga Valley Railroad 38
Tri-Cities Historical Museum 169
Trolley Museum of New York 225
Trolleyville, U.S.A. 257
Tweetsie Railroad 238

U
Union Pacific Collection 198
U.S. Army Transportation Museum 338

V
Valley Railroad Company 75
Valley View Model Railroad 107
Verde Canyon Railroad, L.C. 8
Virginia & Truckee Railroad Co. 201
Virginia Museum of Transportation 340

W
Wabash Frisco & Pacific Railway
   "The Uncommon Carrier" 190
Walker Transportation Collection Beverly
   Historical Society & Museum 156
Walkersville Southern Railroad 154
Wanamaker, Kempton & Southern, Inc. 284
Washington Park & Zoo Railway 271
Waynoka Historical Society 265
West Coast Railway Heritage Park 376
West Florida Railroad 87
Western Development Museum 399
Western Maryland Railway Historical
   Society, Inc. 153

Western Maryland Scenic Railroad 150
Western Minnesota Stream
   Thresher's Renunion 183
Western Vancouver Island
   Industrial Heritage Society 372
West Shore Rail Excursions 286
West Virginia Northern Railroad 353
Whetstone Valley Express 313
Whippany Railway Museum 212
White Mountain Central Railroad 203
White Pass & Yukon Route 4
White River Railway. 15
Whitewater Valley Railroad 108
Willamette Shore Trolley 272
Wilmington & Western Railroad 81
Wilmington Railroad Museum 244
Winnipesaukee Scenic Railroad 204
Wiscasset, Waterville & Farmington
   Railway Museum .140
Wyoming Transportation Museum
   and Learning Center 365

Y
Yakima Electric Railway Museum 350
Yakima Valley Rail and Steam Museum 348
Yreka Western Railroad .58
Yolo Shortline Railroad Company 57
York Durham Heritage Railway 394
Yosemite Mountain Sugar Pine Railroad 29
Yukon's Best Railroad Museum 266
Yuma Valley Railway 13